||| || |||||||||||||||||||||||||||||| ||| || |||

✓ **KU-204-565**

The illuminated Hôtel de Ville

narrowly failed 1995 referendum on separation transformed the city into a pitched battlefield over linguistic and territorial rights. It seems virtually everyone can speak French, while the younger generation of Francophones also speak *l'anglais* – certainly a blessing for English-speaking visitors, who should have no problem finding someone who speaks the language.

The duality of Montréal's social mix is also reflected in its urban make-up. Sandwiched between the banks of the St Lawrence River and the forested, trail-covered rise of Mont Royal (233m high, but a "mountain" in the minds of Montrealers) the heart of the city is an engaging melange of old- and new-world aesthetics. Busy Downtown, with its wide boulevards lined by sleek office towers and rambling shopping malls, is emblematic of a typical North American metropolis, while just to the south, Vieux-Montréal preserves the city's unmistakable French heritage in its layout of narrow, cobblestone streets and town squares. Closer investigation belies both these cliches, however, for there are charming nineteenth-century churches dotted about Downtown, while the bulk of Vieux-Montréal's buildings are actually the fruits of the Anglophone merchant class that made its fortunes off the country's plentiful natural resources and later during the Industrial Revolution, when the nearby Lachine Canal was "Canada's Pittsburgh". Ironically, the impetus for the canal – the Lachine Rapids in the St Lawrence River – was the reason for the city's early success in the first place: Montréal was as far as ships could travel into the interior, and so became a major port and trading centre.

It's the street-level vibe that makes Montréal such a great place to visit. Like the homegrown Cirque du Soleil, Montréal has a ceaseless and contagious energy that infuses its café culture, the thrilling, into-the-wee-hours nightlife and the boisterous summer festivals – celebrating jazz, comedy, music and film. Nowhere captures the city's free-spirited ethos better than Plateau Mont-Royal, the trendiest neighbourhood in town and effective meeting-point of Montréal's founding and immigrant cultures. Here, the best restaurants, bars and clubs hum and groove along boulevard St-Laurent,

▲ Basilique-Cathédrale Marie-Reine-du-Monde

| INTRODUCTION | WHAT TO SEE | WHEN TO GO

5

Fact file

- Montréal, founded in 1642, is the third-largest French-speaking city in the world (after Paris and Kinshasa).

- What Montrealers consider "north" is actually northwest – this is because the street grid was set up parallel to the St Lawrence, which flows northeast where it passes Vieux-Montréal. The further "north" you go from there, the greater the house number in addresses. Boulevard St-Laurent divides the city into east and west.

- On average, it snows nearly every second day during December, January and February. The heaviest snowfall on record was on March 4, 1971 – the 102cm that dropped that day is nearly half the average snowfall for the whole year.

- The population of the city of Montréal is 1.6 million, of which 54 percent have French as a mother tongue, 17 percent English and 29 percent another language (a fifth of these are Italian). The population of greater Montréal, including the off-island cities and suburbs, is just over 3.5 million.

- The roughly triangular Île de Montréal covers nearly 500 square kilometres and is dominated by Mont Royal – known by everyone as "the mountain". The island has 267km of shoreline, surrounded by the St Lawrence River to the south and east and the Rivière des Prairies to the northwest.

- Montréal's top three most-attended events are Just for Laughs (*Juste pour Rire*), Festival de Jazz and Divers/Cité.

the symbolic divide between the city's French and English communities, all under the watchful gaze of the city's most prominent landmark: the cross atop Mont Royal that recalls Montréal's initial founding as a Catholic colony.

What to see

Invariably, most first-time visitors head straight for **Vieux-Montréal**, the oldest part of the city, where the continent's finest collection of seventeenth- to nineteenth-century buildings line the atmospheric streets between rue St-Antoine and rue de la Commune. Sights are clustered around a number of public spaces, and **Place d'Armes**, dominated by the radiant **Basilique**

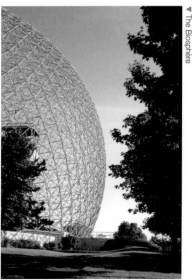

▲ The Biosphère

Montréal

written and researched by

Arabella Bowen and John Shandy Watson

ROUGH
GUIDES

NEW YORK · LONDON · DELHI

www.roughguides.com

Contents

Taste of Montréal
colour section following
p.112

Summer festivals
colour section following
p.208

Montréal colour maps
following p.320

◄◄ Illuminated Marché Bonsecours ◄ The Plateau's Coloniale Street

Introduction to

Montréal

Montréal is by far Canada's most cosmopolitan city. Toronto may have the country's economic power and Vancouver its most majestic scenery, but the centuries-old marriage of Protestant English and Catholic French cultures that defines Montréal has given the city a dynamic allure that is unique in North America. Its captivating atmosphere combines the best of both traditions, tempered with the Scottish merchants and Irish workers who built much of the city and also the diverse mix of Italians, Greeks, Eastern Europeans, Jews, Chinese and Portuguese who have put down roots in various neighbourhoods over the last century. And yet Montréal's free-spirited ambience – at once laid-back and highly style-conscious – is a product of the city itself rather than merely a sum of its multiethnic parts.

Ever since the French first flew the flag here in the 1600s, the struggle for the city's soul has centred on – and largely set apart – its English and French factions. As such, Montréal has always been a pivotal player in the tense politics of Québec separatism, which reached its lowest point in the late 1960s, when the Front de Libération du Québec waged a terrorist campaign on the city. This occurred in the wake of legislation that enshrined French-language dominance in Québec, causing English-Quebecers to flee in droves, tipping the nation's economic supremacy from Montréal to Toronto. After decades of linguistic dispute, though, a truce appears to have at last settled in, and nowadays it's hard to believe that little more than a decade ago a

4

■

Notre-Dame, is the best place to start from. The neighbouring streets are home to historic museums as well as the delicately steepled **Chapelle Notre-Dame-de-Bon-Secours** and the silver-domed **Marché Bonse-cours**, one of the city's best-known landmarks. In the district's southwest corner, the excellent **Musée d'Archéologie** provides a good introduction to Montréal's three and a half centuries of history, while the reclaimed land of the **Vieux-Port**, running the length of Vieux-Montréal along the St Lawrence River, is lined with promenades, parks and a number of harbourfront attractions.

Between Vieux-Montréal and the mountain, you'll find Montréal's modern **Downtown**, centred on the east–west artery **rue Ste-Catherine**, and filled with a collection of department stores, hotels, restaurants and cinemas. Nearby, the scaled-down (but still massive) rendition of St Peter's – the **Basilique-Cathédrale Marie-Reine-du-Monde** – as well as the warm-hued interior of **St Patrick's Basilica** contrast with the more sober Protestant churches dotted about. Although no longer the tallest of Montréal's skyscrapers, the cross-shaped **Place Ville Marie** seems to tower over the city; it sits atop the shopping mall that began the **Underground City's (RÉSO)** network of pedestrian tunnels linking the Métro system to shopping centres, offices and cultural institutions. The foremost example of the latter is the complex of theatres that, along with the **Musée d'Art Contemporain de Montréal**, comprises **Place des Arts**, half a dozen blocks east of Place Ville Marie.

The west end of Downtown overlaps the **Golden Square Mile**, the historic enclave of Montréal's wealthy Anglophone elite, which clings to the southern slopes of the mountain. This neighbourhood's contributions to the city include a number of sumptuous mansions and such public institutions as **McGill University** and the **Musée des Beaux-Arts** facing onto rue Sherbrooke, the premier address for upscale galleries and boutiques. By contrast, the eastern edges of Downtown are marked by the small yet bustling **Chinatown** and the bars and cafés of the **Quartier Latin**, stomping ground of students from the Université du Québec à Montréal. A

▼ Calèche in Vieux-Montréal

similarly vibrant energy infuses the **Village**, the openly gay and lesbian district further east along rue Ste-Catherine.

The Plateau Mont-Royal district on the mountain's eastern flank mixes Montréal's typically down-to-earth quality with hip style and ethnic charm. The largely Francophone neighbourhoods of the Plateau lie to the east of the chic boutiques and cafés of **rue St-Denis** – ideal for people-watching – while a panoply of ethnic businesses and trendy restaurants are clustered on and around **boulevard St-Laurent**, more commonly known as "The Main". Rising above Downtown but best accessed from the Plateau, **Parc du Mont-Royal** is the city's largest park, wound about with trails and terrific views over the city. The **Oratoire St-Joseph** and its massive dome rise above the western flank of the mountain, while to the north, a pair of vast cemeteries give way to tony, Francophone **Outremont** and the Greek and Jewish communities of **Mile End**. Further north still, **Little Italy** is a major foodie destination, as much for its espresso and Italian dishes as for the enticing produce stalls and gourmet shops surrounding the **Marché Jean-Talon**.

Some of Montréal's chief tourist attractions are a bit far from the centre, but remain easily accessed via the Métro. In the city's east end, the **Stade Olympique**, with its unique inclined tower, lies between the **Biodôme**,

Franglais

Despite Québec's linguistic battles, there's often a great deal of crossover between English and French and it's not uncommon to hear Montrealers switching from one to the other in the course of a single conversation. Francophones and Anglophones have also each picked up words and phrases from the other's language – a combination of French and anglais dubbed "franglais". So while you might hear a Montréalais say something like, "Je suis allé à un party ce weekend – c'était full fun", it's no less natural for a Montrealer to throw in French expressions while making plans for the evening: "Let's try to grab a seat on the terrasse for the cinq à sept before heading to that new resto on the Plateau – we'll need to grab a bottle of wine at the dep along the way, though."

featuring four ecosystems under one roof, and the enormous **Jardin Botanique**, notable for its replica Chinese and Japanese gardens and creepy-crawly **Insectarium**. To the south, in the middle of the St Lawrence opposite the Vieux-Port, visitors and locals alike head to **Parc Jean-Drapeau**, consisting of **Île Ste-Hélène** and man-made **Île Notre-Dame**, for its green spaces, amusement park, casino and racing track (built for the Grand Prix). West of Downtown is the staid Anglophone enclave of **Westmount**, while strung along the **Lachine Canal** to the south are a few workaday communities, notably **Pointe St-Charles** and **St-Henri**, which grew up during the area's Industrial Revolution heyday. An excellent bicycle path runs through these neighbourhoods, from the Vieux-Port to the canal's end at the former fur-trading post of **Lachine**.

Beyond Montréal, two enchanting regions – the **Eastern Townships** (Les Cantons-de-l'Est) and the **Laurentian mountains** (Les Laurentides) – provide excellent year-round escapes with plenty of activities (especially top-notch skiing), away from the teeming city centre. In contrast to Montréal, **Québec City**, around 250km northeast, seems immune to outside forces, its walled old-town steadfastly embodying the province's four-century-old French roots. Perched atop a promontory with a commanding view of the St Lawrence and laced with winding, cobblestone streets flanked by seventeenth- and eighteenth-century stone houses, it ranks as the country's most romantic and beautifully situated city.

The thistle and the shamrock

Much is made of the history of the English and French in the development of Montréal, but there are two other emblems on the city's flag (which you can see flying above Place d'Armes – see p.68): in addition to the English rose and French *fleur-de-lis*, the other quadrants contain a **thistle** and a **shamrock**. The former represents the **Scottish** settlers, notably the wealthy landowners and merchants who were responsible for building much of what you see in Vieux-Montréal and grand houses such as shipping magnate Sir Hugh Allan's Ravenscrag (see p.61). Their names are still visible throughout Downtown, from streets such as rue McTavish to the university founded by James McGill. Although there were also influential Irish businessmen, the majority of **Irish** immigrants were poor refugees from the potato famine, who didn't fare much better in the unhealthy slums of Pointe St-Charles. By the mid-nineteenth century, they comprised a fifth of Montréal's population and provided the backbone (along with their French Catholic brethren) for the industrial revolution along the Lachine Canal. They've also left visible traces in the city, from the glorious St Patrick's Basilica (see p.54) to the even older St Patrick's Day Parade (see p.224).

When to go

▼ "The Main", heart of the Plateau

Montréal's climate is one of extremes – bone-chilling **winter** temperatures morph into sweaty summer highs with barely an iota of spring to ease the transition. Though tourist authorities are fond of minimizing the true extent of the city's winters, the season is in fact bitterly cold; temperatures often fall well below the zero mark and snowfalls don't dust the city – they bury it. Though a boon for avid skiers and snowboarders, the period between November and April can be positively grim for everyone else. That said, if you're here during a cold snap, the labyrinthine Underground City (RÉSO) provides an escape from the elements and spending the afternoon tucked inside a cozy café is a wonderful antidote.

The transition from winter to **summer** passes almost unnoticed, and locals quickly replace their complaints about the cold to gripes about the humidity. The population seems to double come summer as the city's residents come out of hibernation; still, despite the heat and the crowds, late June through August is one of the best times to visit, thanks in part to a rotating menu of wild festivals. Likewise, Montréal can be simply glorious during the **autumn** months. Though it's cooler in the evenings, the days remain quite warm and, best of all, the changing leaves set the city ablaze with bursts of yellows, oranges and reds. Indeed, the season is perfect for hikers as the provincial parks resonate with colour, though traipsing up Mont Royal can be just as splendid.

Average monthly temperatures and rainfall

	Jan	Feb	Mar	Apr	May	June	July	Aug	Sept	Oct	Nov	Dec
Max°C	-6	-4	2	11	19	23	26	29	20	13	5	-3
Min°C	-15	-14	-7	1	7	13	15	19	9	4	-2	-11
Max°F	22	24	36	51	65	74	79	84	68	55	41	27
Min°F	5	8	20	33	45	54	60	67	49	38	28	12
Rain (mm)	63.3	56.4	67.6	74.8	68.3	82.5	85.6	104	86.5	75.4	93.4	85.6
Rain (inches)	2.5	2.2	2.7	2.9	2.7	3.3	3.4	4.1	3.4	3.0	3.7	3.4

23

things not to miss

It's not possible to see everything that Montréal has to offer in one trip – and we don't suggest you try. What follows is a selective taste of the city's highlights: memorable restaurants, lively festivals, engaging museums and exciting outdoor activities. They're arranged in five colour-coded categories to help you find the very best things to see, do and experience. All entries have a page reference to take you straight into the Guide, where you can find out more.

01 **Jardin Botanique** Page **112** • Head east to see the pagoda-dotted Chinese Garden and serene Japanese Garden, the highlights of this sprawling botanical oasis.

02 Musée d'Archéologie et d'Histoire de Montréal

Page **79** • Filled with remains from Montréal's earliest days, this fascinating museum lies on the site of the colony's founding in 1642.

03 The Village Page **89** • The

heart of Montréal's gay and lesbian community, this vibrant neighbourhood offers an abundance of restaurants, cafés, bars and shops.

04 See and be seen on a terrasse Page **161 & 171** •

For both café society and after-work 5 à 7 drinkers, Montréal's patios fill up when the warm weather arrives and keep going until the wee hours.

05 Historic churches Page **71** •

The city abounds with graceful chapels and churches, in addition to the bolder architecture of its four cathedrals, including the Basilique Notre-Dame (pictured).

06 Strolling the Plateau
Page **92** • Checking out the distinctive architecture of the Plateau's staircase-lined streets and back-lane courtyards, called "Balconville" by locals, is as good an excuse as any to explore this hip neighbourhood.

07 Fripperies
Page **204** • Bin-diving at any of Montréal's funky second-hand clothing shops is bound to turn up distinctive looks – at bargain prices – that will set you apart from the crowd back home.

08 Snack on a fresh Montréal bagel
Page **206** • Fans say the city's bagels are better than New York's. Decide for yourself by joining the queues at the Mile End bagel bakeries and tasting one straight from the oven.

09 Grand Prix
Page **213** • The thunder of Formula 1 cars reverberates throughout the city, as do the accompanying festivities Downtown.

10 Mont Royal
Page **102** • At 233 metres, the "mountain" is hardly deserving of the name, yet its many trails, stunning views and central location make it a more-than-worthwhile destination.

11 Vieux-Quebéc Page 253 •
Much of New France's history is bound up within the fortification walls encircling the beautiful and atmospheric Old Québec.

14 Festival International de Jazz de Montréal Page 225 •
Montréal's storied jazz scene is celebrated at this massive annual concert series, which draws big names and hundreds of thousands of visitors from all over the world.

12 Marché Jean-Talon
Page 207 • This market at the heart of Little Italy overflows with fresh produce, bread, cheeses and meats seven days a week.

13 Jean-Paul Riopelle
Page 56 • The influential Québécois artist's vibrant abstracts are splashed about both the Musée d'Art Contemporain (pictured) and the Musée des Beaux-Arts.

15 Mont Tremblant Page 240 •
This sprawling resort complex in the Laurentians north of Montréal offers luxurious lodgings and almost a hundred ski runs.

16 Dinner at a bistro
Page **155** • With its bold and brash atmosphere, Vieux-Montréal restaurant *Holder* provides a convivial way to ease into French bistro cuisine.

17 Château Ramezay
Page **75** • This 300-year-old manor house is as much an artefact of the city's history as the exhibits inside, especially the ornate mahogany-panelled Salle de Nantes, where concerts are held.

18 Biking the Lachine Canal
Page **125** • Once the centre of Montréal industry, this waterway has been rehabilitated with a lengthy, picturesque walking and biking trail.

19 Les Cantons-de-l'Est
Page **245** • The rolling foothills of the Eastern Townships are dotted with charming villages such as North Hatley, and active travellers can head to the lakes and forested peaks for hiking, canoeing, skiing and more.

20 Oratoire St-Joseph Page 105 •
This copper-domed edifice, an awe-inspiring tribute to religious devotion, towers over the western slopes of Mont Royal.

22 Relaxing in Parc Lafontaine
Page 96 • Take a break from sightseeing at this urban oasis, where you can lie in the sun, take a boat out on the ponds, or even catch a free play at the outdoor Théâtre de Verdure.

21 Montréal Canadiens Page 211 •
Though the Canadiens are a long way from their glory days, seeing them play at the Centre Bell is still an action-packed, invigorating way to spend an evening.

23 Vieux-Montréal architecture Page 67 •
Every turn of a corner reveals architectural details in Old Montreal's jumble of narrow, lamp-lit streets lined with eighteenth-century houses and elaborate nineteenth-century commercial buildings.

Basics

Basics

Getting there

From most places in North America – and from anywhere overseas – the fastest and easiest way to get to Montréal is to fly to Aéroport de Montréal-Trudeau (YUL). If you are coming from anywhere within 500–600 kilometres of the city, however, a train, bus or car journey may be cheaper and, after factoring in airport formalities, just as quick.

Airfares always depend on the **season**, with the **highest** being around June to early September, when the weather is nicest; you'll get the best prices during the **low season**, November to February (excluding mid-December through the New Year when prices are hiked up and seats are at a premium); during the **shoulder seasons** the smaller crowds and moderate prices are balanced out by the uncertainty of good weather. Note also that flying on weekends ordinarily adds a bit to the round-trip fare; price ranges quoted throughout this section assume midweek travel and a Saturday night stay.

If you have already arrived from overseas or live in Québec, Ontario or the northeast US, there are a number of alternatives to the hassles of flying. The most comfortable route is to take a **train** – VIA Rail operates frequent services in the Windsor–Québec City corridor, and Amtrak provides a direct train from New York and a train–bus combo from Washington. If you're on a budget, a **long-distance bus** trip is the cheapest way to get to Montréal, with Greyhound services from the US and a number of Canadian carriers also available.

Flights from the US and Canada

There are frequent daily flights from Toronto and other **Canadian cities** like Ottawa, Québec City and Halifax. **Air Canada** provides by far the most comprehensive service, reaching all parts of the country through its flagship brand and regional Air Canada Jazz. Its no-frills Tango fares aim to compete with increasing **competition** from low-cost carrier **WestJet**; in addition to lower prices, the airline also services smaller

Canadian cities and parts of Florida, Arizona and Hawaii. For the time being, Air Canada's higher published fares are somewhat irrelevant in the face of their almost weekly seat sales, Web specials and last-minute offers; revisit the airline's website regularly (or sign up for its email alerts) to be sure of getting a good deal. One bonus to all the competition is that one-way fares are indeed now available for half the price of a return.

Fares tend to vary widely. You should be able to fly from Toronto for around C$350 including taxes; maritime cities start at just under C$400. Out west, Calgary to Montréal runs to $570–750 and Vancouver ranges from $650 on a discount airline to around $825 in economy on Air Canada.

Service **from the US** is also competitive, particularly on **United** (which code-shares with Air Canada) and **American Airlines**; both have a good number of daily flights from the eastern hubs of Atlanta, Boston, Chicago, Cincinnati, New York, Philadelphia and Washington, DC. There are fewer direct flights from the south and west – you might have to change planes to get a time and price to suit. Expect to pay US$260–300 from New York, Boston or Washington, DC; US$300–350 from Chicago; US$450–580 from Miami and US$430–550 from LA.

Flights from the UK and Ireland

Of the **major carriers**, only Air Canada and British Airways offer directly scheduled flights for the seven-and-a-half-hour trip from London to Montréal, although you can often get a cheaper fare by connecting through a major European or US hub, which adds a few hours to your journey. KLM often has the best deals – and it's worth paying a bit extra to fly via Amsterdam than Detroit's dreadful airport. **Charter airlines** like Thomas Cook Airways and Air Transat offer consistently cheaper fares but only fly direct from May to October.

You'll have to change planes regardless if you're travelling from one of the UK's **regional airports**, either via London, Toronto or a US or European hub; again, prices vary – expect to pay anywhere from the same rates as if flying directly from London to a couple of hundred pounds more. Prices from the UK vary widely, with flights out of **London** as cheap as £300 in low season (though £350–400 is more typical) but you'll be hard pressed to find much below £550 in the peak summer season. Shop around on a few of the online booking engines to get an idea of which airlines have seat sales; prices can also vary considerably depending on routing and time of day (you'll usually be less jet-lagged with a daytime return and higher prices reflect the demand for these flights).

There are no direct flights **from Ireland**; the best routes connect through London. Count on €510–570 in low season and upwards of €600–800 in summer.

Flights from Australia, New Zealand and South Africa

There are no direct **flights** to Montréal from Australia, New Zealand or South Africa. For the 24-hour haul from Australia or New

---

Fly less – stay longer! Travel and climate change

Climate change is a serious threat to the ecosystems that humans rely upon, and air travel is among the fastest-growing contributors to the problem. Rough Guides regard travel, overall, as a global benefit, and feel strongly that the advantages to developing economies are important, as is the opportunity of greater contact and awareness among peoples. But we all have a responsibility to limit our personal impact on global warming, and that means giving thought to how often we fly, and what we can do to redress the harm that our trips create.

Flying and climate change

Pretty much every form of motorized travel generates CO_2 – the main cause of human-induced climate change – but planes also generate climate-warming contrails and cirrus clouds, and emit oxides of nitrogen, which create ozone (another greenhouse gas) at flight levels. Furthermore, flying simply allows us to travel much further than we otherwise would do. The figures are frightening: one person taking a return flight between Europe and California produces the equivalent impact of 2.5 tonnes of CO_2 – similar to the yearly output of the average UK car.

Fuel-cell and other less harmful types of plane may emerge eventually. But until then, there are really just two options for concerned travellers: to reduce the amount we travel by air (take fewer trips – stay for longer!), and to make the trips we do take "climate neutral" via a carbon offset scheme.

Carbon offset schemes

Offset schemes run by ⓦ www.climatecare.org, ⓦ www.carbonneutral.com and others allow you to make up for some or all of the greenhouse gases that you are responsible for releasing. To do this, they provide "carbon calculators" for working out the global-warming contribution of a specific flight (or even your entire existence), and then let you contribute an appropriate amount of money to fund offsetting measures. These include rainforest reforestation and initiatives to reduce future energy demand – often run in conjunction with sustainable development schemes.

Rough Guides, together with Lonely Planet and other concerned partners in the travel industry, are supporting a **carbon offset scheme** run by climatecare.org. Please take the time to view our website and see how you can help to make your trip climate neutral.

ⓦ**www.roughguides.com/climatechange**

Zealand, you'll need to change planes at least once – and more likely twice – depending on the airline and routing; the same is true of the twenty-hour trek from South Africa.

Most flights from **Australia and New Zealand** are via the West Coast – principally Los Angeles, though some pass through San Francisco or Vancouver – and you may need to change planes again on the way to Montréal. There are often deals from the big Asian carriers via their home airports, which can allow for an interesting stopover, depending on the city, often at no extra charge. It's also worth considering a stopover in Honolulu or the South Pacific.

Sydney offers the most choice for flights **from Australia** and, along with Melbourne, is the cheapest city to fly from – you'll pay as much as A$1000 more from Perth, for instance. Fares for flights to Montréal vary seasonally, and you can expect to pay A$2400–3300 (and up). It's well worth considering purchase of an air pass and connecting via Los Angeles, which costs around A$800–1000 less than a ticket straight through to Montréal – you'll pay just over A$1500 if you hit upon a good fare.

From New Zealand, the best deals are out of Auckland – you'll need to factor in an extra NZ$200 from Wellington and NZ$400 from Christchurch. Fares through to Montréal are in the NZ$2800–3500 range. As with Australia, you may be better off flying directly to Los Angeles and using an air pass from there; flights to LA cost NZ$1800–2400.

From South Africa, you'll fly east and most often connect in a US hub like New York or Washington, DC, though you may occasionally find yourself switching planes in Europe. Johannesburg is the most affordable departure city, with flights around R17,000 in low season and R30,000 in high season.

Trains

Travelling by train from eastern Canada, Toronto, Ottawa and Québec City is a viable, if more time-consuming, alternative to flying. Operated by **VIA Rail**, the trains are comfortable but have about as much character as air travel; that said, you'll likely be too busy gawking at the passing scenery to notice. In addition to economy service, the busier routes have VIA1 first-class cars – the higher price covers free booze and good-quality meals rather than any extra space to stretch out. Students with an ISIC card cop a 35 percent discount, while anyone can save 25–35 percent (depending on route) by booking at least five days in advance (there are only limited seats at this rate, though, so book well ahead).

Visitors arriving in Montréal from the US on **Amtrak** can count on ten-hour rides from New York and fifteen-hour trips from Washington, DC (including an hour by bus from St Albans, VT). All things considered, it's often more time- and cost-effective to drive from the US than take the train (see p.26).

Rail passes

If you plan seeing cities outside of Montréal on your trip, it might be worth investing in a **rail pass** that covers transit to other parts of Canada and even the United States. VIA Rail's ten-day **Corridor Pass** includes Toronto, Québec City, Ottawa and Niagara Falls from $265 ($239 for students), while its twelve-day **Canrailpass** will get you from coast to coast over a thirty-day period from $508 ($457 for students). If you want to combine Canada and the United States, the thirty-day **North America Rail Pass** covers both on Amtrak and VIA Rail from $815–1149 ($734–1034 for students).

Buses

The scope of North America's **bus** services is as vast as the continent itself – something you may want to think about before considering travelling from, say, San Diego to Montréal, an epic, three-day-plus journey. But if you're on a tight budget, the US$149 fare (if purchased a week in advance) may be compelling – though be sure to factor in three days' worth of food and drink – plus you get to see a whole lot of country in between. A similar Canadian odyssey from Vancouver takes just as long, but, if you purchase two weeks in advance, costs just C$137 – a third of the regular fare.

For most travellers, however, the bus is only bearable for a day at most. The more common trips to Montréal are **from Toronto** on Coach Canada, with an express ride lasting six and a half hours ($88); Greyhound makes the two-hour-and-twenty-minute trip **from Ottawa** ($33.85 day of; $16.50 with seven-day advance purchase); and Orléans Express handles most routes in **Québec**: the Québec City express takes two hours and twenty minutes ($40, $34 with student discount).

From the US, Adirondack Trailways and Greyhound compete on the New York to Montréal run, offering half a dozen seven-hour trips per day (US$76.50). Greyhound subsidiary Vermont Transit Lines runs most trips from Boston, also at around seven hours a pop; Greyhound itself covers travel from the rest of the US. Count on about twelve hours from Washington, DC, as you'll need to transfer in New York. Keep in mind, too, that border crossings can delay your arrival time.

The **Moose Travel Network** provides a completely different experience – a mini-coach service aimed at backpackers, it hits the major destinations on the travellers' circuit between May and mid-October (for winter packages, see p.24). The jump-on, jump-off Loonie Pass package stops in Montréal, Montmorency Falls and Québec City for $160 ($150 with ISIC or hostelling discounts).

Airlines, agents and operators

Most airlines and discount travel agencies now allow you to book your tickets **online**, cutting out the cost of agents and middlemen, though many do charge a small handling fee. Good deals can also be found through auction sites, but you should read the fine print carefully. Airlines themselves often offer lower rates online than by phone, and good last-minute deals can be found on undersold flights, so be sure to include them in your search as well.

Online booking

Ⓦ www.cheaptickets.com (in US) Ⓦ www.expedia.ca (in Canada)

Ⓦ www.expedia.co.uk (in UK) Ⓦ www.expedia.com (in US)

Ⓦ www.expedia.com.au (in Australia)

Ⓦ www.hotwire.com (in US)

Ⓦ www.lastminute.com (in UK)

Ⓦ www.au.lastminute.com (in Australia)

Ⓦ www.us.lastminute.com (in US)

Ⓦ www.opodo.co.uk (in UK)

Ⓦ www.orbitz.com (in US)

Ⓦ www.priceline.com (in US)

Ⓦ www.travelocity.co.uk (in UK) Ⓦ www.travelocity.com (in US)

Ⓦ www.travelocity.ca (in Canada) Ⓦ www.zuji.com.au (in Australia) Ⓦ www.zuji.co.nz (in New Zealand)

Airlines

Aer Lingus US and Canada ☎ 1-800/IRISH-AIR, UK ☎ 0870/876 5000, Ireland ☎ 0818/365 000, Ⓦ www.aerlingus.com.

Air Canada ☎ 1-888/247-2262, UK ☎ 0871/220 1111, Ireland ☎ 01/679 3958, Australia ☎ 1300/655 76, New Zealand ☎ 0508/747-767, Ⓦ www.aircanada.com.

Air France US ☎ 1-800/237-2747, Canada ☎ 1-800/667-2747, UK ☎ 0870/142-4343, Australia ☎ 1300/390-190, Ⓦ www.airfrance.com.

Air New Zealand Australia ☎ 13 24 76, Ⓦ www.airnz.com.au; New Zealand ☎ 0800/737 000, Ⓦ www.airnz.co.nz.

Air Transat Canada ☎ 1-877/872-6728, Ⓦ www.airtransat.com.

Alitalia US ☎ 1-800/223-5730, Canada ☎ 1-800/361-8336, UK ☎ 0870/544 8259, Ireland ☎ 01/677 5171, New Zealand ☎ 09/308 3357, Ⓦ www.alitalia.com.

American Airlines ☎ 1-800/433-7300, UK ☎ 0845/7789 789, Ireland ☎ 01/602 0550, Australia ☎ 1300/650 7347, New Zealand ☎ 0800/887 997, Ⓦ www.aa.com.

Austrian Airlines US☎ 1-800/843-0002, UK ☎ 0870/124 2625, Ireland ☎ 1800/509 142, Australia ☎ 1800/642 438 or 02/9251 6155, Ⓦ www.aua.com.

bmi US ☎ 1-800/788-0555, UK ☎ 0870/607 0555, Ireland ☎ 01/407-3036, Ⓦ www.flybmi.com.

British Airways US and Canada ☎ 1-800/AIRWAYS, UK ☎ 0870/850 9850, Ireland ☎ 1890/626 747, Australia ☎ 1300/767 177, New Zealand ☎ 09/966 9777, Ⓦ www.ba.com.

Continental Airlines US and Canada ☎ 1-800/523-3273, UK ☎ 0845/607-6760, Ireland ☎ 1890/925-252, Australia ☎ 2/9244-2242, NZ ☎ 9/308-3350, International ☎ 1-800/231-0856, Ⓦ www.continental.com.

Delta US and Canada ☎ 1-800/221-1212, UK ☎ 0845/600-0950, Ireland ☎ 1850/882-031 or 01/407 3165, Australia ☎ 1-300-302-849, New Zealand ☎ 09/379 3370, Ⓦ www.delta.com.

easyJet UK ☎0905-8210905, ⊛www.easyjet .com.

EgyptAir US ☎1-800/334-6787 or 212/315-0900, Canada ☎416/960-0009, UK ☎020/7734 2343, Australia ☎1300/309-767, ⊛www.egyptair.com.eg.

JAL (Japan Air Lines) US and Canada ☎1-800/525-3663, UK ☎0845/774 7700, Ireland ☎01/408 3757, Australia ☎02/9272 1111, New Zealand ☎09/379 9906, ⊛www.jal.com or ⊛www.japanair.com.

KLM (Royal Dutch Airlines) UK ☎0870/507 4074, Australia ☎1300 303 747, New Zealand ☎09/309 1782, ⊛www.klm.com.

Lufthansa US ☎1-800/645-3880, Canada ☎1-800/563-5954, UK ☎0870/837 7747, Ireland ☎01/844 5544, Australia ☎1300 655 727, New Zealand ☎09/303 1529, ⊛www.lufthansa.com.

Qantas Airways US and Canada ☎1-800/227-4500, UK ☎0845/774 7767, Ireland ☎01/407 3278, Australia ☎13 13 13, New Zealand ☎0800/808 767 or 09/357 8900, ⊛www.qantas .com.

Royal Air Maroc ☎1-800/344-6726, UK ☎0207/307-5800, ⊛www.royalairmaroc.com.

SAS (Scandinavian Airlines) US ☎1-800/221-2350, Canada ☎1-800/221-2350, UK ☎0870/6072 7727, Ireland ☎01/844 5440, Australia ☎1300/727 707, ⊛www .scandinavian.net.

South African Airways South Africa ☎0861/359 722, ⊛www.flysaa.com.

Swiss USA and Canada ☎1-877/359-7947, UK ☎0845/601 0956, Ireland ☎1890/200 515, ⊛www.swiss.com.

Thomas Cook Airlines UK ☎0870/750 0316, ⊛www.thomascook.com.

United Airlines US ☎1-800/241-6522, UK ☎0845/844 4777, Australia ☎13 17 77, ⊛www .united.com.

US Airways US and Canada ☎1-800/428-4322, UK ☎0845-600-3300, Ireland ☎1890-925065, ⊛www.usair.com.

WestJet US and Canada ☎1-888/WEST-JET, UK and Ireland ☎0800/5381-5696, ⊛www.westjet .com.

Agents and operators

Australian Pacific Touring Australia ☎1800/675 222 or 03/9277 8555, New Zealand ☎09/279 6077, ⊛www.aptours.com. Long-established, award-winning operator running package tours and independent travel. Montréal is one stop on a ten-day Niagara Falls to Québec City coach tour; longer trips include the Rockies or US destinations. May–Sept only.

Canadian Affair UK ☎0870/075 3000, ⊛www .canadian-affair.com. Good-quality and consistently cheap charter flights from the UK to Montréal on Thomas Cook Airways (late May to Oct). Also accommodation packages, self-drive itineraries and car and motorhome hire.

Classic Journeys ☎1-800/200-3887 or 858/454-5004, ⊛www.classicjourneys.com. Walking trips with an emphasis on culture. Six-day itinerary includes Québec City, small towns and countryside in Charlevoix and the inevitable whale-watching cruise in the Saguenay. Six days for US$2395.

Contiki US and Canada ☎1-888/CONTIKI, UK ☎020/8290 6777, Australia ☎02/9511 2200, New Zealand ☎09/309 8824, ⊛www.contiki.com. Tour operator for18- to 35-year-olds only. Montréal and Québec City are included in a couple of multi-city US & Canada bus tours for around US$155 per day.

Cosmos ☎1-800/276-1241, ⊛www .cosmosvacations.com. Planned vacation packages with an independent focus. Eight-day bus tour of Ontario and Québec's major cities for US$930.

ebookers UK ☎0800/082-3000, Ireland ☎01/488-3507, ⊛www.ebookers.com. Low fares from the UK and Ireland with an extensive selection of scheduled flights and package deals.

Flightcentre Canada ☎1-888/WORLD-55, ⊛www.flightcentre.ca, US ☎1-866/WORLD-51, ⊛www.flightcentre.us, UK ☎0870/890 8099, ⊛www.flightcentre.co.uk, Australia ☎13 31 33, ⊛www.flightcentre.com.au, New Zealand ☎0800 243 544, ⊛www.flightcentre.co.nz. Rock-bottom fares from the UK, Canada, Australia and New Zealand.

Globespan UK ☎0870/556 1522, ⊛www .globespan.com. UK-based agent for Air Transat charter flights to Montréal (late May to Oct). Also car and motorhome hire.

Globus ☎1-866/755-8581, ⊛www .globusjourneys.com. Planned vacation packages such as a nine-day bus tour of Ontario and Québec's major cities for US$1469 plus a longer option that takes in the northeast US.

Kuoni Travel UK ☎01306/747 002, ⊛www.kuoni .co.uk. Award-winning major tour operator running flexible package holidays to long-haul destinations worldwide. Especially good deals for families. Offers an eleven-night Eastern Explorer coach tour to Montréal, Québec City, Ottawa, Niagara Falls and Toronto.

Lee Travel Ireland ☎021/427 7111, ⊛www .leetravel.ie. Flights and holidays worldwide from Ireland.

Maupintour ☎1-800/255-4266, ⊛www .maupintour.com. Luxury independent and escorted tours that take in Québec's big cities and scenic countryside.

Moose Travel Network ☎416/504-7514 or 1-888/816-6673, ⓦwww.moosenetwork.com. Backpacker outfit that runs hop-on and -off seven-day coach tours to Montréal, Québec City, Mont Tremblant and Ottawa from $449 in summer/winter.

STA Travel US ☎1-800/781-4040, Canada ☎1-888/427-5639, UK ☎0870/1630-026, Australia ☎1300/733 035, New Zealand ☎0508/782 872, ⓦwww.statravel.com. Worldwide specialists in independent travel; also student IDs, travel insurance, car rental, rail passes and more. Good discounts for students and those under 26.

Suntrek Tours ☎1-800/SUNTREK, ⓦwww .suntrek.com. Soft-adventure specialists who offer a two-week camping tour of the northeast US and eastern Canada that includes a couple of days in Montréal and Québec City (US$932).

Talpacific Australia ☎1300/137 727 or 02/9244 1850, New Zealand ☎0800/888 099, ⓦwww .talpacific.com. Australian and New Zeland travel-deals specialist with deals like two-night Montréal or Québec City breaks.

Thomas Cook UK ☎0870/750 0512, ⓦwww .thomascook.co.uk. Long-established one-stop UK travel agency for package holidays, city-breaks or flights, with bureau de change issuing Thomas Cook–branded traveller's cheques, plus travel insurance and car rental.

Trailfinders UK ☎0845/058 5858, Ireland ☎01/677 7888, ⓦwww.trailfinders.com. One of the best-informed and most efficient agents for independent travellers in the UK and Ireland.

Travel Bag UK ☎0870/890 1456, ⓦwww .travelbag.co.uk. Discount deals worldwide from the UK.

travel.com.au and travel.co.nz Australia ☎1300/130 482 or 02/9249 5444, ⓦwww.travel .com.au, New Zealand ☎0800/468 332, ⓦwww .travel.co.nz. Comprehensive online travel company, with discounted fares from Australia and New Zealand.

Travel4Less UK ☎0871/222 3423, ⓦwww .travel4less.co.uk. Good discount airfares, bargain global city-breaks and discounted package deals from the UK, including cruises, fly-drives and ski holidays in the Laurentians. Part of lastminute.com.

Travelmood UK ☎0870/66 45 66, ⓦwww .travelmood.com. Discounted flights to Montréal from the UK.

Trek America ☎1-800/221-0596, ⓦwww .trekamerica.com. Walking and soft-adventure tours all over the US, Canada and Mexico, year-round, for 18–38-year-olds. Montréal figures in their two-week summer-only "Canada Pioneer" trip, priced from US$1160.

Trek Holidays ☎1-800/661-7265, ⓦwww .trekholidays.com. Canadian agent that handles a vast array of deals from adventure companies worldwide. Their winter seven-day Ice Hotel trip covers Québec City, four days of backcountry snowshoeing and cross-country skiing, an overnight at the Ice Hotel and finishes in Montréal, from $2370.

USIT Northern Ireland ☎028/9032 7111, ⓦwww.usitnow.com, Ireland ☎0818/200 020, ⓦwww.usit.ie. Ireland-based specialist in student, youth and independent travel – flights, trains, study tours, TEFL, visas and more.

World Travel Centre Ireland ☎01/416 7007, ⓦwww.worldtravel.ie. Excellent worldwide fares from Ireland.

Rail contacts

Amtrak US ☎1-800/872-7245, ⓦwww.amtrak .com.
STA Travel US ☎1-800/781-4040, Canada ☎1-888/427-5639, UK ☎0870/1630-026, ⓦwww.statravel.com.
VIA Rail Canada ☎514/989-2626 or 1-888/842-7245, ⓦwww.viarail.ca.

Bus contacts

Adirondack Trailways US ☎1-800/858-8555, ⓦwww.trailways.com.
Coach Canada US and Canada ☎1-800/461-7661, ⓦwww.coachcanada.com.
Greyhound US ☎1-800-231-2222, Canada ☎416/367-8747, ⓦwww.greyhound.com.
Moose Travel Network Canada ☎416/504-7514, US ☎1-888/816-6673, ⓦwww.moosenetwork.com.
Orléans Express US and Canada ☎1-888/999-3977, ⓦwww.orleansexpress.com.
STA Travel US ☎1-800/781-4040, Canada ☎1-888/427-5639, UK ☎0870/1630-026, Australia ☎1300/360 960, New Zealand ☎0508/782-872, ⓦwww.statravel.com.
Vermont Transit Lines US ☎1-800/552-8737, ⓦwww.vermonttransit.com.

Arrival

With direct international flights from across Canada and the US, as well as many European cities, Montréal is an easy city to get to. A number of rail lines also converge on the city, bringing VIA Rail trains from the rest of Canada and Amtrak trains from the US. Orléans Express buses link the city with other Québec destinations, while a variety of companies handle transborder routes. The train station is right downtown, while the bus station is just to the east, and both are well integrated into the city's efficient public-transport system. Numerous *autoroutes* provide a relatively quick way to reach Downtown, though access to the island, via the Tunnel Lafontaine and many bridges, suffers from traffic bottlenecks at rush hour.

By air

All flights on major airlines touch down at **Aéroport de Montréal-Trudeau** (☎514/394-7377 or 1-800/465-1213, ⓦwww.admtl .com), 25km west of Downtown. The airport's layout is simple, with the domestic and international wings connected by a large concourse on the upstairs Departures level and separated by a long corridor on the ground-floor Arrivals, where currency exchange and car-rental desks are available outside the baggage-claim areas. ATMs are dotted throughout.

The cheapest way to get Downtown is by **local bus** ($2.75), a complicated, 60–90-minute journey you don't want to think about unless you're on an extremely tight budget. From outside the terminal catch #204 to the Dorval bus and train station due south of the airport. From there, switch to either one of the infrequent commuter trains downtown or bus #211 (or Métrobus #190 or #221 during rush hour) to Métro Lionel-Groulx, from where you can take the orange or green line Downtown.

Instead, most visitors opt for the straightforward and luggage-friendly **Aérobus shuttle** (☎514/931-9002; three hourly, daily 7–2am; tickets from the booth just outside the terminal between domestic and international Arrivals), which drops passengers off at the Downtown Aérobus Station (adjacent to the main train station) and main bus station in 35 to 45 minutes. Included in the $13 fare ($22.75 return) are free minibuses that connect the Aérobus Station with forty hotels in Downtown, Vieux-Montréal and the Quartier Latin.

Taxis queue up outside Arrivals and will take you anywhere within the wider Downtown area (from Vieux-Montréal to around avenue des Pins, between Atwater and Papineau) for a flat rate of $35 ($50 for limousines) plus tip; other destinations are metered.

By bus

The main terminus for long-distance buses to the city, **Station Centrale d'Autobus Montréal** (central bus station), lies on the eastern edge of the Quartier Latin, at 505 boul de Maisonneuve E (☎514/842-2281), and connects directly with Métro Berri-UQAM. It's a pretty impersonal spot, though there are adequate facilities for visitors, including ATMs, newsstands, a café/restaurant, pay-Internet terminals, currency exchange, lockers and left luggage for larger items. The area outside the station can be a bit sketchy at night – if you are carrying luggage, head directly to the Métro or catch one of the taxis that queue up outside the station. Buses from Québec City also stop at the Longueuil terminus on the South Shore, at the end of the yellow Métro line.

By train

VIA Rail and Amtrak **trains** loop south of Downtown before diving under Place Bonaventure to reach the main terminus, **Gare Centrale** (central station), located at 895 rue de la Gauchetière O in the heart of Downtown. Once inside the grand main concourse, you'll find a labyrinthine food court, ATMs, newsstands, Internet kiosks and

Driving in Québec

Road signs in Québec are the same as elsewhere in North America but usually in French. Drivers can make a right turn at a red light except on the island of Montréal. Unless indicated otherwise, maximum speed limits are 100kph on *autoroutes*, 80kph or 90kph on other highways and 50kph in built-up areas. Slower speeds are advisable in adverse winter conditions; throughout the colder months, snow tires are a necessity.

An International Driving Permit is recommended, although it is not legally required for visits of less than six months. A minimum of $50,000 third-party liability insurance is required. Nonresidents may be covered for compensation under the province's no-fault insurance if driving a vehicle registered in Québec or a province or US state with a reciprocal arrangement – see p.36 for further details.

Note that motorists are not only prohibited from using radar detectors, they may not even be carried in your car. Seatbelts are compulsory for all passengers. Finally, do not drive under the influence of alcohol – penalties are steep and often include jail time; the maximum legal alcohol-to-blood ratio for driving is 0.08 percent.

left-luggage facilities (for ticketed passengers only; $3/24hrs, $6 oversized; Mon–Fri 7am–7.15pm, Sat & Sun 7.30am–7.15pm). The station is connected to the rest of the city via the Underground City (RÉSO; see box p.49), which also links it to Métro Bonaventure and other Métro stations. If you have a lot of luggage, you might want to avoid the trek to the Métro and take a taxi instead – follow the signs to the covered taxi rank.

By car

A network of **autoroutes** (expressways or motorways) funnel into Montréal from all directions, and, apart from rush hour and bottlenecks on the bridges from the south shore, traffic generally flows quite smoothly. The two main freeways **from Ontario**, Hwy-401 from Toronto and Hwy-417 from Ottawa, converge just west of the island, from where Hwy-40 and Hwy-20 continue straight across Montréal and extend eastward to

Québec City. **From the US**, a number of interstate highways provide access to Montréal from the south. I-87 travels straight up from New York City, becoming Hwy-15 as it crosses the border. If you're coming from Boston, I-93 to I-89 (which becomes Hwy-133) provides the most direct route; alternatively, take I-91 (Hwy-55 in Québec), which leads to Hwy-10, the main route through the scenic Eastern Townships.

Roadside assistance is available from the CAA – the Canadian Automobile Association (☎514/861-5111 or 1-800/CAA-HELP for emergency assistance, ⊛www.caaquebec.com) – who have reciprocal agreements with the AAA and motoring groups from other countries. The Ministère des Transports (☎1-888/355-0511, ⊛www.mtq.gouv.qc.ca) has information on road conditions as well as a detailed online map; local English radio stations, like CJAD (800 AM), broadcast up-to-date traffic reports.

Getting around

If you're not planning to stray too far from the city centre, you can easily get around in Montréal without a car. Walking is certainly your best bet in Vieux-Montréal, where narrow streets and nightmarish parking and driving conditions prevail, but the frequent and fairly speedy Métro and buses make excellent options for seeing the rest of the city. Taxis are plentiful and relatively cheap. In the warmer months, cycling is an excellent way to get a flavour of the city.

By Métro

The clean and quiet **Métro** is run by the **STM** (Société de transport de Montréal; ☏514/288-6287, ⓦwww.stm.info), whose website and phone line provides detailed journey information. Free maps of the Métro and bus network are also available at most stations – if they've run out, drop by the system's main information desk at Métro Berri-UQAM, opposite the turnstiles nearest to the Station Centrale d'Autobus exit.

The four lines that make up the public-transit system are colour-coded, with the last stop on each line used to denote your direction – refer to the back of this guide for a colour plan of the system. The two most heavily used lines pass through Downtown – the **green line** snakes along from west to east, heading out past the Stade Olympique, while the **orange line** makes a large "U", with the arms heading north from Downtown on either side of the mountain. The east–west **blue line** runs north of the mountain, intersecting with the orange line at Snowdon and Jean-Talon stations. The **yellow line**, which only has three stops, is the best way to get to Parc Jean-Drapeau; transfer from the orange or green lines at Berri-UQAM station. Service starts at 5.30am daily on all lines. The last trains on the blue line are at 12.15pm; the others stop running at 12.30am (1am on Saturdays).

Useful bus routes

#11 (Montagne) From Métro Mont-Royal across the top of the mountain.

#24 (Sherbrooke) From Métro Sherbrooke through Downtown and Westmount to Métro Villa-Maria.

#36 (Monk) From Métro Square-Victoria along rue Notre-Dame past the Marché Atwater to Métro Angrignon.

#51 (Édouard-Montpetit) From Métro Laurier via Outremont and past the Oratoire to Métro Snowdon and beyond.

#55 (St-Laurent) From Place d'Armes in Vieux-Montréal to Little Italy via the Main.

#80 (Du Parc) From Métro Place-des-Arts alongside the mountain to Outremont and Mile-End; #129 (Côte-Ste-Catherine) follows the same route before veering off north of the mountain.

#144 (Av des Pins) From Métro Atwater to Métro Sherbrooke along the mountain's south flank and past Molson Stadium.

#165 (Côte-des-Neiges) and #166 (Queen Mary) From Métro Guy-Concordia along the mountain's west side for access to the main gate of Cimetière Notre-Dame-des-Neiges and the Oratoire.

#167 (Casino) Follows a circuit around the islands from Métro Jean-Drapeau.

#535 (R-Bus Du Parc / Côte-des-Neiges) Rush-hour service that combines the #80 and #165 routes via boulevard René-Lévesque.

Single tickets cost $2.75 but you can buy a strip of six tickets for $11.75 at retail outlets such as pharmacies and *dépanneurs* (cornershops) throughout the city as well as at the stations themselves. If you're planning to make more extensive use of the Métro and bus system, it's worth investing in a **Tourist Card** – the one-day pass is $9 from Downtown stations (but is only available at Berri-UQAM and Bonaventure stations from November to March). If you want something longer than that, the **CAM Hebdo** (a weekly commuter pass) is $18.50, giving you more days for a bit more money than the three-day tourist card at $17; the only drawback is that the pass is valid starting Monday and ends on the following Sunday.

By bus

The city's fleet of **buses** supplements the Métro system, filling in the gaps between the lines and fanning out into the suburbs. Prices are the same as for the Métro (exact fare required if paying cash rather than using a ticket) and if you want to transfer from one bus to another or on to the Métro, ask the driver for **une correspondance** (transfer) when you pay your fare. If you're planning to hop on a bus after exiting the Métro, pick up a transfer from one of the machines on the other side of the turnstiles. Bus stops indicate which Métro station the bus is heading towards, and many also have a unique telephone number you can call for the schedule for that particular stop. A limited number of routes operate after midnight; these vary from the daytime routes and are marked on the back of the STM map mentioned above.

By car

You don't really need a car when visiting Montréal unless you're planning a day out from the city. If you do insist on **driving**, avoid Vieux-Montréal where the narrow streets make life difficult and parking can be a pain (for advice on your best options, see box, p.68). Downtown traffic can be a bit slow, and, while you might have difficulty finding a metered spot, there's plenty of parking otherwise. There are numerous open-air lots (which the city hopes to reduce) and more secure underground parking as

well – the car park below Dominion Square is one of the most central.

In most of the city, traffic doesn't pose too many problems outside of rush hour, which is at its worst at *autoroute* junctions and the bridges off the island that form natural bottlenecks. If you're driving in the winter, make sure you have snow tires and antifreeze and know how to control a skid in icy conditions; in general, drive more cautiously than you would on dry roads.

Montréal is one of the only places in North America where you cannot turn right at a **red light** – and with good reason. Montréal drivers are renowned in Canada for their laissez-faire driving skills, and for them it often seems that the word "arrêt" on the red, octagonal signs is not a literal translation of "stop". Otherwise, signage in the city conforms to North American norms, albeit in French, although you're likely to have the most difficulty deciphering those related to parking – even Francophone Montrealers get caught out occasionally by the bewildering array of **parking restrictions** at certain hours, days of the week or months of the year. In residential areas, pay especially close attention to signs indicating if a resident's permit is required. Be aware that during and after a snowfall, extra no-parking signs are temporarily installed so that snow-removal crews can do their job.

If you need a **rental car**, you'll find plenty of competition at the airport and throughout Downtown (see p.228 and box opposite). You'll need to have a credit card, and an International Driver's Permit is recommended. Some car rental firms won't accept drivers under 25; others will charge a premium for younger drivers (minimum 21 years old). It may be worth booking a fly-drive package if you plan to do a lot of driving, but if you're only planning a day or two out of the city it will likely cost more and you'll have to worry about parking the beast.

Allô-Stop (☎514/985-3032, ⓦwww.allo-stop.com), is a **ride-sharing** service that matches drivers with passengers for destinations within Québec. Membership costs $6 per year, and you pay for your share of petrol – it's about $16 to Québec City, which also has a branch (☎418/522-0056); other destinations within the province are also available.

Car rental agencies

Alamo ☎1-800/462-5266, ⓦwww.alamo.com.

Avis ☎1-800/331-1212, ⓦwww.avis.com.

Budget Canada ☎1-800/268-8900, ⓦwww.budgetcanada.com, US ☎1-800/527-0700, ⓦwww.budgetrentacar.com.

Discount ☎1-800/263-2355, ⓦwww.discountcar.com.

Dollar US ☎1-800/800-3655, ⓦwww.dollar.com.

Enterprise Rent-a-Car ☎1-888/261-7331, ⓦwww.enterprise.com.

Hertz ☎1-800/654-3001, ⓦwww.hertz.com.

Kangouroute ☎1-888/768-8388, ⓦwww.kangouroute.net.

National ☎1-800/227-7368, ⓦwww.nationalcar.com.

Thrifty ☎1-800/847-4389, ⓦwww.thrifty.com.

Via Route ☎514/871-1166, ⓦwww.viaroute.com.

Taxis

Taxis are relatively cheap and easy to find Downtown and everywhere on the main roads, and they can also be found at taxi ranks near the larger hotels and transport termini. The largest and most reliable of the city's taxi fleets are Taxi Diamond (☎514/273-6331) and Taxi Co-op (☎514/725-9885). **Fares** start at $3.15 and the meter clocks another $1.45 for each kilometre travelled, or 55¢ per minute at a standstill. A short ride within Downtown will cost around $7; factor about $12–14 to the Plateau. Trips between Downtown and the airport are a fixed $35 ($50 in a limousine). A fifteen-percent tip is standard.

Cycling

Cycling is a great way to get a feel for the city's many neighbourhoods and get a bit of exercise while trekking out to more distant attractions. The main places to **rent** a bike are in Vieux-Montréal (see p.215) – handy for checking out the industrial landscapes along the Lachine Canal or exploring the islands – and the Plateau, where you'll find a number of bike shops near the rue Rachel bike path that runs from the mountain out to the Stade Olympique.

Most of the city's **bike paths** have two lanes side by side, separated from the traffic by a curb or a series of waist-high posts; be careful at intersections, especially when you are travelling counter to the main flow of traffic. In addition to the rue Rachel path, the other well-used path runs north–south from Vieux-Montréal on rue Berri, with a detour through Parc Lafontaine, north of rue Sherbrooke. For car-free cycling, the paths on the islands and the route along the Lachine Canal are both good options, though the latter gets congested with bladers and Sunday cyclists. For further details, see Chapter 16, "Sports and outdoor activities".

You can bring your bike onto the front car of the **Métro** at any time outside of rush hour (Mon–Fri before 10am and 3–7pm); as there are no lifts, be prepared to hike it up stairs and/or escalators.

By boat

Although it's less convenient (and more expensive) than taking the Métro, the passenger **ferry** that runs from the Quai Jacques-Cartier in the Vieux-Port to Île Ste-Hélène affords striking views of Montréal's skyline. The ferry runs hourly from mid-May to early October (☎514/281-8000 for schedules) and the twenty-minute ride costs $4.50 each way.

The media

English-language print media in Montréal isn't too strong on quality news reporting but does provide good local coverage (in both mainstream and alternative varieties) and up-to-date listings on events around town. Television is broadly similar to that in the US but with some home-grown programming and international shows. Likewise, radio is pretty middle-of-the-road; tune into university radio or the CBC for the most interesting broadcasts.

Newspapers and magazines

The city's only English daily **newspaper, The Montreal Gazette** ($1 weekdays, $2 Saturday; ⓦwww.montrealgazette.com), has been keeping locals abreast of all the latest news for over two centuries and contains fairly comprehensive entertainment listings; watch out for special supplements tied to the starts of major festivals. Its national and international coverage is fairly patchy – for better quality news, pick up the Toronto-based **Globe and Mail** or **National Post**. The best place to find out what's happening entertainment-wise are the free **alternative weeklies** – the two tabloid-size English papers, **Hour** (ⓦwww .afterhour.com) and the **Montreal Mirror** (ⓦwww.montrealmirror.com), are virtually indistinguishable in content; they both come out on Thursdays and are available in newsstands all over town. Their French counterparts are **Voir**, the most respected of the lot, and **ici**. Look in cafés and bookstores for other free magazines that cover various cultural and nightlife scenes, specific neighbourhoods or gay and lesbian issues. There have also been sporadic attempts at city lifestyle magazines; however, none of these seem to stick around for long. You'll find the latest English publications and foreign newspapers and magazines at the shops below.

News and magazine stands

Metropolitan News Agency 1109 Cypress ☏514/866-9227.
Multimags 370 rue Laurier O ☏514/272-2554; 652 rue Ste-Catherine O ☏514/666-5081; 3552 boul St-Laurent ☏514/287-7355; 825 ave Mont-Royal E ☏514/523-3158.

Le Point Vert 4040 boul St-Laurent ☏514/982-9195.

Radio

On the **radio**, CBC One (88.5 FM) is the national broadcaster's flagship station, with programming focusing on news and commentary, while CBC Two (93.5 FM) plays classical music. For rock, stick to the FM dial: CHOM (97.7 FM) and MIX 96 (95.9) are the best of a mediocre lot, though if you can pull in "The Buzz" (WBTZ at 99.9 FM) from across the border you'll get a more alternative bent. If you want some Francophone rock along with North American chart-toppers, try CKOI (96.9 FM) or RockDétente (107.3 FM). English talk-radio stations are on AM frequencies – try CJAD (800 AM) to hear what has the local "angryphones" up in arms this week; it's also a good source for news, sports, weather and traffic reports, as is the all-news station 940 News (940 AM). McGill University's student-run CKUT (90.3 FM) has a hit-or-miss schedule of music and spoken word covering all genres.

Television

Despite the primacy of French in the city, there are three local English-language **TV stations**: CBC on channel 6, CFCF (CTV) on channel 12 and CKMI (Global) on channel 46. The main French channels are Radio-Canada (2), TVA (10), Télé-Québec (17) and Télévision Quatre-Saisons (35). If you have a TV in your hotel room, it's most likely hooked up to **cable** – the channels for the above stations will vary depending on which cable company the hotel deals with. You'll also have access to the whole range of US networks as well as sports and music video channels and international news broadcasters like the BBC and CNN.

Travellers with disabilities

Montréal is one of the best places in the world to travel if you have mobility problems or other physical disabilities. All public buildings are required to be wheelchair-accessible and provide suitable toilet facilities, almost all street corners have dropped curbs, and public telephones are specially equipped for hearing-aid users. The city's main failing in this regard is with public transport: the Métro is inaccessible to wheelchair users, although this is offset somewhat by a system of adapted-transport buses.

Most **airlines**, both transatlantic and internal, will do whatever they can to ease your journey and will usually allow attendants of more seriously disabled people to accompany them at no extra charge – Air Canada is the best-equipped carrier.

All VIA Rail **trains** can accommodate wheelchairs that are no larger than 81cm by 182cm and weigh no more than 114kg, though 48-hours notice is required. They offer an excellent service and will help with boarding and disembarking. Those who need an attendant can apply for a two-for-one fare with a "Disability Travel Card"; it's available under "National Programs" from the Easter Seals / March of Dimes National Council (☎514/866-1969, ⓦwww.esmodnc.org). You can download an application form, which must be signed by a health professional, from their website.

Although **buses** are obliged to carry disabled passengers if their wheelchairs fit in the luggage compartment, access is often difficult. However, you can arrange to have an elevator-platform-equipped bus on most intercity routes in Québec. Nearly all bus companies accept the two-for-one *Carte à l'accompagnement* (to accompany card), and drivers are usually extremely helpful. Contact the Québec Bus Owners Association for more information and card forms, which must be submitted at least a month in advance (☎418/522-7131, ⓦwww.apaq.qc.ca). The larger **car-rental companies** can provide cars with hand controls at no extra charge, though these are only available on their most expensive models; book one as far in advance as you can.

Montréal is also blessed with an organization that works to make tourist facilities accessible: **Kéroul** (☎514/252-3104, ⓦwww.keroul.qc.ca) provides information, and publishes the *Le Québec Accessible* ($19.95) guide to accommodation, attractions and other services in the city and around the province. Much of their documentation is in French, however, so it may also be worth contacting the Canadian Paraplegic Association (CPA), who can provide a wealth of information on travelling in Canada (see below). The provincial tourist office is also an excellent source of information on accessible hotels, motels and sights. As well, keep an eye out for the tourist and leisure companion sticker (TLCS, also known by its French acronym VATL), which allows free access for the companion of a person living with a disability or a mental health problem when they visit tourist and leisure activity sites. For a list of participating establishments, visit ⓦwww.vatl.qc.ca.

Contacts in Canada

Canadian Paraplegic Association
☎1-800/720-4933, ⓦwww.canparaplegic.org.
Their main office is at Suite 230, 1101 Prince of Wales Drive, Ottawa, Ontario K2C 3W7 ☎613/723-1033, ⓕ613/723-1060; however, there are branches in most other provinces. Comprehensive resources for persons with spinal cord injuries and other disabilities; their website has hundreds of links to useful sites.
Kéroul Box 1000, Station M, 4545 ave Pierre-de-Coubertin, Montréal, Québec H1V 3R2 ☎514/252-3104, ⓕ514/254-0766, ⓦwww.keroul.qc.ca. Provides information on the accessibility of accommodation and attractions around the province; they also offer tour packages to various Québec destinations.

Travel essentials

Costs

Montréal ranks among the cheaper of Canada's major cities, and while the Canadian dollar has grown stronger, it's still less expensive to visit than, say, London or New York.

Accommodation will eat up the largest chunk of your budget – unless you take advantage of Montréal's pricier gastronomic restaurants or go full-tilt on the nightlife front. Aside from a no-frills youth hostel or student residence room, count on spending around $50–75 for a budget one- or two-star hotel. Many of these places can be fairly grim and it's worth spending closer to $100 for B&B accommodation (the large breakfasts go some way to making up the difference) or one of the city's charming small hotels. Downtown and even more so in Vieux-Montréal, you'd be hard-pressed to find a decent place below $150, and you're looking at over $300 for the most spectacular properties. Many hotels offer promotional deals in the off-season.

You can get by on as little as $20 a day for **food** if you stick to cheap fry-up breakfasts, a sandwich for lunch and a fast-food shawarma (kebab) pita, noodle dish or pizza by the slice for dinner. That would be a shame, though, as Montréal has a fantastic array of restaurants that are cheaper than ones of comparable quality in Europe or America's foodie capitals. Figure on around $50 a day for moderately priced meals and a drink or two, though you can easily spend that on dinner alone (double it for a quality bottle of wine) at finer places.

In restaurants, it's customary to **tip** fifteen percent of the total before taxes. If there's a group of you, the restaurant may insist on adding the tip to your bill. Bar staff expect fifteen percent tip, as do taxi drivers and hairdressers. For porters, doormen and bellhops, tip $1 per bag; ditto per drink at a bar – even if you get it from the bartender yourself.

Passes

If you're planning to see a lot of museums while in Montréal, you'll also save money by picking up one of three passes. The **Carte Musées Montréal** (Montréal Museums Pass; Ⓦ www.museesmontreal.org), covers access to some 32 attractions, including the Musée des Beaux-Arts, the Centre Canadien d'Architecture and the Musée d'Archéologie, for $35 ($45 including three-day Métro pass), over three consecutive days; you can buy it at participating museums or at either of the tourist information centres listed on p.40 and most city hotels. The main attractions east of Downtown aren't included, however; to see the Biodôme, Jardin Botanique and Insectarium, get the Nature Package for $20.50, or add on a trip up the Stade Olympique's tower with the Get an Eyeful pass for $31.50.

Both the federal and provincial governments get their share of **taxes**: the 6 percent GST (TPS in French) goes to the former and the 7.5 percent QST (TVQ in French) the latter.

Youth and student cards

Once obtained, various **youth/student ID cards** soon pay for themselves in savings. Full-time students are eligible for the International Student ID Card (ISIC; ⓦwww .isiccard.com), which entitles the bearer to special air, rail and bus fares and discounts at museums, theatres and other attractions. The card costs $16, US$22, £7, A$18 and NZ$20. You only have to be 26 or younger to qualify for the International Youth Travel Card, which costs US$22/£7 and carries the same benefits. All these cards are available in Canada from Travel CUTS (known as Voyages Campus in Québec), in the US from STA and Travel CUTS, and from STA in the UK, Australia and New Zealand.

Crime and personal safety

In contrast to comparable-sized cities in the US, there's very little street crime in Montréal. You shouldn't have any problems in terms of personal safety if you stick to the main parts of town, though it's obviously advisable to be cautious late at night. During the day, the usual rules apply: don't flash money around or leave bags unattended or visible in your car.

The main exceptions are the drug-dealing areas around Parc Émilie-Gamelin and to the east of the bus station and the red-light district along rue Ste-Catherine, near boulevard St-Laurent (although this is relatively tame by American standards and much of the activity is being pushed away eastwards). Also, avoid the larger parks late at night. Public transit is generally safe at any time of the day – any problems tend to be well out in the suburbs.

Montréal is generally a safe place for **women**, though the usual common sense rules apply: avoid walking alone late at night outside of well-lit, populated areas. Don't take short-cuts through parks or vacant lots and, when walking along the sidewalk, stay close to the curb and away from dark nooks in buildings and alleyways. Women who are travelling on city buses at night can take advantage of the "Entre deux arrêts" service, whereby you can ask the bus driver to let you off between stops after 7.30pm (9pm May–Aug).

Theft is also uncommon, though it's obviously a good idea to be on your guard against petty thieves. Always keep an eye on your luggage at bus and train stations; secure your things in a locker when staying in hostel accommodation or in a safe at hotels; and if you need to leave valuables in your car, stow them in the trunk and park in a well-lit area. If you are unlucky enough to be attacked or have something stolen, phone the **police** on ☎911 or ☎514/280-2222 for non-emergencies. If you're going to make an insurance claim or traveller's cheque refund application, ensure the crime is recorded by the police and make a note of the report number.

Electricity

Electricity in Québec is 110V. Visitors from outside of North America will need to bring a converter.

Entry requirements

Citizens of the EU, the EEA and most Commonwealth countries travelling to Canada do not need an entry visa – all that is required is a valid passport. Technically at least, United States citizens only need some form of photo identification plus proof of US residence and citizenship (eg a birth certificate), but given the heightened state of security on all North American borders, you would be well advised to present a passport. Note that a US driver's licence alone is insufficient proof of citizenship.

All visitors to Canada have to complete a **customs declaration card**, which you'll be given on the plane or at the US/Canada border. At point of entry, the Canadian immigration officer will check the declaration card and decide the **length of stay permitted**, up to a maximum of six months, but usually not more than three. The officers rarely refuse entry, but they may launch into an impromptu investigation, asking how much money you have and what job you do;

they may also ask to see a return or onward ticket or e-itinerary. If they ask where you're staying and you give the name and address of friends, don't be surprised if they check. Note also that, although passing overland between the US and Canada is usually straightforward, there can sometimes be long delays.

For visits of **more than six months**, **study trips** and stints of temporary **employment**, contact the nearest Canadian embassy, consulate or high commission for authorization prior to departure (see opposite for contact details). Once inside Canada, if an extension of stay is desired, written application must be made to the nearest **Canada Immigration Centre** well before the expiry of the authorized visit.

Duty-free

As for **duty-free allowances**, visitors arriving in Québec who are 18 years of age or older may import, duty- and tax-free and for personal use, either 1.5 litres of wine, 1.14L of liquor or spirits, or 24 x 355 ml cans or bottles of beer, ale or their equivalent.

Canadian high commissions, consulates and embassies

An official list of all Canada's **high commissions**, **consulates** and **embassies** abroad, including email and postal addresses and telephone numbers, is to be found on ⓦ www.dfait-maeci.gc.ca/world/embassies /menu-en.asp.

Canadian consulates abroad

Australia Canberra High Commission ☎ 02/6270 4000; Melbourne Consulate ☎ 03/9653-9674; Perth Consulate ☎ 08/9322 7930; Sydney Consulate General ☎ 02/9364 3000.
Ireland Dublin Embassy ☎ 01/417 4100.
New Zealand Auckland Consulate ☎ 09/309 3690; Wellington High Commission ☎ 04/473 9577.
South Africa Johannesburg High Commission ☎ 27-11-442 3130; Cape Town Consulate General ☎ 27 (21) 423-5240; Durban Consulate ☎ 27 (31) 303-9695; Pretoria High Commission ☎ 27 (12) 422-3000.
UK London High Commission ☎ 020/7258 6600.
USA Washington, DC, Embassy ☎ 202/682 1740; Consulates General in Atlanta, Boston, Buffalo, Chicago, Dallas, Denver, Detroit, Los Angeles, Miami, Minneapolis, New York and Seattle. Consulates in Anchorage, Houston, Raleigh, Philadelphia, Phoenix, San Diego and San Francisco.

Gay and lesbian travellers

Montréal is one of the most progressive cities in the world when it comes to **gay and lesbian** rights. The province of Québec was one of the first to recognize same-sex unions, in 2002 – the federal government of Canada followed suit in 2005 – making Montréal a popular gay wedding destination. That said, the city has long been on the gay party circuit thanks to major annual events like Black and Blue (October), Red Weekend (mid-February), Bal des Boys (New Year's Eve) and Divers/Cité (August), Montréal's annual Gay Pride event. See Chapter 13,

Crossing the US/Canada border

Recently there has been a lot of confusion in the US about what is needed to cross the **US/Canada border**. American visitors crossing the border in either direction do not need a **passport**. However, they may be asked to verify their citizenship with either a passport or a birth certificate, as well as a photo ID. Naturalized US citizens should carry a naturalization certificate, and permanent US residents who are not citizens should carry their Alien Registration Receipt Card (Green Card). Non-American visitors to Canada crossing into the US for a simple day-trip should be aware of all visa regulations and/or residency requirements for both countries and have the proper paperwork, or else risk being stranded at the border. Worthy sites to consult for relevant information include **Transports Québec** (ⓦ www.mtq.gouv.qc .ca), **Canadian Border Service Agency** (ⓦ www.cbsa.gc.ca) and US **Department of State** (ⓦ travel.state.gov).

"Gay Montréal", for more information on gay events, bars, accommodation and the like.

Health

While Canada has excellent health care service, nonresidents are not entitled to free health care, and medical costs can be astronomical, depending on the treatment. If you have an accident, medical services will get to you quickly and charge you later.

Doctors and **dentists** can be found listed in the *Pages Jaune (*Yellow Pages), but for **medical emergencies** (as well as fire and police) call ☎911. If you are bringing medicine prescribed by your doctor, carry a copy of the prescription – first, to avoid problems at customs and immigration; second, for renewing medication with Canadian doctors, as required.

As you would expect, Montréal has scores of **pharmacies.** One chain, PharmaPrix, has two central Plateau locations: 3861 boul St-Laurent (☎514/844-3550) and 1 Mont-Royal E (☎514/284-1865). Its competitor, Jean Coutu, has a downtown branch at 677 rue Ste-Catherine O (☎514/289-0800).

Canada requires no specific vaccinations and the only issue you may have to contend with in Québec are irritants like **blackflies** and **mosquitoes** – which are only prevalent if you go camping in backcountry like Mont-Tremblant and Oka. If you are planning a wilderness expedition, you'd be well-advised to take three times the recommended daily dosage of **vitamin B complex** for two weeks before you go and to take the recommended dosage while you're in Canada; this cuts down bites by up to 75 percent.

Once you're there, **repellent creams** and **sprays** may help – the ointment version of Deep-Woods Off is the best brand, with 95 percent DEET – as will wearing long socks, trousers and sleeved shirts. Other tricks include burning coils or candles containing allethrin or citronella. Once bitten, an **antihistamine cream** like Phenergan is the best antidote.

Medical resources for travellers

US and Canada

Canadian Society for International Health Ⓦwww.csih.org. Extensive list of travel-health centres.

CDC Ⓦwww.cdc.gov/travel. Official US government travel-health website.
International Society for Travel Medicine Ⓦwww.istm.org. Has a full list of travel-health clinics.

Australia, New Zealand and South Africa

Travellers' Medical and Vaccination Centre Ⓦwww.tmvc.com.au, ☎1300/658 844. Lists travel clinics in Australia, New Zealand and South Africa.

UK and Ireland

British Airways Travel Clinics ☎012776/685-040 or Ⓦwww.britishairways.com/travel/healthclinintro/public/en_gb for nearest clinic.
Hospital for Tropical Diseases Travel Clinic ☎020/7387-5000 or ☎0845/155-5000, Ⓦwww.thehtd.org.
MASTA (Medical Advisory Service for Travellers Abroad) Ⓦwww.masta.org or ☎0113/238-7575 for the nearest clinic.
Travel Medicine Services ☎028/9031 5220.
Tropical Medical Bureau ☎1850/487 674, Ⓦwww.tmb.ie.

Insurance

You'd do well to take out an **insurance policy** before travelling to Canada to cover against theft, loss, and illness or injury, especially as Canada's generally excellent health service costs nonresidents anything from $50 to $1000–2000 a day for hospitalization. There is no free treatment to nonresidents but if you do have an accident, medical services will get to you quickly and charge you later.

Before paying for a new policy, however, it's worth checking whether you are already covered: some all-risks home insurance policies may cover your possessions when overseas, and many private medical schemes include coverage when abroad. For residents from elsewhere in Canada, provincial health plans usually provide full coverage for hospitalization but for a visit to a physician you need to pay up front and seek reimbursement later. Holders of official student/teacher/youth cards in Canada and the US are entitled to meagre accident coverage and hospital in-patient benefits. Students will often find that their student health coverage extends during the vacations and for one term beyond the

Rough Guides travel insurance

Rough Guides has teamed up with Columbus Direct to offer you **travel insurance** that can be tailored to suit your needs. Products include a low-cost **backpacker** option for long stays; a **short break** option for city getaways; a typical **holiday package** option and others. There are also annual **multi-trip** policies for those who travel regularly. Different sports and activities (trekking, skiing etc) can usually be covered if required.

See our website (⊛www.roughguidesinsurance.com) for eligibility and purchasing options. Alternatively, UK residents should call ☎0870/033-9988; US citizens should call ☎1-800/749-4922; Australians should call ☎1-300/669 999. All other nationalities should call ☎+44 870/890 2843.

date of last enrollment. Some credit-card companies also offer coverage if your holiday is purchased using your card; however, coverage is generally minimal.

If you are **driving** to Montréal, you must have at least $50,000 liability coverage. Under the Société de l'Assurance Automobile du Québec (SAAQ) insurance scheme, you are fully covered if injured in a Québec-registered automobile (including rental cars). If your car isn't registered in Québec (or a Canadian province that has a reciprocal agreement), or you are a pedestrian or cyclist, you can also claim compensation to the degree that the accident wasn't your fault. For more information, visit the SAAQ website (⊛www.saaq.gouv.qc.ca) or call ☎1-800/361-7620.

Internet

You won't have a problem checking your email or surfing the **Internet** while in Montréal, as the city is extremely well-connected – as it should be, considering it's among Canada's foremost telecommunications centres. Consequently, many cafés offer wireless service, while others allow you to log on to on-site terminals for as little as 10¢ per minute or $5 per hour. A list of **WiFi**-enabled cafés and restaurants is maintained by Île sans fil (⊛www.ilesansfil.org); if you left your laptop at home, drop by one of the **cyber cafés** listed below, a couple of which are open around the clock.

Internet cafés

Café Planète 163 av Mont-Royal E ☎514/844-2233.

Centre d'affaires Montréal 4117a boul St-Laurent ☎514-844-0388.
Netopia 1737 rue St-Denis ☎514/286-5446. Open 24hrs.
Net 24 2157 rue Mackay ☎514/845-9634. Open 24hrs.

Laundry

While you're unlikely to be in Montréal long enough to require **laundry** services, they're easily procurable at most hotels, especially the higher-end ones. If you're more inclined to wash your own unmentionables, you'll find a good concentration of laundromats on the Plateau; one of the best all-around options is **Buanderie Net-Net**, 310 rue Duluth E (☎514/844-5811), where you can wash and fold for around $8, or let them do it for you in 24 hours for 89¢ per pound.

Mail

The main Downtown **post office** is at 1250 rue University (Mon–Fri 8am–5.45pm). Most other post office opening hours are Monday to Friday 8.30am to 5.30pm, though a few places are open on Saturday between 9am and noon. Service counters are also found inside larger stores, pharmacies and the like, so look out for Postes Canada / Canada Post signs or look up the nearest outlet (☎1-866/607-6301, ⊛www.canadapost.ca). Newsstands, pharmacies, hotels and souvenir shops usually sell stamps either individually or in a pack of six or so.

Letters and postcards under 30g cost 51¢ to mail in Canada, 89¢ to the US and $1.49 to international addresses. If you're posting letters to Canadian addresses, always include the recipient's postal code or your mail may never get there.

Letters can be sent **poste restante** to any Canadian main post office by addressing them c/o Poste Restante. Make a pickup date if known, or write "Hold for 15 days", the maximum period mail will usually be held. After that time the post is returned to sender, so it's a good idea to put a return address on any post. Take some form of ID when collecting.

Maps

The tourist information offices (see p.40) provide a comprehensive **map** of Montréal's main sightseeing areas, which, along with the maps in this guide, should be sufficient for your needs. If you're planning to use city buses, the free map available from the STM (see p.27) covers the whole island but lacks the detail you'd need for driving. If you're a member of a motoring organization, it's worth checking to see if they provide maps free of charge; otherwise, there are a number of commercial options (see below). You can also download maps: Transports Québec has a road map of the province (Ⓦwww.mtq.gouv.qc.ca – click on "Inforoutière"), while the city website has plans of districts and tourist areas (Ⓦwww .ville.montreal.qc.ca – click on "Discovering Montréal") and the STM has detailed (if dated) maps of the areas surrounding each Métro station (Ⓦwww.stm.info/English /metro/a-mapmet.htm) as well as various transit maps.

MapArt produces the best general map of the city, a fully indexed map of the island with an enlargement of the Downtown area; Rand McNally produces one at a similar scale. Larger-scale maps that cover the main tourist areas (essentially the same area as the enlargement on the map mentioned above), and highlight attractions, hotels and the like, include MapArt's *Downtown Montréal Map* ($5.95) and *Montréal Fast Track Map* ($9.95), plus American Map's laminated *Insight FlexiMap* ($8.95) and National Geographic's *Montréal Destination Map* ($8.99). MapArt also publishes a series of street atlases of Montréal and the surrounding area.

Money

The **Canadian currency** is the dollar ($), made up of 100 cents (¢) to the dollar. Coins are issued in 1¢ (penny), 5¢ (nickel), 10¢ (dime), 25¢ (quarter), $1 and $2 denominations; the $1 coin is known as a "loonie", after the bird on one face, the $2 coin is mostly called the "twoonie". Paper currency comes in $5, $10, $50, $100, $500 and $1000 denominations. Although US dollars are widely accepted, the exchange rate is rarely favourable – it's mostly on a one-for-one basis, even though the US dollar is worth more than its Canadian counterpart – and you're better off exchanging it at a bank or similar, rather than going shopping with it.

As regards **exchange rates**, at the time of writing C$1 is worth US$0.88, £0.47, A$1.16, and €0.69. For the most up-to-date rates, check the currency-converter website Ⓦwww.oanda.com. You can **exchange currency** at private outfits at the airport and in tourist areas; the best are **Calforex**, 1250 rue Peel (☎514/392-9100), and **Thomas Cook**, Centre Eaton, 705 rue Ste-Catherine O (☎514/284 7388). Large downtown **banks** also exchange currency; Banque Royale, Banque de Montréal, CIBC, Banque TD-Canada Trust, Banque Scotia, Banque Nationale and Banque Laurentienne are the major banks and are generally open Monday to Friday 10am–4pm (it's very rare to find one open on Saturday). All of them are equipped with *guichets automatique* (**ATMs**) which accept Plus- and/or Cirrus-networked cards (all are on the Canadian Interac system). Make sure you have a personal identification number (PIN) that's designed to work overseas. You'll also find ATMs at *caisses populaires* (credit unions), bars, restaurants, some Métro stations and elsewhere. Most machines charge a fee of $1 or $2 in addition to any banking fees your home institution may charge. ATMs also accept **credit cards**; all major cards, including MasterCard, Visa and American Express, are widely accepted in Montréal.

Opening hours and public holidays

As a general rule, most **museums** are open from 10am to 5.30pm, though many are

Official public holidays

January
1: New Year's Day
March/April
Good Friday
Easter Monday
May
Monday preceding May 25: Fête des Patriotes (Victoria Day)
June
24: Fête St-Jean-Baptiste
July
1: Canada Day
September
1st Monday: Labour Day
October
2nd Monday: Thanksgiving
November
11: Remembrance Day (partial holiday)
December
25: Christmas Day
26: Boxing Day

which have shorter winter hours or close altogether. Many attractions have extended opening hours for the **summer season**, which typically begins on the weekend nearest the Fête St-Jean and extends until Labour Day, though some may commence summer operations as early as the Fête des Patriotes and/or carry through to Thanksgiving in October. Note that Canada's Thanksgiving is a month earlier than the American one and coincides with Columbus Day in the US.

Banks, schools and government buildings close on **public holidays** although many shops, restaurants, museums and sights remain open (in fact, many museums that are normally closed on Mondays open on holidays).

Phones

Unlike in Europe, local calls made from a private residence or commercial establishment in Canada cost nothing at all to make – and it's just 25¢ for unlimited conversations on **public telephones**. If you'll be making a number of calls and don't feel like carrying around a stack of quarters, pick up a prepaid La Puce **phone card** from Bell-Canada outlets, newsagents and the Centre Infotouriste; the card comes in a variety of denominations and works like a debit card – insert it into phones with a yellow card-reader and you'll be deducted the cost of the call. Bell's other cards are better for long-distance and international calls, but there are a variety of competing cards and access numbers. Many public telephones also accept credit cards though you'll be charged at a higher rate; collect calls to elsewhere in Canada and the US can likewise be costly. Commercial establishments often have toll-free (freephone) numbers, which begin with 1-800, 1-866, 1-877 or 1-888. Otherwise, local phone numbers are ten digits long, including area code – 514 represents Montréal, 450 the outskirts – and all ten numbers need to be composed to make a call.

closed one day of the week (usually Monday) and may be open late one day during the middle of the week (often free of charge). Government **offices**, including post offices, are open during regular business hours, typically 8.30 or 9am until 5 or 5.30pm, Monday to Friday. **Shops** are generally open Monday to Friday 10am–6pm (with many staying open as late as 9pm on Thursday and Friday), Saturday 11am–5pm and Sunday noon–5pm. Smaller specialty shops may be closed Sunday and/or Monday.

Montrealers tend to dine a bit later than the rest of North America, so **restaurants** are typically open until around 11pm; quite a few open for dinner at 6pm, especially on weekends. Many diner-type places, however, close earlier in the evening (or much later, if they cater to the nightlife crowd). Places that specialize in breakfasts open early, between 6am and 8am and shut mid-afternoon. **Bars** open anywhere between 11am and mid-evening and continue serving until 3am in most cases. Clubs don't open their doors until around 10pm and, except for after-hours clubs, shut at 3am.

Time of year makes a big difference to opening times of information centres, museums and other attractions, many of

If you want to use your own **mobile** in Canada, you'll need to check with your service provider as to whether it will work abroad. It's unlikely that a mobile bought for use outside Canada or the US will work in Montréal, so if you expect to be making a lot of local calls, it's worth investing in a

Useful telephone numbers

Emergencies ☎911 for fire, police and ambulance.

Police ☎514/280-2222 for non-emergencies.

Operator ☎0.

Directory assistance (local) ☎411.

Directory assistance (long-distance) ☎1 + area code + 555-1212.

Directory assistance (toll-free numbers) ☎1-800/555-1212.

Area codes ☎514 Montréal; ☎450 off-island suburbs, Lower Laurentians and western areas of the Eastern Townships; ☎819 Upper Laurentians and rest of Eastern Townships; ☎418 Québec City.

International and long-distance dialling

Montréal From the US and Canada, dial 1 + 514 + number; from overseas, dial your international access code + 1 + 514 + number.

US and Canada 1 + area code + number.

UK 011 + 44 + city code + number.

Ireland 011 + 353 + city code + number.

Australia 011 + 61 + city code + number.

New Zealand 011 + 64 + city code + number.

Note that the initial zero is omitted from the area code when dialling the UK, Ireland, Australia and New Zealand from abroad.

---

temporary SIM card from Canadian wireless providers like Fido ($30; ☎1-888/481-3437, ⓦwww.fido.ca) or Rogers ($25; ☎1-800/575-9090, ⓦwww.rogers.ca); once inserted into your phone, all you'll need to do is buy a pre-paid phone card (denominations start at $10) to make calls from your new local phone number. You can pick up both at La Cabine Téléphonique, 705 rue Ste-Catherine O (☎514/282-2063), a Downtown cell phone store located near the Centre Eaton.

Visitors from other parts of Canada may be able to make local calls at the same rates as in their home area code. If that's the case, you're better off not answering an incoming call and instead phoning the caller right back; otherwise you, and possibly they as well, will pay long-distance charges. Some US phones will only work within the region designated by the area code in the phone number (212, 415, etc) – check with your service provider whether this applies to your phone.

In the UK, you'll generally have to inform your phone provider before going abroad to get international access switched on. There are usually hefty charges even for local calls as well as extra charges for incoming calls when in Canada. If you want to retrieve messages while you're away, you'll need a

new access code from your provider. Most UK mobiles – as well as those in Australia and New Zealand – use GSM, which gives access to most places worldwide, except Canada and the US. For further information about using your phone abroad, check out ⓦ www.telecomsadvice.org.uk/features /using_your_mobile_abroad_roaming.htm.

Time

Montréal is in North America's Eastern **time zone**, four hours behind Greenwich Mean Time from the first Sunday in April to the last Sunday in October, and five hours behind the rest of the year. Unlike most cities in Canada, however, times for events, performances, store openings and the like, are usually cited according to the French 24-hour system, with 17h meaning 5pm and 20h30 meaning 8.30pm, and so forth.

Tourist information

The main tourist information office in Montréal is the Downtown **Centre Infotouriste** located in the Dominion Square Building facing Square Dorchester, just south of rue Ste-Catherine (daily: late June to early Sept 8.30am–7.30pm; early Sept to late June 9am–6pm). Run by

Calling home from abroad

Note that the initial zero is omitted from the area code when dialing the UK, Ireland, Australia and New Zealand from abroad.

US and Canada international access code + 1 + area code.
Australia international access code + 61 + city code.
New Zealand international access code + 64 + city code.
UK international access code + 44 + city code.
Ireland international access code + 353 + city code.
South Africa international access code + 27 + city code.

Tourisme Québec, it has loads of brochures and information on Montréal sights (including free maps and the useful **Montréal Official Tourist Guide** booklet) and those of the rest of the province, making it an excellent stop if you're planning to do some travelling outside the city. In addition, there's an accommodation service and a counter where private companies offer currency exchange, car rental and city tours – most bus tours depart from directly in front of the office.

The city-run tourist office, the **Bureau d'Information Touristique de Vieux-Montréal**, is on the corner of Place Jacques-Cartier at 174 rue Notre-Dame (early June to early Sept 9am–7pm; early Sept to early June 9am–5pm). There are also a number of smaller information offices or kiosks dealing with specific districts – these are described in the relevant sections of the Guide.

Tourist offices

Bureau d'Information Touristique de Vieux-Montréal 174 rue Notre-Dame E ☎514/874-9553 or 1-877/266-5687, ⓦ www.vieux.montreal.qc.ca or www.tourism-montreal.org.

Tourisme Québec 1255 rue Peel, Suite 100 ☎514/873-2015 or 1-877/266-5687, ⓦ www .bonjourquebec.com.

The City

The City

Downtown Montréal

Although **Downtown Montréal** lacks the charm of Vieux-Montréal or the edginess of the Plateau, it's dotted with enough old churches and museums to more than fill a few days' exploration. Besides historical and cultural attractions, Downtown affords plentiful opportunities for both **shopping** and **nightlife**, especially along **rue Ste-Catherine**, where many of Montréal's best cinemas, music venues, bars and clubs are found.

The main thoroughfares Downtown run east–west, giving it a long, rectangular shape bounded by rue Sherbrooke to the north, rue St-Antoine to the south and boulevard St-Laurent to the east, beyond which it merges with the Quartier Latin (see p.85). The western border is harder to define, as it overlaps with the remnants of the historic Anglophone enclave once known as the **Golden Square Mile**.

Downtown Montréal

A number of public spaces, such as **Square Dorchester** and **Place du Canada**, break up Downtown's long stretches of commercial establishments, which helps keep the area from feeling too claustrophobic. The centrally located cruciform skyscraper and attendant plaza of **Place Ville Marie** mark the southern end of the city's truncated "Champs d'Elysées", while to the east can be found **Christ Church Cathedral**, the **Musée d'Art Contemporain de Montréal** and the performance halls of **Place des Arts**. South of there are the bustling restaurants and shops of Montréal's small **Chinatown**.

Some history

For the first couple of centuries of Montréal's existence, most development was concentrated in Vieux-Montréal and the *faubourgs*, residential areas clustered outside the gates of the former city walls. At the start of the nineteenth century, when rue Ste-Catherine was laid out, the area that is now Downtown was little more than a spread of farms. But within a few decades, rue Ste-Catherine was lined with townhouses, schools and churches, and by the 1840s had become the city's main commercial thoroughfare. Houses continued to be built along the side streets, with middle-class neighbourhoods sprouting up and the wealthier nabbing prime estates on the mountain's slopes for their mansions.

In 1865, the first horse-drawn streetcars began running along rue Ste-Catherine year-round, leading to Downtown's expansion as the Anglophone population moved further north and west into villa and rowhouse subdivisions

△ Musée des Beaux-Arts

clutching at the skirts of the wealthy's estates, and financial institutions began to make their mark. It wasn't long before Downtown became increasingly urbanized, spurred by the opening of the Gare Windsor in the 1880s and the first of the big department stores around Square Phillips a decade later. In the 1890s, electric streetcars began running along rue Ste-Catherine, making it the largest commercial artery in Canada by the time Ogilvy opened its doors at its present location on the corner of rue de la Montagne in 1912. The following decades saw the advent of the big movie palaces, theatres and cabarets that would become a part of the fabled nightlife that drew Prohibition escapees from the US for riotous weekends. Hotels and restaurants cropped up on middle-class residential side-streets such as rue Peel, while businesses as well as shops began choosing Downtown instead of Vieux-Montréal for their headquarters (notably Sun Life's giant wedding cake of a headquarters, built between 1914 and 1933).

Montréal's answer to New York's Rockefeller Center, the signature Place Ville Marie skyscraper and the vast climate-controlled shopping centre at its base, opened in 1962 (the year construction on the Métro began), with Royal Bank as its principal tenant. This coup sealed Vieux-Montréal's fate: the other large, conservative banks followed the Royal Bank's lead in the ongoing exodus from the old city to Downtown. An explosion of other major works in the 1960s, including Place des Arts and a number of other office towers, completed Downtown's transformation as the city's cultural and business centre. The first phase of the Métro went into operation in 1966, linked to ten Downtown buildings (including the monstrous Place Bonaventure) that formed the nucleus of the now famous Underground City (RÉSO) (see p.49), just in time for Expo '67 and Montréal's debut as an "international city".

Most of the rest of Downtown's present-day character was formed in a massive construction boom in the Eighties and early Nineties, when McGill College was widened and a number of skyscrapers shot up to rival Place Ville Marie in height and add to the Underground City (RÉSO) with their lower-floor shopping malls and passageways. Today, the process continues towards

Downtown's fringes with the towers of the Cité du Commerce Électronique (E-Commerce Place) near the Centre Bell and the filling in of the gap between Downtown and Vieux-Montréal with the Quartier International development. But other than a recessionary blip in the mid-1990s that caused quite a few boarded-up shopfronts, rue Ste-Catherine continues to be Downtown's bustling commercial heart.

Square Dorchester and Place du Canada

Square Dorchester, on the east side of rue Peel between rue Ste-Catherine and boulevard René-Lévesque, is a good place to get your bearings as Montréal's main **Infotouriste** office (late June to early Sept daily 8.30am–7.30pm; early Sept to May 9am–6pm; ☎514/873-2015 or 1-877/266-5687, ⓦwww .bonjourquebec.com) is located in the Dominion Square Building on the square's north border. Originally a Catholic cemetery, the area was first laid out as Dominion Square in 1872 and subsequently partitioned by the widening of Dorchester Boulevard, with the southern half becoming Place du Canada (see below). Controversy erupted after the boulevard – whose moniker honoured Lord Dorchester, the British governor for much of the late 1700s – was renamed **boulevard René-Lévesque** following the premier's death in 1987. The northern half of the square was later called Square Dorchester in order to appease Anglophones.

Lording over the eastern side of the square is the grey-granite **Édifice Sun Life**, built in 1918 and for a quarter of a century the largest office building in the British Commonwealth. The building's principal tenant for many decades – the Sun Life Assurance Company – was among the many Canadian firms that moved their head offices out of Montréal around the time of the 1980 referendum on sovereignty. Today, the cool marble and minimalist decor in the large lobby behind the massive bronze doors speak of old money.

The similarly monumental **Windsor Hotel** that once mirrored the Sun Life building hosted a procession of royalty in its time, but was mostly destroyed in a fire. The streamlined Tour CIBC skyscraper replaced the main part of the hotel in 1962 and was briefly the country's tallest building until eclipsed by Place Ville Marie later that year. In the 1906 annex that was spared, you can still see the opulent chandelier-lit Peacock Alley, a gilt marble hall that links the two formal ballrooms.

Separated from Square Dorchester by boulevard René-Lévesque, the southern half of Dominion Square was renamed **Place du Canada** in 1967, Canada's centennial year. Its name made it an appropriate rallying point for national unity during the 1995 referendum on separation, when, three days before the vote, some 300,000 federalists gathered here in the largest political demonstration the country has ever seen. The square – mostly covered in asphalt, with a few bits of greenery – is dotted with various memorials and monuments, including an imposing bronze statue of **Sir John A. MacDonald**, Canada's first prime minister, but most items of interest lie on the periphery.

Basilique-Cathédrale Marie-Reine-du-Monde

Dominating Place du Canada's eastern perimeter is the **Basilique-Cathédrale Marie-Reine-du-Monde** (Cathedral-Basilica of Mary Queen of the World; daily 7am–7.30pm except during mass at 7.30am, 8am, 12.10pm & 5pm; ☎514/866-1661, ⓦwww.cathedralecatholiquedemontreal.org; Métro Bonaventure), a scaled-down version of St Peter's in Rome that includes faithful copies of the original's massive portico and copper dome. Although many think the statues

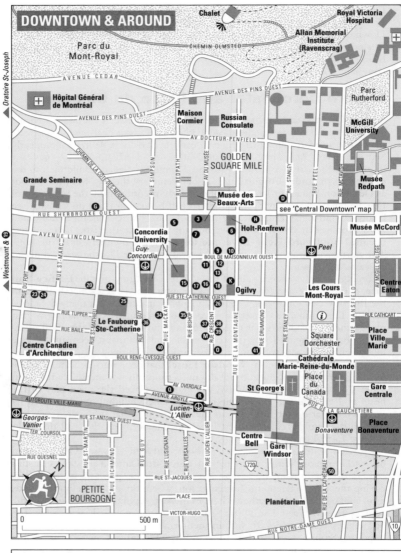

ACCOMMODATION

L'Appartement Hôtel	E
Auberge de Jeunesse Internationale de Montréal	Q
Casa Bella	F
Château Versailles	G
Hôtel de la Montagne	K
Hôtel Y des Femmes (YWCA)	O
Hyatt Regency	L
La Maison du Prêt d'Honneur	N
Manoir Ambrose	D
McGill University Residences	A & B
Petite Auberge les Bons Matins	R
Quality Hotel Downtown	C
Quality Inn Downtown	M
Les Résidences Universitaires UQAM	I
Ritz-Carlton	H
Le St-Malo	J
Travelodge Montréal -Centre	P
W Montréal	S

RESTAURANTS & CAFÉS

3 Amigos	21
Bar-B-Barn	36
Bâton Rouge	28
Ben and Jerry's	12
Le Café des Beaux-Arts	3
Café Imagination	2
Le Café du Nouveau-Monde	29
Café République	18 & 22
Café Tramezzini	8
Les Chenêts	7
Ciné-Express	24
Eggspectation	10
Hong Kong	46
Idée Magique	45
Il Cortile	5
Jardin de Jade	44
Kafeïn	17
Katsura	6
Lotté-Furama	42
Maison VIP	43

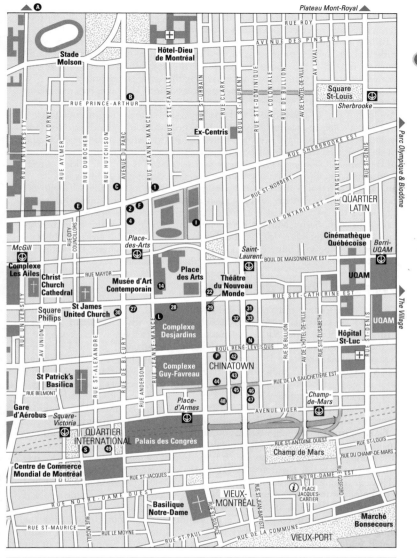

Plateau Mont-Royal

Parc Olympique & Biodôme

The Village

Map labels

Stade Molson
Hôtel-Dieu de Montréal
Square St-Louis
Sherbrooke
RUE ROY
AVENUE DES PINS EST
RUE PRINCE-ARTHUR
Ex-Centris
RUE SHERBROOKE EST
QUARTIER LATIN
McGill
Place-des-Arts
Cinémathèque Québécoise
Berri-UQAM
Saint-Laurent
BOUL DE MAISONNEUVE EST
Complexe Les Ailes
Christ Church Cathedral
RUE MAYOR
Musée d'Art Contemporain
Place des Arts
Théâtre du Nouveau Monde
UQAM
RUE STE-CATHERINE EST
Square Phillips
St James United Church
UQAM
Complexe Desjardins
BOUL RENÉ-LÉVESQUE
Hôpital St-Luc
St Patrick's Basilica
Complexe Guy-Favreau
CHINATOWN
RUE DE LA GAUCHETIÈRE EST
Place-d'Armes
Champ-de-Mars
Gare d'Aérobus
Square-Victoria
QUARTIER INTERNATIONAL
Palais des Congrès
Champ de Mars
RUE ST-ANTOINE OUEST
RUE ST-LOUIS
RUE DU CHAMP-DE-MARS
Centre de Commerce Mondial de Montréal
RUE ST-JACQUES
RUE NOTRE-DAME EST
VIEUX-MONTRÉAL
PLACE JACQUES-CARTIER
Basilique Notre-Dame
Marché Bonsecours
RUE ST-MAURICE
RUE LE MOYNE
RUE ST-PAUL
RUE DE LA COMMUNE
VIEUX-PORT

BARS & CLUBS

Montréal Pool Room	32	Les 3 Brasseurs	26	Magnétic Terrasse	K
Pho Bang New York	47	Benelux	1	McKibbin's Irish Pub	15
Prêt à Manger	20	Brutopia	39	Newtown	11
Queue de Cheval	41	Cock 'n' Bull Pub	23	Nyks	30
La Rotonde	14	Club Soda	31	SAT	33
Ruby Rouge	48	Club Vatican	16	Sharx	25
Toqué	49	Comedy Nest	19	Sir Winston Churchill
		Comedyworks	35	Pub (Winnie's)	13
		Hurley's Irish Pub	38	Spectrum	27
		Jimbo's Pub	35	Station 1160	40
		Madhatter Saloon	37	Stogies	9

Time Supper Club	50
Upstairs	35
Vinyl Lounge	4

crowning the facade are of the Apostles (as is the case with St Peter's), the thirteen figures actually represent the patron saints of the parishes that donated them.

Bishop Ignace Bourget commissioned the building to replace the previous cathedral, St-Jacques, which was located in the present-day Quartier Latin and burned in 1852. He chose St Peter's as the inspiration to emphasize the dominant role of Catholicism in what was then the largest city in the new Dominion of Canada. Construction was delayed until 1870 due to a number of factors, including the uproar over his chosen site – a predominantly Protestant Anglophone neighbourhood – and services did not finally begin until 1894.

Inside it's not as opulent as you might expect from the grand exterior (and million-dollar price tag – a record at the time for Montréal), with the exception of the high altar of marble, onyx and ivory that's surmounted by a reproduction of Bernini's baldachin over the altar in St Peter's. As in Rome, the gilded copper baldachin's spiralling columns support an altar canopy topped by statues of angels. Back towards the entrance along the eastern aisle is the Chapelle des Souvenirs, which contains various relics collected by the enthusiastic Bourget, including the wax-encased remains of the immensely obscure St Zoticus, an early Christian martyr. Midway between the altar and the rear, the small marble-laid Chapelle Funéraire des Évêques holds the tombs of the city's archbishops and bishops (open Thurs 1.30pm–5pm). Paintings throughout the cathedral depict prominent members and events of the early colony.

West of Place du Canada

Opposite the southwestern corner of Place du Canada, at the intersection of rues Peel and de la Gauchetière, the Victorian **St George's Anglican Church** (Tues–Sun 8.30am–4pm, Sat from 9am; ☎514/866-7113, ⓦwww.st-georges.org) is the only one of the six Protestant churches constructed around Dominion Square between 1865 and 1875 to remain standing. Its solid Neo-Gothic exterior gives way to a lofty interior with vaulting double hammer-beam trusses that rise in a series of arches to support the gabled roof. A tapestry used at the Queen's coronation in Westminster Abbey in 1953 contrasts nicely with the darker wood fixtures, including the altar and choir hand-carved from English oak. Free guided tours are available from early July to late August (Tues–Sat 9am–4pm).

Gare Windsor, the large Romanesque Revival structure facing the church's main entrance on rue de la Gauchetière, was Montréal's main rail terminus from 1887 until 1938, helping draw much business to Downtown away from Vieux-Montréal. Just inside the doors on rue de la Gauchetière is a plaque bearing an eloquent tribute to the employees of the railway who perished in World War I (the eulogy is repeated on the monument – a statue of an angel lifting a soldier to heaven – at the end of the otherwise bland concourse).

Although it continued to serve as a terminus for commuter trains until the mid-1990s (trains now stop a block to the west), the station's demise was finally sealed with the construction of the **Centre Bell** on the western side of the courtyard at 1200 rue de la Gauchetière O (☎514/925-5656 or 1-800/363-3723, ⓦwww.centrebell.ca; Métro Lucien-L'Allier or Bonaventure). This 21,000-seat amphitheatre is home to ice hockey's **Montréal Canadiens** (or "Habs"), the team that's won the most Stanley Cups in the history of the National Hockey League. When there isn't a hockey game, it's the place for rock concerts, classical music performances and family entertainment. Guided tours focusing on the legacy of the Habs take place in English daily at 11.15am and 2.45pm (1hr15min; $8) and can be purchased at the box office or the boutique, where fans can pick up a hockey jersey or other Canadiens paraphernalia.

Rue Ste-Catherine

Retrace your steps to Square Dorchester and head north on rue Peel (see p.50). You will quickly come to the corner of what has been the city's main commercial thoroughfare since the early 1900s, **rue Ste-Catherine**. The intersection of the two is the busiest in the city, and along the stretch east of here are the main shopping centres and department stores overlying the core of the **Underground City** (see box below). Exclusive boutiques and mid-priced chain stores interspersed with souvenir shops and fast-food outlets line the street westward as far as rue Guy, after which the area becomes a bit more downmarket. There's a similar trailing off in quality east of Square Phillips (see p.53) before things perk up around the entertainment district anchored by Place des Arts (see p.54). But for all its consumerist gloss, rue Ste-Catherine still has seedy bits scattered throughout, with peepshows and strip clubs enlivening the streetscape.

The Underground City (RÉSO)

Montréal's expansive **Underground City** – recently renamed RÉSO (pronounced ray-zo), the French word for network, was planned as a refuge from outrageously cold winters and humid summers. It began with the mall beneath Place Ville Marie in the 1960s. Montrealers flooded into the first climate-controlled shopping arcade, and, spurred by the opening of the **Métro** in 1966, the Underground City duly spread. With each newly constructed commercial development linking to the complex, it now has 32km of passages – the largest such subterranean network in the world – providing access to the Métro, major hotels, 1700 shops (including most Downtown malls), transport termini, thousands of offices, apartments and restaurants and a good smattering of cinemas and theatres to boot. Around half a million people pass through it each day, mostly on their way to and from work – the sixty building complexes linked to the system contain eighty percent of Downtown's office space. Calling it a "city" is appropriate because of the way that it has developed gradually, with each addition bringing its own design style to the network, but it is also misleading because each component is privately owned, and anything undesirably urban, like beggars or protest marches, are excluded.

In the largest section of the system, you can walk all the way from the Centre Bell to La Baie – over a kilometre in a straight line, but several times that below ground with all the twists and turns that take you past a year-round skating rink, along the train station's grand concourse and through a shopping mall built below the foundations of Christ Church Cathedral. And from Cours Mont-Royal in the northwest, you can wend your way as far as the Centre de Commerce Mondial on the edge of Vieux-Montréal. A recent series of links now connects this to the other major axis, between the Palais des Congrès (the city's mammoth convention centre) and Place des Arts. The third main component is the area around Métro Berri-UQAM, which includes the bus station and the pavilions of the Université du Québec à Montréal (UQAM).

Although tourist-office hype makes the Underground City sound somewhat exotic, don't plan to make a day out of visiting: the reality is pretty banal and most Montrealers use it solely as a way to get from place to place. It does offer a variety of experiences, though, from bustling Métro concourses and brightly lit shopping malls to long stretches of depressing, empty, brown-brick corridors, all of it connected by a convoluted circuit of escalators and stairs that lead to sudden expanses of glass providing unexpected views outside. And if you want cheap and quick food, check out the **food courts** on the lowest floor of any of the malls en route – also handy for public toilets.

Rue Peel

Largely residential until the 1920s, **rue Peel** has now become one of the main north–south Downtown routes, stretching from the Lachine Canal to the verge of the mountain, where a series of steps lead to the chalet and lookout (see p.104). Half a block north of rue Ste-Catherine at no. 1430 stands **Martlet House**, one of the city's architectural curiosities, replete with battlements and a fake portcullis, and apparently modelled on a sixteenth-century Scottish castle. Built in 1929 for Seagram – the Bronfman-owned liquor company that made a fortune during the

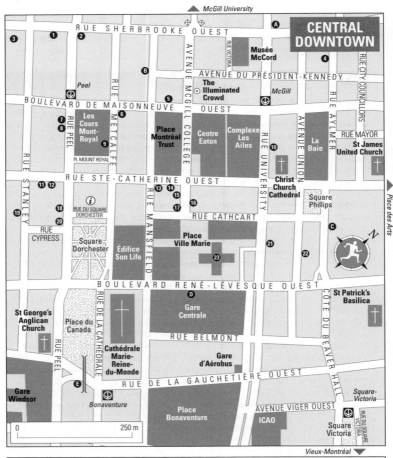

ACCOMMODATION		RESTAURANTS & CAFÉS				BARS & CLUBS	
Le Germain	B	Basha	13	Ferreira Café Trattoria	8	Alexandre et Fils	7
Marriott Château		Ben's Delicatessen	6	Garçon	1	Altitude 737	23
Champlain	E	Boccacinos	16	Le Parchemin	10	Club 6/49	12
Fairmont The		Brûlerie St-Denis	3	Reuben's Deli	11 & 14	House of Jazz	4
Queen Elizabeth	D	Café Presto	19	Sushi Shop	5 & 17	McLean's Pub	18
Royal Victoria College	A	Chez Éric	22	Takara	9	Peel Pub	20
Le Square Phillips	C	Le Commensal	15	Zen	2	Le Vieux Dublin	21

Sin City

Though certainly not to everyone's tastes, strip clubs are – and have been since the early part of the twentieth century – an integral part of Montréal's entertainment scene and can, in fact, be found right on the main Downtown commercial streets, rather than relegated to a destitute tenderloin district as is often the case in major cities. Back in the old days, dancers like Lili St Cyr were even accorded a sort of legendary status. Even if much of the style (and talent) is absent from today's performances, having been replaced by dancers who peel their clothes off rather than put on a show and by conveying more than a whiff of sleaze (especially in the clubs that allow "contact dances"), a few Downtown clubs still pack them in.

If you're interested in seeing a "show", expect to encounter typical businessman crowds, alongside some more down-at-the-heel types – entrance after all is free, with a one-drink minimum (the doorman also expects a $2 tip). Most popular – and most obvious – of all is probably *Super Sexe*, 696 rue Ste-Catherine O (☎514/861-1507; Métro McGill); you'll hardly fail to notice the massive neon sign across from the Centre Eaton (see p.52), or, once inside, the "erotic bed" on stage.

Montréal's hedonistic reputation extends beyond merely looking, though – recent years saw a big rise in the swingers' scene, with members-only clubs being quite open about things (after tussles with the police, they secured a Supreme Court victory in 2003 legalizing swingers' clubs, subject to certain restrictions). If you're a "lifestyler", you can find out more from the Québec Swingers Association (☎514/990-5723, ⓦwww.aeqsa.com) and even book a room at the *Auberge le 1082*, at 1082 boulevard Rosemont (☎514/272-1082, ⓦhttp://le1082.com), the only officially recognized swingers' hotel in Québec and site of the city's only coed sauna. Montréal's gay saunas (see p.187) are definitely more renowned, mind you. For more on the city's underbelly laid bare, pick up the free quarterly *Montréal Confidential* magazine.

Prohibition era in the United States – it's now occupied by the McGill Alumni Association (and closed to the public). Opposite stands the elegant **Cours Mont-Royal** (1455 rue Peel), the largest hotel in the British Commonwealth when completed in 1922 and a catalyst for the street's commercialization. Although no longer a hotel, it's worth going inside to gawk up at the fourteen-storey-high atria (surrounded by condos and offices), and to check out the lower four floors of shops, where a number of expensive designers jostle with stores geared to club kids.

Place Ville Marie

Heading back to rue Ste-Catherine and continuing east a block, you'll come across Downtown's most visible landmark, the silver, cross-shaped **Place Ville Marie**, designed by I.M. Pei, Montréal's first truly defining skyscraper. Although a number of the city's other towers have reached similarly lofty heights, the 46-storey skyscraper remains one of the city's defining features with its powerful searchlights strafing the night sky. Sadly, there is no public viewing deck – in fact, none of Montréal's skyscrapers have one – but for the price of a drink at *Altitude 737* (see p.169) you can check out the city from the top floor; the entrance is on the rue University side of the tower.

The base of the tower is integrated into the shopping mall that was the catalyst for the Underground City (RÉSO – see box, p.49). Set in the pavement in the centre of the mall's landscaped roof is a granite compass indicating true north. It's not particularly exciting in itself, but because the city's street grid is tilted 45 degrees, most Montrealers would argue that north actually lies in the direction of avenue McGill College (which is geographically to the northwest). Now you can prove them wrong. Ignoring the compass and looking "north" beyond Gerald Gladstone's abstract copper sculpture, *Female Landscape*, you'll see one of Downtown's best **views**. Framed by office towers are the gates leading to McGill University's main campus, with the cross atop the mountain visible in the distance beyond.

In the opposite direction, you can see the dully modernist *Fairmont the Queen Elizabeth Hotel* (see p.136), directly south of Place Ville Marie. Surprisingly enough, it was in room 1742 of this hotel where John Lennon and Yoko Ono held their Bed-In for Peace and recorded *Give Peace a Chance* on June 1, 1969.

Avenue McGill College and around

Redesigned in the early 1980s as a wide, tree-lined boulevard, **avenue McGill College** extends north from Place Ville Marie and bustles with cafés that overflow onto the wide sidewalks alongside occasional art displays, buskers and street vendors. One block north of rue Ste-Catherine, on the eastern side of the street, stands one of the city's most notable sculptures – Raymond Mason's larger-than-life *The Illuminated Crowd*. The numerous white fibreglass figures, facing an illumination (both in the literal and metaphorical sense of "seeing the light"), are meant to represent the fragility of man – only a short distance separates the healthy folk in front from the particularly gruesome figures furthest from the light. Ironically, the character at the front of the group is pointing across to the other side of the street, where Léa Vivot's charming bronze sculpture, *The Secret Bench*, depicts two youngsters cosying up to one another at the end of a park bench. Further along, the boulevard terminates at the gates to the expansive campus of McGill University (see p.60).

Back on rue Ste-Catherine and just east of avenue McGill College, you'll be confronted with another juxtaposition. Across the road from the families streaming out of Centre Eaton – a large shopping mall with a pretty run-of-the-mill selection of shops and restaurants – is a two-storey-high neon sign fronting *Club Super-Sexe*, featuring scantily clad "superwomen" (see box, p.51). Adjacent to the Centre Eaton is an Italianate building with shop windows set within ornamental columns and arches – this was where the venerable Eaton's department store stood for seven decades until the chain went into receivership in 1999. The building's current tenant, the Complexe Les Ailes shopping mall, has carved up the interior with a striking elliptical atrium. The mall's real must-see, however, will be the ninth-floor restaurant, *Le 9*, an Art Deco marvel designed in 1931 by Jacques Carlu to resemble the *Ile de France* transatlantic liner – if it ever reopens.

Christ Church Cathedral

The seat of Montréal's Anglican diocese, **Christ Church Cathedral**, one block east of the Centre Eaton at 635 rue Ste-Catherine O (daily 8am–6pm; ☏514/843-6577, ⓦwww.montreal.anglican.org/cathedral; Métro McGill), is best remembered by many Montrealers as the "floating church". For most of 1987, the cathedral was supported on concrete struts while, underneath, developers tunnelled out the glitzy **Promenades de la Cathédrale**, a boutique-lined part of the Underground City (RÉSO), whose commercial rents pay the cathedral's bills. The land behind the church has also been leased out to the same end, and the resulting La Place de la Cathédrale, a mirrored, postmodern office tower, now reflects the symmetry of the 1859 church's tripartite Neo-Gothic facade.

The cathedral's other architectural oddity is its steeple – the original stone spire threatened to crash through the roof and was replaced by a replica of aluminium plates moulded to look like stone. Inside the cathedral, soaring Gothic arches are decorated with representations of angels and the Evangelists, while the carved foliage is typical of what grew on Mount Royal. The copy of *The Last Supper* that hangs in the chancel was saved from the fire that destroyed the earlier church on rue Notre-Dame by the derring-do of a soldier who cut it from its frame with his sword. The cathedral's most poignant feature, though, is mounted to the left of the pulpit: the small *Coventry Cross*, made from nails salvaged from the bombed Coventry Cathedral in Britain. The cathedral makes for a good spot to escape Downtown's bustle, especially during the concerts on Saturdays (occasionally other days as well) throughout the year; they're usually free but a small donation is expected.

One of the best features of the church is actually outside it – around back, where you'll find benches set about a small and well-manicured public **garden**, centred around a trickling fountain that helps shut out the sounds of the city. The stone building separating the garden from rue University was the church's **rectory**, but has since been converted into the airy *Le Parchemin* restaurant (see p.152).

Square Phillips and around

Spreading back from rue Ste-Catherine another block east from Christ Church, **Square Phillips** has little in the way of greenery. Instead, the square offers a line of market stalls towered over from the centre by a bronze statue of **Edward VII** sculpted by Louis-Philippe Hébert, who also sculpted the pulpit at the Basilique Notre-Dame and had a lock on most public art commissions at the turn of the century. Thomas Phillips, a prominent merchant who bought the land in 1840, decreed that the buildings around the square should be the most beautiful in Montréal, and although they fall short of fulfilling his wish – the east side is a forgettable mishmash of cheap modern styles – a couple of the buildings do fit the bill. The 1894 **Henry Birks and Sons building**, a jewellery store on the square's west side, has, behind the smooth-cut, sand-coloured stone of its facade, a lovely interior full of marble columns supporting a frothy cream ceiling. On the square's north side, the distinctive dark red-sandstone building with the arched windows that dates from 1890 now houses **La Baie** (The Bay), a department store descended from the Hudson's Bay Company, which operated the trading forts throughout the Canadian wilderness from the seventeenth to nineteenth centuries. To the south, the **Canada Cement Company Building**, defined by its Ionic columns and a scallop-motif parapet, is (somewhat) notable for being the first reinforced-concrete office building in Canada.

Immediately east of Square Phillips, the **St James United Church** at 463 rue Ste-Catherine O (daily 10am–4pm; ☎514/288-9245) is the most surprising newcomer to Downtown's cityscape. The church had been tucked away for decades behind a row of shopfronts, with only its pair of steeples – one unusually suspended atop flying buttresses – on view to passers-by from the 1920s until as recently as 2006, when the stores were torn down to reveal its impressive 1889 red-sandstone bulk, complete with unusual frieze of rabbits and owls, and rose window. While restoration continues to its exterior, it's worth ducking in to see the cherrywood interior; it's especially appealing during one of the summer organ recitals (Tues 12.30pm; free).

Scattered about the upper floors of the mercantile building across the street at 460 rue Ste-Catherine O are eight contemporary art galleries showcasing the work of mainly younger artists working in a variety of styles and media – check out Occurrence on the third floor for large-scale social commentary pieces. You can find more of the same at **Édifice Belgo**, a bit further east at no. 372, whose fifth floor also houses the Association des Galeries d'Art Contemporain (AGAC) (suite 521; ☎514/861-2345, Ⓦwww.agac.qc.ca), who have information on the various gallery shows around town. Note that most of these galleries are only open towards the end of the week (generally Wed–Sat noon–5pm).

St Patrick's Basilica

Of Montréal's four basilicas, **St Patrick's**, a block south and east from Square Phillips at 460 boul René-Lévesque O (daily 8.30am–6pm; ☎514/866-7379, Ⓦwww.stpatricksmtl.ca; Métro Square-Victoria or McGill), receives the least attention. However, when the first Mass was celebrated, appropriately enough on March 17, 1847, the church must have been an imposing sight on the hill overlooking Vieux-Montréal, where its Irish parishioners lived. Enter from the main south entrance, where the rather drab Gothic exterior gives way to a dramatic interior full of warm hues. Although at first glance the dozen pillars supporting the vault appear to be a red, veined marble, they are in fact each crafted from pine trees 30m tall. The combination of the pillars' polished glow, along with the cream and peach colour of the ceiling and walls decorated with shamrocks and fleurs-de-lys contrasts with the cool and distant tones of the **sanctuary**. It's hard to miss the elaborate sanctuary lamps over the main altar – the larger of the two weighs almost a tonne and is surrounded by two-metre-tall angels.

Place des Arts and around

A couple of blocks east of Square Phillips, rue Ste-Catherine slopes down towards **Place des Arts**, Montréal's leading performing arts centre, opened in 1963 and home to events like the famous Festival International de Jazz de Montréal (see p.225). Place des Arts comprises five performance halls and the **Musée d'Art Contemporain de Montréal** in an ensemble of buildings set around a large plaza, with a series of gardens and fountains and a wide set of steps creating a seating area for tired tourists and for spectators during outdoor

△ Place des Arts

concerts. Note that the entrances to all the performance halls are via an underground concourse, best entered directly from the Métro Place-des-Arts or at 175 rue Ste-Catherine O, where information on cultural events is available in the lobby. For details of Place des Arts' resident symphony, ballet, theatre and opera companies, see Chapter 14, "Performing arts and film".

Plans are afoot to rename the one-kilometre area around the Place des Arts – from rue Sherbrooke to the north, boulevard René-Lévesque to the south, rue City Councillors to the west and rue Berri to the east – as the **Quartier des Spectacles** (Performance Quarter), after the 25 cultural venues that occupy these few blocks. At press time, only a few superficial, temporary projects had borne fruit, but the ambitious plans include building a new symphony hall in the Place des Arts complex (due in 2011) and an overall sprucing up of the neighbourhood's public spaces. For the latest information, check Ⓦwww .quartierdesspectacles.com.

Musée d'Art Contemporain de Montréal

Occupying the west side of Place des Arts, the **Musée d'Art Contemporain de Montréal** (late June to early Sept daily 11am–6pm, Wed until 9pm; closed Mon mid-Sept to late June; $8, free Wed evenings; Ⓣ514/847-6226, Ⓦwww .macm.org; Métro Place-des-Arts) was Canada's first museum devoted entirely to contemporary art. The city's foremost showcase for work produced by Québécois painters and sculptors since 1939, the museum also has a number of pieces by other Canadian and international artists. The collection overlaps with that of the Musée des Beaux-Arts and the Musée National des Beaux-Arts du Québec (see p.268) a fair bit, so don't be surprised when you see the same names (and occasionally very similar paintings, like those by Borduas and Riopelle – see box, p.56) cropping up again from one museum to the next. If you're not really into contemporary works – or don't fancy the temporary exhibition on show – head to the Musée des Beaux-Arts instead.

The building design is fairly low-key, although a photograph of a pair of lips smiling down from the rooftop adds a light-hearted touch. Inside, a two-storey rotunda links all of the museum's main components, including the *La Rotonde* restaurant (see p.152), whose terrace is often filled with diners enjoying live music. The exhibit space is divided into two wings, one of which hosts temporary exhibitions of major artists, while the other displays recent acquisitions of contemporary works alongside highlights of contemporary Québécois art culled from the 6000-item permanent collection.

Besides paintings, the museum's collection is also impressively stocked with sculpture, photography, video and installation art, and also features the occasional multimedia performance. There is also a small, hard-to-find **sculpture garden**, entered through a partially hidden doorway in the last room of the temporary-works wing in the museum's northeast corner. Although there's only a handful of pieces here, it's worth seeking out for the totem-pole-like Henry Moore bronze of an abstract human form, *Upright Motive no. 5*, standing amidst the greenery.

The long-term exhibition of works from the Forties to the Sixties – known as the **Place à la Magie** – occupies four small interconnected rooms in the museum's southeast corner, to your immediate left as you reach the top of the stairs. Among the most significant pieces in the museum's collection are those of **Paul-Émile Borduas**, founder of the influential group, Les Automatistes (see box, p.56). Scoot through the first gallery to the side room devoted to his output – you can follow his progression clockwise as his realistic early works give way to increasingly gestural pieces like the *Surrealist Artist's Palette, or 3.45*

Les Automatistes

Along with the formation of the Contemporary Art Society in 1939, the initial impetus of contemporary art in Montréal came with **Alfred Pellan**'s return from Paris after World War II broke out, bringing with him the main strands of the **avant-garde** – Cubism, Fauvism, Primitivism and Surrealism. Although parallel to the evolution of Abstract Expressionism in New York around this time, the art scene in Montréal developed along a divergent path thanks to one artist in particular.

A rival of Pellan, **Paul-Émile Borduas** drew upon the theory of automatism (automatic writing) espoused by surrealist poet André Breton and applied it to his painting, repudiating figurative art for a visual expression drawn from the subconscious mind. He and his group of followers, dubbed **Les Automatistes** in a review of their second Montréal show in 1947, published a landmark manifesto *Refus global* (Total Refusal) the following year, sparking outrage among the establishment. The manifesto's challenging of the conformist, Church-dominated society and demand for freedom of artistic expression and "resplendent anarchy" influenced a generation of Québécois and kindled the spirit that led to the Quiet Revolution and secularization of Québec in the following decades. For a mimeographed text that saw only 400 copies printed, it had a profound impact on cultural thinking in Québec that extended well beyond art.

Many of Québec's best-known artists were among the signatories, including Françoise Sullivan, Pierre Gauvreau, Marcelle Ferron and Jean-Paul Mousseau, who instigated the incorporation of nonrepresentative art in the Métro's stations. **Jean-Paul Riopelle** left the group in 1950, developing his Pollock-like lyrical abstraction, slathering his canvases with thick blobs of colour overlaid with paint drizzles, before adopting a palette knife to produce the large-scale mosaic-like works that are among the most collectible in Québec. Other Automatistes such as **Fernand Leduc** later joined the Mondrian-influenced **Les Plasticiens** (Neo-Plasticists), producing works further abstracted to a unity of form, colour and line.

You can catch these artists' works at the province's big three art museums – in addition, the Musée des Beaux-Arts National du Québec devotes a room solely to Riopelle (see p.269), the Musée d'Art Contemporain sets aside space for Borduas (see p.55) and the Musée des Beaux-Arts showcases both painters (see p.62).

(State of Mind, Composition with Eggs), awash in broad stokes of glistening colour and resembling an aurora borealis. By the early 1950s, his palette became more muted, with ever-increasing volumes of slathered whites, culminating in his best-known paintings – abstracts reduced to black blobs on a field of thick white paint, as seen in *United (no. 34), (Cornerstone)*.

Fellow Automatistes represented in the main gallery include **Jean-Paul Riopelle**, most notably his untitled 1949 piece filled with thick dabs of colour overlaid with drizzles of black and white. His later paintings, like *Landing*, burst with vibrant energy and colour, laid on sharply with a palette knife to produce a mosaic-like effect.

The two other rooms that round out the collection display other Automatistes, like **Guido Molinari**, whose rigorous abstract pieces are typified by ruler-straight bands of vertical colour – a great example of which, *Mutation Quadri-Violet*, with its gradient colour scheme, dates from 1966 – and **Marcelle Ferron**, whose stained-glass piece reflects reds and blues onto the gallery floor, but pales next to her large-scale panels that adorn the Champ-de-Mars Métro station (see p.75). Likewise, the monochromatic landscape of **Jean-Paul Lemieux**'s *Winter Moon* – which depicts just the moon, dark sky and a flat grey plain – though evocative, doesn't convey the radical style changes throughout his career that are better displayed at the Musée National des Beaux-Arts du Québec (see p.269). Sculpture of the period is represented by a pair of vertical abstract sculptures by two Montrealers – both **Yves Trudeau**'s *La Cité*, made of welded segments of iron tubes, and the cut and welded metal planes of **Ivanhoé Fortier**'s *Sublunar Tower*, cast shadows that are almost as interesting as the sculptures themselves. A small antechamber houses delightful collage works; **Charles Gagnon**'s *Box No. 4* is particularly charming, with its youthful schoolboy photo accompanied by paper plates and kitten wallpaper, swathed together with red paint.

East of Place des Arts

As you follow rue Ste-Catherine east from Place des Arts, the blocks get increasingly seedy and there's not much of note along this stretch as far as sightseeing goes. The present-day **Théâtre du Nouveau Monde**, at the corner of rue St-Urbain, was once the notorious Gayety Burlesque Theatre, where Lili St-Cyr performed (see p.51). Though the building was given a sleek style update by Dan Hanganu (architect of the Musée d'Archéolgie) and is fronted by a trendy café, the plays are mainly from the classical French canon (see p.196). Further along rue Ste-Catherine, the intersection at **boulevard St-Laurent** has been a longtime hangout for prostitutes and is surrounded by some of the city's larger concert venues. Things don't get much more wholesome between here and the Quartier Latin, what with places like the nightclub **Les Foufones Électroniques** (literally, "The Electric Buttocks" – see p.182), although the area is gradually cleaning up as the Université de Québec à Montréal encroaches from the west. Plans to clean up the area are nothing new, however – citizens were complaining about its seedy, red-light-district character as long ago as the 1840s. The area is safe to enough to walk through in the daytime and even at night with a modicum of common sense, but if you're footsore you can skip it by taking the Métro two stops from Place-des-Arts station to Berri-UQAM in the Quartier Latin (see p.85).

Complexe Desjardins and south

Place des Arts marks the northern point on one of the main axes of the Underground City (RÉSO), with a tunnel connecting it to **Complexe Desjardins**, a collection of office towers and the *Hyatt* (see p.137) surrounding a shopping mall just across rue Ste-Catherine. The complex's enormous central atrium hosts exhibitions on subjects of mainly local interest. You can surface at the south side of the complex to explore Chinatown or continue to the hulking **Palais des Congrès** (🌐www.congresmtl.com), the city's main conference centre built over the Autoroute Ville-Marie (Hwy-720) opposite the northern edge of Vieux-Montréal. If you're passing through, be sure to check out the centre's surreal *Lipstick Forest*, an installation of neon-pink concrete casts of actual trees, along its northwestern side. The new square fronting the centre's multicoloured western facade, **Place Jean-Paul-Riopelle**, was designed around the artist's *La Joute* (the Joust) fountain, where a group of bronze sculptures is surrounded by water – and licked by flames (on the hour).

Chinatown

A block south of rue Ste-Catherine and just north of Vieux-Montréal, a large Chinese gate rises above boulevard St-Laurent, replete with temple-like roofs and Chinese characters and flanked by a pair of white marble lions, one of several gates that mark the entrances to Montréal's small **Chinatown**. Although

△ Chinatown entrance

the Chinese immigrants who constructed the nation's railway lines settled here in the mid- to late nineteenth century, their descendants later dispersed throughout the city, leaving Chinatown to evolve into a primarily commercial and cultural centre. The traffic-choked blocks on boulevard St-Laurent contain a chaotic mix of produce shops and cheap but good restaurants, with crowds picking through the vegetables amid delivery vans double-parked along the sidewalks.

Extending westward as far as the plaza in front of the Palais des Congrès, the car-free portion of rue de la Gauchetière is quieter, though no less busy as crowds of pedestrians search out a place for dim sum or an evening meal (for reviews, see p.152). Many of the city's Chinese residents also venture here from the suburbs, outnumbering the tourists as they stock up at grocery shops selling dry goods and herbal remedies. If you're coming here by train, Métro Place-des-Armes is the nearest stop.

Although it's not a patch on the far more impressive Chinese Garden at the Jardin Botanique (see p.112), **Place Sun-Yat-Sen**, a granite-paced square at the corner of rues Clark and de la Gauchetière, offers a respite from the commercial bustle with cultural shows and impromptu street performances. Performances take place on the raised stage area, guarded by a dragon and with polished stone panels engraved with Chinese landscapes as a backdrop, while the east side of the square is bordered by a small pavilion inspired by palatial Imperial architecture.

The Golden Square Mile and around

The **Golden Square Mile**, a dignified neighbourhood of limestone mansions that cascades down the slopes of Mont Royal and is encroached upon by Downtown's western core, was Montréal's epicentre of English privilege at the beginning of the twentieth century. Its name derives from the area it covers, roughly one square mile – from rue University west to rue Guy, and avenue des Pins south to boulevard René-Lévesque – and from the riches of its residents who, at the neighbourhood's zenith in 1900, possessed 75 percent of Canada's wealth.

Things are slower paced and more genteel in the area just north and west of Downtown, which has retained much of its character and where you can easily spend an afternoon visiting **rue Sherbrooke**'s heavyweight cultural institutions, such as the **Musée McCord d'Histoire Canadienne** opposite **McGill University**. The university spreads up Mont Royal's slopes, where it occupies a number of stately mansions in the core of the Golden Square Mile. This enclave's gentrified airs extend west through a district of chic boutiques and pricey art galleries towards the venerable **Musée des Beaux-Arts**.

South of here, there's no coherent identity to the area where the western edge of Downtown and the Victorian townhouses of the Golden Square Mile overlap, and the nightlife of rues Bishop and Crescent gives way to **Concordia University**'s urban campus and studenty residential area. It's worth the trek, though, to the impressive **Centre Canadien d'Architecture**, in the Shaughnessy Village neighbourhood to the southwest.

Some history

Originally settled by fur merchants like James McGill – who maintained a summer home here and an "everyday house" in Vieux-Montréal – shipping, railroad and banking magnates began colonizing the Mile for year-round living in the 1860s. Upon arrival, they built ostentatious mansions, embellishing them with an array of cornices, ornamental cherubs and bas-relief detailing that loudly announced their economic standing. But after the 1929 stock market crash, many of these residents were forced to flee west to smaller – but still relatively lavish – homes in nearby Westmount (see p.123). The neighbourhood's character changed drastically as the Downtown core spread, and skyscrapers sprouted up where mansions once had been. Thankfully, much of the area north of rue Sherbrooke has remained relatively untouched, and most of the mansions there maintain their sumptuous facades – even though they've nearly all been turned into university faculties, hospital wings and apartments. You can take a virtual tour of McGill's holdings in the district at Ⓦ http://cac .mcgill.ca/campus.

Musée McCord d'Histoire Canadienne

Near Downtown's centre, close to the corner of rue University at 690 rue Sherbrooke O, sits the **Musée McCord d'Histoire Canadienne** (Tues–Fri 10am–6pm, Sat & Sun 10am–5pm, Mon 10am–5pm, closed Mon in winter except holidays; guided tours Sat 2pm; $12, free Sat before noon; ☎514/398-7100, Ⓦ www.mccord-museum.qc.ca; Métro McGill), a handsome, early twentieth-century limestone building that faces its one-time administrator, McGill University. The three-storey museum, dedicated to Canadian history, was inaugurated in 1921 following the donation of wealthy magistrate David Ross McCord's collection of 15,000 artefacts and moved to its present location in the 1960s. The current collection numbers nearly a million objects, photos and documents, although the majority of these only come out during high-calibre temporary exhibitions. However, you can also view much of the collection on the museum's website – the slide show of famous Montrealers in fancy-dress ball costumes is a hoot.

A cedar *gayang* (totem pole) greets you on the way to the second floor, where more than 800 pieces are displayed in **Simply Montréal**, a permanent exhibition addressing the city's social and commercial development. Though lacking cohesiveness – it seems as if nearly every aspect of Montréal life is touched on in only a few rooms – the exhibit does have its strong points. Photos confirming the worst you've heard about the city's punishing winters accompany displays of furry mitts, an image of a tram converted into a snowplough and mid-nineteenth-century ice skates – all of which reveal how Montrealers adapted to, and even enjoyed, the climate. The real stunners, though, are the gritty floor-to-ceiling black-and-white **photographs** of the city taken by William Notman at the turn of the nineteenth century. These anchor the displays in galleries three and four and provide the exhibit's most visceral contrasts: an image of rue St-Jacques bustling with streetcars and *calèches* is around the corner from a forlorn shot of workers' houses, with sagging wood frames and crooked stone chimneys. Equally sterling are the **aboriginal items**, such as a collection of wampum beads once used as trading currency and a delicately carved and painted Iroquois baby-carrier. The delightful array of memorabilia from elite Montréal families shows off things like an intricately detailed mourning necklace, with its onyx and pearl pendant, worn to honour the dearly departed. The gift shop is worth a look-in as well for its books on Canadiana and native and folk-art items.

McGill University

While the expansive campus of Québec's first English-language university, **McGill University** (☎514/398-6555, ⓦwww.mcgill.ca; Métro McGill or Peel), spreads from rue Sherbrooke up to Mont Royal, and west from rue University to rue Peel, the main thrust of the university lies behind the semicircular **Roddick Gates** that enclose the top of avenue McGill College. The gates' colonnades open onto the campus's main road, lined with grassy quads on either side, and on the right a **statue** of founder James McGill surveys the land. The main road leads directly to the Neoclassical **Arts Building**, the campus's first (1843), situated on a slight promontory at the northern end of the campus. It's distinguished from the rest by McGill's red-and-white flag atop its cupola – stand on the front steps for a fine view of Downtown and the surrounding campus.

McGill was the greatest beneficiary of the Golden Square Mile's decline, inheriting a number of mansions vacated by the neighbourhood's wealthy merchants. Along with the stone facades of the main university buildings, these give the grounds a dignified air, and the picturesque setting on the slopes and foreground of Mont Royal produces a quietude that's unexpected so close to the bustle of Downtown.

Musée Redpath

Before reaching the Arts Building, the main road splits, with the western fork cresting in front of the **Musée Redpath** (Mon–Fri 9am–5pm, Sun 1–5pm; free; ☎514/398-4086, ⓦwww.mcgill.ca/redpath; Métro McGill), an unusual museum devoted to zoological and ethnological pursuits. The 1882 Greek Revival structure in which it is housed lays claim to being the province's first custom-built museum. Upstairs there's an impressive two-storey-high oval atrium with a wraparound mezzanine.

Architecture aside, though, this is an odd place all in all, featuring a hodge-podge collection of stuffed and fossilized creatures, geology specimens and ethnological tidbits, with a few interesting relics tucked here and there. There's the briefest of glimpses of marine life as you enter, including a massive "fragment" of a bowhead whale skull, but the main collection is upstairs in the Dawson Gallery, where a seven-metre-long menacing *Albertosaurus* dinosaur skeleton known as "Zeller" strides over the atrium's centre. The surrounding panels detailing the evolution of various species throughout the eras lend an educational aspect to the array of fossils and minerals, but the more recently departed animals at the far end are more diverting (and are as close as you're likely to get to some of Canada's wildlife). Here, stuffed birds of prey perch between windows overlooking the mountain, foregrounded by a commanding wolf, sly coyote and a whooping crane (whose eyes seem to follow you), as well as the requisite beaver. Peer into the top floor landing's shelves of cultural artefacts and you'll see some spooky Kongo sculptures from Africa and ancient Egyptian sarcophagi behind the glass; a computer screen shows a CT scan of the mummy's insides. Extending out from the landing, the mezzanine's rounded walls provide a round-the-world trip through other ancient cultures.

Rue Sherbrooke

For decades, the stretch of **rue Sherbrooke** between rue University and rue Guy that forms the core of the Golden Square Mile was known as Canada's Fifth Avenue, as it was home to the country's choicest boutiques. Although the strip lost its five-star rating when much of the city's money shifted to Toronto years ago, it retains elements of its former shopping glory nonetheless: Ralph Lauren hobnobs with Escada and Giorgio Armani, as well as Holt Renfrew, Canada's answer to Neiman Marcus. Those allergic to high-priced clothiers will still enjoy a stroll down this length of rue Sherbrooke, as impressive ornamental

A house-hunting detour

The Golden Square Mile's most noteworthy mansions are on the slopes of Mont Royal north of rue Sherbrooke, cradled by lush foliage and Mont Royal's rugged rock face. The roads around here are quite steep – although the superb views of Downtown along the way offer plenty of excuses for a breather. Begin by heading to the north end of rue McTavish, McGill campus's western artery, to avenue des Pins ouest. On the north side of the street at no. 1025 looms **Ravenscrag**, a magnificent Tuscan-style villa, now home to a psychiatric institute, but originally built for shipping magnate Sir Hugh Allan in 1864. Hemmed in by a weighty stone and wrought-iron gateway, the mansion's two sprawling wings connect to a central watchtower that rises high above the roofline. Allan himself often stood in the windowed tower to observe his ships docking at the port far below, and for decades its rough-cast stone facade welcomed Montréal's finest, along with royalty like Japan's Prince Fushimi, to waltzes in the grand Second Empire ballroom.

The most attractive of the fine mansions absorbed by McGill on the south side of avenue des Pins was built for Sir Hugh's brother, Andrew. The red-brick **Maison Lady Meredith** at no. 1110 has a Romanesque Revival influence, and leading architects of the day, Edward and William Maxwell, took a more light-hearted approach than with their mannered Musée des Beaux-Arts, with conical turrets and a looping arch pattern in the brickwork. Ten minutes further west at no. 1418 stands the **Maison Cormier**, its handsome Art Deco facade decorated with a sleek female statue above the door. Former Prime Minister Pierre Elliott Trudeau died here in 2000, and it is still occupied by his family. Across the street at no. 1415 is the former **Cuban Consulate**'s digs, recently converted into condos. The location hints at the longstanding friendship between Trudeau and Fidel Castro – a bond so strong that Castro was a pallbearer at Trudeau's funeral.

Four residences back, east along avenue des Pins, a long set of stairs on the south side of the street leads down to avenue du Musée. The three eclectic mansions closest to the base of the stairs on the left form the **Russian Consulate**, and it's thought the United States was closely monitored from here during the Cold War. Whatever the Soviets were up to, they clearly didn't want anyone knowing about it: when fire broke out in 1987, they kept the firemen outside for fifteen minutes while they loaded document-filled boxes into waiting cars. From here, it's a five-minute walk to the bottom of avenue du Musée and the Musée des Beaux-Arts.

details, like demonic gargoyles, wrought-iron entrance grilles and detailed bas-relief carvings, add to the street's architectural panache. Beginning as far east as the Musée McCord, a series of plaques highlights the most notable buildings still in existence with photos and a historical overview.

Of the many structures in this area converted to commercial purposes, **Maison Alcan**, the aluminium giant's headquarters just west of rue Peel at no. 1188, is the most impressive, integrating a pair of nineteenth-century townhouses and an old, 1920s-era, red-brick hotel into an office building clad, naturally enough, in aluminium. Inuit and other sculptures are scattered about the atrium connecting the buildings, and there's a sunny garden and café in back that's good for a rest.

One of the finest examples of the street's heyday is the Beaux-Arts expanse of the **Ritz Carlton** hotel (see p.137), built in 1911 and announcing its grandeur with a sinuous frieze of acanthus leaves and twinkling lights from the entranceway's chandeliers. The accommodations for the street's permanent residents in bygone times were almost as grand – a number of colossal apartment buildings were erected for those who couldn't afford to maintain a Golden Square Mile mansion – notably across the street at no. 1321, where the aptly named **Appartements Le Château** rises like a fortress, topped by battlements, turrets and copper roofs.

Musée des Beaux-Arts

Canada's oldest art museum – it was inaugurated in Square Phillips in 1879 – the **Musée des Beaux-Arts** (Tues 11am–5pm, Wed–Fri 11am–9pm, Sat & Sun 10am–5pm; free, except special exhibits $15, half-price Wed after 5pm; ⓣ514/285-1600, ⓦwww.mbam.qc.ca; Métro Guy-Concordia) moved to its rue Sherbrooke location in 1912. It's renowned for the excellent quality of its visiting exhibits and the sheer size of its collection, which now spans two buildings (1379 and 1380 rue Sherbrooke O, connected by an underground passageway) and 65 rooms. Seeing everything on display could easily take a full day, but doing so need not be a priority as the permanent collection is actually rather spotty. Certain aspects, like the post-1945 contemporary-art collection, are of high calibre, as are many of the pieces by the likes of Picasso, Rodin, Renoir and Dalí. Unfortunately, these are surrounded by many lesser-known and inferior works often grouped in a seemingly haphazard fashion. The collection does get moved around a lot, so if you're intent on finding a particular piece, do ask at the reception counters located on the buildings' main floors, where you can also pick up a museum map.

Pavillon Jean-Nöel Desmarais

The blockbuster temporary exhibits and the best of the permanent collection are housed in the modern **Pavillon Jean-Nöel Desmarais** on the south side of rue Sherbrooke O. Designed by Moshe Safdie, the pavilion merges the red-brick facade of a pre-existing apartment building alongside a new postmodern wing built of Vermont marble and incised with a sloping glass roof supported by a lattice of tubular aluminium.

Begin on the fourth floor, where pieces from the museum's collection of **European decorative arts** and **Old Masters** from the twelfth to nineteenth centuries are on display; visit the rooms clockwise to get the clearest sense of chronological order, starting with the room furthest to the left of the elevators. The oldest works are **religious paintings and sculptures**, beginning in the foyer with an almost marionette-like *Christ on the Cross* sculpted in twelfth-century Italy, and continuing in the first gallery, which has a Jan de Beer triptych with pastoral overtones as the centrepiece. Straight ahead and in a small room to the left is a dimly lit collection of works, including the almost cartoon-like drunkards of *Return from the Inn* by Bruegel the Younger.

The adjoining rooms, furthest from the entrance, feature a good selection of sixteenth- and seventeenth-century **Dutch and Flemish art**. Amongst the still lifes and high-key portraits, scenes capture the varied lives of commoners; the visceral imagery of Lucas van Valckenborch's *A Meat and Fish Market (Winter)* and Rubens' rollicking pastoral *Landscape with Shepherds and Shepherdesses* being two fine examples. The room to the far right displays Rembrandt's *Portrait of a Young Woman*, her face brilliantly illuminated against an almost black background, next to Emmanuel de Witte's more artfully situated *Interior with a Woman Playing Virginals* – seeing it through a doorway adds an extra layer to the sequence of rooms and delightful play of light in the painting itself.

Back towards the entrance and adjacent to the first room, the portraits, pastoral views and allegorical scenes seem to be linked only by time period, spanning the mid-seventeenth to late eighteenth centuries. The best of the lot are English painter Thomas Gainsborough's immense *Portrait of Mrs George Drummond* and the small, gold-tinted *Interior of San Marco, Venice* by Canaletto.

The progression continues via a passageway to the museum's east side, where French works prevail; en route a tiny antechamber houses Goya's simple *Portrait of Carlos Lopez Alltamirano*, showing the judge in his robes and inscribed by the artist himself. Once in the French galleries, look for the hurried brushstrokes speaking of the urgency of the flight of Honoré Daumier's *Women Pursued by Satyrs*. The final gallery culminates with a couple of the collection's stand-outs: James Tissot's splendid oil painting *October*, which features an elegant young lady tucked amongst golden autumn foliage, hanging next to the hypnotic stare of the little girl in William Bouguereau's *Crown of Flowers*.

The temporary exhibition halls that mount the museum's high-calibre shows are down a floor. To the right of the elevators here are two small galleries where a **Sacred Africa** exhibit, showcasing several pieces from the Cirque du Soleil's collection (see p.194), will remain on view until 2010. The thrust of the evocative pieces are spiritual accoutrements. Stand-outs include a nineteenth-century Congolese ceremonial wooden staff with what looks to be a set of bellows at its base, a *Memorial Ibis* that appears to be shaped from driftwood and thought to be from a royal mausoleum in Madagascar, and a menacing *Janus-Faced Headdress* from Nigeria fashioned of wood, leather and metal spikes.

Back on the ground floor, in four small rooms through the rear doors, is the museum's fine collection of **Impressionist** and **twentieth-century European** artworks. The first gallery finds Monet's rosy-hued *A Cliff at Pourville in the Morning* hanging across from Albert Charles-Lebourg's *The Pont Marie at Sunset, Paris*, with its sky aglow. The second, and exceedingly sparse, chamber is where a gloomy Degas hangs with three Renoirs; the latter's *Vase of Flowers* overflows with vibrant colours. Rodin's soft white marble sculpture *The Sirens* anchors the third room, its sensuous contours matched by Kees van Dongen's redolent *Woman on a Sofa*, the sitter's furs and arm bangles oozing a certain personal decadence. The final gallery here hosts works by Giacometti, Matisse, Otto Dix, Picasso and Dalí, whose pre-Surrealist *Portrait of Maria Carbona* is positively chaste in comparison to Picasso's sexually charged *Embrace*, a Cubist take on entwined lovers.

In the basement, the superb post-1945 **contemporary art** collection has a strong accent on works by Canadian artists. Abstract painter Jack Bush and hyperrealists Alex Colville and Christopher Pratt are all represented, but the best of the pieces belong to **Québécois artists**. Look for Claude Tousignant's acrylic *Gong 96*, depicting a pastel-hued bull's-eye – stare at it too long and you may go cross-eyed. Jean-Paul Riopelle has an entire room devoted to his work: the drizzled lines and daubs of primary colour that stand out against the blacks in *Crosswind* mark the beginning of his trademark style, best exhibited in his magnificent oil painting *Gravity*, with hundreds of geometric daubs of colour surrounding a stark white centre. Riopelle's art is given as much emphasis as that of fellow **Automatiste** Paul-Émile Borduas (see box, p.56), who gets an entire gallery in the back. Examine Borduas' pieces counterclockwise to follow his artistic progression – early works are much more fluid and brighter than later pieces, which are sparsely coloured but highly textured. Borduas' work culminates with *The Black Star*, its putty-coloured background heavily sculpted and layered with his painting knife.

Gallery of Ancient Cultures

Slightly jarring after the vivid colours of the contemporary works are the much older products of ancient civilizations, worth at least a cursory look as you pass through the **underground tunnel** between the museum's two buildings. Grouped by region, the **Gallery of Ancient Cultures**' displays begin on your left with masks, shields, carved figures and other ritual objects from Oceania and Africa, followed by a number of Asian and Islamic pieces, notably the glazed Persian ceramics and tableware, which include a handsome thirteenth-century ewer with a lapis lazuli glaze. On the right side of the passageway, pre-Columbian treasures range from a *zapotec* (funerary urn) to carved stone objects used for ball games.

Pavillon Michal et Renata Hornstein and Pavillon Liliane et David M. Stewart

Designed by architects Edward and William Maxwell, the elegant Beaux-Arts temple of art on the north side of rue Sherbrooke ouest comprises two joined pavilions. Its wide steps lead past a colonnaded portico to the original half of the building, the **Pavillon Michal et Renata Hornstein**, whose main hall's majestic grand staircase leads to the upstairs *salles* hosting temporary exhibitions. In back, the Hornstein fuses with a more modern annex, the **Pavillon Liliane et David M. Stewart**, which contains the thrust of the museum's Canadian collection on its upper floor, a wide-ranging survey of decorative arts below and a small showcase of Greco-Roman and Near Eastern and Egyptian art on the ground floor.

Straight ahead after you've ascended the Hornstein's grand staircase, the **Canadian collection** occupies the second-floor galleries of the Pavillon Stewart annex. The furthest gallery to the left is busy with **Inuit carvings**. Look for Joe Talirunnilik's tiny soapstone *Migration*, showing a boat positively jammed with fleeing passengers; a variation on this piece sold for $278,500 in 2006, a record price for an Inuit carving.

The main gallery's collection of pre-1945 **Canadian paintings** is less than spectacular and confusing to boot, as numerous dividing walls break up the flow. The most worthy collection here is the series of landscapes by the **Group of Seven**, a group of Canadian artists that set the standard for landscape paintings throughout much of the twentieth century. Tom Thompson, the instigator of the group's creation, has several works here, including his magnificent *In the Northland*, which resonates with the orange hues typical of northern Canadian autumns. Also of note are Lawren Harris's moody landscapes of simple, rounded rock forms in the far north, typified in *Morning, Lake Superior*.

Don't miss the side gallery devoted to **Alfred Laliberté**, whose discovery of Rodin while at the École des Beaux-Arts in Paris is evident in his angry-looking *Dollard des Ormeaux*. The successor to Louis-Phillipe Hébert as the main sculptor of public art in the first half of the twentieth century, Laliberté captures numerous aspects of Québécois life in the works on display here, as well as in the 200 bronzes commissioned for the Musée du Québec (see p.268). Also worth a look are the four trippy **Alfred Pellan** works at the back of the gallery – his *Mad Love (Homage to André Breton)* is particularly psychedelic, with its heart painted in realistic blood-red.

The entire floor below the Canadian collection spans more than five centuries of **furniture and domestic objects** – to get here from the Hornstein's main hall, pass to either side of the grand staircase. Some of its most impressive and oldest pieces are the intricately inlaid wooden panels depicting prominent Romans that date from 1420s Siena. The rest of the first gallery's eclectic contents include an elaborate seventeenth-century Spanish writing cabinet, an ornate Rococo dragon-headed sleigh from France and delicate faïence porcelain. The Neoclassical and Victorian furniture in the next two galleries are not as memorable as the Art Deco stained-glass peacock-motif window and snake-wrapped floor lamp towards the end. If frou-frou isn't so much to your taste, you'll better appreciate the large collection of **twentieth-century design** that rounds out the exhibition. Gerrit Rietveld's classic *Red-Blue Chair* gives way to fabulously shaped creations like Marcel Breuer's sinuous wood-laminate *Isokon* lounge chair and Eero Saarinen's cow-patterned *Womb* armchair. Other twentieth-century luminaries who are also featured for their furniture and household objects include Alvar Aalto, Charles and Ray Eames, Isamu Noguchi, Arne Jacobsen and Ron Arad.

After all of this decorative and Canadian art, the two rooms back near the street entrance are a bit of a disconnect, focusing as they do on Greco-Roman and Near Eastern and Egyptian arts of the sort you'd expect to see downstairs in the Gallery of Ancient Cultures (see opposite). A fifth-century Syrian mosaic floor depicting two sheep with knotted tails flanking the tree of life, and several Near Eastern plaster funeral masks from the first and second centuries are the highlights here. After you leave the museum, be sure to check out the colourful sculptures by Keith Haring – 3-D versions of his signature humanoid figures – that enliven the Hornstein's eastern side on avenue du Musée.

Quartier du Musée and Concordia University

The southern verge of the Golden Square Mile may be a mishmash of architectural styles and purposes where it interweaves with Downtown but there are a few distractions en route to the excellent architecture centre located here (see p.66). The area immediately around the Musée des Beaux-Arts, dubbed the **Quartier du Musée** by the tourist authorities, contains some fine remnants of the Square Mile's golden age, elaborated on in the free two-hour tour of the district that departs from the museum's main lobby (mid-June to late Aug Wed–Sun 2pm; ☎514/288-6176, ⓦ www.quartierdumusee.com). Included in the itinerary is **rue Crescent**, where the row of nineteenth-century townhouses below rue Sherbrooke hosts some of the city's most upscale boutiques. Closer to rue Ste-Catherine, bars and dance clubs catering to a mix of Anglophone office workers, students and tourists proliferate (see p.169).

A block to the west are the profoundly ugly structures that make up the nucleus of **Concordia University**'s urban campus: the 1960s-era vintage Henry F. Hall Building appears to be clad in urinals – perhaps the inspiration for the use of what appear to be bathroom tiles for the exterior of the postmodern J.W. McConnell Building, opposite. The latter's saving grace is the preserved **Royal George Apartments**, a 1912 Renaissance Revival building on rue Bishop adorned with white-glazed, terracotta floral detailing. Behind its facade but entered through the main building at 1400 boul de Maisonneuve O is the **Leonard and Bina Ellen Art Gallery** (Tues–Fri noon–6pm, Sat until 5pm; free; ☎514/848-2424 ext 4750, ⓦhttp://ellengallery.concordia.ca; Métro Guy-Concordia), whose collection of contemporary art alternates with student shows. Hurrying along to rue Ste-Catherine and rue Guy leads to the university's new **EV Complex** anchoring the north-eastern corner; the contemporary seventeen-storey glass tower now houses Concordia's engineering and visual arts departments and boasts a stellar, floral glass mural conceived by a former student on its eastern facade. Catty-corner to this is the **Faubourg Ste-Catherine**, at 1616 rue Ste-Catherine O, a city mall that's lost some of its gloss in recent years, but still houses a decent food court on its upper floors, making it a good place to grab a quick bite.

Centre Canadien d'Architecture (CCA)

Situated in the neighbourhood of limestone houses and low-slung red-brick apartment blocks known as Shaughnessy Village, on the outskirts of the Golden Square Mile a couple of blocks southwest from the Faubourg, stands the **Centre Canadien d'Architecture (CCA)**. Its significant collection of architectural prints, drawings and scale models is housed in an immensely formal building set back from landscaped grounds at 1920 rue Baile (Wed–Sun 10am–5pm, Thurs until 9pm; $10, free Thurs after 5.30pm; ☎514/939-7026, ⓦwww.cca.qc.ca; Métro Guy-Concordia). The severe, grey-limestone facade is broken up by an aluminium allusion to a parapet and very few windows, a minimalist approach echoed in the angular metal-and-glass portico over the entrance to the grounds themselves. But what the CCA lacks in detail on its side facing rue Baile, it more than makes up for on the side that fronts boulevard René-Lévesque. Here, two Golden Square Mile–era houses collectively known as the **Shaughnessy House** have been ingeniously incorporated into the building, and their refurbished interiors offer the most luxurious places in the city to sit and rest. Outfitted with marble fireplace mantles and archways supported by grooved columns, the setting may make you linger long enough to forget about seeing the exhibits. One-hour guided tours of the building and the Shaughnessy House are offered in English on weekends (Sat & Sun 1.30pm) with the price of admission.

The CCA mounts anywhere from three to eight exhibitions a year using pieces from its archives and elsewhere – past shows have focused on the works of Frank Lloyd Wright, Frederick Law Olmsted and Carlos Scarpa, with whimsical displays on Disney theme parks and garden implements also receiving critical acclaim. If you're in town between exhibits, there is no permanent collection to tour as such, and though museum staff insist the architecture of the Shaughnessy House fulfills that function, it alone isn't worth the entry price; that said, if you are into design and architecture books, the museum's bookstore is a must, and it's free of charge. Outside, the CCA's **gardens**, on the south side of boulevard René-Lévesque, are also open to the public (daily 6am–midnight; free), and are scattered about with an incongruous collection of fragments of buildings, miniature temples and other architectural allusions designed by local artist/architect Melvin Charney.

Vieux-Montréal

The clichés that abound about **Vieux-Montréal** (Old Montreal) are a bit misleading. Yes, there are stretches of cobblestone streets and eighteenth-century residences which make it feel like an old French village – and an extremely well-kept one at that – but the bulk of the original city is actually characterized by tall, dark canyons of nineteenth- and early twentieth-century commercial buildings built by the English and Scottish. Likewise, the sight of Victorian lampposts and the sound of horse-drawn *calèches* echoing off the stone structures can produce a Dickensian reverie – until it's broken by the occasional car rumbling down the area's narrow lanes. The neighbourhood's delights lie more in turning down its small, secretive streets and in ogling the Industrial Revolution–era embellishments – deeply rusticated stone walls, fanciful carved garlands or serious-looking busts – adorning many of the facades in Canada's one-time financial powerhouse. Even the buzz and cheesiness of the more touristy bits have an infectious appeal, especially the sense of anticipation that builds on Wednesday and Saturday summer evenings when the whole circus shuffles down to the Vieux-Port to ooh and ah the fireworks (see p.225).

Roughly coinciding with the limits of the old town walls, Vieux-Montréal is braced by rue St-Antoine (and the Quartier International) to the north, rue Berri to the east, rue McGill to the west and the St Lawrence to the south. Relatively compact, it is best visited on foot, and you could easily spend a day (and evening, when the landmark buildings are artfully illuminated) just strolling the streets and squares, starting with **Place d'Armes**, the old heart of the city, framed by buildings from the main epochs of Montréal's history. Much of that history was determined by the forces of commerce and the Church, represented here by lavish banks and the soaring **Basilique Notre-Dame**, while the edifices of government, including the ornate **Hôtel de Ville**, lie east along **rue Notre-Dame**. It passes the jostling tourist centre of Vieux-Montréal, **Place Jacques-Cartier**, adjacent to one of the neighbourhood's best museums: the **Musée du Château Ramezay**, which showcases hundreds of fascinating artefacts dating from the city's fur-trading days through to its financial zenith.

The old city's other, and more attractive, main thoroughfare, **rue St-Paul**, runs parallel to and south of rue Notre-Dame, extending from the intimate **Chapelle Notre-Dame-de-Bon-Secours** and silver-domed **Marché Bonsecours** (both of which also face onto the Vieux-Port and the St Lawrence) in the east to the Old Customs House in the west. The latter is part of the excellent **Musée d'Archéologie**, whose main building is located on the precise spot of Montréal's founding in 1642 and full of centuries-old artefacts excavated from the soil beneath.

Vieux-Montréal was not only the birthplace of the city's institution as a Catholic mission (see box, p.72) but was also Canada's financial and commercial hub up until the mid-twentieth century. As businesses moved to the present Downtown area, the old city was largely left to decay until the decision to hold Expo '67 on the islands facing Vieux-Montréal (see p.117) helped bring people back into the neighbourhood, kick-starting a long process of refurbishment that has made it into a tourist magnet (which locals often disdained). But since the explosion of boutique hotels and condo-conversions a few years ago that spurred the opening of new gastronomic restaurants and flashy lounges, the area has become popular with more and more Montrealers year round. And the recent completion of the **Quartier International** business district has bridged the gap where the open trench of the Autoroute Ville-Marie once severed the old town from the rest of the city.

After the heady history of Vieux-Montréal, the **Vieux-Port** (Old Port), wedged between rue de la Commune and the St Lawrence, makes a great place to chill out, its car-free parkland providing plenty of places to sit and watch the crowds pass by. Its quays offer terrific views and, with the **Centre des Sciences de Montréal** and its **IMAX Theatre**, a good escape if the weather turns bad, especially if you've got kids in tow.

Place d'Armes and around

Start exploring at **Place d'Armes**, the square braced by rues St-Jacques and Notre-Dame that was once the financial centre of the city but which now banks mostly on tourism, thanks to its location directly in front of the Basilique Notre-Dame. In the colony's early days, the square served as both a cemetery and a common battlefield – the most legendary confrontation saw a supposedly unarmed Paul de Chomedey, Sieur de Maisonneuve, take on an armed Iroquois chief in 1644 and emerge victorious. A century later, French regiments surrendered their arms here in 1760, after the British captured the city.

Vieux-Montréal practicalities

The best way to get to Vieux-Montréal is by the **Métro**'s orange line – Place-d'Armes is the most central station, due north of the eponymous square; to the east, Champ-de-Mars is the closest to Place Jacques-Cartier, while Square-Victoria serves the western end of the district. A **bicycle path** runs south to the end of rue Berri, but you'll have to dodge pedestrians after it then turns west to run the length of the Vieux-Port. If you bring your **car**, there are parking lots on Quai King-Edward and Quai de l'Horloge ($3 per half-hour, up to $15 for 12 hours), but traffic can be a nightmare, especially during the fireworks displays (see p.225) and other big events. A better bet is the parking garage under the Chaussegros de Léry building just east of the Hôtel de Ville or under the Centre de Commerce Mondial or Palais des Congrès, both accessible from rue St-Antoine.

The city-run **tourist office** is located on the northwest corner of Place Jacques-Cartier (see p.73 for details). Vieux-Montréal's official website is ⓦ www.vieux .montreal.qc.ca. For information on activities in the Vieux-Port, there's a counter in the front of the large pavilion on Quai Jacques-Cartier (mid-May to late Sept) and on the port area's website: ⓦ www.quaysoftheoldport.com.

Horse-drawn *calèches* can be hired at Place d'Armes, on rue Notre-Dame est near the Hôtel de Ville and along rue de la Commune at various points, including the bottom of Place Jacques-Cartier ($45/30min, $75/1hr). If you'd prefer to hoof it, there are also regular **walking tours** of the district and the city publishes a self-guided tour booklet, *Discover Old Montreal*, available at the tourist office and Vieux-Montréal museums for $5.99.

VIEUX-MONTRÉAL | Place d'Armes and around

2

VIEUX-MONTRÉAL

Quartier Latin ▲

Métro Champ-de-Mars ▲

Chinatown ▲

Downtown ▲

Square-
Victoria ▲

Quai de
l'Horloge

VIEUX-PORT   Promenade du Vieux-Port

Quai
Alexandra

0   250 m

ACCOMMODATION
Auberge Alternative
du Vieux-Montréal
Auberge Bonaparte
Auberge Bonsecours
Auberge Les Passants
du Sans Soucy
Auberge de la
Place Royale
Auberge du Vieux-Port
Le Beau Soleil
Casa de Matéo
Hôtel Gault
Hôtel Nelligan
Hôtel Place d'Armes
Hôtel St-Paul
Inter-Continental
Marriott SpringHill
Suites   O
Pierre du Calvet   I
W Montréal   E

**RESTAURANTS &
CAFÉS**
Ben and Jerry's   K
Bio Train   M
Bonaparte   J
Boris Bistro   J
Café du Château   H
Le Cartet   G
Casa de Matéo   L
Chez L'Épicier   C
Claude Postel   N
Club Chasse et Pêche   B

Cluny
Da Emma   F
Eggspectation   D
Garde Manger   I
Holder   A
Java U
Masala
Olive et
Gourmando   3
Le Petit
Moulinsart   14
Pizzédélic   7
Scola Pasta   27
Stash Café
Titanic   10
Toqué   4

BARS & CLUBS
Les 3 Brasseurs   13
Café des Éclusiers   30
La Cage aux
Sports   18
Le Cigare
de Pharaon   21
Cobalt   19
Les Deux Pierrots   25
Le Jardin Nelson   17
Modavie   11
Pub St-Paul   15
Les Remparts   16
Suite 701   K
                                C

Centre des
Sciences de
Montréal

Musée d'Archéologie
et d'Histoire de Montréal

Old Customs House

Place Royale

Centaur Theatre

Basilique
Notre-Dame

Aldred
Building

Place
D'Armes

Séminaire
de Saint-Sulpice

Banque
de Montréal

Banque
Nationale

Banque
Royale

Centre de Commerce
Mondial de Montréal

Palais des Congrès

QUARTIER
INTERNATIONAL

La Joute

PLACE JEAN
PAUL RIOPELLE

Place
d'Armes

Palais de
Justice

Old
Courthouse

Édifice
Ernest-Cormier

Champ de Mars

Hôtel de Ville

Place
Vauquelin

Château
Ramezay

Place
Jacques-
Cartier

Marché
Bonsecours

Lieu Historique
Sir-George-
Étienne-Cartier

Maison du
Calvet

Chapelle
Notre-Dame-de-
Bon-Secours

Centre
d'Histoire
de Montréal

Youville
Stables

Place de la
Grande-Paix

Place D'Youville

Hôpital Général des
Soeurs-Grises

Musée Marc-
Aurèle Fortin

RUE ST-DENIS
RUE ST-LOUIS
RUE ST-ANTOINE EST
AUTOROUTE VILLE-MARIE
RUE GOSFORD
RUE DU CHAMP-
DE-MARS
RUE NOTRE-DAME EST
RUE ST-VINCENT
RUE ST-GABRIEL
RUE ST-JEAN-BAPTISTE
BOULEVARD
ST-LAURENT
RUE ST-DIZIER
RUE DE
BRÉSOLES
COURS
LE ROYER
RUE ST-SULPICE
RUE LE ROYER
RUE BONSECOURS
RUE ST-PAUL EST
RUE DE LA COMMUNE EST
RUE ST-FRANÇOIS-XAVIER
RUE ST-PAUL OUEST
RUE ST-JACQUES
RUE ST-ANTOINE OUEST
RUELLE DES
FORTIFICATIONS
AVENUE VIGER OUEST
RUE DE L'HÔPITAL
RUE DU ST-SACREMENT
RUE ST-PIERRE
RUE ST-MAURICE
RUE NORMAND
RUE NOTRE-DAME OUEST
RUE DOLLARD
RUE DES RÉCOLLETS
STE-HÉLÈNE
RUELLE MOYNE
RUE DU PORT
RUE WILLIAM
RUE MCGILL
RUE DES SOEURS-GRISES
LONGUEUIL
RUE KING
RUE ST-HENRI
RUE DE WELLINGTON

▲ & Parc des Écluses
▲ & Lachine Canal
▲ & Cité Multimédia

N

69

The square's centrepiece is a century-old **fountain** commemorating the founding of Montréal, capped by a strident flag-bearing statue of de Maisonneuve. Among the key figures of the early colony represented on the base of the fountain, designed by sculptor Louis-Philippe Hébert, is Pilote, the dog whose barking allegedly warned de Maisonneuve and his troops of the impending 1644 Iroquois attack. You can see the Montréal flag fluttering nearby, its four emblems – French fleur-de-lys, English rose, Scottish thistle and Irish shamrock – recalling the nations that built the city.

There's not much to the square itself – most items of interest are in the buildings that face onto it, such as the domed shrine of the **Banque de Montréal**, which is located on the north side at 119 rue St-Jacques O. Founded in 1817 by local Scottish merchants, it served the entire nation until the Bank of Canada was created in the 1930s. The current structure, built three decades after the bank was founded, is credited with initiating rue St-Jacques' development as the "Wall Street of Canada". The Banque de Montréal was by far the most glorious bank in the area; outwardly modelled on the Pantheon in Rome, it has interior chambers that reek of opulence with deluxe marble counters, gleaming bronze fittings and dark green syenite columns with gilt Corinthian capitals supporting an ornate coffered ceiling. Off to the left of the main entrance, a small **Numismatic Museum** (Mon–Fri 10am–4pm; free) displays old account books, banknotes and coins – be sure to check out the cheque written on sealskin. Several of the other banks that comprised Canada's Wall Street presided over the blocks of **rue St-Jacques** west of the square, their ornate facades adorned with carved garlands, elaborate lintels and detailed cornices – a style exemplified by the **Banque Royale** at no. 360, the tallest building in the British Commonwealth when erected in 1928 and possessing a central banking hall of almost cathedral-like grandeur.

The east side of Place d'Armes is equally imposing, starting with the red-sandstone building on the northeast corner built in 1888 for the **New York Life Insurance Company**. At eight storeys high, it was the city's first skyscraper, though you won't be able to check out the view – access is limited to the dimly lit lobby, whose ceiling is stamped with handsome copper mouldings. Next door, at 507 Place d'Armes, the 23-storey Art Deco **Aldred Building** is the city's finest example of the ziggurat style made famous by the Empire State Building, both completed in 1931, the set-back roof the result of a 1929 city ordinance mandating that structures over ten storeys design their building profiles to maximize the amount of sunlight let onto nearby streets. Its streamlined verticality and simplified ornamentation marked the first shift away from the classically inspired architecture that still gives Vieux-Montréal much of its character. The Art Deco detailing continues inside the lobby, where a stained-glass window casts a golden hue on the copper and brass friezes of swallows sitting atop telegraph poles.

The ugly black monolith housing the **Banque Nationale** on the west side of the square would be nothing more than an eyesore but for its symbolic importance. Towering over its neighbours, the 1967 building is seen as representing the power of the Francophone business class over their former oppressors, the Church and the English. Its vault, the black granite box jutting out on the opposite side from Place d'Armes, is suspended in the air to make it near impossible to break into. Until the tower's installation, little thought was given to conserving the architectural heritage here, so at least one positive aspect is that it provided a catalyst to change the planning laws to emphasize the conservation of the neighbourhood's historic character.

Basilique Notre-Dame

Framing Place d'Armes to the south is the twin-towered, Gothic-Revival **Basilique Notre-Dame** (daily 8am–4.30pm; $4; ☎514/842-2925, ⓦwww .basiliquenddm.org; Métro Place-d'Armes), church of the Catholic faithful since 1829 – the largest religious building in North America at the time. It made such an impression on its architect, a Protestant Irish-American named James O'Donnell, that he converted to Catholicism six months before its inauguration. He died a year later and is buried in a rather unprepossessing (and inaccessible) grave in the church basement.

The basilica is for some reason often compared to Notre-Dame-de-Paris, but more closely resembles Westminster Abbey, thanks to its severe towers, named La Persévérance and La Tempérance (neither is open to the public). Persévérance, the westernmost of the two, holds the twelve-tonne Jean-Baptiste bell affectionately called *le Gros Bourdon* (the Big Bumblebee), which required twelve bell-ringers to get it moving before electricity was installed. Though rarely rung nowadays – former Prime Minister Trudeau's state funeral in 2000 was a notable exception – its low rumbling peals could be heard as far as 25km away in the days before urban development blocked the sound.

The lushness of the vast interior comes as a surprise after the stern exterior. For its first four decades or so it was equally austere until Victor Bourgeau drew inspiration from the Ste-Chapelle in Paris to embellish it in a lush French Catholic manner. The basilica positively explodes with colour, the wooden mouldings above the 3500-seat vault painted in dense blues, reds, golds and greens. The vibrant blue ribs, adorned with hundreds of gold-leaf stars, give the impression of sitting under a midnight sky, while light from three rose windows located, unusually, in the ceiling combine with flickering votive candle flames to create a sense of intense warmth and intimacy. The rich hues of the stained-glass windows portray the colony's early days – to the right of the altar, de Maisonneuve carries the cross to the top of the mountain.

About halfway toward the altar, you'll find an ornately decorated staircase leading up to the pulpit; the base is guarded by Louis-Philippe Hébert's exceptional woodcarvings of the prophets. Backlit in brilliant cobalt-blue light, the soaring altar itself is a masterpiece of detailing by Frenchman Henri Bouriché, whose exquisite sculptures of biblical figures themed on the Eucharist have Christ's crucifixion as the focal point.

Behind the altar lies the surprisingly bright and modern **Chapelle Sacré-Coeur**, fondly referred to as the Wedding Chapel – up to five weddings a day are held here on summer weekends. Destroyed by an arsonist in 1978, the ground floor's delicately carved walls and richly embellished capitals supporting the mezzanine were reconstructed to the original design, while the upper layers – including a pine-panelled vault that fairly glows – are decidedly modern. Against the back wall, an enormous 16-metre-high bronze altarpiece by Charles Daudelin depicts man's progression from birth to heaven, the gates of which are represented by the sweeping wings of a dove over Christ's head.

Time your first visit so that you can catch the "**And then there was light**" *son et lumière* spectacle (Tues–Sat evenings, times vary; $10; ☎514/842-2925 ext 226, ⓦwww.therewaslight.ca), which details the early history of the church and colony on giant screens before they are drawn back to reveal the interior architecture in all its glory, with artful lighting emphasizing its architectural features. The basilica provides an equally resplendent setting for concerts by the Orchestre Symphonique de Montréal and other classical ensembles (see p.191). Otherwise, to get the most out of your visit, take one of the free twenty-minute guided tours that start every half-hour or so from the reception desk near the entrance.

Séminaire de St-Sulpice

Adjoining the presbytery on the western side of the basilica is Vieux-Montréal's oldest building, the mock-medieval **Séminaire de St-Sulpice**, whose main doorway is topped by North America's oldest public clock, installed in 1701. The central part of the building dates from 1685 and was built as the headquarters of the Paris-based order of Sulpician priests that instigated Montréal's establishment as a religious colony and held title to the island for two centuries (see box below). There is no public access to the building: two dozen Sulpicians still live there today and maintain the basilica.

Rue St-Sulpice, rue le Royer and the Palais de Justice

From the basilica, head south along **rue St-Sulpice**, a street rife with history. Many of the continent's first explorers lived here, and while some of the houses

Messieurs de Montréal

Montréal was originally conceived and run as a French religious colony, a plan that entailed the conversion of the many Natives – particularly Iroquois and Algonquin – to Catholicism. This momentous task fell to a group of missionaries, the **Messieurs de St-Sulpice**, an order of Sulpician priests trained in a seminary outside Paris.

It was a question of finances and determination more than anything else that led the Sulpicians to win spiritual dominion of Montréal. Their supporters had deep pockets and, crucially, eagerly emptied them when informed of the personal spiritual rewards to be gained from the practice. The first four priests to arrive came ashore in 1657 with a tidy sum of 75,000 *livres* and went on to found the parish of Notre-Dame. Their influence stretched beyond the sacred when they were given title to the island as its *seigneurs* in 1663, allowing them to rent it out to tenants. This system hampered efforts by industrial and mercantile barons to develop the land and, in tandem with other reforms, the Sulpician's right of seigneury was rescinded in 1859.

Headquartered at the **Séminaire de St-Sulpice**, the society's seemingly endless funds had a lasting impact on the city's public face. On a civic note, they contributed to the city's urban planning – one needed roads, after all, to get the faithful to church, school and hospital – and the creation of many Montréal streets, like **rue St-Paul** (see p.76), can be credited to Sulpician leader François Dollier de Casson. Domestically, the Sulpicians funded the creation of the **Maison St-Gabriel** (see p.127), the eventual home and school of the *filles du roi* – women sent from the motherland to help populate the colony (see p.129). The priests would also assure their longevity by training newcomers at a facility built for the purpose in 1840, the **Grand Séminaire**, located northwest of Downtown; over six thousand priests have studied in its hallowed halls since its inception.

Not surprisingly, the most obvious remnants of Sulpician rule are the churches the order's alms helped erect. The most significant of these can still be visited in Vieux-Montréal: the **Chapelle Notre-Dame-de-Bon-Secours**, which received construction subsidies from the priests, and the 1829 **Basilique Notre-Dame**, arguably the Sulpicians' most lasting contribution to Montréal architecture and religious history. The basilica is certainly their only sanctified domain today – managed by what few Sulpician priests remain in Montréal.

are today still private residences – those that aren't have been converted into shops – they are embellished with a variety of sometimes hard-to-spot historical plaques. Daniel Greysolon, Sieur du Lhut – the man for whom Duluth, Minnesota, was named – lodged in the corner building at 88 rue Notre-Dame in 1675. Also, the Le Moyne brothers, who founded the American cities of Biloxi, Mobile and New Orleans, as well as the colony of Louisiana, were born and raised at no. 404.

About halfway down the street on the east side is **rue le Royer**, an austere courtyard lined with late nineteenth-century warehouses that recall Montréal's past as a major shipping port. The site of Montréal's first hospital, it was run by nuns, who later made a fortune building the warehouses and then renting them out (the proceeds helping to fund their new hospital near the mountain. They were converted into offices and apartments in the late 1970s, the first such repurposing of old properties, which sparked the revival of Vieux-Montréal.

Walking to the courtyard's far end will bring you to boulevard St-Laurent, from which it's a short block north to the intersection with rue Notre-Dame. Running the length of Vieux-Montréal and along the south side of Place d'Armes, **rue Notre-Dame** is home to the city's main administrative bodies. The region east of boulevard St-Laurent is presided over by the mammoth **Palais de Justice**, the courthouse that handles most legal cases today. Its predecessor lies in its shadow: the **Old Courthouse**, at 155 rue Notre-Dame E, which was built by the British in 1856 and designed to look like a Greek temple, now holds municipal offices. The third storey and incongruous grey dome were added 35 years later. Across the street, at no. 100, the colonnaded **Édifice Ernest-Cormier** held criminal trials after the courts were separated in 1926. Massive bronze doors embossed with the symbols of justice guard the entrance to what had served a long spell as a music conservatory before resuming a judicial calling as the Court of Appeal a couple of years ago. Other

than the grand travertine-clad lobby, it's off limits to the public. Further along, at no. 160, the **Maison de la Sauvegarde**, built in 1800 with a rough-hewn limestone facade, high chimneys and steeply pitched roof and dormers, is one of the last houses built in the local French style, which persisted for four decades after the English conquest. Typical of the period, shops occupied the ground floor and the merchant and his family resided above.

Place Jacques-Cartier

The main activity on rue Notre-Dame est is found east of the courthouses, around the cobble-stoned **Place Jacques-Cartier**, which served as the city's public market from 1804 to 1960 and

△ Fieldstone facade on rue St-Paul

stretches down to the Vieux-Port (see p.81). The only echo of its former use are the few small stalls selling flowers and prints at the square's north end daily throughout the summer. Most of the action now is in the form of buskers and artists hustling for change from the crowds that swarm to the square's bustling restaurants and terrace-fronted cafés. The city-run tourist office (early June to early Sept daily 9am–7pm; early Sept to early June daily 9am–5pm, except closed 1pm–2pm Nov–April and all day Mon & Tues Nov–March) occupies the stone building at the square's northwest corner, while off its lower reaches is tiny **rue St-Amable**, infested with water-colour-hawkers but providing access to a shady courtyard where jewellery stalls offer some decent artisan-crafted pieces.

The **Nelson Monument** at the north end of the square features a likeness of Admiral Nelson atop a drab column one-third the height of its better-known London counterpart. The statue is interesting less because of its composition than the controversy that continues to dog it. Funded by a group of Montréal Anglophones delighted at Nelson's defeat of the French at Trafalgar in 1805, it later became a source of sovereignist ire, reminding some of British colonialism. A faction plotted to blow the statue up as early as 1890, and grumbling about it continued well into the 1970s, when the surrounding taverns were hotbeds of sovereignist activity. Debate renewed as recently as 1997, when the city proposed moving it to a faraway Anglophone neighbourhood. Public opposition allowed Nelson to keep his spot, although he had to come down from his perch for two years for cleaning. It turned out Nelson was so weather-ravaged he had to be replaced; the statue there now is actually a reproduction of the original (which is on display in the Centre d'Histoire de Montréal; see p.80).

Place Vauquelin and Champ de Mars

Facing Place Jacques-Cartier on the north side of rue Notre-Dame, the intimate **Place Vauquelin** features the Francophone answer to the Nelson Monument: a statue of French naval commander Jean Vauquelin, who harried the British during the Seven Years' War. Once the site of the city jail, Place Vauquelin has been a public space since 1858 and is outfitted with a pretty fountain surrounded by stone and wood benches.

A fortified city

Even though Vieux-Montréal was a walled fortress for over a century, all that remains of the **fortifications** that once surrounded it are stretches in the Champ de Mars and an extensive chunk inside the Musée d'Archéologie et d'Histoire. The first wall, a 2800-metre-long row of cedar posts, was erected in 1687 to protect against Iroquois attack. The structure ended up being more useful as firewood, and by 1713 it was deemed an insufficient barrier against the city's new enemy: the British. Construction on new walls began soon after, and by 1744 the city was wrapped in a stone cocoon that measured about 4m high in places. Those thirty-odd years of labour proved unnecessary, though; the war they were built to defend against was fought in Québec City in 1759 (see p.253). When the British took over the colony, they dropped Montréal as the military centre and focused on fortifying the capital. In 1796, a public petition requested that the walls, by then unkempt and blocking the town's expansion, be demolished. The public's will was approved in 1801, and the walls came down after an act was passed to advance the city's "Salubrity, Convenience and Embellishment" – official-speak for urban development.

At the square's north end, a set of stairs leads down to the **Champ de Mars**, a grassy expanse named for the god of war, though the only action it ever experienced consisted of military drills. By the 1820s, the park became a public promenade that Montrealers took to in their finest Sunday dress and was also, ironically, the city's favoured spot for public hangings. Though converted into a car park in the early twentieth century, it was transformed back into parkland in honour of the city's 350th anniversary, when remains of the **stone fortifications** that once surrounded the city were excavated (see box, opposite) – you can see the parallel scarp and counterscarp cutting through the grass.

Hôtel de Ville

East of Place Vauquelin hulks the immense **Hôtel de Ville** at 275 rue Notre-Dame E (Mon–Fri 8am–5pm; free; Métro Champ-de-Mars). The building itself is quite opulent for a city hall, with its mansard roof and turreted entranceway, and the interior is just as impressive after renovations following a serious fire in 1922 were undertaken in the Beaux-Arts style. These produced the grand two-storey-high Hall of Honour adorned with bronze railings and marble pilasters and overhung with an immense (and hideous) bronze chandelier. The bronze statues of a man sowing seed and a woman carting a wooden bucket flanking the entrance foyer were done by Alfred Laliberté and intended as a reminder of Québec's agrarian past. If the municipal government isn't in session, take a peek into the council chambers, where five stained-glass windows depict Montréal at the beginning of the twentieth century in mauve-tinted hues. Free one-hour guided tours are available between late June and mid-August (Mon–Fri 10am–4pm).

The Hôtel de Ville's second-floor balcony was chosen by French **President de Gaulle** as the launchpad for his incendiary rallying cry, "Vive le Québec libre!" during his state visit to Expo '67. His words left the city's Anglophones reeling at the thought that Québec was on its way to independent status and rekindled Francophones with a political fervour that peaked with the 1970 October Crisis (see p.285). French presidents have since then stayed notably mum – publicly anyway – as to their views on Québec's independence.

Musée du Château Ramezay and around

The history of the **Château Ramezay** (June–Aug daily 10am–6pm; Sept–May Tues–Sun 10am–4.30pm; $8; ☎514/861-3708, ⓦwww.chateauramezay.qc.ca; Métro Champ-de-Mars), the low fieldstone manor house opposite the Hôtel de Ville at 280 rue Notre-Dame E is as interesting as the articles now on display in its many chambers. When built in 1705 for the eleventh governor of Montréal, Claude de Ramezay, it was the finest of the colony's two hundred homes. It then served as the North American headquarters of the Compagnie des Indes Occidentales, a fur-trading company, before passing into the hands of the British after the conquest in 1760. Fifteen years later, Benjamin Franklin and his cohorts set up shop here during the fleeting American invasion and attempted to persuade the young colony to join the United States.

Since 1895, the Ramezay has served as a historical **museum**, and its lack of pretension is tremendously appealing. Many of the displayed artefacts from the eighteenth and nineteenth centuries have a genuinely used feel about them – an eighteenth-century missionary's prayerbook is weather-stained and a fireman's hat is creased and chipped from wear. These items contrast with the glistening beaver-pelt top hat and other well-preserved relics of the upper classes. Their portraits hang alongside old maps, like Lord Dorchester's 1795 vision of Québec with very un-Québécois county names like Kent and Buckinghamshire. Nearby is a Dion-Bouton, a turn-of-the-century luxury car that apparently so confused city authorities that they refused to provide a carriage permit for it, instead granting the owner a bicycle licence – a state of affairs rectified a few years later when it received the province's first licence plate, "Q1". In the whitewashed vaults downstairs, the exhibits take on more of an educational slant, recreating domestic scenes that include a kitchen with a dog-powered roasting spit.

But even if these don't interest you, the Ramezay's reconstruction of the **Salle de Nantes** of the Compagnie des Indes Occidentales is alone worth the entrance fee. The two-room salon has walls of rich mahogany imported from a private mansion in Nantes, France, lavishly textured with rose trellises, cherubs and musical instruments. It's the work of Germain Boffrand (principal architect for Louis XIV and Louis XV), and the Ramezay honours the salon's musical theme by putting on concerts here every month or so (free with museum admission; call ☎514/861-3708 for information).

Fieldstone walls surround the small **garden** (free) in back, laid out in a manner typical of eighteenth-century New France; in summer, you can observe the gardens while sitting at the terrace café (see p.154) or take part in a workshop exploring music (Sat 1–5pm) or artisanal crafts such as soap-making (Sun 1–5pm).

Lieu Historique Sir-George-Étienne-Cartier

A five-minute walk east from Château Ramezay brings you to the edge of Vieux-Montréal. At 458 rue Notre-Dame E, the **Lieu Historique Sir-George-Étienne-Cartier** (late May to early Sept daily 10am–6pm; early Sept to late Dec & April to late May Wed–Sun 10am–noon & 1–5pm; $3.95, $6.15 includes theatrical presentation; ☎514/283-2282, ⓦwww.parkscanada.gc.ca /cartier; Métro Champ-de-Mars) comprises two adjoining houses that were inhabited by the Cartier family between 1848 and 1871. Sir George-Étienne Cartier was one of the fathers of Confederation, a moderate reformer who persuaded the French Canadians to join the Dominion of Canada. Today, leaders of Québec nationalism decry Cartier as a collaborator, and the displays in the east house diplomatically skirt over the issue of whether he was right or wrong and instead emphasize his role in the construction of Canada's railways. Such conservatism is carried out in a decidedly bizarre fashion, however: the fact that the Muppet-like figures representing the founding fathers on the main floor are meant to portray Cartier's political bedfellows is only made clear when explained by a guide (fortunately, staff members are happy to provide some context).

The stuffily decorated rooms filled with original domestic objects in the west house vividly recreate the period when Sir George lived here, though the monologues by fictitious house staff that start playing once you walk into the rooms are a bit hokey. They do, however, dish out the odd bit of salacious gossip, like Cartier's penchant for staying at the nearby Rasco Hotel rather than at home. To make the most of it, time your visit for one of the theatrical perform-ances that take place daily in summer, weekends otherwise (call or see website for days and times).

Rue St-Paul and around

One block south of the Cartier museum is one of the city's oldest and most attractive thoroughfares, **rue St-Paul**, which runs parallel to rue Notre-Dame the length of Vieux-Montréal. The nineteenth-century commercial buildings and Victorian lampposts that line rue St-Paul look much the same today as they did back when Charles Dickens stayed at the **Rasco Hotel** (now an office building) at nos. 281–295 in 1842. Many of the street's storefront windows house upscale art galleries, antique stores and clothing boutiques, with some tacky souvenir shops thrown in. But if you walk around to the back of these buildings on rue de la Commune – which parallels rue St-Paul just to the south and faces the Vieux-Port – you'll note that several of them resemble warehouses from the rear. It's an architectural trompe l'oeil that reflects the habits of the time, when goods were delivered to the back and sold in the front.

The street's most attractive building is the three-storey **Maison du Calvet**, at 409 rue St-Paul E, built in 1725 for the American Revolution supporter Pierre du Calvet. The house, now part of the inn that bears his name (see p.140), is the city's finest example of French domestic architecture, retaining two of the style's most distinctive characteristics: exterior stone walls that extend past the rooftop and "S"-shaped irons inset into the walls. The walls were built higher to prevent blazes from spreading between houses, and the irons are anchors, connecting to rods that hold the opposing fieldstone walls in place.

Catty-corner to the Maison du Calvet, the splendid silver-domed **Marché Bonsecours** at 350 rue St-Paul E (ⓦ www.marchebonsecours.qc.ca), is Vieux-Montréal's quintessential marketplace. Erected in 1846 as an interior counterpart to Place Jacques-Cartier's outdoor market, its upper floor served a very brief stint as United Canada's House of Parliament and was Montréal's City Hall for a few decades in the 1800s. Produce stalls bustled on the ground floor until 1964. After being taken over entirely by municipal offices, the building was restored to its former duty as a marketplace in 1992 and now houses very high-priced designer boutiques and commercial art galleries. If you're looking for more affordable shopping, try the blocks west of boulevard St-Laurent, where galleries offer anything from incredibly cheesy landscapes to vibrant contemporary works and even oriental art.

Chapelle Notre-Dame-de-Bon-Secours

Facing Maison du Calvet at 400 rue St-Paul E is the delicate and profusely steepled **Chapelle Notre-Dame-de-Bon-Secours**, its fieldstone walls supporting six copper-and-stone spires of various heights. The location near the St Lawrence earned it the nickname of the Sailors' Church, and mariners would endow it with model ships as thanks for having safely reached the shore – many of these are still on display as votive lamps hanging in the nave. The chapel, which served as Montréal's first church, was initiated by **Sœur Marguerite Bourgeoys** (see below) in 1655. The structure you see today, though, postdates her by some seventy years as it was rebuilt in 1771 following a serious fire. Inside the chapel, white marble panels and pilasters lend it an airy feel while overhead the vault's light grey and sepia tones make it hard to discern what are structural arches or merely painted decoration; this bit of trompe l'oeil, painted by François-Édouard Meloche in the 1880s, was only rediscovered in the 1990s. In a glassed-in chapel to the left of the marble main altar is Bourgeoys' tomb – her remains were only transferred to the church in 2005 – surmounted by an ornate altar that highlights the tiny wooden statue of the *Virgin and Child* given to her in 1672.

Musée Marguerite-Bourgeoys

Adjacent to the chapel, a **museum** (May–Oct Tues–Sun 10am–5.30pm; Nov to mid-Jan & mid-March to April 11am–3.30pm; $6, $8 with archeological tour; ⓣ514/282-8670, ⓦ www.marguerite-bourgeoys.com; Métro Champ-de-Mars) devoted to Bourgeoys adds a touching note; one small room is filled with

58 handcrafted miniature doll scenes that tell her life's story, from birth to death. She arrived in Montréal in 1653 and quickly set to work as a teacher, was founder of the colony's first school (in a stable donated by de Maisonneuve) and driving force behind the chapel's construction. She also established the farm and vocational school in Pointe St-Charles that helped women (including the King's Wards – see p.129) to establish homes and adapt to the harsh life of the colony. For all this, she was known as the "Mother of the Colony" and her piety eventually led her to become Canada's first saint, in 1982.

The museum itself isn't all that exciting, but it's the only way to gain access to the narrow staircase leading up 69 steps to the small **aerial chapel**, which gives excellent views over the port and the crammed network of streets around the church. A further flight leads to an open-air belvedere with glorious views.

Pointe-à-Callière and Place Royale

Montréal is one of those rare cities that can pinpoint the exact location on which it was founded: **Pointe-à-Callière** a triangular spit of land that juts out into rue de la Commune (the shoreline of the St Lawrence in the mid-1600s) at the western edge of Vieux-Montréal, a ten- to fifteen-minute walk from the Marché Bonsecours along rue St-Paul or rue de la Commune. But while the founding's location is clear, the precise date of the event is slightly murky – the only thing for sure is that it happened mid-May, 1642. It proved an ill-fated spot, prone to flooding, so the colony was moved a little to the north across the Petite Rivière St-Pierre (now channelled below Place d'Youville), near present-day **Place Royale**. From its earliest days, Place Royale was a meeting space, serving first as an Indian campground, then the site for annual fur-trading fairs in the colony's early days, and later as a marketplace and a public square replete with fountain and gardens fronting the Neoclassical Customs House. It may appear fairly drab today but beneath the raised expanse of granite paving stones lies one of the Musée d'Archéologie's highlights.

△ Dome of Marché Bonsecours and steeple of Chapelle Notre-Dame-de-Bon-Secours

Musée d'Archéologie et d'Histoire de Montréal

Visible the length of the Vieux-Port, the splendid main building of the **Musée d'Archéologie et d'Histoire de Montréal**, 350 Place Royale (late June to early Sept Mon–Fri 10am–6pm, Sat & Sun 11am–6pm; early Sept to late June Tues–Fri 10am–5pm, Sat & Sun 11am–5pm; $12; ☎514/872-9150, ⓦwww .pacmuseum.qc.ca; Métro Square-Victoria) rises up from the point of de Maisonneuve's landing, looking much like a ship that's run ashore. Inside the contemporary limestone structure, the boat motif carries on with finishing touches like portholes that are inset in the entrance floor, and industrial stairwells connecting the building's four levels. The name of the edifice equally captures its shipping theme – it's known as the **Éperon** (Cutwater).

The museum has three main components: the Éperon, the underground **archeological crypt** and the **Old Customs House**, a Neoclassical building from the 1830s that backs on to rue St-Paul. Temporary exhibits are hosted on the upper floors of the Éperon and the Customs House, and the café and terrace on the second floor of the former offer great views of the port (though not as impressive as the vista from the tower, from where you can also look over Vieux-Montréal). The crypt is a series of underground passageways and rooms – all of which connects the basements of the Éperon and Customs House buildings, passing below Place Royale en route – and is where you'll find the museum's stellar collection of archeological finds excavated from the soil surrounding the buildings between 1983 and 1992.

Before heading to the subterranean exhibits, start your visit with the 18-minute-long multimedia history presentation in the Éperon's main-floor theatre. By far the best way to experience the rest of the museum is on one of the free hour-long guided tours that begin at the ground-floor ticket desk (Sat 2.30pm, but call ahead as this may change). Otherwise, the interactive map downstairs can help you get your bearings.

Once downstairs, the most riveting find is a Catholic **cemetery** dating from 1643 – the oldest vestiges of the original settlement – discovered during the construction of the present-day Éperon building in 1989. Some 38 bodies were buried on this site, although only seven of the gravesites have been unearthed thus far. You can see the impressions left in the clay by the coffins but not the remains – the one skeleton not washed away by centuries of floods has been removed. Traces of three generations of buildings dating back as far as 1796 can be found layered on top of one another within the labyrinth of foundations, interspersed with exhibits of beads, eighteenth-century wine bottles and other artefacts left behind by the site's occupants. As you descend to the sewer, keep an eye out for the subterranean windows – evidence that the street level today is three metres higher than it was centuries ago.

Further along (as you pass below Place d'Youville), a walkway takes you over an eighteenth-century water main and sewage system lined with cobblestones, the tamed **Petite Rivière St-Pierre**, which threatened the first inhabitants with inundation – during the spring thaw, the sewer still gets filled. Beyond that, an exhibition chamber contains five intricate scale models of the surrounding area from different time periods. Set under glass below the floor, they illustrate the area's history from when only Natives roamed the grassy shores up to the late 1800s and provide some guidance to the jumble of stone remains nearby, below Place Royale itself. Beside the privy pipe of an inn built in 1800 on the ruins of the fortifications, steps lead to a catwalk passing over and through earlier foundations, where spotlights highlight traces of seventeenth-century stockade posts and a stretch of an eighteenth-century cobblestone street. From here, you can take the stairs up to the Old Customs House, home of the museum's gift shop and a chaotic exhibition extolling Montréal's neighbourhoods and cultural groups.

Place d'Youville and around

Directly west of the archeology museum stands **Place d'Youville**, a narrow public square constructed atop the former watercourse of the little river (and later sewer) that is still visible from inside the museum. The square's eastern end was renamed **Place de la Grande-Paix** in 2001, to mark the tricentennial of the Great Peace of Montréal, a treaty signed here to end the conflict between the Natives and French settlers. Passing the century-old "Founder's Obelisk", keep an eye out for the entrance to the **Youville Stables** on your left. The name is a misnomer – the 1825 complex of gardens, shady courtyard and stone buildings, which today houses yuppified offices and a restaurant, was in fact a warehouse – the stables were next door. It's a nice enough place to stop in if you're walking by, but not worth going out of your way for.

Opposite, and dividing the square in two, is a converted red-brick fire station housing the **Centre d'Histoire de Montréal** (Tues–Sun 10am–5pm; $4.50; T514/872-3207, W www.ville.montreal.qc.ca/chm; Métro Square-Victoria), which focuses on the city's social history. On the ground floor, displays depict Montréal from the first European settlement to its present expansions – fine for a sketchy overview but not terribly engaging. There are a few bits of ephemera worth keeping an eye out for: Jackie Robinson's baseball bat, kitsch Expo '67 souvenirs and the 1810 statue of Nelson that once overlooked Place Jacques-Cartier. Temporary and permanent exhibitions in the warren of rooms upstairs (including a kitchen circa 1950) attempt to capture daily life in Montréal – the most amusing of these displays is the mock tram with historic street scenes scrolling past the windows as a driver's voice calls out the stops.

Covered by a barren car park for years, the western half of Place d'Youville is undergoing a $3.5-million restoration as a public square due to be completed in 2008. Plans include elements to highlight that the marketplace that once stood here also served as the first Parliament of United Canada, from 1844 until it was torched by Tory rioters in 1849. To the south, between rues St-Pierre and Normand, the **Hôpital Général des Soeurs-Grises** cared for the colony's sick and old, as well as orphaned children, though all that remains of the original H-shaped structure is the west wing and half of the late seventeenth-century chapel's stone walls – its original footprint is marked out in paving stones on rue St-Pierre. Next door, the **Musée Marc–Aurèle Fortin**, at no. 118 (Tues–Sun 11am–5pm; $5), is a small gallery dedicated to the prolific Québécois landscape painter of the early to mid-twentieth century who considered himself the first to found a "Canadian school" that wasn't influenced by Europeans. Judging by the mundane works inside, he probably could have used the help.

The Quartier International

Place d'Youville terminates at **rue McGill**, which separates Vieux-Montréal from the converted warehouses that host software startups, condos and exhibitions at the **Fonderie Darling** arts centre, 745 rue Ottawa (Wed–Sun noon–8pm, Thurs noon–10pm; $2; free Sun T514/392-1554, W www.quartierephemere .org), in the **Cité Multimédia** to the west.

Rue McGill was recently spruced up as a more pedestrian-friendly conduit to the Vieux-Port by the same urban-design team behind the **Quartier International**, a revamped district between Downtown and Vieux-Montréal that, until a few years ago, was mostly a wasteland of parking lots and the open trench carved by the Autoroute Ville-Marie (Hwy-720) and is now a business and institutional district bracketed by a pair of attractive green spaces. Head north past rue St-Jacques to reach the first of these, where rue McGill opens out into **Square Victoria**. A bronze statue of Queen Victoria presides over the southern half of the square, looking across to Hector Guimard's sinuous Art Nouveau **Métropolitain entrance**, built for the Paris original and donated to Montréal for the Métro's inauguration in 1967. Located on the site of the old Haymarket, the square began to acquire its commercial character in 1845 with the construction of Morgan's store, but the architectural unity has become less coherent over the years, with the former Second Empire and Neo-Renaissance buildings giving way to modern structures like the **Tour de la Bourse**, the 47-storey stock exchange tower with black glass framed by massive concrete piers, designed by Luigi Moretti and Pier Luigi Nervi in the early Sixties. More sympathetic was the 1991 **Centre de Commerce Mondial**, a "horizontal skyscraper" at the square's southeast corner uniting diverse historic buildings with a soaring block-long atrium that illuminates a graceful fountain adorned by Amphitrite, Poseidon's wife, near its western end and a chunk of the Berlin Wall to the east.

An equally grand atrium, with a 43m-high glass wall supported by white tree-like trusses, runs through the **Centre CDP Capital**, linking the northern half of Square Victoria with one of the city's newest public spaces, **Place Jean-Paul Riopelle**. Named after the influential Québécois artist (see box, p.75), it provides a showcase for his grandest project: *La Joute* (The Joust), which comprises a central fountain surrounded by thirty rough-hewn bronze sculptural works in a shallow pool. A panel nearby describes the individual elements: good luck determining which of the abstract forms corresponds to which name. True to the artist's wishes, the ensemble comes to life in the evenings for an hourly "show" that incorporates jets of water, flames and veils of mist.

The kaleidoscopic glass facade of the hulking **Palais des Congrès** (Ⓦwww .congresmtl.com), the city's main conference centre, provides a colourful backdrop to *La Joute* – inside, be sure to check out the surreal *Lipstick Forest*, containing electric-pink concrete casts of actual trees, in the centre's northwest corner. Its southern side, along rue St-Antoine, incorporates a number of historic facades, including the Art Deco Tramways building (this was the hub of the city's tram network) and, at no. 181, a 1908 fire station, behind which you'll find **Monopoli** (Wed–Fri noon–6pm, Sat noon–5pm; free; ☎514/868-6691), a gallery devoted to showcasing contemporary architecture in the city.

The Vieux-Port

Running the full length of Vieux-Montréal, between rue de la Commune and the St Lawrence, the **Vieux-Port** (Old Port) was once the most important harbour in Canada; its strategic location at the head of the Lachine Canal connected ships with the Great Lakes and assured its maritime dominance for centuries. The construction of the St Lawrence Seaway in 1959 – allowing ships to bypass the canal altogether – ended the Vieux-Port's glory days, leaving it to deteriorate for three decades. Refurbishment came about in the early 1990s as part of the city's 350th birthday celebrations, and the parkland that was developed turned this kilometre and a half stretch of waterfront into one of

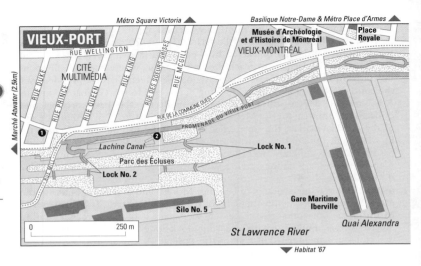

Inside the map:

VIEUX-PORT

Métro Square Victoria ▲

Basilique Notre-Dame & Métro Place d'Armes ▲

Musée d'Archéologie et d'Histoire de Montréal

Place Royale

RUE WELLINGTON

VIEUX-MONTRÉAL

CITÉ MULTIMÉDIA

RUE DUKE

RUE PRINCE

RUE QUEEN

RUE KING

RUE DES SŒURS-GRISES

RUE McGILL

Marché Atwater (2.5km)

RUE DE LA COMMUNE OUEST

PROMENADE DU VIEUX-PORT

❶

❷

Lachine Canal

Lock No. 1

Parc des Écluses

Lock No. 2

Silo No. 5

Gare Maritime Iberville

0   250 m

St Lawrence River

Quai Alexandra

▼ Habitat '67

Montréal's most idyllic playgrounds (recently rebranded as the "Quais du Vieux-Port" for some reason). The area is graced with superb promenades for strolling, biking, rollerblading or cross-country skiing that offer spectacular vistas onto the waterfront to the south and the former warehouses lining rue de la Commune to the north (see p.215 for places that rent wheels).

Traces still remain of the port's former shipping duties in the ghostly junkyard remnants of grain elevator **Silo no. 2**, at the port's eastern end, and the **Tour de l'Horloge**, a watchtower completed in 1922. But these sights are largely overlooked by those in search of summertime activities, like pedal-boating the calm waters of the **Bassin Bonsecours**, a protected reservoir that cascades into the St Lawrence. Fronting the massive Silo no. 5, the narrow **Parc des Écluses** marks the start of the Lachine Canal – reopened to pleasure boats only a few years ago – and its **bike path**, which embarks from the port's westernmost end. Overlooking the first set of locks, a striking wedge-shaped pavilion is home to a waterside terrace café and viewing balcony, where you can get a glimpse of the **Flora International** exhibition (mid-June to early Oct Mon–Thurs 10am–6pm; $12.50; Fri–Sun 10am–8pm; $14.50; ☎514/333-5672, ⓦwww .floramontreal.ca; Métro Square-Victoria). Set to occupy the park until the end of the decade, this annual horticultural show runs for nearly four months and presents some 45 gardens showcasing everything from urban spaces (planting for rooftops or balconies) to the latest contemporary trends. It is as much educational and commercial as it is a place to wander around or admire the greenery from an on-site café terrace.

The Vieux-Port's activity all but dies out come winter, or at least moves indoors to the cavernous halls on the **Quai King-Edward**, where a portside hangar incorporates the interactive science exhibits of the **Centre de Sciences de Montréal** and its **IMAX theatre**.

Quai King-Edward and the Centre des Sciences de Montréal

The lively **Quai King-Edward** at the southernmost end of boulevard St-Laurent is the hub of the Vieux-Port and a good place to start your waterfront explorations. The area immediately west of the quay is lined in early summer with a row of stalls occupied by *les bouquinistes*, whose stock of antique books

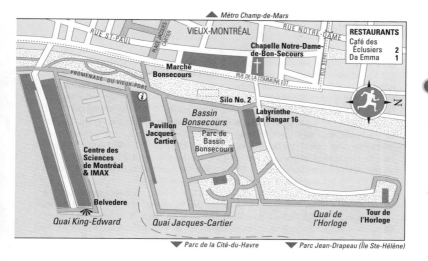

▲ Métro Champ-de-Mars

VIEUX-MONTRÉAL

RUE ST-PAUL

PLACE JACQUES-CARTIER

RUE NOTRE-DAME

RUE DE BERRI

RESTAURANTS
Café des
Éclusiers   2
Da Emma   1

Chapelle Notre-Dame-de-Bon-Secours

PROMENADE DU VIEUX-PORT

Marché Bonsecours

RUE DE LA COMMUNE EST

Silo No. 2

Pavillon Jacques-Cartier

Bassin Bonsecours

Parc de Bassin Bonsecours

Labyrinthe du Hangar 16

Centre des Sciences de Montréal & IMAX

N

Belvedere

Quai King-Edward

Quai Jacques-Cartier

Quai de l'Horloge

Tour de l'Horloge

VIEUX-MONTRÉAL | The Vieux-Port

▼ Parc de la Cité-du-Havre   ▼ Parc Jean-Drapeau (Île Ste-Hélène)

and etchings occasionally yields a find. The real estate to the east of the quay is equally colourful, with caricaturists and musicians on hand to amuse passers-by. If you want to get away from the hubbub, walk to the southernmost end of the quay and take the stairs over the car park to reach a quiet **lookout** point.

Here, you can get a rare panoramic view of the city stretching north to the mountain and south to the islands of the St Lawrence. To your right and across from the Vieux-Port, on a long spit jutting into the St Lawrence, are the staggered Cubist blocks that comprise **Habitat**, a unique apartment complex built for Expo '67 by Moshe Safdie, who later designed the new pavilion at the Musée des Beaux-Arts (see p.62). Next to Habitat is the **Parc de la Cité-de-Havre**, a little-known getaway accessible by car or bicycle via industrial rue Mill at the port's western end; the bridge you see links these to Île Ste-Hélène and Île Notre-Dame (see Chapter 7, "Parc Jean-Drapeau"), in the middle of the St Lawrence.

The port's main indoor attraction is the **Centre des Sciences de Montréal** (mid-June to early Sept Mon–Fri 9.30am–5pm; Sat & Sun 10am–5pm; early Sept to mid-June Mon–Fri 9am–3.30pm, Sat & Sun 10am–5pm; exhibit $10, film $12, both $17; ☎514/496-4724, ⓦwww.montrealsciencecentre.com; Métro Place-d'Armes), located in a revamped industrial hangar on Quai King-Edward (keep an eye out for the panels describing the high-tech design elements of the centre). Divided into a number of exhibition halls, the interactive science museum is geared mainly towards families and focuses on the themes of Life, Information and Matter, with displays heavy on multimedia technology – interactive touch screens and audio and video players are scattered throughout. As this guide went to press, plans were underway to revamp all of the permanent exhibits (visit the website for the latest news), except for the interactive movie game, which is a popular draw for teens. If you don't have kids, take a free peek at the displays of high-tech proto-types in the corridors or head instead for the seven-storey film screen of the complex's **IMAX Theatre** – even the 2D films can give you vertigo. English screening times for both the game and the cinema vary, so check ahead.

Quai Jacques-Cartier and Quai de l'Horloge

Heading eastwards, the next pier along is the **Quai Jacques-Cartier**. There are no attractions per se here but you'll find an information booth in the warmer

All aboard!

Although you can appreciate the Vieux-Montréal skyline from a number of vantage points, including Île Ste-Hélène (see p.117) and the bridges that access the island, it's quite a different sensation to view the port from the water as earlier arrivals to the city often did. The cheapest (though briefest) glimpse you'll get is aboard the hourly ferry to Parc Jean-Drapeau (T514/281-8000 for schedules; $4.50 each way), which departs from Quai Jacques-Cartier. For a more lingering view, try one of the following options:

Amphi-Bus T514/849-5181, W www.montreal-amphibus-tour.com. From May to October, you can see Vieux-Montréal by land and by water from a customized military landing craft. The one-hour-long narrated tour costs $26 ($39 during the two-hour fireworks tour); departures are from the corner of boulevard St-Laurent and rue de la Commune (late June to early Sept hourly 10am–midnight; otherwise four daily) or the Centre Infotouriste (late June to early Sept four daily).

Le Bateau Mouche T514/849-9952 or 1-800/361-9952, W www.bateau-mouche .com. Daytime cruises give fine views onto the Vieux-Port and the skyline before circling around Île Ste-Hélène (four daily, 1hr, $18; one daily, one and a half hours, $24), while longer dinner cruises travel downriver to the Îles de Boucherville before returning to the lit-up city (three and a half hours, $84–140 including tip). Departures during the mid-May to mid-October season are from Quai Jacques-Cartier.

Croisières AML T1-800/563-4643, W www.croisieresaml.com. A variety of cruises on Le Cavalier Maxim are available with or without meals, ranging from one and a half to four hours ($25–40) and departing from Quai King-Edward. If you want to party on board, check out their schedule of midnight–3am cruises ($30 and up), featuring different themes and DJs.

Croisières Evasion Plus T514/364-5333 or 1-866/639-4242, W www.evasionplus .com. Four-hour cruises departing from Quai Jacques-Cartier start at $99 for a five-course dinner, more for a bigger spread or during the fireworks. They also run six-and-a-half-hour cruises to Québec City for $139 and up, one way (a same-day return by bus is $40 extra).

months, grounds that host summertime concerts and the departure points for ferries to Parc Jean-Drapeau (see box, p.118) and various river cruises (see box, above). A walkway at the end of the pier gives a great view of Alexander Calder's colossal grey planar sculpture, *Man*, and the tracery of the Biosphère on Île Ste-Hélène, and connects to the more tranquil **Parc du Bassin Bonse-cours** with its bridges arching over pedal-boaters in summer ($5.65 per half-hour per person; reservations T514/282-0586) and ice-skaters in winter. The pavilion here has a terrace for families at ground level and a lounge-bar on the upper terrace for a 5 à 7 cocktail with a view.

The easternmost, L-shaped pier, **Quai de l'Horloge**, has a kids' playground and activities at Hangar 16 (see p.220). It serves as the departure point for Saute-Moutons' wild and wet excursions to the Lachine Rapids (see p.125) is presided over by the simple **Tour de l'Horloge** (mid-May to early Sept daily 10am–7pm; free), a sandstone clocktower that rises 65m above sea level. The views of Vieux-Montréal, the islands and Mont Royal from its highest platform are superb, but it's a workout to get there – there are nearly 200 steps, and the last fifty or so are quite narrow and steep. The lookout point on the grounds immediately east of the tower is an excellent spot to watch the annual fireworks competition (see p.225).

3

The Quartier Latin and the Village

B efore rue Ste-Catherine plunges from Downtown into the eastern suburbs, it passes through the **Quartier Latin**, the haunt of Francophone university students, and the **Village**, home to the city's gay and lesbian community. Both are exciting, vibrant districts filled with cafés, restaurants and boutiques and thronged with revellers passing from bar to bar in the evenings. And while both have also undergone a number of changes through the years, they seem to have gone in opposite directions – whereas the Quartier Latin has changed from a district of the intellectual bourgeoisie in the nineteenth century to having a more downmarket, studenty vibe, the formerly working-class, industrial Centre-Sud district from which the Village evolved is on the upswing as gentrification sets in.

Quartier Latin

Like its Parisian counterpart, Montréal's bohemian **Quartier Latin**, on the eastern edge of Downtown, bounded roughly by boulevards St-Laurent and René-Lévesque and rues Sherbrooke and St-Hubert, derives its name from the fact that in the late nineteenth century the area's large student population studied in Latin. The Université de Montréal was based here before it moved north of the mountain, and the scholastic tradition continued with the foundation of the **Université du Québec à Montréal (UQAM)** in 1969, now attended by more than 40,000 students. For most visitors, though, the Quartier Latin's main appeal lies in just wandering through the boutiques or grabbing a drink at one of the many street-side terraces clustered on the stretch of **rue St-Denis** between rue Sherbrooke and rue Ste-Catherine to the south.

Rue St-Denis and around

Rue St-Denis has long been the main street for the city's Francophone residents. Above rue Sherbrooke is the preserve of the well-heeled, while the lower stretches have a rawer edge thanks to the younger crowd who study and party here. You can begin your tour in the thick of things from Métro

Berri-UQAM, but for a better introduction proceed south from Métro Sherbrooke for an overview of the street scene as rue St-Denis descends from the ridge that marks the edge of the Plateau. The district's Victorian grey-stone houses, topped with turrets and fanciful parapets, visible above the shopfronts, have seen much better days since they were constructed in the 1860s. The focus here is now much more at the street level, where terraces spill out from the numerous cafés and bars in order to accommodate the throngs of customers.

Otherwise, the area's principal attractions are its cultural institutions lodged between boulevard de Maisonneuve and rue Ste-Catherine, including the

ACCOMMODATION				RESTAURANTS & CAFÉS			
Alexandre Logan B&B	E	Hôtel St-Denis	I	Area	24	Kilo	34
Angelica Blue	M	Le House Boy	L	Bangkok	21	Ô Chalet	47
Auberge Cosy	G	Le Jardin d'Antoine	B	La Brioche Lyonnaise	20	O'Thym	22
Auberge Le Pomerol	F	Maison Brunet	P	Chez Gatsé	6	La Paryse	9
Bed & Breakfast du Village	K	Manoir des Alpes	J	Le Commensal	14	Au Petit Extra	2
Hotel Bourbon	H	Manoir St-Denis	C	Confusion	16	Pho Viet	17
Castel Saint-Denis	A	Les Résidences		Croissant de Lune	11	Le Resto du Village	45
La Conciergerie Guest House	Q	Universitaires UQAM	N	Ella Grill	46	Saloon	33
Gîte Saint-Dominique	O	VIP Loft	D	Fou d'Asie	13	Spirite Lounge	3

symmetrical Beaux-Arts **Édifice St-Sulpice** at 1700 rue St-Denis. Built in 1915 as a library for the Sulpicians, it became a founding part of Québec's national library half a century later. Unfortunately, all you can see are glimpses of the ornate stained-glass windows and skylights through the door since it closed after its state-of-the-art successor opened a block east at 475 boul de Maisonneuve E in 2005. The **Grande Bibliothèque**'s (Tues–Fri 10am–10pm, Sat & Sun 10am–5pm; ⓦ www.banq.qc.ca) nearly $100-million price-tag wasn't without controversy, nor was the overlooking of more daring designs in favour of the one chosen: a long box clad in strips of luminous green frosted

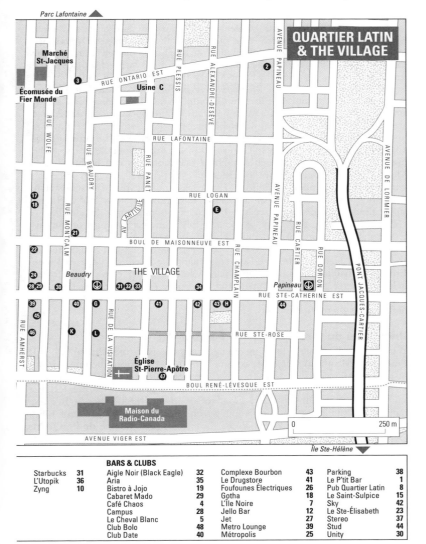

BARS & CLUBS						
Starbucks	**31**	Aigle Noir (Black Eagle)	**32**	Complexe Bourbon	**43**	Parking	**38**
L'Utopik	**36**	Aria	**35**	Le Drugstore	**41**	Le P'tit Bar	**1**
Zyng	**10**	Bistro à Jojo	**19**	Foufounes Électriques	**26**	Pub Quartier Latin	**8**
		Cabaret Mado	**29**	Gotha	**18**	Le Saint-Sulpice	**15**
		Café Chaos	**4**	L'Île Noire	**7**	Sky	**42**
		Campus	**28**	Jello Bar	**12**	Le Ste-Élisabeth	**23**
		Le Cheval Blanc	**5**	Jet	**27**	Stereo	**37**
		Club Bolo	**48**	Metro Lounge	**39**	Stud	**44**
		Club Date	**40**	Métropolis	**25**	Unity	**30**

glass that emphasise its linearity. It was a design choice that was to provoke further problems as a number of the glass panels have shattered, forcing the authorities to erect unsightly fences around the structure until they can figure out how to ensure its safety. Bringing a number of collections together, the new library stores more than four million works, and you can consult all the documents published in Québec dating back more than two centuries. The lofty interior, with sections cordoned off by walls of birch slats, is worth ducking into as a cool air-conditioned respite or to check out the free art exhibitions, and, if you've got kids, to take advantage of the "Espace jeunes" children's section for a story break or to use the CD and DVD booths (obtain a free day pass at the reception desk; ID required).

Continuing back down rue St-Denis, the culture on display takes a more populist turn. One of the city's grand old theatres, the **Théâtre St-Denis** at no. 1594, lies behind a streamlined modern-style facade, though some of the basketweave brickwork of the original 1900 structure is visible from across the street. When it's not hosting the comedy galas during the Just for Laughs festival (see p.226), it's the place to see Broadway-style performances. Nearby, at no. 1564 are the **Office National du Film du Canada** (National Film Board of Canada) and its unique, robotic video jockey, and the **Cinémathèque Québécoise** around the corner at 335 boul de Maisonneuve E (for both, see p.198), which hosts repertory film screenings, festivals and related exhibitions. The latter also has a couple of free permanent exhibitions: "Do Not Adjust Your Set" records the history of the medium through a hundred televisions donated by broadcaster Moses Znaimer, ranging from the earliest juke-box-sized clunkers to space-age sets from the Seventies lifted from *The Jetsons* and the first TV wristwatch. Adjoining it is an exhibition on animation, ranging from old-school zoetropes and spinning discs to sketches, cells and video clips from the past decades.

The only bit of green space in the area lies immediately south of the bus terminal, a block east of St-Denis between boulevard de Maisonneuve and rue Ste-Catherine. Here, Melvin Charney's whimsical steel sculptures of architectural elements mounted on stilts mark the northern edge of **Place Émilie-Gamelin**, a gently sloping park where summer concerts are often held. It's a nice place to be during the day, but keep in mind that there are drug dealers to be found here as well, and the park is best avoided later at night unless there's a show on.

Université du Québec à Montréal (UQAM)

With seemingly a new building going up every year, the **Université du Québec à Montréal (UQAM)** continues to spread out from the intersection of rue St-Denis and rue St-Catherine, where its most interesting building is located. The modern red-brick **Pavillon Judith-Jasmin** incorporates the south transept and ninety-metre-high steeple of the 1858 Église St-Jacques, built on the site of the city's cathedral, which burned in the great fire of 1852 that ravaged much of the district. Inside the pavilion, **La Galerie de l'UQAM** (Sept to mid-June Tues–Sat noon–6pm; free; Ⓦ www.galerie.uqam.ca; Métro Berri-UQAM), easiest to find from the 1400 rue Berri entrance, showcases artworks from its students as well as more established contemporary artists.

The university's other main sight, the **Centre de Design de l'UQAM** (Sept–May Wed–Sun noon–6pm; free; Ⓦ www.centrededesign.com; Métro Berri-UQAM), a block west at 1440 rue Sanguinet, mounts exhibitions on architectural, industrial, graphic and urban design themes. The Dan Hanganu–designed building itself, with its stark, deconstructed facade of steel, glass and concrete, fits this premise quite well.

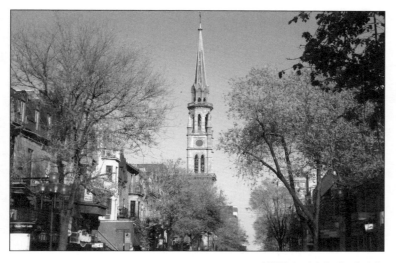
△ UQAM steeple in the Quartier Latin

Chapelle Notre-Dame-de-Lourdes

Facing the old Église St-Jacques church's south transept at 430 rue Ste-Catherine E, the stocky Romanesque **Chapelle Notre-Dame-de-Lourdes** (Mon–Fri 7am–6pm, Sat & Sun 9.30am–6.30pm; ☎514/842-4704; Métro Berri-UQAM), ornamented with white marble detailing on its smooth grey-stone facade, goes unnoticed by most of the people hurrying past. But if you look up, you'll notice the gold-leaf statue of the Virgin, *La Vierge dorée*, gleaming in the sun, returned after a lengthy restoration to her perch atop the roof gable on her 2004 centenary. The interior of the Sulpicians' 1881 church is worth pausing for, its vault heavily embellished in soft hues leading to a large cupola that seems to be supported by the angels painted on the pendentives where the arches intersect. Beyond the ornate altar, the side-lit statue of a young Mary was the first major work by the prolific sculptor of public monuments, Louis-Philippe Hébert.

The Village

The **Village**, the heart of the city's gay and lesbian community, begins around **rue Amherst**, a few blocks east of the Quartier Latin, and extends along **rue Ste-Catherine** as far as rue Papineau, just shy of the massive green girders of the Pont Jacques-Cartier. Montréal's gay district was once centred on rue Stanley Downtown, but the city pressured bar owners out of the area in the run-up to the 1976 Olympics. The bars relocated to this run-down part of rue Ste-Catherine, and appearances have gradually improved, as has the city's attitude towards the gay community – the local Métro stop, Beaudry, even incorporates the colours of the rainbow flag into its design. The **information centre** opposite Place Émilie-Gamelin, on the second floor of 576 rue Ste-Catherine E (Mon–Fri 9am–5pm, weekends in summer and during major events; ☎514/522-1885 or 1-888/595-8110, ⓦwww.outtravel.ca; call ahead as they may be moving), is similarly targeted towards gay visitors. The Village occupies part of the Centre-Sud district – a working-class neighbourhood built up during the Industrial Revolution. With the exception of the Molson brewery, whose neon sign glows to the southeast near the St Lawrence, though, much of the Centre-Sud's industrial heritage has disappeared, been repurposed (as in the case of the Usine C theatre space, which occupies a one-time jam factory) or taken over by new industries such as media – Radio-Canada, TVA and Télé-Québec all have broadcast studios in the area.

Rue Amherst

Over the past decade or so, **rue Amherst** has become something of a twentieth-century design mecca, with a cluster of shops selling 1930s to 1970s furniture and decorative arts, notably along the east side of the street north of boulevard de Maisonneuve. Rue Amherst's retro shops have an architectural counterpart in the pair of Art Deco buildings located where the strip peters out at rue Ontario. On the northeast corner, the blooming flowers and pyramids of fruits and vegetables add colour to the stalls fronting the first of these, the streamlined orange-brick **Marché St-Jacques**, a former market building that now houses municipal offices.

Cross to the west side of rue Amherst to see the other Art Deco structure, the **Écomusée du Fier Monde**, at no. 2050 (Wed 11am–8pm, Thurs & Fri 9.30am–4pm, Sat & Sun 10.30am–5pm; $6; ☎514/528-8444, ⓦwww .ecomusee.qc.ca; Métro Beaudry). It occupies a former public bath, whose more fanciful facade is patterned in cream-coloured brick, with a stern bust peering from the elaborate keystone in the entrance arch. It hints at the graceful arches that soar over the light-filled interior, where rotating exhibitions ranging from artworks to historical themes (often with a gay slant) are held in the former pool, the depth markings still visible in the tiles. The permanent exhibition, which runs along the mezzanine and covers the social and industrial history of the formerly working-class neighbourhood, doesn't warrant the admission fee on its own – if there's no temporary show on, you can still get a good peek at the interior from the reception desk.

Rue Ste-Catherine and around

The blocks of **rue Ste-Catherine** between rues Amherst and Papineau form the heart of Montréal's gay and lesbian community, and it's here that you'll find the majority of the city's **gay bars and clubs**. Scattered throughout are numerous restaurants that are equally popular with the media types working for the big French-language broadcasters in the vicinity. Listings of bars and clubs, as well as community resources and gay-friendly accommodation, can be found in Chapter 13, "Gay Montréal" (see p.184). Just by wandering along rue Ste-Catherine, you can't miss the activity – most bars open their windows wide to the streets in the warmer months and couples wander blithely hand-in-hand past rainbow-flag-decked shopfronts while an unending stream of cars cruise by.

Largely commercial- and nightlife-oriented, there's not much in the way of sights on this stretch of rue Ste-Catherine itself – the main exception being **Station C** at the corner of rue Plessis, a colonnaded stone building that began as a post office in 1912, was the one-time home to the legendary *K.O.X.* nightclub in the 1990s and, after occasionally being used as a performance and exhibition space, reopened as a sex club in summer 2006. It's worth exploring the side streets, which in this neighbourhood are lined with attractive townhouses and well-tended gardens. The most interesting of these streets is **avenue Lartigue**, northeast of the Métro via rue de la Visitation and boulevard de Maisonneuve. Its winding path, reminiscent of an English mews, derives from the route the workers took to the early factories, whose owners weren't too concerned whether the streets lined up or not.

A block south of rue Ste-Catherine at 1201 rue de la Visitation, the **Église St-Pierre-Apôtre** (daily noon–4pm; guided tours available upon request ☎ 514/524-3791) is a delicate 1851 Neo-Gothic church supported by flying buttresses and topped by a slender tin-plated steeple (at 71m, one of the highest in the city). It was the first commission for Victor Bourgeau, who went on to design hundreds of other buildings, including the Marie-Reine-du-Monde cathedral. Within its finely embellished interior lies the "Chapel of Hope", dedicated to those who have died of AIDS. A less successful AIDS memorial marks the corner of rue Ste-Catherine and rue Panet; many locals think the **Parc de l'Espoir**, with its concrete expanse ranged with black granite blocks and plain metal poles sporting now-ratty ribbons of remembrance, was better left as green space. A couple of blocks to the east at the corner of rue Alexandre-DeSève, the gaudy extravagance of the Complexe Bourbon's hotel, bars and cafés goes some way to recalling "Gay Paree" – if it were to be recreated by a theme-park developer or Vegas casino designer, that is.

THE QUARTIER LATIN AND THE VILLAGE | Rue Ste-Catherine and around

Plateau Mont-Royal and north

N o neighbourhood is as emblematic of Montréal as **Plateau Mont-Royal**, a dense urban area that manages to capture the city's duelling English and French traditions, as well as its immigrant legacy. Plateau Mont-Royal, called just "the Plateau" by most, occupies **Mont Royal**'s eastern flank; the edge of the plateau where the land drops down towards the St Lawrence is clearly visible along the district's southern border, rue Sherbrooke. It extends east as far as rue d'Iberville and north to the Canadian Pacific Railway tracks, with the exception of the area's northwest corner, which is taken up by the Mile End neighbourhood. **Mile End** runs alongside the former town of **Outremont**, its bagel bakeries and Greek tavernas a stone's throw from the latter's trendy cafés and fine food shops. Further to the north, **Little Italy**, as its name suggests, is the heart of Montréal's Italian community and has a terrific public market as well.

Plateau Mont-Royal and around

The Plateau's tight grid of streets was laid out in 1860, shortly after the first horse-drawn trams began trundling through what had been a mostly rural landscape. The district's main arteries developed along the tram routes, prompting the building boom of the Plateau's characteristic townhouses. While the eastern half of the Plateau has remained steadfastly Francophone, the western part has been home to a rotating cast of immigrants (see box, p.99) since the late 1800s. It became popular with students and artists in the last decades of the twentieth century, although, as of late, yuppies have been the largest group of arrivals, causing rents to skyrocket and pushing the young creative types who made the neighbourhood so trendy to other areas, such as Mile End.

While pretty much devoid of standard tourist attractions, the neighbourhood is nonetheless a fabulous place to wander about. The main drags – **avenue du Mont-Royal**, **rue St-Denis** and especially **boulevard St-Laurent**, or "The Main" – hum with a constant energy, and the area is home to many of the city's finest restaurants, bars and clubs. Add to that a wide selection of trendy boutiques and charming green spaces, **Square St-Louis** and larger **Parc Lafontaine** in particular, and you've got yourself a great day out.

Avenue du Mont-Royal, rue St-Denis and around

The Mont-Royal Métro station exits directly onto Place Gérald-Godin, a paved plaza named after the Québécois poet whose poem *Tango de Montréal* is excerpted on the wall of a nearby building. The brightly coloured **information kiosk** opposite the station dishes out brochures and maps of the area throughout the summer (late June to early Sept daily 10am–6pm; Ⓦ www.mont-royal.net). **Avenue du Mont-Royal**, running along the north side of Place Gérald-Godin, has become increasingly gentrified over the past decade or so, with a collection of boutiques, cafés and restaurants catering to a diverse, though still mainly Francophone, population. But as you head further east (the frontier being pushed further each year), things become increasingly downmarket, reflecting the district's traditionally working-class population.

To get a flavour of the distinct, early twentieth-century residential architecture typical of the Plateau, take a stroll down some of the side streets that branch off avenue du Mont-Royal to the east, notably avenue de Christophe-Colomb and rue Fabre. Wrought-iron balconies, ornate parapets and *tourelles* (turret-like dormers) adorn the brick and grey-stone townhouses, but the most notable features are the parallel lines created by rows of exterior staircases repeating endlessly into the distance – built outside despite the snow and ice, in order to save interior space. Search out the back lanes of this neighbourhood where the dynamic landscape of washing lines, tin-covered sheds, circular fire-escape staircases and balconies wrapped around U-shaped courtyards reflect a more intimate side of life – dubbed "Balconville" by locals.

Many of the same architectural details appear on the facades of the more bourgeois townhouses lining **rue St-Denis**, which intersects avenue du Mont-Royal two blocks west of the Mont-Royal Métro station. Long *the* shopping street for the city's Francophones, rue St-Denis continues to draw well-heeled shoppers with its array of fashion boutiques, French-language bookstores, interior-design shops and a multitude of cafés, bars and bistros. It's a great spot for a stroll as the chic stores are mostly one-of-a-kind places that put a lot of effort into their window displays – they need to, given the competing distraction of the terraces where Montrealers linger over bowls of *café au lait* and check out the people passing by.

A couple of blocks south of avenue du Mont-Royal, and just west of rue St-Denis, is the 1912 Italian Baroque–style **Église St-Jean-Baptiste**, 309 rue Rachel E (Ⓣ 514/842-9811), the Plateau's most impressive church and one of the city's largest. Its smooth stone facade, fronted by classical columns and pediment, leads to a spacious interior that can accommodate up to 3000 worshippers, a third of them in the unusual circular mezzanine. A magnificent baldachin of gilded wood and pink marble rests atop the white marble altar, although the Casavant organ that runs the length of the choir above the entrance is the most notable feature – certainly during the regular concerts held here.

A block further south, rue St-Denis crosses red-brick-paved **avenue Duluth**. To the west spreads a funky mix of reasonably priced restaurants, twentieth-century antique shops and spots appealing to more alternative types – a folk café, ethnic arts-and-crafts boutiques and a store that sells drums for tam-tam percussionists. Lined with *apportez votre vin* (bring your own wine) restaurants

PLATEAU MONT-ROYAL

Mile End ▲   Little Italy ▲

RUE GILFORD
RUE DE GRAND-PRÉ
RUE DROLET
RUE VILLENEUVE OUEST
RUE JEANNE-MANCE
AV DE L'ESPLANADE
RUE ST-URBAIN
RUE CLARK
BOULEVARD ST-LAURENT
RUE ST-DOMINIQUE
RUE COLONIALE
AVENUE DE BULLION
AV DE L'HÔTEL-DE-VILLE
AVENUE HENRI-JULIEN
RUE GILFORD
RUE DE BIENVILLE
RUE ST-DENIS

Maison de Culture

AVENUE DU MONT-ROYAL OUEST

Mont-Royal

Sanctuaire Très St-Sacrement

AVENUE LAVAL

AVENUE DE L'ESPLANADE

RUE MARIE-ANNE OUEST

Parc Jeanne-Mance

Parc du Portugal

Parc des Amériques

Église St-Jean-Baptiste

RUE RACHEL OUEST

AVENUE DE CHÂTEAUBRIAND
RUE ST-HUBERT
RUE ST-CHRISTOPHE
RUE BERRI
RUE RIVARD

AVENUE DULUTH OUEST

RUE BAGG

Hôtel-Dieu de Montréal

RUE NAPOLÉON

AVENUE HENRI-JULIEN
RUE DROLET
RUE ST-DENIS

Schwartz's

RUE ST-CUTHBERT

BOULEVARD ST-LAURENT
RUE ST-DOMINIQUE
AVENUE COLONIALE
RUE DE
BULLION

RUE ROY EST

AVENUE DES PINS EST

RUE JEANNE-MANCE
RUE STE-FAMILLE
RUE ST-URBAIN
RUE CLARK

RUE PRINCE-ARTHUR OUEST

RUE PRINCE-ARTHUR EST

Ex-Centris

Square St-Louis

Sherbrooke

RUE MILTON

AVENUE DE L'HÔTEL-DE-VILLE

RUE SHERBROOKE EST

McGill University ▲
Parc du Mont-Royal ▲

94

Place des Arts & ▼   Quartier Latin ▼

ACCOMMODATION

Anne ma Soeur Anne	D
Auberge Chez Jean	C
Auberge de la Fontaine	B
Bienvenue Bed & Breakfast	F
Boulanger Bassin B&B	A
Casa Bella	P
Château de l'Argoat	M
Doubletree Plaza	L
Gîte Plateau Mont-Royal	N
Hôtel Godin	O
Hôtel de Paris	J
Kutuma	G
Linsey's B&B for Women	E
À la Maison de Pierre et	
Dominique	H
Aux Portes de la Nuit	I
La Résidence du Voyageur	K

RESTAURANTS & CAFÉS

Amelio's	77
L'Avenue	11
La Banquise	29
Beauty's	5
Bières & Compagnie	17
La Binerie Mont-Royal	6
Brunoise	56
Le Café Cherrier	64
Café Santropol	40
Caffè ArtJava	8
ChuChai	34
La Colombe	46
Le Continental	31
Côté Soleil	48
Crêperie Bretonne Ty-Breiz	26
Aux Deux Marie	21
Eduardo	43
Eurodeli	65
L'Express	52
Folies	7
Fonduementale	22
Les Gâteries	75
Globe	78
Jano	54
La Jardin de Panos	38
Khyber Pass	44
Laïka	35
Laloux	59
Maestro SVP	67
Mañana	68
Meu Meu	14
Moishe's	49
Mondo Fritz	51
La Montée de Lait	1
Na Brasa	37
Le Nil Bleu	61
Ouzeri	2
Au Pied de Cochon	45
Pintxo	58
La Piton de la Fournaise	39
Pizzédélic	13
Au P'tit Lyonnais	18
Le P'tit Plateau	19
Red Thai	73
Ripples	53
St-Viateur Bagel & Café	9
La Selva	20
Senzala	27
Soupesoup	41
Tasca	42
Time Boutique Café	76

BARS & CLUBS

Balattou	16
Barfly	33
L'Barouf	30
Barraca	12
Bifteck St-Laurent	62
Bily Kun	10
Blizzarts	47
B Side	66
Café Campus	70
Central Station	15
Copacabana	50
Divan Orange	24
Else's	57
Exit	74
À Gogo Lounge	63
Laïka	35
Living	4
Miami	55
Passeport	32
Le P'tit Bar	72
Quincaillerie	28
Réservoir	36
Rouge	69
Sofa	25
Tokyo	60
La Tulipe	3
Vol de Nuit	71
El Zaz Bar	23

(see p.159) the blocks east of rue St-Denis make for the most pleasant, scenic route for the ten-minute walk to Parc Lafontaine.

Parc Lafontaine

The Plateau's central park, **Parc Lafontaine** (daily 6am–midnight; Métro Mont-Royal or Sherbrooke), offers a green respite from the crowded streets nearby. Its western half features a promenade that makes for a lovely stroll around two large man-made ponds, while to the east a network of lamp-lit pathways are shaded by tall trees. Locals swarm to the park in warmer times to bask in the sun, take a lazy turn on a pedal-boat or cruise around on rollerblades. Two of the city's main bike paths converge here, intersecting next to the aptly sited **Maison des Cyclistes** (see p.216) facing the park's northern edge. The outdoor **Théâtre de Verdure**, on the western side of the ponds, regularly stages free summertime performances that range from classical concerts to Shakespeare (see p.191). In winter, the frozen-over ponds create a perfectly romantic scene for **ice-skating** (see p.214).

Square St-Louis and rue Prince-Arthur

Back on rue St-Denis and heading south, you'll pass an enormous silver-domed edifice built as the Institut des Sourdes-Muettes (a home for deaf-mutes) and typical of the city's late nineteenth-century architecture; it now houses government offices. Just before rue St-Denis crosses rue Sherbrooke into the Quartier Latin (see p.85), it adjoins **Square St-Louis**, Montréal's most attractive square. The elegant ensemble of grey-stone Victorian residences with fanciful *tourelles* – some painted in vivid red or purple – that border it were originally occupied by the city's Francophone elite. Accordingly, the square itself has a formal layout, centred around a large fountain with pathways radiating outward beneath the overarching trees. Some of those hanging out here are a bit scruffy – but they tend towards the hippyish rather than thuggish, and you shouldn't encounter any problems other than offers to buy substandard pot (and an increased police presence has diminished that likelihood).

On the opposite side of avenue Laval from the square begin the five pedestrianized brick-paved blocks of **rue Prince-Arthur**, lined with mostly mediocre restaurants and bars with plenty of outdoor seating. Tourists crowding around the street performers and artists' stalls here can make it a bit difficult to navigate, but even Montrealers occasionally get caught up in the hubbub and park themselves on a terrace shaded by umbrellas with a pitcher of sangría to watch the busy parade. Though the relentless hawking for customers and the small souvenir shops dotted about reflect the street's surrender to tourism, a bit of the old 1960s anarchic spirit shows up on the frequent occasions when the fountain with sculpted lily pads halfway along gets spiked with washing powder.

The Main

The pedestrianized part of rue Prince-Arthur ends at the equally crowded **boulevard St-Laurent** (Ⓦ www.boulevardsaintlaurent.com; Métro Sherbrooke or Saint-Laurent; bus #55), usually jammed with revellers passing to and from the many bars and restaurants on the city's most famous strip. Appropriately known as "**The Main**", boulevard St-Laurent is the traditional divide between the Catholic, French-speaking east side of the city and the Protestant, English-speaking west side (designated in 1792 as the official divide from which streets are numbered). It captures much of the city in microcosm, reflecting its ethnic diversity and attracting citizens of all stripes with its pulsing vibe. The nonstop stream of automobile traffic moving northward echoes the movement of the immigrants who walked up the Main from the port, stopping, as legend has it, when they heard their own language being spoken. Eastern Europeans, Jews, Greeks, Hungarians, Portuguese and Latin Americans have all passed through, leaving behind a trail of wonderful shops and restaurants. The "discovery" of the area's cheap rents and ethnic flavour by artists and students in the 1970s and 80s gave it a hip reputation that has led to rapid gentrification on the stretch above rue Sherbrooke, though the continuing tug-of-war between the various communities further along has kept the area dynamic and interesting. **FRAG**, a series of graphic panels installed at various sites along boulevard St-Laurent by artists' group ATSA, captures aspects of the Main's history; the accompanying text and podcasts can be downloaded at Ⓦ www.atsa.qc.ca/pages/frags2home.asp.

There's not really anything specific to see here – the Plateau's sole museum, the nearby **Musée des Hospitalières de l'Hôtel-Dieu de Montréal** at 201 av des Pins O (mid-June to mid-Oct Tues–Fri 10am–5pm, Sat & Sun 1–5pm; mid–Oct to mid-June Wed–Sun 1–5pm; $6; Ⓣ 514/849-2919, Ⓦ www .museedeshospitalieres.qc.ca), appeals really only to history buffs with its collection of artefacts relating to the founder of the original hospital in Vieux-Montréal in the colony's early days, Jeanne Mance (who, unusually for that period, was not a nun), as well as religious and medical paraphernalia. Instead, the street's charm is appreciated by just wandering along – though you might want to check out trendy **ex-Centris**, the multimedia cinema and stylish café at no. 3536 on the Main's flashiest block of clubs and *m'as-tu vu?* ("did you see me?") restaurants between rues Sherbrooke and Prince-Arthur.

Behind the cinema's colon-naded facade are bizarre ticket booths where you're face-to-face with a video image of the ticket-seller (eerily, real human hands pass you your ticket).

Northwards from rue Prince-Arthur, you'll find some of the Main's former incarnation – bakeries, butchers, kitchenware and fabric shops in early commercial buildings like the 1892 Baxter Block on the west side – struggling in vain against the tide of new bars and cafés advancing from the south. One classic storefront that won't be going anywhere soon, though, is **Schwartz's**, a tiny deli further up the Main at no. 3895. No visit to the city would be complete without a classic Montréal smoked-meat sandwich, and this unassuming spot, open since 1930, is the best place to tuck into one (see p.159). The Main's mutability shows up again where the

△ Café terraces on rue St-Denis

garment trade's former digs have given way to some of the city's trendiest furniture showrooms further north, on the blocks between a couple of small parks that interrupt the commerce. A faux Central American temple-gate serves as a backdrop to occasional concerts in the **Parc des Amériques** at the corner of rue Rachel, while the **Parc du Portugal** at the corner of rue Marie-Anne more successfully reflects the local Portuguese community with its glazed tiles and central gazebo. Leonard Cohen owns a house opposite the latter, near the house at 30 rue Vallières, which he donated as a centre for zen meditation (sessions by reservation; ☎514/842-3648, Ⓦ www.centrezendelamain.ca).

North of the Plateau

To the northeast of the mountain, the Francophone elite have long inhabited the tony enclave of **Outremont**, which reluctantly merged with Montréal as part of the creation of the "Mega-City" (see p.287). The former town abuts the **Mile End** neighbourhood, settled by Greek immigrants in the 1950s and considered an increasingly desirable place by a crowd of students and arty types looking for the atmosphere that once characterized the Main, prior to its gentrification. Further north, a different ethnic flavour infuses **Little Italy**, home to some of Montréal's best espresso and a major foodie destination as well, thanks to the bustling **Marché Jean-Talon**.

Outremont

The neighbourhoods to the northwest of the Plateau are a bit of an odd couple, their markedly different characteristics nonetheless linked by a couple of main streets full of shops and restaurants. **Outremont** has long been the abode of the island's wealthy Francophones, the houses increasing in grandeur as they scale the northeast slopes of the hill for which it is named, and more modest as you head to the northern boundary at the rail tracks just beyond avenue Van-Horne. The main shopping and promenading street for Outremont's stylish set is lively **avenue Laurier**, full of chic cafés, restaurants and upscale boutiques. The main north–south commercial street, avenue du Parc, is actually in adjacent Mile End (see below), but for a fix of Outremont's stately old homes you can walk north from avenue Laurier along **avenue Bloomfield**. The Gothic-Revival Église St-Viateur at the intersection of the two marks the start of one of the area's most attractive residential streets. Pass leafy Parc Outremont and striking Beaux-Arts Académie Querbes, now a primary school, before reaching **avenue Bernard**, where, as with avenue Laurier, fashionably attired bourgeois Franco-phones promenade past artsy cafés and swish boutiques and restaurants on the western, Outremont portion of the street.

Mile End

Formerly the town of St Louis, **Mile End** was annexed by Montréal in 1909 as the city's population exploded. Extending north to the rail lines and blending with the Plateau towards avenue du Mont-Royal, the neighbour-hood's pronounced ethnic character and cheaper rents are drawing the students, artists, musicians and businesses that you might once have found lower down on the Main, earning it the "new Plateau" label. The pavement

The Main's ethnic flavour

While much of boulevard St-Laurent, aka "The Main", gets its traffic nowadays from boutique-shoppers and café-dwellers, strolling various pockets still affords a taste – quite literally – of the city's various immigrant waves. Food, as is to be expected, played an important role in Montréal's ethnic communities, and, unsurprisingly, some of the most lasting contributions they made to the city's social fabric are the grocery stores and restaurants that still line the street. Come hungry to get the best samples.

The perfect place to get a flavour for the neighbourhood is at the central part of the Main, an area bounded to the south by avenue des Pins and to the north by avenue du Mont-Royal. It's here, in the heart of the Plateau neighbourhood, that you'll find Montréal's greatest concentration of ethnicities. The Main's original inhabitants were newcomers from **Eastern Europe** – including a large Jewish population fleeing the pogroms of late nineteenth-century Russia – while more recent arrivals hail from Latin America, Africa and Portugal; all of these groups are huddled together in a few short and easily walkable blocks.

Heading north from avenue des Pins, you'll hit upon La Vieille Europe at no. 3855, a fantastic cheese and meats shop that caters to the Old World community, across the street from Berson and Sons, a Jewish tombstone-maker that's been in business for four generations. The overlapping communities on the Main are something of a palimpsest, with traces of the older Jewish community – left behind when later generations moved to the suburbs – intermingling with the rotisseries of the **Portuguese**, who settled throughout the area in the 1950s. In addition to the rotisseries, you'll find cafés on avenue Duluth full of old Portuguese men watching football and the Santa Cruz church on the corner of rues St-Urbain and Rachel, the site of riotous festivals on saints' feast days.

terraces and expensive, but delectable, fine-food emporia of **avenue Laurier** continue east from Outremont, past rue Hutchison, the western border of Mile End. Oddly enough, avenue Laurier's flair doesn't spill over onto the main drag, **avenue du Parc** (which the mayor is trying to rename; see p.288) – as soon as you turn the corner, the shops and restaurants to the north and south are cheap rather than chic.

For the next couple of blocks north, the places of interest lie on the side streets – Jewish bagel bakeries are the main draw on **avenue Fairmount** and **rue St-Viateur**, not far from the city's largest community of Hasidic Jews. Don't expect to see much in the way of an architectural presence – the Hasidic synagogues tend to be in modest dwellings and the synagogues of the other Jewish sects were demolished or converted to schools or other uses in the decades since the community moved to western suburbs such as Côte-des-Neiges, Hampstead and Côte-St-Luc. The most impressive religious structure in the area is Catholic, built for Irish parishioners but now home to a mainly Polish flock – though the massive flat dome and narrow flanking towers of the **Église St-Michel-Archange** (also known as the Church of St Michael's and St Anthony's; guided tours July & Aug Tues–Sat 9.30am–6pm; ℡514/277-3300) at the corner of rues St-Viateur and St-Urbain looks like it could have been transplanted here from Istanbul. Elsewhere on rue St-Viateur, the black-clad men with curls peeking out of their hats provide an equally striking contrast to the laid-back students and artists who frequent the quirky shops, family-run restaurants and no-nonsense Italian cafés that are turning this into one of the city's funkier streets. Mile End's commercial flavour is concentrated north of here along avenue du Parc, a bustling stretch

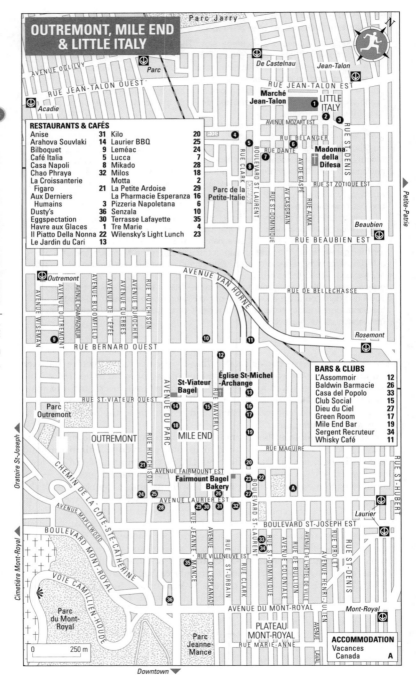

OUTREMONT, MILE END & LITTLE ITALY

RESTAURANTS & CAFÉS

Anise	31
Arahova Souvlaki	14
Bilboquet	9
Café Italia	5
Casa Napoli	8
Chao Phraya	32
La Croissanterie Figaro	21
Aux Derniers Humains	3
Dusty's	36
Eggspectation	30
Havre aux Glaces	1
Il Piatto Della Nonna	22
Le Jardin du Cari	13
Kilo	20
Laurier BBQ	25
Leméac	24
Lucca	7
Mikado	28
Milos	18
Motta	2
La Petite Ardoise	29
La Pharmacie Esperanza	16
Pizzeria Napoletana	6
Senzala	10
Terrasse Lafayette	35
Tre Marie	4
Wilensky's Light Lunch	23

BARS & CLUBS

L'Assommoir	12
Baldwin Barmacie	26
Casa del Popolo	33
Club Social	15
Dieu du Ciel	27
Green Room	17
Mile End Bar	19
Sergent Recruteur	34
Whisky Café	11

ACCOMMODATION

Vacances Canada   A

0   250 m

with excellent Greek restaurants leading to **avenue Bernard**, home to a few funky restaurants and bars.

Little Italy

The vibrant neighbourhood of **Little Italy** is a marvellous place to poke about, especially if you've got food on the brain. The city's largest **outdoor market** is here (see p.207), and the whole area around boulevard St-Laurent between rues St-Zotique and Jean-Talon is dotted with **cafés** and **restaurants** dishing out authentic Italian cuisine and some of the city's strongest coffee (some of the best is provided by the atmospheric *Café Italia*, at 6840 rue Jean-Talon, see p.165). While it's a short ride from Downtown to Métro Jean-Talon, and just a half-hour walk from the Plateau, most people bus it here on the #55 that runs up boulevard St-Laurent. You'll know you've arrived when you see Italian flags waving everywhere. Although the neighbourhood had a palpable Italian presence for a long time beforehand, it really took on its character in the years following World War II when economic migrants left Italy in search of a better future in Canada. And although Montréal's largest Italian districts are now in northeastern suburbs like St-Léonard, Little Italy has retained its authentic feel and is still, aside from the areas described below, a largely residential district.

Hop off the bus at **Parc de la Petite-Italie**, where locals cluster on benches near the large gazebo and which faces the former Église St-Jean-de-la-Croix (converted into condos), notable for its twin bell towers whose cupolas are supported by appropriately Roman-style arches. Stylish restaurants and cafés line the stretch of boulevard St-Laurent north of here, though the family-run trattorias on eastward-running **rue Dante** hold more appeal. The fourteenth-century Italian poet also lends his name to the charming local park that runs alongside the blocky red-brick **Madonna della Difesa church**. The impressive frescoes on the vault and apse are the work of Florence-born Guido Nincheri, whose inclusion of a horse-back Mussolini among the figures to the right of the altar led to his detainment in 1940 as a Fascist sympathizer.

The area's main attraction, **Marché Jean-Talon** (shops: Mon–Wed & Sat 8am–6pm, Thurs & Fri 8am–9pm, Sun 8am–5pm; stalls: times vary; Ⓦwww .marchespublics-mtl.com), lies two blocks to the north. Italian families grew prodigious gardens in their backyards, which surrounded the lacrosse field that stood here, and set up stalls to feed the spectators. These have evolved into the bakers, *fromageries*, fishmongers, cafés and trendy gourmet boutiques that surround the market proper. Built as a Depression-era make-work project, the open-air, covered marketplace brims with colourful fruits, vegetables and flowers picked over by the jostling crowds. A new building at the market's east end has a number of places to graze – there are shopfronts offering everything from game sausages to *gelato* – as well as much-needed underground parking (enter from avenue Henri-Julien) and even a bookshop for foodies. For regional delights, don't miss the selection of over two hundred cheeses, as well as jams, maple-syrup products and locally produced booze, at **Le Marché des Saveurs** (Ⓦwww.lemarchedessaveurs.com) just south of the new market building. From here, it's a five-minute walk northeast to Métro Jean-Talon, next to the Casa d'Italia community centre at the intersection of rues Jean-Talon and St-Denis.

Mont Royal and northwest

The large, rounded hill rising up north of Downtown dominates the city's skyline and its inhabitants' perceptions to the extent that, although it is only 233m high and actually comprises three separate summits – Mont Royal, Westmount and Outremont – everyone simply calls it **the mountain**. Confusingly, locals refer to "the mountain" or "Mont Royal" when talking about the whole mass, just the summit of Mont Royal or even **Parc du Mont-Royal**.

The park is the area's chief attraction, covering the summit of Mont Royal and its southern and eastern slopes. Wound about with heavily used trails, the park draws active Montrealers from all over the city, many of whom stop to ogle the spectacular views of Downtown from the various lookout points.

The largest green space on the mountain, though, is not the park itself, but the two vast **cemeteries** on the northern slopes, which offer a tranquil escape from the city: the woodsy Cimetière Mont-Royal, full of meandering paths, and the more precisely ordered Cimetière Notre-Dame-des-Neiges. Overlooking the latter is the mammoth dome of the **Oratoire St-Joseph**, an unmissable presence on the mountain's northwest side that is visible from miles away due to its enormous dome. It's an important pilgrimage site that is equally worth a visit for nonbelievers. The **Côte-des-Neiges** neighbourhood to the northwest is mostly residential but features an attraction that is less physically monumental yet more emotionally compelling than the oratory: the **Musée Commémoratif de l'Holocauste à Montréal**, its haunting exhibits documenting the horrific experiences faced by Europe's Jews in the concentration camps.

Parc du Mont-Royal

The mountain itself is crowned by **Parc du Mont-Royal** (daily 6am–midnight; Ⓦ www.lemontroyal.com; bus #11 and numerous buses on the periphery), which was established by the city in 1876 as the result of demands for the mountain's protection after a number of its trees were cut for firewood after a particularly harsh winter. Occupying some 544 acres – a fifth of the mountain's total area – it was designed by the American landscape architect Frederick Law Olmsted, whose works include New York City's Central Park and Golden Gate Park in San Francisco. Although the Ice Storm of January 1998 damaged trees to the extent that 4000 had to be felled, it wasn't as catastrophic as Mayor Jean

Drapeau's 1950s "morality cuts" of the underbrush on the summit, which were intended to thwart amorous pursuits, causing Mont Royal to be dubbed "Bald Mountain". Autumn is the best time to visit, when the leaves are a mixed palette of reds, oranges and yellows, while in winter you can wander through a beautiful monochromatic landscape with black tree trunks silhouetted against the snow.

Ascending the mountain

Although you can access the park from various sides, including the top end of rue Peel from Downtown, the most interesting approach on foot or by bicycle is from the Plateau. From the intersection of boulevard St-Laurent and rue Rachel, head west to **Parc Jeanne-Mance**, where a path continues on past soccer fields, tennis courts and a paddling pool to Parc du Mont-Royal's main access point – easy to spot by the **Sir George-Étienne Cartier monument**, topped by a winged angel and guarded by four reclining lions. The surrounding plaza draws large crowds on summer Sundays from noon until dusk for the **Tam Tam**, a large drumming jam session and improvised market with hippyish overtones that's a great place to chill out. Begun by a group of musicians who came to practise here in the late 1970s, the Tam Tam soon evolved into an almost pagan celebration with people dancing uninhibitedly to the incessant rhythms of the drums, while hundreds of Montrealers of all stripes picnic on the surrounding grassy slopes.

North of the monument, **chemin Olmsted**, the gravel path designed by Olmsted for horse-drawn carriages, ascends the 4.5km up to the Chalet and cross in a series of gentle looping slopes. The lazy hour-long stroll up the main path offers several memorable vistas of the city below, but there's a shortcut halfway along if time is limited. Just after the two-kilometre mark, look for the 200-odd steps that lead up to the Chalet (see p.104) – a treacherous climb when covered in snow and ice, and exhausting at any time.

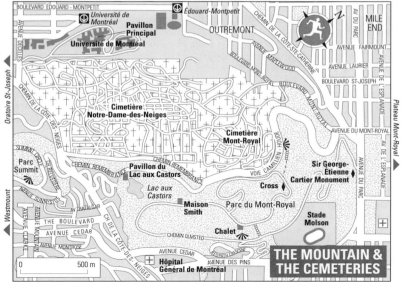

McGill University & Downtown

Atop the mountain

If you stick to chemin Olmsted, the trees open out into a large grassy expanse surrounding the man-made **Lac aux Castors** (Beaver Lake) twenty minutes further along. Pedal-boats ($8 per half-hour) rather than beavers glide across the surface of the former swamp, and the immediate area is popular for winter activities like inner-tube sledding ($8, $4 for children under 13), and skating on the lit trails running amongst the nearby trees. You can rent snowshoes, cross-country skis and ice skates from the pavilion next to Lac aux Castors (☎ 514/843-8240).

On the slope above the lake, the mostly stone abstract sculptures dotted about are a relic of the 1964 sculpture symposium, when a dozen international artists created the works from scratch. The sculptors stayed in the **Maison Smith** (May–Oct Mon–Fri 10am–6pm, Sat & Sun 10am–7pm; Nov to mid-Dec & mid-March to April daily 11am–4pm; mid-Dec to mid-March Mon–Fri 11am–4pm, Sat & Sun 9am–5pm; free; ☎ 514/843-8240, ⊛ www.lemontroyal .com), a squat stone structure further east that now houses an information centre, an exhibition on Mont Royal and a handy café open an hour or so longer. Ask for the brochures detailing various themed walking tours of the mountain or join one of the weekend guided walks (times and prices vary) that depart from here.

Five to ten more minutes of walking up chemin Olmsted brings you to the rustic mountaintop **Chalet** (daily 10am–8pm), part of Olmsted's original plan but not built until the early 1930s, and the nearby thirty-metre-high **cross**, one of the city's most recognizable landmarks and visible from miles around. The Chalet's long, low, stone building is a good spot to warm up on colder days, with a passable canteen (daily 10am–4pm; hours are longer in summer, but they vary), toilets and a gift shop. Keep an eye out for the squirrels nestled in the rafters high up in the large main hall – they're more interesting than the paintings of Montréal history hung high on the walls (although a couple are by Paul-Émile Borduas, you'd be hard-pressed to see anything of the renowned abstract artist's style in them). The chief attraction, though, is the large semicircular plaza in front of the Chalet that offers outstanding **views** of Downtown's skyscrapers and beyond.

Although it's possible to walk east along chemin Olmsted to the base of the cross, it's not nearly as impressive up close. The illuminated metallic structure, erected in 1924 by the St-Jean-Baptiste Society, recalls the wooden one that de Maisonneuve, the founder of Montréal, carried up the mountaintop and planted here in 1643 in honour of the fledgling colony being spared from a flood. Further along, gaps in the trees frame views of the city's northern sprawl and a set of stairs leads down to the lookout on voie Camillien-Houde for a panorama that takes in the Stade Olympique and eastern Montréal.

The cemeteries

The winding paths amidst large pockets of trees and shrubs make the 165-acre Protestant **Cimetière Mont-Royal** (main gate: late May to early Sept Mon–Fri 8am–7pm, Sat & Sun 8am–5pm; Oct–May daily 8am–5pm; south gate: Mon–Fri 9am–4pm, Sat & Sun 9am–2pm; ☎ 514/279-7358, ⊛ www .mountroyalcem.com), founded in 1847, another wonderful place to wander around. Easily accessed from the car park behind the Maison Smith in Parc du Mont-Royal, the cemetery draws relatively few people, and the surrounding ridges help cut out most of the city's noise, making it feel like taking a stroll through a tranquil patch of countryside. The **reception centre**, located at the bottom of the slope next to the north entrance on chemin de la Forêt, off boulevard Mont-Royal, has a guide for birdwatchers (145 species of bird have been spotted here, from tiny sparrows and warblers on up to owls and kestrels) in addition to a map listing the burial sites of prominent citizens – the Molson brewing family's mausoleum is particularly impressive. Among the other memorials, the fireman-topped column that marks the resting place of fire fighters killed on duty is especially poignant, while the simple grave of Anna Leonowens of *The King and I* fame is perhaps the most unexpected.

The adjacent (but not directly connected) **Cimetière Notre–Dame–des–Neiges** (daily April–Oct 8am–7pm; Nov–March to 5pm; Ⓣ514/735-1361, Ⓦwww.cimetierenddn.org) has been the favoured resting place for the city's Catholics since 1855. It is mainly notable, though, for its vastness – with nearly one million resting souls, it is one of the largest cemeteries in North America. There's a gate on chemin Remembrance opposite Lac aux Castors, but for information about the gravesites you'll need to visit the main reception, a fifteen-minute walk away. To get there, head west along chemin Remembrance and turn right on chemin de la Côte-des-Neiges; you can also walk ten minutes from Métro Côte-des-Neiges or take bus #165, #166 or #535 directly to the cemetery from Métro Guy-Concordia Downtown. Among the who's who of Québécois artists and politicians interred here are poet Émile Nelligan and Fathers of Confederation Sir George-Étienne Cartier and Thomas D'Arcy McGee. The most attractive memorial centres on a full-size marble reproduction of Michelangelo's *La Pietà*, located towards the Cimetière Notre-Dame-des-Neiges' northwest corner. Nearby, a gate opens onto avenue Decelles from where it's a five-minute walk to the Oratoire St-Joseph.

Oratoire St-Joseph

Towering over the northwestern slopes of Mont Royal is the immense granite **Oratoire St-Joseph** (daily: late June to late Aug 6.30am–10.30pm; late Aug to late June 7am–9pm; Ⓣ514/733-8211, Ⓦwww.saint-joseph.org; Métro Côte-des-Neiges or bus #51, #165, #166 or #535), a monumental domed shrine constructed between 1924 and 1967 on a promontory set far back from chemin Queen-Mary, rising up from (and incorporating) the earlier 1000-capacity crypt church (1914–17). Upon approaching the main entrance at no. 3800, you may pass pilgrims – in search of physical cures – heading up the structure's hundred-odd steps on their knees. Such displays of devotion are the norm from visitors who often feel divinely inspired by the life of its late founder, Frère André Bessette (see box, p.107). For those unable to scale the steps, the church provides a free (though donations are expected) minibus service.

The sheer size of the structure almost lives up to its mythical aura as a pilgrimage destination. Topped by a remarkable 45-metre-high copper dome, which is surpassed in size only by that of St Peter's basilica in Rome, the interior chambers are so widely dispersed that escalators link the complex's main sights, including the hypnotic **Votive Chapel**, majestic **basilica** and an **exhibition** on Frère André that features one of Montréal's most bizarre spectacles (see p.106). The Oratory also provides a suitably grand space for regular organ and carillon **recitals**.

Rather than charging straight up, head to the information booth to the right of the curving stairs leading to the main portico (until the new visitors pavilion is completed in 2008–09), where you can pick up a detailed guidebook for $2; guided tours are also available (times vary; $5 suggested donation). From here, head to the side entrance on the right side of the complex.

△ Oratoire St-Joseph

The ground-floor **Votive Chapel** is the Oratory's eeriest room – the flames of 10,000 votive candles illuminate a colossal collection of wooden canes, crutches and braces left behind as *ex voto* offerings by pilgrims (their sheer numbers seeming to be directed against visiting sceptics). A central statue of St Joseph with his arms outstretched stands between two doorways leading to a simple room containing Frère André's **tomb**, where parishioners can often be found touching the black marble slab in an attempt to establish a connection with the man.

The landing at the top of the first set of escalators leads to an outdoor terrace with terrific **views** across the northern swathes of the city and to the Oratory's **gardens** of the Way of the Cross, pleasantly landscaped by Frederick G. Todd, the man behind Île Ste-Hélène (see p.117) and Québec City's Plains of Abraham (see p.267); the gardens are dotted with mid-twentieth-century sculptures representing each station.

Tucked away on a mezzanine two levels up from the Votive Chapel is the Frère André **exhibition**. Here, three rooms central to his life have been recreated with their original furnishings. His bedroom, with its tiny bench-like bed and small roll-top desk, illustrates his ascetic ways. The main draw on this floor is on the other side of the exhibition where, amazingly, a gold box atop a marble column holds Frère André's **heart**. It has been preserved as a sign of admiration, and some pilgrims have claimed it has twitched in their presence. Nearby, a gallery holds a life-size Nativity scene and exhibitions drawn from the Oratory's collection of treasures.

Further up is the **basilica**, an enormous space with a soaring domed ceiling supported by angular concrete arches. After the heavy iconography found in the lower levels, the basilica's lack of frills is quite refreshing. Its cruciform layout is ornamented simply by six wooden carvings of the Apostles mounted at the end of each transept and a few stone representations of Christ's procession with the cross, inset in the connecting corridors. A corridor behind the altar accesses the most richly decorated part of the basilica, the **Chapel of the Blessed**

Montréal's miracle man

The founder of the Oratoire St-Joseph, the **Blessed Brother André** (1845–1937) is one miracle away from sainthood. Pope John Paul II recognized the first of his necessary two posthumous miracles in 1982, after a cancer-stricken New Yorker returned home from the Oratory disease-free. Still, André Bessette's early years didn't portend such greatness. At the age of 25, he was asked to leave the religious order of the Holy Cross because he was too sickly to perform the manual labour asked of him. After the bishop of Montréal intervened, André was allowed to stay on as a lay brother and was given the lowest job on the order's totem pole: porter of Collège Notre-Dame, a boys' school facing where the Oratory stands today.

It was here that André's extraordinary curative powers began to show, as after he tended to ailing parishioners, many of them soon healed completely. He attributed his abilities to the oil he applied to their afflictions: an unguent that came from a lamp below a small statue of St Joseph in the college chapel. As knowledge of André's abilities spread, thousands of sick pilgrims began visiting the school. To make room, he built a primitive chapel in St Joseph's name at the top of the future oratory's grounds in 1904, using $200 saved, in part, from tips received for cutting the boys' hair. More than four hundred cures were recorded here in 1916 alone.

Brother André never took credit for the cures pilgrims received, but always deferred to St Joseph's divine generosity. Indeed, André's devotion to St Joseph was so intense that he deemed the chapel an insufficient monument to his patron saint and began canvassing for donations to build the massive shrine that stands today. André never saw it finished – he died in 1937, 18 years before the basilica was inaugurated. Impressively, one million mourners came to see his body laid out in the Votive Chapel.

Sacrament, painted from floor to ceiling in gold leaf and anchored by chunky green-marble columns. The doors to the right lead outside to Frère André's original rustic **chapel** to St Joseph, with decor common to Québec's hinterlands, particularly the cross over the small altar – it's festooned with vanity-mirror light-bulbs. As you leave the chapel, the driveway behind the basilica exits onto Summit Crescent, leading to Summit Circle and the Westmount lookout (see p.125).

Côte-des-Neiges

The neighbourhood overlooked by the Oratory, **Côte-des-Neiges**, is largely residential, populated with families and some of the 50,000-plus students who attend the **Université de Montréal**. You can get a glimpse of the area from the #51 bus, which passes in front of the Oratory and along the length of the university campus as it spreads along the mountain's northern slopes. Its most notable feature is Ernest Cormier's **Pavillon Principal**, a massive yellow-brick Art Deco structure whose tripartite wings frame a central block dominated by the university's signature tower (unfortunately, although the tower promises some incredible views, it is inaccessible). Other than providing visual appeal, however, the campus offers little of interest to visitors, and you're just as well to continue eastward on the bus past the handsome Outremont homes to avenue Laurier (see p.99).

Musée Commémoratif de l'Holocauste à Montréal and the Centre des Arts Saidye Bronfman

About 25 minutes' walk northwest of the Oratory via avenue Victoria is the recently expanded **Musée Commémoratif de l'Holocauste à Montréal**

(Montréal Holocaust Memorial Museum). Located in the same building as the Jewish Public Library at 5151 chemin de la Côte-Ste-Catherine (Mon, Tues & Thurs 10am–5pm, Wed 10am–9pm, Fri 10am–3pm but may vary, Sun 10am–4pm; $8; ☏514/345-2605, ⓦwww.mhmc.ca; Métro Côte-Ste-Catherine or bus #129), the centre is a repository not just of artefacts relating to the Holocaust but also of videotaped testimonies from survivors, many of whom, along with their descendants, live in the area and the suburbs to the west. The museum's exhibits are as poignant as you'd expect, but rather than portraying the Jews sent to the concentration camps merely as victims, it also highlights the many small acts of defiance, through keepsakes like a heart-shaped autograph book crafted as a birthday present for a young woman by her fellow inmates. Other exhibits portray Jewish life before the Nazi rise to power, illustrating just how much was lost – a panel listing five thousand towns and villages inhabited by Jews stands near walls bearing the names of the concentration camps that took their place.

Across the street at 5170 chemin de la Côte-Ste-Catherine, contemporary Jewish culture is the mainstay of the **Centre des Arts Saidye Bronfman** (☏514/739-2301, ⓦwww.saidyebronfman.org; Métro Côte-Ste-Catherine or bus #129), an arts centre that hosts Yiddish- and English-language theatre productions (see p.196) and contains an art gallery presenting contemporary exhibitions (June–Sept Mon–Thurs 9am–7pm, Fri 9am–4pm, Sun 10am–5pm; Oct–May Mon–Thurs 9am–9pm, Fri 9am–2pm, Sun 10am–5pm; free). You can take bus #129 east from here to get to Outremont (see p.98), hopping off as it curves below the chic homes of avenue Maplewood, accessible by stairs from the intersection of chemin de la Côte-Ste-Catherine and avenue Laurier.

Parc Olympique and Jardin Botanique

O n a clear day, the **Parc Olympique**'s striking architectural forms act like a magnet, enticing visitors from Montréal's Downtown to the Hochelaga-Maisonneuve neighbourhood, 7km to the east. Rising on the slope above the district's residential and industrial tracts, the flying-saucer-shaped **Stade Olympique** anchors the site of the 1976 Olympic Games. Climbing up the stadium's eastern side is the **Tour de Montréal**, an inclined tower with city views from its observation deck. The nearby Vélodrome, another relic of the Games, was transformed in 1992 into the **Biodôme**, an engrossing indoor zoo-like attraction conceived around four distinct ecosystems.

While the sheer scale of the stadium may draw your attention at first, the real reward for venturing this far from the urban core is the superb **Jardin Botanique** extending north of it, one of the largest botanical gardens in the world. Among its gardens and greenhouses are a Ming Dynasty replica **Chinese Garden**, a traditional **Japanese Garden** and the unique **Insectarium**, crawling with all manner of six- and eight-legged creatures.

Park practicalities

The easiest way to reach this area from Downtown is the fifteen-minute Métro ride on the green line to the Viau or Pie-IX (pronounced "pee neuf") stations, though you can also get out there by cycling along the rue Rachel bike path – it's about twenty to thirty minutes from rue St-Denis. The gardens and the park cover a huge area, but fortunately a shuttle bus (11am–5pm; free) links each attraction with the Métro Viau stop.

If you plan on seeing more than one attraction out this way, you'll save money by investing in either the "Nature Package", a combo ticket that covers the Biodôme, Jardin Botanique and Insectarium for $20.50, or the "Get an Eyeful" pass, which adds a ride up the Tour de Montréal for $31.50. These are available only at the attractions themselves. **Places to eat** are a bit thin on the ground; while there are cafeterias in the Biodôme and the Jardin Botanique (in the warmer months), your best bet is either to visit the Marché Maisonneuve a few blocks south of the stadium (see p.112) or pack a lunch beforehand for a picnic in the grassy areas to the east of the stadium or in Parc Maisonneuve, adjacent to the Jardin Botanique (be sure to get your hand stamped for re-entry).

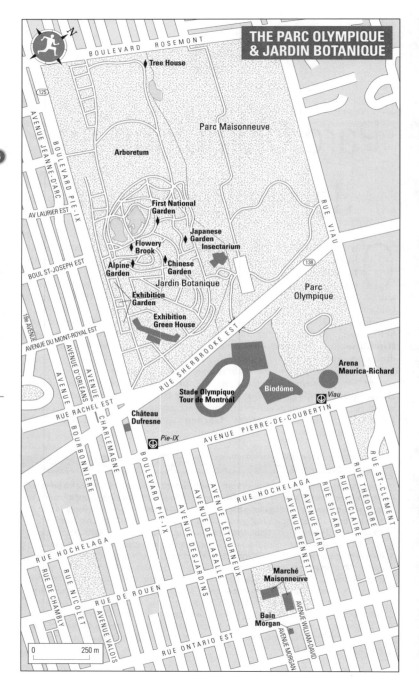

THE PARC OLYMPIQUE
& JARDIN BOTANIQUE

BOULEVARD ROSEMONT

Tree House

125

AVENUE JEANNE-D'ARC

BOULEVARD PIE-IX

Parc Maisonneuve

Arboretum

AV LAURIER EST

RUE VIAU

First National
Garden

Japanese
Garden

Flowery
Brook

Insectarium

BOUL ST-JOSEPH EST

138

Alpine
Garden

Chinese
Garden

18e AVENUE

Jardin Botanique

Parc
Olympique

Exhibition
Garden

AVENUE DU MONT-ROYAL EST

Exhibition
Green House

AVENUE D'ORLEANS

AVENUE

RUE SHERBROOKE EST

Arena
Maurica-Richard

RUE RACHEL EST

Stade Olympique
Tour de Montréal

Biodôme

Viau

CHARLEMAGNE

Château
Dufresne

BOURBONNIERE

Pie-IX

AVENUE PIERRE-DE-COUBERTIN

BOULEVARD PIE-IX

AVENUE DE LASALLE

AVENUE DESJARDINS

AVENUE LETOURNEUX

RUE HOCHELAGA

AVENUE BENNETT

AVENUE AIRD

RUE SICARD

RUE LECLAIRE

RUE THEODORE

RUE ST-CLÉMENT

RUE HOCHELAGA

RUE DE CHAMBLY

RUE NICOLET

RUE DE ROUEN

AVENUE VALOIS

Marché
Maisonneuve

AVENUE WILLIAM-DAVID

Bain
Morgan

AVENUE MORGAN

RUE ONTARIO EST

0   250 m

Leave time as well for a tour of the elegant **Château Dufresne**, a restored Beaux-Arts residence built in the early twentieth century for two brothers who were prominent players in the development of the short-lived, visionary city of **Maisonneuve** to the south.

The Parc Olympique

The 1976 Olympics resulted in one of the city's most recognizable landmarks – and also one of its biggest follies. French architect Roger Taillibert, who also designed the Stade du Parc des Princes in Paris, was enlisted to create the **Parc Olympique**, the Games' massive arena and housing complex, and was told money was no object. Indeed, then-mayor Jean Drapeau even declared: "It is as unlikely that Montréal will incur a debt as for a man to bear a child." Biology has yet to catch up, but the complex ended up costing $1.4 billion (over $2 billion with subsequent maintenance and interest) – the final $15 million of which was paid off only in 2006 – some thirty years after the event itself. In addition to travails with the Kevlar roof and a falling concrete beam in 1991, the stadium's bad luck extended to Canada's Olympic hopefuls – it was the only country not to win a gold medal while hosting the Games.

The Stade Olympique and the Tour de Montréal

At the centre of the Parc Olympique complex looms the **Stade Olympique** (daily early Sept to mid-June 9am–5pm; mid-June to early Sept 9am–7pm; tower $14, tour $8, both $17.75; Ⓦ www.rio.gouv.qc.ca; Métro Viau or Pie-IX), now mostly relegated to hosting a varied line-up of monster truck races and trade shows. It's an impressive sight, with huge concrete ribs rising out of an asphalt expanse to enclose the stadium's shell. Locals refer to the stadium as the "Big O" – ostensibly because of its shape or for the "O" in Olympic, but more often for the money owed for its construction. Adding insult to injury, the **Expos**, the Major League Baseball team that for years threatened to move, in fact did just that and became the Washington, DC, Nationals in 2004. Consequently, only stadium buffs are likely to appreciate the half-hour **guided tours** (Ⓣ 514/252-4737 or 1-877/997-0919 for schedule), which include a stop by – but not a dip in – the Olympic swimming pools.

Adjoining the stadium and rising above it in a graceful arc is the 175-metre-high **Tour de Montréal**, the world's tallest inclined tower. Although it was designed to hold the steel cables that (in theory) would raise the stadium's 65-tonne roof, at the time of the Games it was still just a concrete stump – the upper section was not completed until 1987, and the movable roof was installed soon after (it never really worked properly, though, and was replaced by a fixed roof in 1998). Accessed via the Tourist Hall at the tower's base, the funicular glides quickly up the tower's spine, rewarding riders with views of the Olympic Village en route and a panoramic view across the city from the top – on a clear day you can see as far as the Laurentians 60km to the northwest (see p.233). It's worth noting, however, that you can get an equally striking and arguably better view for free from atop Mont Royal (see p.104).

Biodôme de Montréal

The Parc Olympique's old Vélodrome, the scalloped-roof structure south of the tower, is now the **Biodôme** (daily 9am–5pm, summers until 6pm; $12.75; Ⓣ 514/868-3000, Ⓦ www.biodome.qc.ca; Métro Viau), an engaging environmental museum comprising four distinct ecosystems. Taillibert's design has proven as well suited for its current role as it was for Olympic cycling events, as the large, column-free roof span allows visitors to wander freely through the flora- and fauna-filled zones.

By far the most popular of the attractions here is the hot and humid **tropical rainforest**; keep an eye out for the two-toed sloths, which move so slowly that their fur grows algae, quite unlike the lively golden tamarins and tiny black callimico monkeys that clamber through the trees above. It's hard to miss the screeching scarlet macaws, but you may need to ask one of the keen-eyed guides to point out the shyer creatures. It's noticeably cooler in the **Laurentian forest** portion, where you can look at an actual beaver dam and take a televised peek at the busy animals inside its lodge. Beyond that, in the **St Lawrence marine ecosystem**, petrels, terns and kittiwakes fly overhead, occasionally touching down on an impressive tidal rock pool complete with foaming waves and a multi-coloured population of anemones, crabs, lobsters and starfish. The final **Polar zone** recreates both Arctic and Antarctic ecosystems – puffins bob and dive along a replica Labrador coast, while four different species of penguins waddle amusingly on snow-covered slopes across the way, much to children's delight.

Jardin Botanique de Montréal

With its harsh winters, Montréal seems an unlikely locale for one of the world's largest botanical gardens, but the **Jardin Botanique de Montréal** (daily 9am– 5pm, mid–May to early Sept until 6pm, mid-Sept to late Oct until 9pm; $12.75

Maisonneuve

Most visitors out this way rarely make it to the neighbourhood directly south of the Parc Olympique – but if you have the stamina, it's worth the detour if only to grab lunch at the remarkable **Marché Maisonneuve** (4375 rue Ontario E; Mon–Wed & Sat 8am–6pm, Thurs–Fri until 9pm, Sun until 5pm), the bustling public market that remains the primary focal point of an area that was, from 1883 to 1916, in fact an independent city known as **Maisonneuve**. The original Beaux Arts market is fronted by an expansive square and topped by a copper-covered cupola and chateau-style corner towers. A modern building to the east houses fresh fruit and vegetable stalls, as well as top-notch bakeries and cheese shops; of these, *Première Moisson* is your best bet for a full repast and offers covered outdoor terrace seating in summer months.

The market itself is an unexpected sight in what is otherwise today a working-class neighbourhood. It wasn't always so, however, as Maisonneuve's initial residents were wealthy Francophones who decided they would be better off on their own rather than be amalgamated by Montréal. Influenced by the **City Beautiful** reform movement, prominent citizens constructed wide boulevards – like boulevard Morgan, immediately south of the market – and elegant Beaux Arts public buildings. Architect Marius Dufresne (see p.115) was instrumental in designing many of these, including the market and the nearby **Bain Morgan**, an ornate public bath fronted by classical Ionic columns, a few steps to the south, at 1875 boulevard Morgan.

Civic beauty aside, the local elite had also hoped Maisonneuve would be a model industrial city and, buoyed by its proximity to both the St Lawrence River and railways, the city did indeed succeed as a major independent manufacturing centre for some 35 years. The wealth generated by local industry proved insufficient to support their grand projects, however, which ultimately led to the city's bankruptcy in 1918 and subsequent annexation by Montréal.

Tourisme Hochelaga-Maisonneuve (4375 rue Ontario E ☏514/256-0459) occasionally offers guided tours of the district's few remaining historical buildings.

Tastes of Montréal

Montréal's dining scene is not for the diet-conscious – the city's French legacy has produced a culinary repertoire overflowing with uncommonly rich fare, from foie gras to creamy cheeses. Indeed, the opportunity to savour dishes and wines that are virtually absent from menus elsewhere in this hemisphere – at a fraction of the price you'd expect to pay in Paris or New York – has made Montréal a major gastronomic destination in its own right. But French food isn't the only reason to loosen your belt while in town. Local twists on more lowbrow fare – witness the age-old debate between New York and Montréal over whose bagels are better, the saucy Québécois take on french fries known as *poutine* and the province's award-winning beer – are also worth sampling. However you decide to whet your appetite, Montréal remains one of a handful of cities outside of Europe where lingering over a three-course dinner with wine is often the *raison d'être* of an evening out. As long as you plan on dining late, you'll fit right in.

▲ Fresh bread at Marché Atwater

French fare

You could easily spend an entire visit to Montréal indulging in **French cuisine** – and even when you're not at a restaurant on rue St-Denis doing just that, temptations will present themselves virtually everywhere you go around town, where *patisseries* display flaky croissants, *fromageries* showcase runny cheeses and *chocolatiers* serve up sinfully sweet truffles.

A recent culinary trend known as **cuisine du terroir** – literally "cuisine of the soil" – has emerged in restaurants that focus on regional produce, such as **game** from around the province, **shrimp** from Matane and **duck** from Lac Brome (the fine-feathered creatures are guests of honour at an annual festival – see p.246). The French-influenced cuisine has a lighter *nouvelle cuisine touch* and is often fused with Mediterranean or Asian cooking styles. Likewise, *cuisine du marché* (market cuisine) features market-fresh ingredients, reflected in menus that vary with the season – and even daily, depending on what the chef finds at market that morning. Serious foodies should make a point of visiting these same markets – most notably **Marché Jean-Talon** – to browse the superb regional produce brought in from the countryside each day; the Fédération des Agricotours (⊛www.agricotours.qc.ca) also maintains a complete list of local producers and restaurants.

◄ A Montréal specialty – *poutine*

Comfort food

If you've come for traditional **Québécois cuisine**, you may have to look long and hard, since apart from a few mainstays like *tourtière* (meat pie) and *fèves au lard* (baked beans with fatty bacon), such cuisine is nearly nonexistent in Montréal and Québec City. That said, the province does distinguish itself with local versions of the comfort food

Ten foodie experiences

La Binerie Traditional Québécois fare like *rillettes* and *tourtière*. p.161

La Croissanterie Figaro *Café au lait* and pastries in a setting worthy of Paris. p.164

L'Express Top-notch French cuisine in a classy brasserie ambience. p.162

Fairmount Bagel Bakery Poppy-seed or sesame bagels straight from the oven. p.206

Fonduementale Hearty fondues served in a townhouse restaurant. p.162

Laurier BBQ Rotisserie-style chicken doused in a homemade barbecue sauce. p.165

Mondo Fritz Innovative takes on french fries – and *poutine*. p.159

Milos Superlative Greek fare with an emphasis on seafood. p.165

Schwartz's Smoked meat on rye that's never served lean. p.159

Toqué! Award-winning Québécois fusion with an accent on local ingredients. p.156

▲ *Schwartz's* smoked-meat sandwich

found throughout North America, such as *steamés* – steamed **hot dogs** topped with grated cabbage and tucked into a steamed bun – and **barbecued chicken** which, in Quebec, is spit-roasted rotisserie-style and served in quarters. The fast-food *poutine* (fries smothered in gravy and topped with cheese curd) is another distinctly local standby, available at *casse-croûtes* (snack bars) around the province and often in variations such as Italian *poutine* (with a tomato and meat sauce).

Local delicacies

What many locals consider quintessentially **Montréal delicacies** were in fact adopted from the European Jews who settled here in the early twentieth century. Top of the list is **smoked meat**, beef brisket cured in brine and then smoked (similar to pastrami or corned beef), which is sliced thick and piled high on rye bread. Another Montréal classic is its variation on the rather prosaic **bagel** – denser and chewier than those found elsewhere – which are boiled first in honey water before being baked in a traditional wood-burning oven and sprinkled with sesame seeds.

Rounding out Montréal's more illustrious cuisines are those contributed by **Italian**, **Greek** and **Portuguese** immigrants; the latter two mostly settled north of Downtown, in the Plateau neighborhood and Mile End, while Little Italy has established a

▼ Cakes at Kilo

strong community around Marché Jean-Talon, complete with the requisite trattorias and *caffès* serving up strong espressos and cream-filled cannoli.

Les Bières

In a country otherwise dominated by the Labatt and Molson giants, with their bland, mass-produced brands, Québec distinguishes itself with award-winning **microbreweries** that turn out unique, flavourful brews. Rather than be classified as ales, lagers and the like, beer is differentiated here by **colour** – blonde, *rousse* (red), *ambrée* (amber) and *noir* (dark) – a shorthand that's also commonly used when ordering a pint at a bar. Brands to look out for include Brasserie McAuslan, who craft beers under the **St-Ambroise** and **Griffon** labels at their Lachine Canal brewery, opened in 1989, Les Brasseurs du Nord (producers of Boréale) and Brasseurs RJ (**Cheval Blanc** and **Belle Gueule**). Unibroue, who ramp up the alcohol content for Belgian-style beers **Maudite** and **La Fin du Monde**, also have regular-strength brands like **Blanche de Chambly**, a wheat beer. The best of breed are showcased annually as part of the **Mondial de la Bière** festival held in early June (see p.225).

Brewpubs

Benelux A weekly selection of six beers ranging from pale ale to stout, with seasonal varieties like the aptly named Oktoberfest come fall. p.169

Brutopia Six on tap, including Nut Brown Ale and Raspberry Blonde; stouts and porters also featured on occasion. p.169

Le Cheval Blanc Eight handcrafted brews such as Bleuet (blueberry) and Triple, a 9.5% alcohol-strong beer that's triple brewed over a nine-month period. p.172

Dieu du Ciel Over ten local choices, depending on the season; look for unusual beers like Fumisterie (hemp beer) and Equinox du Printemps (maple scotch ale that's aged in a keg for a year and a half). p.175

Réservoir Six varieties from Ambré de Blé (a wheat beer infused with coriander) to 500 (a sweet dark ale with an 8.5% alcohol content). p.174

Sergent Recruteur Six year-round house brands, including the blonde Raconteuse and a *rousse* called Frousse, plus a roster of 23 seasonal varieties. p.175

May–Oct, $9.75 Nov–April; ☎514/872-1400, ⓦwww.ville.montreal.qc.ca /jardin; Métro Pie-IX), immediately north of the Parc Olympique, is just that, second in size only to London's Kew Gardens. Begun in 1931, the 185-acre site, which comprises some thirty thematic gardens and ten greenhouses, can easily take a full day to explore. The **main gate** at the corner of boulevard Pie-IX and rue Sherbrooke provides the most dramatic approach, passing by a procession of colourful flowerbeds and a statue of founder Frère Marie-Victorin on the way to the Art Deco administration building. Behind the latter is the **reception centre**, where you can find out when the various guided tours of the site (and of specific gardens) take place. Between May and October, a free mini-train travels from the reception centre to the Insectarium and Tree House every fifteen minutes.

The exhibition greenhouses

The reception centre leads to the **Molson Hospitality Greenhouse**, where fan palms, bamboo and other subtropical plants provide a backdrop to introductory displays on plant biology. From here, the rest of the greenhouses branch off in two narrow rows. The hot and humid **east wing** begins with a simulated **tropical rainforest** canopy, the fake tree limbs hosting several types of bromeliads, rootless plants that collect water in their funnel of leaves to survive. The next conservatory may look similar, but the **tropical economic plants** flourishing here – which provide everything from coffee to medicines – help illustrate society's dependency on the rapidly disappearing rainforests. Next door, in the most striking greenhouse, scores of multicoloured **orchids** and **aroids**, including wild calla lilies, appear to have colonized an ancient ruin, the walls of which were actually built from salvaged Vieux-Montréal cobblestones.

The pathways in the east wing are narrow, and, when crowded, you may prefer the more varied and less busy **west wing**. First up is the **begonias and gesneriads** conservatory, whose bright flowers contrast greatly with the **arid regions** room next door, where a desert landscape supports spiky aloe, prickly pear and giant cacti straight out of a Road Runner cartoon. Further on – past the **Hacienda**, which replicates an Hispanic inner courtyard complete with terra-cotta tiles, cacti and palms – the footbridge and ponds of the aptly named **Garden of Weedlessness** create a memorable stage for the impressive Chinese *penjings* (dwarfed trees), tended and pruned with exacting care; while the two-tiered **Main Exhibition Greenhouse** at the end of the west wing showcases everything from springtime perennials to a carved-pumpkin competition at Halloween.

The outdoor gardens and Arboretum

The **Exhibition Gardens**, bordering boulevard Pie-IX, were the first part of the Jardin Botanique to be developed and are laid out in a formal French manner with a central axis interrupted by vine-covered pergolas and decorative fountains. Nearest to the reception centre are the **Perennial Garden** and **Economic Plant Garden**, installed to educate visitors on the practical uses of plants such as indigo and camomile. The axis terminates with a cluster of smaller gardens, including a collection of **poisonous plants** – fortunately fenced off.

The path opposite the Garden of Innovations – a showcase of landscaping trends located midway along the axis – leads to the **Alpine Garden**, where hardy dwarf conifers poke out of the scree and delicate alpine poppies cling to a faux-mountain landscape. A small waterfall flows into a stream, along whose banks lies the English-style **Flowery Brook** garden of lilies, irises and peonies. The brook itself feeds the ponds at the centre of the Jardin Botanique, one of which borders on the **First Nations Garden**, celebrating native-peoples' relationship with the land and also serving as the site of related activities and performances.

Beyond the ponds, and covering more than half of the botanical garden's area, is the sprawling **Arboretum**, a popular spot for local birdwatchers (a leaflet on captive species is available at the reception centre) and, in winter, cross-country skiers. It's at its loveliest in autumn when many of the 200-odd species of trees and shrubs turn fiery shades of yellow and orange. In the far northeast corner here, the **Tree House** interpretation centre holds a unique collection of dwarf North American trees, cultivated in the same manner as Japanese bonsai.

The Chinese and Japanese gardens

The Jardin Botanique's true highlights are those based on the traditional landscaping principles of China and Japan. To get to them, head east from the reception centre, where you'll first come across the **Rose Garden** and then the **Marsh and Bog Garden**, whose lotuses and water lilies are laid out in a grid of ponds with sunken pathways so you can see the plants up close.

From here, a pathway to the left leads through a grand pagoda-like arch guarded by stone lions to the **Chinese Garden**'s entrance courtyard, where a full-moon gate provides a perfect frame for the ensemble of seven pavilions interconnected by pathways and bridges – all often filled with human traffic. The design is a replica of a Ming Dynasty garden, and its most arresting feature is the

△ The Japanese Garden in the Jardin Botanique

Tower of the Condensing Clouds, a delicate fourteen-metre-high pagoda perched on a rocky ridge above a turquoise lake fed by a cascading waterfall. The tree peony blooms – described by Marco Polo as "roses the size of cabbages" – are another startling sight, though you'll only see these bursts of soft pink if you visit in June. Throughout the year, Scotch pine and some twenty species of bamboo provide a green backdrop to magnolias, azaleas and artfully placed stones, many of which were imported from Shanghai and assembled onsite by Chinese landscapers. Equally charming is the Springtime Courtyard full of *penjings* (dwarfed trees), many over 100 years old. The best time to visit is on an autumn evening, when hundreds of Chinese lanterns illuminate the garden.

More serene, the **Japanese Garden** is a short walk to the northeast. The simple compositional elements of water, rock, plants, bridges and lanterns reward you with carefully planned views along the perimeter of its pond – save perhaps from the north side, with the Olympic Stadium in the distance breaking the harmony. The garden might be best appreciated from the **Japanese Garden Pavilion**, especially during the occasional tea ceremonies ($2–6; ☎514/872-1400 for schedule), which also allow access to the *roji* (tea garden); free guided tours are also available. Designed in the style of a traditional family home, the pavilion also has within its precincts a Zen garden and a collection of bonsai, the oldest of which are around 350 years old – almost the age of Montréal itself.

Insectarium

Much shorter-lived than the ancient bonsai are the inhabitants of the nearby **Insectarium** (admission included with Jardin Botanique; ⊛ www.ville .montreal.qc.ca/insectarium), a building to the southeast shaped like a stylized housefly and devoted solely to insects and arthropods. The upper level is the more educationally oriented, with interactive displays on insect physiognomy surrounding a transparent beehive that lets you see the busy inhabitants go about their work of creating intricate honeycombs.

The bulk of the collection is downstairs, where some of the mounted beetles look like beautifully wrought jewellery, though the horned rhinoceros beetles might put you off ever wanting to visit the tropics. The live scorpions, tarantulas and giant centipedes are hardly more comforting, even behind glass. Far more pleasant are the mounted butterflies – though in late February through April, it's more fun to see lives ones in action in the adjacent **butterfly house** where dozens of species flit about unfettered. If you can overcome your fears, the Insectarium also hosts insect-tasting sessions every other year, when local chefs sauté scorpions and wrap other critters in pastry or chocolate (see box, p.116).

Le Château Dufresne

In contrast to the modernistic, fluid forms of the Stade Olympique across boulevard Pie-IX, the Beaux-Arts **Château Dufresne** at 2929 av Jeanne-d'Arc (Thurs–Sun 10am–5pm; $7; ☎514/259-9201, ⊛ www.chateaudufresne.qc.ca; Métro Pie-IX) presents a mannered and dignified sight. Inspired by the Petit Trianon palace at Versailles, the symmetrical facade gives no indication that there are actually two separate residences within, built between 1915 and 1918 for two brothers influential in the development of Maisonneuve (see box, p.112). The west wing housed the mansion's architect, Marius Dufresne, while the east was home to his elder brother Oscar, an industrialist who headed the family's shoe-manufacturing company. After a mid-twentieth-century stint as a religious boys' school, the building was abandoned. Although the chateau was restored as a museum in the late 1970s, restorers are still trying to uncover murals painted over by the Holy Cross Fathers – apparently the images were too provocative for their young charges.

The entrance is in back, where a small exhibit on the history of the building and the Dufresnes gives a bit of context, although the free afternoon guided tours (French: 1.30pm & 3.30pm, English: 2.30pm) best bring the period to life. The tour begins by ascending a staircase to the main foyer of **Oscar Dufresne's residence**, where his visitors must have been impressed by the gold-damask walls and opulent marble staircase. A hallway leads past Oscar's study to a large drawing room designed with business rather than socializing in mind, its decorative restraint limited to a few features like the elaborate

Crunchy snacks

When people speak of Montréal's fine gourmet fare, they're not typically referring to dishes like mealworm-filled biscotti and barbecued locusts. And yet, delectable offerings just like these have graced the menu at the Insectarium for over a decade.

Inaugurated in 1993, the Insectarium's novel **Croque-insectes** (Insect Tastings) event, held every other year, has since attracted over 250,000 brave souls to nibble on creepy-crawlies ranging from ants to scorpions. Sautéed, baked and marinated by chefs trained at the highly regarded Institut de Tourisme et d'Hôtellerie du Québec, the wide-ranging menus have introduced exotic delicacies such as Madagascar morsels (spicy grilled scorpion or stick insects), cricket *basbousa* (couscous and honey cake garnished with crickets) and ant macaroons (infused with coconut). A non-alcoholic drink designed around a multi-legged creature or two is also served up at the **Bug Café** created especially for the event; one year, the elixir of the moment was ant nectar – a "refreshing" quaff of orange juice, bananas, honey and ants.

Officially intended to raise awareness of insects as a high-protein food group common to several African, Latin American and Asian diets, the event now enlists over 100,000 mealworms, upwards of 60,000 crickets and approximately 5000 silkworm pupae just to create the innovative snacks. Somewhat alarmingly, you'll find numerous very-much-alive and squirming examples of the very bugs you're eating in the Insectarium's display cases.

Even if you can't muster the courage to taste some insects yourself, it's still absolutely worth attending just to watch others attempt to do so. It's not very often you see people eating with their eyes scrunched tightly shut – in fear. On the plus side, at $3 for a plate of six snacks, it's one of the best foodie bargains in town.

The event is held over several weekends every other year, including 2007. Check the Insectarium's website (ⓦ www.ville.montreal.qc.ca/insectarium) for full program details and schedule.

candelabra set against the mahogany-panelled walls. Before heading down the hall, check out the small salon to your left – the decidedly secular decoration is the work of Guido Nincheri, the Italian artist whose works feature in more than a dozen Montréal churches (see p.101). Keep an eye out for the "modern" touches in what initially appear to be classical scenes on the pastel-shaded walls – the painted nude in one is framed by electricity poles, still a novelty back in the early 1900s.

A winter garden occupies the rear of Oscar's apartment, and through the breach made in the partition wall you can see its mirror image in **Marius Dufresne's residence**. Once inside the second brother's home, you'll notice almost immediately that it's less austere, and the eclectic mix of styles and comfortable design indicate a more intimate and domestic lifestyle. There's also more scope for whimsy, as the "Turkish lounge", with its bacchanalian frieze, plush cushions and hookah, attest. Recent renovations have uncovered another of Nincheri's works here – an eye-catching ceiling fresco of an angel and an elegant woman among the clouds.

7

Parc Jean-Drapeau

The roars and rumbles that spill out from the city's amusement park and annual auto races do much to obscure the more simple outdoor pleasures found at **Parc Jean-Drapeau**, the collective name of the two islands across from the Vieux-Port. The former Parc des Îles was renamed a few years ago to commemorate former Mayor Jean Drapeau, the man responsible for Expo '67, who died in 1999. With a combined 660 acres of green space – dotted with canals, parks, public art and an astounding number of groundhogs – the park is a popular urban escape, especially during the summer months as the breeze from the St Lawrence provides a welcome respite from the heat. Breaking up all the greenery are various buildings left over from the **1967 World's Fair** (the Universal Exposition whose theme was "Man and His World" and which is best known as simply Expo '67) that drew some fifty million visitors to **Île Ste-Hélène** and **Île Notre-Dame**. The National Archives of Canada has a detailed website (Ⓦwww.collectionscanada.ca/expo/index-e.html) about the event – don't skip the intro or you'll miss the hilarious Expo '67 theme song.

Île Ste-Hélène

Île Ste-Hélène, named after the wife of explorer Samuel de Champlain, who stumbled onto its shores in 1611, is the larger and more historic of the park's two islands. The island was the last French possession in North America to be surrendered to the British in 1760; sixty years later, they built a military garrison along its shores, but eventually ceded the island to Canada. Montréal purchased it in 1908, promising to turn the land around the old military camp into a public park.

The city made good on its vow, and the island now provides visitors with ample spots to lounge about and picnic. Designed by Frederick G. Todd, who also landscaped the gardens at the Oratoire St-Joseph (p.105) and Québec City's Plains of Abraham (p.267), the park spreads out around a 45-metre-high grassy hillock, and is circled by one main road, the chemin du Tour de l'Île. The biggest draw, **La Ronde** (the city's **amusement park**), lords over its easternmost point, while the remains of the **military fort** are nearby along the northern shore. On the southern side looms the aluminium sphere that encloses the **Biosphère**, an engaging ecological museum that should not be confused with the Biodôme (see p.111). Right near the Métro, the **aquatic complex** is a good place to let kids expend energy and cool off (see p.118), while club kids can expend energy

Island practicalities

Parc Jean-Drapeau is easily reached from Downtown. The most efficient way is on the **Métro**'s yellow line to the Jean-Drapeau station on Île Ste-Hélène. Île Notre-Dame is accessible from here by walking over one of the two **bridges** that connect the islands or by taking bus #167 that stops to the left of the Métro station's exit and makes a tour of both islands. From mid-May to early October, a ten-minute **ferry** ride connects Île Ste-Hélène with the Quai Jacques-Cartier in the Vieux-Port (call ☎514/281-8000 for schedules; $4.50 each way; discounts available for/with entry to the Musée Stewart and Biosphère). The **bike path** from the Vieux-Port will get you here in about thirty minutes; head west and take the turn-off to Cité du Havre that passes under Hwy-10 and over the Pont de la Concorde; access is not available during the week surrounding the major motorsports events. From the Village, you can take the bike path on the Pont Jacques-Cartier (accessible from rue Cartier), which affords sky-high views of Downtown. If you're heading back after dusk, you may want to pop your bike on the Métro instead (see p.27). You can also **drive** over either of the two bridges – though on-island parking is scarce and costs $10–$12, $15 at La Ronde.

A seasonal **information booth** (late June to late Aug daily 9am–7pm; ☎514/872-6120, ⊛www.parcjeandrapeau.com) just outside the Métro gives out maps of the islands. While it's possible to walk around the islands, riding a bike or rollerblading are the best ways of getting around (see pp.215–216).

There are a couple of touristy restaurants and basic, overpriced *casse-croûtes* (snack bars) on the islands. The best of the latter is *Chez Tommy*, near the foot of Pont de la Concorde just north of the casino, which serves burgers, *poutine*, fish and chips and the like, and shares a terrace with a kiosk dispensing soft ice-cream. Your best bet, though, is to pack a picnic.

and chill out at Sunday's **Piknic Electronik** (see box, p.181) on the belvedere below Calder's *Man* (see box, p.120).

La Biosphère

As you loop around to the left after exiting the Métro, you can't miss Buckminister Fuller's twenty-storey-high geodesic dome – built to house the United States pavilion during Expo '67 – rising ominously out of the greenery. Composed of thousands of interlocking aluminium triangles, the sphere was left to decay following the World's Fair and lost its protective acrylic cover to fire in 1976. It was spruced up in 1992, and the **Biosphère** (June–Sept daily 10am–6pm; Oct–May Mon & Wed–Fri noon–5pm, Sat & Sun 10am–5pm; $9.50, $15 with Musée Stewart; ☎514/283-5000, ⊛www .biosphere.ec.gc.ca; Métro Jean-Drapeau) moved in as an interactive centre with a focus on water ecosystems, the St Lawrence and Great Lakes in particular. The environmental focus is reflected in the ticket price – there's a 25 percent discount with proof you arrived by public transit (such as a Métro transfer) or bicycle.

Using the raised platforms that remained inside the dome, the Biosphère created a structure resembling an oil rig with several interior halls dedicated to watery pursuits. Several of the permanent installations employ a playful tone that aims to amuse as much as educate, notably the Water Wonders hall, which provides loads of ways for kids – and mischievous adults – to get wet (towels are thoughtfully provided). These include an Archimedes screw (a millennia-old invention used to draw water up an incline), a tipping toilet and a chance to walk on water. Further exhibitions, experiments, activities and films (including one you get to star in) reinforce the message. Still, the best reason to visit the Biosphère may just be the view of the city and islands through the dome's metallic trusses from the fourth-level observation deck.

Fort de l'Île Ste-Hélène and Musée Stewart

A twenty-minute walk from the Biosphère around the winding chemin du Tour de l'Île will get you to the grounds of Montréal's only **fort**, its U-shaped layout situated close to the river's edge. Built by the British between 1820 and 1824 as a defence against the threat of American invasion, its four low-lying buildings are made of stone culled from the island's core and surrounded by fortifications indented with loopholes and parapets. On the parade grounds within its walls is a heavy bronze **cannon** bearing George II's royal coat of arms; lost during a storm in 1760, it was recovered in 1957 during the creation of the St Lawrence Seaway.

The complex never saw battle and got heavy use as an ammunitions storehouse instead. The British withdrew in 1870, and Canadian soldiers patrolled

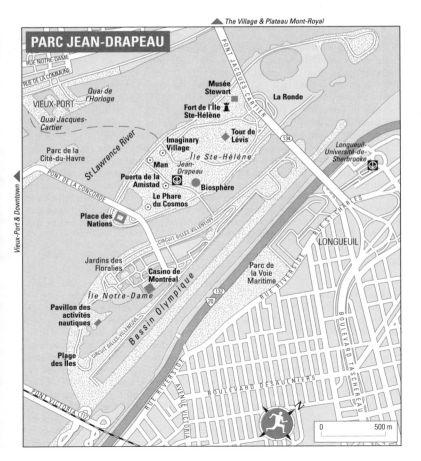

The Village & Plateau Mont-Royal

PARC JEAN-DRAPEAU

RUE NOTRE-DAME
RUE DE LA COMMUNE
Quai de l'Horloge
VIEUX-PORT
Quai Jacques-Cartier
Parc de la Cité-du-Havre
PONT DE LA CONCORDE
St Lawrence River
Musée Stewart
Fort de l'Île Ste-Hélène
La Ronde
PONT JACQUES-CARTIER
Tour de Lévis
Imaginary Village
Île Ste-Hélène
Man
Jean-Drapeau
Puerta de la Amistad
Biosphère
Le Phare du Cosmos
Place des Nations
CIRCUIT GILLES-VILLENEUVE
Jardins des Floralies
Casino de Montréal
Île Notre-Dame
Bassin Olympique
Parc de la Voie Maritime
LONGUEUIL
Pavillon des activités nautiques
Plage des Îles
PONT VICTORIA (112)
Longueuil-Université-de-Sherbrooke
RUE ST-CHARLES
RUE RIVERSIDE
BOULEVARD DESAULNIERS
AVENUE VICTORIA
BOULEVARD TASCHEREAU

Vieux-Port & Downtown

0   500 m

7

Public art on the islands

Among the more unique attractions in Parc Jean-Drapeau are several mammoth pieces of **public art**, their soaring steel and stone forms providing a striking contrast to the surrounding verdant landscape. While dotted about both islands, the most exceptional examples are clustered on the western tip of Île Ste-Hélène, including Mexican sculptor **Sebastián**'s fiery-red *Puerta de la Amistad*, on the chemin du Tour de l'Île west of the Métro (straight ahead as you exit). The openings between its three columns play tricks on the eyes – depending on where you stand, one shrinks and the other expands. Around 100m northwest, the grey-steel stabile *Man*, by **Alexander Calder**, stands at 20m high and 29m wide; it was the largest work ever produced by the American sculptor, and its lumbering mass of sweeping wings and curved angles is poised over a belvedere with terrific views across to the city. Over by the ferry wharf, five white-granite pillars rising high up from the ground comprise Portuguese sculptor **João Charters de Almeida**'s *Imaginary Village*, which looks strangely like a modern version of Roman ruins. A path leads south from Calder's piece to **Yves Trudeau**'s *Phare du Cosmos*, a 9.5-metre-high sculpted robot whose chunky torso sits atop a tripod base. His head and body used to move, but nowadays his mini-telescopic eyes are permanently transfixed on the Pont de la Concorde.

the fort until the end of World War II, when the barracks served as a prison camp for some 250 Nazis and Canadian deserters. Opened as the **Musée Stewart** (mid-May to mid-Oct daily 10am–5pm; mid-Oct to mid-May Wed–Sun 10am–5pm; $10, $15 with Biosphère; ℡514/861-6701, Ⓦwww .stewart-museum.org; Métro Jean-Drapeau) in 1955, the fort is staffed in the summer by costumed guides who lead informative, 45- to 60-minute tours and run loads of activities for kids. To make the most out of a summer visit, arrive in the early afternoon, when actors dressed as a ceremonial military corps perform drills on the parade grounds. The only building open to the public is the museum itself, laid out chronologically in the former storehouse. Inside, there's an extensive collection of military memorabilia, full of uniforms and their accoutrements – French *justeaucorps* and pointy tricorn hats included – and all manner of threatening pistols, revolvers, rapiers and bayonets, some of which are etched with their original owner's insignias. In addition, there are domestic and scientific objects, a sizeable collection of antique globes and a diorama of the old town illuminated by a video history lesson.

La Ronde

The shrieking sounds that can be heard all over the island's eastern point emanate from **La Ronde** (mid- to late May Sat & Sun 10am–8pm; early to mid-June daily 10am–8pm; mid-June to late Aug daily 10am–10.30pm; Sept Sat & Sun noon–8pm; Oct Sat noon–8pm, Sun noon–7pm; rides: $36.04 plus tax; ℡514/397-2000, Ⓦwww.laronde.com; Métro Jean-Drapeau and bus #167). Sold by the city to Six Flags in 2001, who have since invested $75 million in it, this amusement park has shed its run-down image but at the price of increased corporatization – picnic hampers were banned in 2003, causing a local outcry (food is allowed as long as it's not in a cooler). The line-ups for most of the forty-plus rides are usually short and the diversions good fun – a decades-old favourite is Le Monstre, the world's highest wooden double-track roller coaster, though recent addition Goliath tops it in terms of height (53m) and speed (110kph). Close behind in thrills is Orbite, a rocket-launch simulator that shoots passengers 45m in the air before dropping them with a stomach-lurching

△ Alexander Calder's sculpture *Man*

plummet. With synchronized concert performances, La Ronde is also a good spot to watch the spectacular fireworks competition held every June through July (see p.225).

Île Notre-Dame

The man-made island **Île Notre-Dame** rose from the St Lawrence in the mid-1960s, its elongated teardrop shape consisting solely of silt and rock dredged from the riverbed and the construction of Île Ste-Hélène's Métro line. Today, its major draws are the massive **casino** complex along the shores of its lake and, for a couple of long summer weekends, motorsports, with the most hoopla surrounding the **Canadian Grand Prix** Formula One fixture. It was joined in 2002 by the **Molson Indy** (latterly, the **Grand Prix of Montréal** Champ Car race), though at press time it seemed almost certain that the second international venue for the **NASCAR Busch Series** races would supplant the latter. Any of these speed-fests turn the island into a giant pit-stop of fumes, screeching tires and concession stands, and make much of the island inaccessible to visitors. For more on the track's history and attending races, see Chapter 16, "Sports and outdoor activities". Île Notre-Dame is almost completely encircled by the 4.42km **Circuit Gilles-Villeneuve** racetrack, a fast street circuit that is open to the public for rollerblading, cycling and cross-country skiing, when not in use by racecar drivers. Stretching alongside its entire length, the Olympic rowing basin provides the venue for regattas and the annual dragon boat races (late July; Ⓦ www.montrealdragonboat.com). More idyllic, though, are Île Notre-Dame's **parklands** – its 300 acres are ideal for strolling as they're delightfully laced with canals overarched with wooden footbridges.

Casino de Montréal

The diamond-shaped building that held Expo '67's French pavilion presides over Île Notre-Dame like the centrepiece of a giant engagement ring. Shielded from the sun by aluminium shards, the five-storey building is a marvel of concrete, steel and glass, and served a stint as the Palais de Civilisations, a museum showcasing treasures from ancient cultures, before being reconfigured as a **casino** (℡514/392-2746, Ⓦ www.casinos-quebec.com; Métro Jean-Drapeau and bus #167) in 1993. It quickly proved too small to serve its growing clientele and was expanded in 1996 to include the sawed-off pyramid (formerly home to Expo '67's Québec pavilion) to the east. The casino is now host to a whopping 3200 slot machines and 115 gaming tables, and the place teems with players around the clock. A free shuttle bus runs directly to the casino from the Centre Infotouriste (see p.45) on the hour in summer (May–Oct 10am–7pm).

The beach and gardens

Most of Île Notre-Dame's outdoor activities are clustered around the casino and clearly signposted along the island's footpaths. The chunk of land immediately north of the casino envelops the perennially blooming **Jardins des Floralies**, a dozen gardens landscaped by various nations for the 1980 Floralies Internationales flower show, laced with willow-shrouded canals and leafy parklands whose benches and calming fountain invite lingering stays. Further along, on the Parterre de l'Île Notre-Dame, you can sample the sounds and tastes of a variety of cultures throughout July and August at Les Week-ends du Monde festivities run by the city (Ⓦ ville.montreal.qc.ca/weekendsdumonde).

Southwest of the casino, you'll find the city's only central beach, the **Plage des Îles** (late June to late Aug 10am–7pm; $7.50, $4.50 after 4pm; ℡514/872-6120), forming a sandy crescent moon along the southern edge of the man-made lake in the island's centre, whose waters are naturally purified by the nearby reed beds. You can rent pedal-boats and other watercraft to cruise the lake and the Floralies' canals at the **Pavillon des activités nautiques** (same hours; ℡514/872-0199, Ⓦ www.optionpleinair.com), beyond the beach's north end, from $14 per hour.

8

Westmount and the Lachine Canal

To experience a small-town atmosphere not easily found in central Montréal, head out to the city's western neighbourhoods. **Westmount**, which borders Downtown's western fringes and is an independent city again after a brief merger with Montréal, has a picturesque English feel, complete with Victorian houses and tree-lined streets. The mansions belonging to the city's Anglo-Saxon elite look down – literally – from here over the city's poorer neighbourhoods flanking the banks of the **Lachine Canal**. Both **Pointe St–Charles** and **St–Henri** are throwbacks to the industrial era, their landscapes crossed by railroad tracks and dominated by tenement housing. Aside from the former's seventeenth-century Maison St-Gabriel, and the teeming Marché Atwater and "antique alley" of the latter, the area's main draw is the **Lachine Canal bike path** that starts from the Parc des Écluses in the Vieux-Port. At the western end of the 14km bike path lies the town of **Lachine**, a once booming fur-trade burg whose skyline is a miniature version of Vieux-Montréal's, silver dome and church spires included.

Westmount

The wealthy residential city of **Westmount**, which tumbles down from the slopes of the mountain's western peak, became the new epicentre of Anglo-Saxon wealth after the stock market crash of 1929 forced Golden Square Milers to settle permanently into their one-time summer cottages. The choicest of these grand "cottages" remain perched high up on the mountain slopes, and while it's a hike to see them, the views from up top make the effort well worth it.

Westmount's few notable sights are clustered within a seven-block radius of avenue Greene, which is lined with upscale boutiques and presided over by a triad of impersonal black-steel and tinted-glass towers designed by Mies van der Rohe and collectively known as **Westmount Square**. The Atwater Métro station's underground passageway connects to the Square's shopping concourse, from where you can exit onto avenue Greene. Once outside, turn right and then left onto boulevard de Maisonneuve to reach Westmount's architectural standout at the corner of rue Clarke, the chunky Romanesque **Église**

WESTMOUNT

▲ Oratoire St-Joseph

Cimetière Notre-Dame-des-Neiges

Parc Summit

RESTAURANTS

Calories	3
Kaizen	2
Taverne sur le Square	1

Parc King George

Hôtel de Ville

Victoria Hall

Westmount Library

Parc Westmount

Église St-Léon

Atwater

Westmount Square ❶ ❷

Forum Pepsi

❸ Place Alexis-Nihon

Marché Atwater & Lachine Canal ▼

St-Léon anchored by a gabled bell tower. The church's interior is a visual feast of Italian marble floors, columns embellished with Florentine mosaics and superbly coloured frescoes, painted by the prolific Guido Nincheri (whose secular, allegorical paintings adorn the Château Dufresne; see p.115), on every inch of the domed ceiling. Nincheri's altar painting is the most intriguing work on display here, as it shows the church's namesake standing with Attila the Hun; he's hardly the personage you'd expect in a religious portrait, but it turns out that St Leo (the fifth-century Pope Leo I) was instrumental in convincing Attila to leave Italy.

One block north of the church, and another block west on rue Sherbrooke ouest, is the Neo-Tudor **Hôtel de Ville** (City Hall) at no. 4333. There's not much to see inside; more action is found at the rear, where locals, doffed in sporty whites, frequently play croquet or lawn bowls on the village green in the summer. West of here is one of the oldest public libraries in the province, the 1899 Westmount Library, 4574 rue Sherbrooke O (Mon–Fri 10am–9pm, Sat & Sun 10am–5pm, closed Sun mid-June to early Sept), its leaded windows engraved with the names of influential writers and philosophers. There's a cheerful domed **greenhouse** (Mon–Fri 10am–2.30pm, Sat & Sun 10am–4.45pm) adjoining the library with goldfish-filled pools and park benches; the door at its western end leads to the ground-floor atrium of **Victoria Hall,** where local artists' works are showcased. More upscale boutiques are found a few blocks west of the library on rue Sherbrooke ouest.

To the Westmount lookout

No one road leads directly up to Westmount's **lookout**, a fifteen-minute walk away. From the library, head northward through Parc King-George to avenue Westmount, and take it eastward until you reach avenue Aberdeen. From here, strike north again to the curvy **avenue Bellevue**, Westmount's most enchanting street. Its heady hairpin turns wind past gingerbread houses, ivy-covered brownstones and stone cottages before reaching **avenue Sunnyside**, home to the neighbourhood's ritziest private residences. The rambling medieval-looking mansion at no. 14 is perhaps the grandest of all – its gabled peaks poke through the trees behind a finely crafted gridiron gate etched with blooming lilies. Across the street, a set of steep stairs leads to the lookout on rue Summit Circle, where an impressive panorama takes in the gabled roofs of the tony neighbour- hood, the expanse of industrial lands bordering the St Lawrence and, poking out of the river valley, the distant Monteregian Hills – of which Montréal's mountain is the westerly outpost. The 45-acre **Summit Park** behind the lookout is an unlandscaped, wooded nature park and bird sanctuary that's particularly popular with birdwatchers in the month of May, when high concentrations of passerines stop here during migration. If you continue westward on Summit Circle, you'll arrive at Summit Crescent, which accesses the rear of the Oratoire St-Joseph (see p.105).

The Lachine Canal and around

Although Montréal's early importance owed much to the Lachine Rapids that prevented further navigation westward, the need for a route through to the Great Lakes led to a number of attempts to provide a water link, beginning with the Sulpicians' failed 1689 effort. Others went bankrupt in subsequent attempts, including the merchants whose 1819 project was sparked by the development of the competing Erie Canal. The province finally took over the construction of the **Lachine Canal**, built between 1821 and 1825 and extending from the Vieux-Port to **Lachine**, 14km to the west, on the shore of the St Lawrence where it widens out as Lac St-Louis. The canal soon attracted so many factories to the communities bordering it, such as **Pointe St-Charles** and **St-Henri**, that it was expanded twice, and from the mid-eighteenth to the mid-nineteenth centuries the area served as Canada's industrial heartland, lined with steel foundries, sugar and flour refineries, factories, warehouses, and rail- and shipyards.

At the canal's peak, just before the 1929 crash, it was used by 15,000 ships annually. But the construction of the St Lawrence Seaway all but obliterated the canal's usefulness; it was closed and mostly filled in by 1970. Now a National Historic Site, it was taken over in 1978 by Parks Canada and cycling paths were built along the derelict industrial landscape, but the area's real turnaround came in the late 1990s as various government bodies pumped $100 million into the area, reopening the canal to pleasure-boat traffic in 2002 (for land and water tours and rentals, see box p.127). Alongside this, private devel- opments have converted the former factories and warehouses into offices for high-tech firms and expensive condos, and further projects such as marinas and

For years, the Lachine Canal was mainly the preserve of active Montrealers who came to bike or blade its length. But thanks to the reopening of the locks and the area's increasing popularity, you can now cruise its waters or take a walking tour of the industrial legacy that most people obliviously whiz past. In tandem with the Pôle des Rapides (℡514/364-4490, ⊛www.poledesrapides.com), the tourist body for the whole region surrounding the canal, Parks Canada operates a number of **info kiosks** (hours vary – see below) and runs free **guided tours** in the National Historic Site (mid-May to early Sept; ℡514/283-6054 or 637-7433, ⊛www.parkscanada.gc.ca /lachinecanal) centred on the canal itself. In addition to info on area attractions, the kiosks provide a free map (a more useful one is available for $2).

From east to west, there's an information kiosk at Écluse St-Gabriel (lock no. 3; late June to early Sept daily 10am–5.30pm), whose weekend tours cover the area's industrial heritage. Further along, the kiosk at the foot of the pedestrian bridge leading from Marché Atwater is the departure point for daily tours detailing the canal's history and urbanization, as well as weekend bike tours. Two kilometres further west, there's another info booth at the Écluse Côte-St-Paul (lock no. 4; same hours). If you've worked up a thirst by now, you might consider a pint (and barbecued snack) at the nearby *Terrasse St-Ambroise* (Mon–Fri 11am–10pm, Sat & Sun 11am–8pm), accessible from the bike path or 5080 rue St-Ambroise; it's run by the Brasserie McAuslan, a local brewery that also offers occasional tours of their facilities (℡514/939-3060 for schedule, ⊛www.mcauslan.com; $10). Finally, you can also find out more about the canal at its terminus, Écluse de Lachine (lock no. 5), where, in addition to tours, the Lachine Visitors Services Centre (mid-May to early Sept daily 9.30am–5pm) has an exhibition of historic photos and a snack bar to boot. En route, keep an eye out for panels that are illustrated with historic photos and give more in-depth accounts of the canal's former life.

The nearest Métro stations to the sector of the canal in front of the Marché Atwater are Charlevoix and Lionel-Groulx, while the handiest station for the Vieux-Port end is Métro Square-Victoria. Numerous bus routes also traverse the area.

Cycling the canal

The cycle paths that run along the canal are popular with Montrealers and visitors alike, to the extent that it can be slow going on sunny summer weekends – if your main goal is exercise, go early in the morning. The path begins at the Vieux-Port,

waterside cafés are in the works. For now, it's still refreshingly untouristy, and the impressive hulks of factories and warehouses provide a backdrop to a great spot to exercise, though guided tours allow the more cerebral to delve into the canal's industrial heritage.

Pointe St-Charles

Slightly more than a kilometre west of the Vieux-Port lies gritty **Pointe St-Charles**, a community severed from Downtown by the Lachine Canal and a string of major highways. The Pointe, as it's affectionately called, developed a rough reputation thanks to a largely Irish, working-class population that first settled here in the early 1800s to help build the canal and later worked in the now-defunct factories along its shores. Though pretty run-down nowadays (despite pockets of gentrification), the Pointe's Irish legacy is ever-present in the shamrocks that emblazon the neighbourhood's bar and cornershop signs and in the wrought-iron Celtic crosses ornamenting the gables of **Grace Church** at 2083 rue Wellington.

where you can rent **bicycles** and **rollerblades** (see p.215 & p.216) and extends westward for 14km to the canal's terminus in Lachine, passing locks, swooping under bridges (the steep grades may be a problem for first-time bladers) and crossing back and forth between the north and south banks. Plan on a minimum of two hours for the full circuit if you're in good shape and cycling outside the busiest times. The grassy Parc René-Lévesque, a peninsula that juts out from the end of the bike path into Lac St-Louis, and adds about 3km to a round trip, has a fantastical collection of 22 contemporary sculptures and offers prime views onto Lachine's attractive skyline. For a change of scene on the way back, follow the des Berges cycle path along the banks of the St Lawrence past the Lachine Rapids and the islets of the Parc des Rapides migratory bird refuge, favoured by herons and bitterns. Pick up a cycling map beforehand at one of the info kiosks (see above) for a list of repair shops and amenities – as well as how to navigate your way back to the canal if you make a detour.

On the water
Don't even think about swimming in the canal (it's prohibited anyway), as its sediment is legendarily polluted after a century of use as the backbone of "Canada's Pittsburgh". There are plenty of options to **cruise** along its surface, though. The most sedate way to experience it is the glass-topped boat *L'Éclusier*, which departs from in front of the Marché Atwater (see p.207) and travels eastward through the St-Gabriel locks to Peel basin and back with a Parks Canada guide providing an Industrial Revolution history lesson on the two-hour cruise (mid-May to mid-Oct Sat & Sun 1pm & 3.30pm; late June to early Sept daily; $16.75; ☎514/846-0428, ⓦwww .croisierecanaldelachine.ca); there are also pricier brunch and dinner cruises. *Le Petite Navire* also offers ninety-minute cruises embarking from the Quai Jacques-Cartier in the Vieux-Port (late June to early Sept Thurs–Sun 2pm; $21.95; ☎514/602-1000, ⓦwww.lepetitnavire.ca).

If you'd rather chart your own course (and forgot to bring your own boat with you), you can hire **pedal-boats** (from $10/hr) and electric **motorboats** (from $35/hr) from Aventures H₂O (☎514/842-1306, ⓦwww.h2oadventures.com) on the south side of the canal just east of the footbridge from the Marché Atwater. Here you can also hire **kayaks** (starting at $15/hr) at your own pace or opt for a two-hour lesson and tour ($35 Wed evening; $39 Sun afternoon).

Maison St-Gabriel

In the Pointe's south end at 2146 Place Dublin stands the neighborhood's main attraction, the **Maison St-Gabriel** (late June to early Sept Tues–Sun 11am–6pm, early April to late June & early Sept to mid-Dec Tues–Sun 1–5pm, last tour one hour before closing; $8, $12 Sun, $4 site only, Sat 11am & noon free; ☎514/935-8136, ⓦwww.maisonsaint-gabriel.qc.ca; Métro Charlevoix and bus #57 or Métro Square–Victoria and bus #61), a picturesque duo of seventeenth-century fieldstone buildings tucked behind a monstrous 1960s apartment complex. The lovely manor house, trimmed by two stone chimneys and capped by a petite bell tower, once served as the school and residence of the King's Wards (see box, p.129); livestock was sheltered in the rustic barn nearby. The estate's location is unexpected, given the Pointe's industrial tenor, but there was little else around when Sœur Marguerite Bourgeoys purchased the land in 1668 and founded the school, a decade after initiating the Chapelle Notre-Dame-de-Bon-Secours (see p.77). Besides housing her order of nuns, the house also served as a neighbourhood school and farm.

The current house dates from 1698 – the original burned five years earlier – and opened as a **museum** in 1966. Members of the congregation founded by

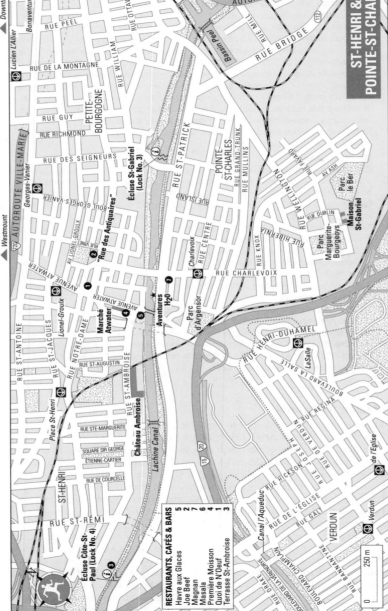

▲ Vieux-Montréal   ▲ Vieux-Port   Pont Victoria ▲

RUE NAZARETH

AUTOROUTE BONAVENTURE

↑ Downtown

Bonaventure

↑ Lucien L'Allier

RUE PEEL

RUE DE LA MONTAGNE

RUE PEEL

RUE OTTAWA

RUE WILLIAM

10

Bassin Peel

RUE MILL

RUE BRIDGE

112

ST-HENRI &
POINTE-ST-CHARLES

RUE GUY

RUE RICHMOND

PETITE-
BOURGOGNE

RUE DES SEIGNEURS

RUE ST-PATRICK

Écluse St-Gabriel
(Lock No. 3)

ℹ

POINTE-
ST-CHARLES

RUE GRAND-TRUNK

RUE MULLINS

RUE CHARLES

AUTOROUTE VILLE-MARIE

Georges-Vanier

BOUL GEORGES-VANIER

720

RUE ISLAND

RUE CENTRE

RUE WELLINGTON

AV. FAVARD

AV. ASH

Parc
le Ber

◄ Westmount

AVENUE ATWATER

Lionel-Groulx

AV. LIONEL-GROULX

RUE VINET

2 "Rue des Antiquaires"

1

RUE DUBLIN

Charlevoix

RUE CHARLEVOIX

Parc
Marguerite-
Bourgeoys

Maison
St-Gabriel

Pont Champlain & Île des Sœurs ►

RUE KNOX

RUE HIBERNIA

4 Marché
Atwater

5

★ H₂O
Aventures

7

Parc
d'Argenson

RUE ST-ANTOINE

RUE ST-JACQUES

RUE NOTRE-DAME

RUE ST-AUGUSTIN

AVENUE ATWATER

RUE ST-AMBROISE

Place St-Henri

Château Ambroise

RUE STE-MARGUERITE

SQUARE SIR GEORGE
ÉTIENNE-CARTIER

RUE DE COURCELLE

ST-HENRI

RUE ST-RÉMI

Écluse Côte-St-
Paul (Lock No. 4)

ℹ

3

Lachine Canal

RUE HENRI-DUHAMEL

LaSalle

BOULEVARD LA SALLE

RUE REGINA

15 20

RUE HICKSON

Canal l'Aqueduc

RUE DE L'ÉGLISE

RUE GALT

RUE DE VERDUN

VERDUN

RUE BANNANTYNE

de l'Église

Verdun

◄ Lachine 8km

RESTAURANTS, CAFÉS & BARS
Havre aux Glaces   5
Joe Beef   2
Magnan   7
Masala   6
Première Moisson   4
Quoi de N'Oeuf   1
Terrasse St-Ambroise   3

0   250 m

When France settled Québec in the mid-1600s, the majority of residents were male bachelors recruited to defend against Iroquois attack; the few women on hand were either married or in the service of the church. The lack of eligible women vexed the men, who responded by carousing with native women. This behaviour was quickly deemed unsuitable, and a scheme was soon hatched to provide the colony with "honest" wives. King Louis XIV sent almost 800 women, who became known as the **King's Wards** (*filles du roi*), to New France between 1663 and 1673. Most of these women were orphans who, in return for their services, had their passage paid for and received a royal dowry of useful household items that enhanced their marriage value.

The first contingents were dispersed between Montréal, Québec City and Trois Rivières, but many of the post-1668 arrivals resided at the Maison St-Gabriel. There, under the guidance of Sœur Marguerite Bourgeoys and members of her congregation, the girls learned domestic skills while awaiting betrothal.

The plan was a success: the colony's population doubled between 1666 and 1672, enabling the king to phase out the programme which, in any case, had proved a drain on the royal treasury.

Bourgeoys give informative, hour-long guided tours (mandatory; on the hour) of the rooms, each boasting unique pieces dating from the early eighteenth century. Most unusual among the items on display are the two large shelf-like sinks made of black stone, cleverly designed to drain outside through the stone wall. The girls' dormitory is also of interest as its tiny canopy beds are stacked high with pillows so the girls would sleep virtually upright lest death come and take them while lying down – a common superstition at the time – and, more prosaically, to aid digestion. During summer Sundays, the grounds are given over to concerts, costumed performances and weaving and lace-making demonstrations (call for information). Next to the neighbouring barn, which hosts temporary historical exhibitions, the New France–style farmhouse garden's plots of vegetables, herbs and medicinal plants can only be visited on a guided tour (included in entry fee).

St-Henri

The neighbourhood of **St-Henri**, northwest of the Pointe between the Lachine Canal and Westmount, is perfect for a pit stop if travelling along the canal's bike path (see box, p.126). Visible across the canal from the trail is the Art Deco **Marché Atwater** (Mon–Wed 8am–6pm, Thurs 8am–8pm, Fri 8am–9pm, Sat & Sun 8am–5pm; Ⓦ www.marchespublics-mtl.com), which is highlighted by a large clocktower and holds a public market brimming with stalls selling mouthwatering foodstuffs. One of the finest is Première Moisson, a delectable gourmet shop at the market's southern end selling heavenly patés – among other sundry treats like dainty pastries and prepared salads – that are perfect for lunching in their conservatory or along the canal. Also worth a peek is the section of rue Notre-Dame ouest just north of the market, between rue Atwater and rue Guy, known as "rue des antiquaires" due to the numerous **antique shops** (see p.200) that line the street; frustratingly, most are closed on Sunday.

While browsing is the main trade in St-Henri nowadays, the neighbourhood's blue-collar history has its origins in leather tanneries. Though there's little left of the bygone era, its working-class roots are still evident a few blocks west of the market on **rue St-Augustin**, a narrow residential street with a clutch of

△ Lachine waterfront

quaint clapboard houses at the rue St-Ambroise end dating from the 1870s and the inspiration for Gabrielle Roy's *The Tin Flute*. Some have recently been covered with unattractive aluminium siding, but the restored private residences at nos. 110 and 118 exude a rustic charm with their small front porches, tiny dormer windows and brightly painted exteriors. Across the railroad tracks just to the west, the **Château St-Ambroise** (Ⓦ www.chateaustambroise.ca) is perhaps one of the best examples of the area's renewal. Housed in the 1882 red-brick Dominion Textile building, the former factory is home to three hundred work studios for artists, creative agencies and start-ups, as well as the Galerie d'Art St-Ambroise (Tues–Fri noon–5pm or by appointment; Ⓣ 514/487-0935, Ⓦ www.galerie-st-ambroise.com), a commercial, contemporary art gallery with a dozen shows a year, and a decent café-restaurant, *L'Ambroisie*, with a terrace (unfortunately, it's the one in the parking lot rather than the lovely residents' garden with a domed pergola overlooking the canal).

Lachine

The canal (and its bike path) ends in its namesake, the scenic town of **Lachine**, which sits on land granted to Robert Cavelier de La Salle in 1667 by the Messieurs de St-Sulpice, the priests that held the title to Montréal for nearly two centuries (see box, p.72). La Salle was so obsessed with finding a passage to China that Montrealers of the time mockingly referred to his territory as "La Chine" (China) – the name stuck even though he never found the route. He somehow managed to chart Louisiana instead.

Lachine grew up to be an important fur-trading post due to its location near the **Lachine Rapids**, which hindered ships from travelling to Montréal prior to the canal days; shipments were unloaded here for transportation to Montréal by land. Those days are remembered in Lachine's major attraction, the **Commerce-de-la-Fourrure-à-Lachine**, an interactive historical museum lodged in a former fur storehouse; the once unnavigable rapids are now plied by rafts and jet boats (see p.217). While the resulting wealth contributed to the steeples and domes that make the skyline so attractive, the rest of the former town (merged with Montréal on January 1st, 2002) is an uninteresting suburban sprawl.

Lieu historique national du Commerce-de-la-Fourrure-à-Lachine

The **Commerce-de-la-Fourrure-à-Lachine** (Fur Trade at Lachine) occupies an attractive low-lying fieldstone building near the Lachine waterfront at 1255 boul St-Joseph (April to mid-Oct daily 9.30am–12.30pm & 1–5pm; mid-Oct to Nov Wed–Sun 9.30am–12.30pm & 1–5pm; $3.95; ☎514/637-7433, Ⓦwww .parkscanada.gc.ca/fur; Métro Angrignon and bus #195). Built in 1803 as a storehouse for the country's leading fur-trading company, the North West Company, today the museum is jam-packed with hands-on exhibits dealing with the fur trade. The costumed mannequins guarding some of the displays are pretty cheesy, but you do get to handle some exquisite furs, the softest of which are beaver – a nearby price list notes a keg of rum bought three. There's also a weigh-station that determines your qualifications as a *voyageur*; their measurements were capped at 178cm and 63kg (5'7"/139lbs) so as not to upset the canoe in which they spent up to eighteen hours a day. A fine example of their water transport, a twelve-metre-long birchbark canoe, is also on display.

Listings

Listings

9

Accommodation

Montréal definitely does not lack for **accommodation**, as it has thousands of available rooms, and more options show up each year. However, even as the number of rooms has increased, so has the number of visitors to the city, which has effectively put an end to the days of being able to score cheap rooms in upmarket **hotels** year-round. During the **high season**, which runs from mid-May to early September, and briefly again around Christmas, you should reserve well in advance – especially if you're coming on Grand Prix weekend (mid-June) or during the Jazz Festival (late June to early July). Throughout the rest of the year, though, when vacancies are higher, good weekend specials can sometimes be found, and many small hotels offer weekly rates. The main exception is accommodation aimed at **gay travellers** (see p.186), which fills up quickly on the big party weekends throughout the year.

In many of the **smaller hotels**, there is often a fair amount of variety – room size, view, brightness, bath or shower – in rooms available for around the same price. In any event, don't hesitate to ask to see a couple of a hotel's rooms in order to find one that best suits you. One other thing to check when booking a room is what type of **breakfast** will be served – a continental breakfast can be as skimpy as a croissant and coffee, while a "continental buffet", "deluxe continental" or "continental plus" might include yoghurt, cheese, cold cuts and fruit. A full (or American) breakfast should include eggs and other hot dishes, but may be served as a buffet. Note that with the introduction of the smoking ban in 2006, all of the city's accommodations are now smoke-free.

Due in large part to rising hotel rates, **bed and breakfasts** are becoming increasingly popular, and many of them are tucked into handsome grey-stones in ideal locations like the Plateau and Quartier Latin. Budget-conscious travellers also have a good selection of options, as Montréal's universities open the doors to their residence halls in summer, and there are also several decent **hostels** to choose from.

You can also check the Tourisme Montréal website (Ⓦ www.tourisme-montreal .org) for packages and last-minute deals; they don't handle online bookings, but Tourisme Québec (Ⓣ 1-877/266-5687, Ⓦ www.bonjourquebec.com) does; you can also book upon arrival at the Centre Infotouriste (see p.45).

Accommodation **prices** vary throughout the year, with the highest rates from mid-May to early September, and again around Christmas. The prices given in this chapter for hotels and B&Bs reflect the average price you can expect to pay for the least expensive double-occupancy room in high season, excluding special offers and price-gouging during the Grand Prix weekend and Jazz Festival. Especially with the big chains, prices can fluctuate quite a bit at any time of year based on capacity, and it's always worth checking for discounts and packages. The prices do not include federal and provincial **taxes**, which come to about 14 percent plus there's an additional 3–percent hotel tax.

Hotels

The major weakness of Montréal's hotel scene is a shortage of quality **mid-range** rooms – we've listed the best of a small supply below. If you're willing to spend at least $150 a night, there are plenty of quality **upmarket hotels** to choose from. And if you're on a tight budget, somewhat shabby **bargain hotels** abound, many of them fortunately concentrated in energetic neighbourhoods like the **Quartier Latin** and on the edge of the **Plateau**. Hotels around the bus station in the Quartier Latin are especially cheap, but keep in mind the immediate area is a popular drug–dealing spot that attracts unsavoury types day and night. **Downtown** finds an assortment of the usual international **chains** geared towards corporate travellers, with a few winning independent hotels thrown into the mix. In contrast, **Vieux–Montréal's inns** and its many **boutique hotels** are intimate and wonderfully atmospheric, but at a price – you're paying for the history of your surroundings as well as exclusive amenities.

Downtown

For the locations, refer to the maps on on p.46 & p.50.

L'Appartement Hôtel ☎514/284-3634 or 1-800/363-3010, ⓦwww.appartementhotel .com; Métro McGill or Place-des-Arts. Recently renovated studios, one-bedroom and two-bedroom apartments with kitchenettes, a/c, phones and TVs, on the border of Downtown and the Plateau. Daily, weekly and monthly rates include continental breakfast and access to the sauna, roof deck and adjacent indoor pool, though parking is extra. $156.

Château Versailles 1659 rue Sherbrooke 0 ☎514/933-8111 or 1-888/933-8111, ⓦwww.versailleshotels.com; Métro Guy-Concordia. Spacious, individually decorated rooms in this complex of four grey-stones built in the 1800s. The deluxe suites have classy touches like chandeliers and gas fireplaces, while the sleek standard rooms have perks like CD players, modem hook-up, bathrobes and fancy toiletries. Book early, as this place is extremely popular, and ask about the various specials when doing so. Continental buffet breakfast included. $185.

Fairmont the Queen Elizabeth 900 boul René-Lévesque 0 ☎514/861-3511 or 1-800/257-7544, ⓦwww.fairmont.com/queenelizabeth; Métro Bonaventure. The grande dame of Montréal's big hotels, the *Fairmont the Queen Elizabeth* doesn't quite command

the same kind of clientele as it did in 1969 when John Lennon and Yoko Ono staged their "Give peace a chance" bed-in here. Nowadays, its thousand-plus rooms play host to convention-goers, and the place can seem quite desolate when nothing corporate is going on. $329.

Le Germain 2050 rue Mansfield ☎514/849-2050 or 1-877/333-2050, ⓦwww.hotelgermain.com; Métro Peel or McGill. Every last detail in this boutique hotel has a designer touch to it – the airy rooms feature dark woods, down duvets and a sheer glass wall that divides the bedroom from the shower (there is a wrap-around shower curtain for privacy-seekers). In-room extras like CD player, free Wi-Fi, bathrobes and fresh fruit just add to the overall package. Buffet breakfast included. $245.

Hôtel de la Montagne 1430 rue de la Montagne ☎514/288-5656 or 1-800/361-6262, ⓦwww .hoteldelamontagne.com; Métro Peel. The lobby is something out of an *Arabian Nights* fantasy: two large sculpted elephants guard the front desk while a nearby flowing fountain, complete with rotating golden water-nymph, shines under a massive crystal chandelier: tacky and yet somehow classy. After this spectacle, though, the guestrooms are four-star standard. The lively singles' bar, *Thursdays*, is on the ground floor (the main entrance faces onto the rue Crescent strip) but the choicest spot for a drink is next to the pool on the twentieth-floor *Magnétic Terrasse* (see p.169). Breakfast included in price on weekends only. $199.

Hyatt Regency 1255 rue Jeanne-Mance ☎514/982-1234 or 1-888/633-7313, ⊛www .montreal.hyatt.com; Métro Place-des-Arts. A glass elevator silently whisks you up the outside of the building to the third-floor lobby with granite floors so polished they squeak. The 600 expansive rooms are quietly elegant and come with large work areas, Wi-Fi and down blankets; the sunny indoor pool faces Place des Arts. When the Jazz Festival is on (see p.225), you won't find a better location – the third-floor terrace overlooks the main stage, though check to see that it won't be closed for private functions during your stay. $279.

Manoir Ambrose 3422 rue Stanley ☎514/288-6922 or 1-888/688-6922, ⊛www .manoirambrose.com; Métro Peel. Two adjoining nineteenth-century Victorian houses on a quiet street, offering affordable accommodation with character and lots of stairs. The pleasant, high-ceilinged rooms have a/c, TVs and Wi-Fi, and most have private bathroom. Continental breakfast included. $105 (shared bath); $120.

Marriott Château Champlain 1050 rue de la Gauchetière 0 ☎514/878-9000 or 1-800/200-5909, ⊛www.marriotthotels.com; Métro Bonaventure. Popular with executive travellers as it's huge, well-appointed and connected to the Underground City (RÉSO – see p.49), this chain hotel's most distinctive features are the rooms' unusual half-moon windows. Ask for quarters facing Place du Canada – the views are excellent. $235.

Quality Hotel Downtown 3440 av du Parc ☎514/849-1413 or 1-800/424-6423, ⊛www .choicehotels.ca; Métro Place-des-Arts. Not exactly Downtown, this moderately priced hotel is just up the street from the summer festival action and handy for the Plateau as well. Rooms have either two doubles or a queen and sofabed, free local calls and Internet. It's pet-friendly – useful if you want a four-legged excuse to get some exercise on the mountain. Alternatively, visit the *Pullman* wine bar and tapas lounge downstairs – quite a bit flashier than the chain's image suggests. $145.

Quality Inn Downtown 1214 rue Crescent ☎514/878-2711 or 1-800/424-6423, ⊛www .choicehotels.ca; Métro Guy-Concordia. This reliable chain hotel gets packed during the June Grand-Prix weekend as its rue Crescent location puts guests right in the thick of the three-day F1 street party (see p.213). All the rooms are junior suites with two double beds or a king and pull-out sofa and can sleep three or four. Street-facing rooms have private balconies with a bird's-eye view of the festivities. Continental breakfast included. $160–180.

Ritz-Carlton 1228 rue Sherbrooke 0 ☎514/842-4212 or 1-800/441-1414, ⊛www.ritzcarlton .com/hotels/montreal; Métro Peel. Standard luxury chain accommodation. Still, the lobby is spectacular, the charming garden-side restaurant is a lovely oasis in summer, and the hotel is conveniently located near the city's finest shopping. $265.

△ The Ritz-Carlton

Le Square Phillips 1193 Place Phillips ☎514/393-1193 or 1-866/393-1193, ⊛www .squarephillips.com; Métro McGill. More stylish than your average apartment-hotel, the high-ceilinged studios and suites are done up in creams, taupes and dark wood accents and have full kitchens, dining tables and high-speed Internet access. Ask for a room overlooking the square. Cheaper weekly and monthly rates available. $197.

Le St-Malo 1455 rue du Fort ☎514/931-7366, ⊛www.hotel-saint-malo.com; Métro

Guy-Concordia or Atwater. A reasonably priced option on the western edge of Downtown. The building lacks charm, but its thirteen rooms are bright, comfortable and come with cable TV. Some rooms have a/c; the cheapest are on the small side. $90.

Travelodge Montréal-Centre 50 boul René-Lévesque O ☎514/874-9090 or 1-800/363-6535, ⊛ www.travelodgemontreal.ca; Métro Place-d'Armes or St-Laurent. There's not a lot of character to the small rooms here, but it's modern, clean and well located on the outskirts of Chinatown, close to Vieux-Montréal. Cable TV, in-room coffeemaker and Wi-Fi included. $99.

Vieux-Montréal

For the locations, refer to the map on on p.69.

Auberge Bonaparte 447 rue St-François-Xavier ☎514/844-1448, ⊛ www.bonaparte.com; Métro Place-d'Armes. A handsome upscale inn, steps from the Basilique Notre-Dame, built in 1886 and shaded by smart burgundy awnings. Inside, the quarters are decked out with wrought-iron headboards, hardwood floors, high ceilings and French dormer windows. The more expensive rooms overlook the private gardens of the Séminaire de St-Sulpice and have jacuzzis. The ground-floor restaurant serves up rich French fare (see p.154). Breakfast included. $165.

Auberge Bonsecours 353 rue St-Paul E ☎514/396-2662, ⊛ www.aubergebonsecours .com; Métro Champ-de-Mars. Set back in a courtyard behind *Le Beau Soleil* B&B (see p.142), this seven-room inn occupies the former stables buildings and has a lovely breakfast room with exposed stone walls. The quarters are decorated with colourful bedspreads and eclectic furnishings, like wrought-iron tables and painted Indian wardrobes, all of which help to compensate for some of the hotel's more questionable modern renovations. $195.

Auberge Les Passants du Sans Soucy 171 rue St-Paul O ☎514/842-2634, ⊛ www.lesanssoucy.com; Métro Place-d'Armes. This charming inn is full of nice touches like flowerpots on the windowsills and lace curtains throughout. Brass beds and hardwood floors contribute to the romantic atmosphere, and some rooms have wooden beams and stone walls. Breakfast, served in a sky-lit nook, is included. $155.

Auberge de la Place Royale 115 rue de la Commune O ☎514/287-0522, ⊛ www .aubergeplaceroyale.com; Métro Square-Victoria or Place-d'Armes. The standard rooms have exposed stone walls and queen beds, but look onto a back lane. Pay a bit more and you can get a view of the Vieux-Port, along with a four-poster bed and a whirlpool bath. All the rooms, though, are a bit dowdy. A full breakfast, served on a sidewalk terrace in summer, is included. $175.

Auberge du Vieux-Port 97 rue de la Commune E ☎514/876-0081 or 1-888/660-7678, ⊛ www .aubergeduvieuxport.com; Métro Place-d'Armes. This waterfront hotel dates from 1882 and is dotted with 27 high-ceilinged rooms offering spectacular views onto the Vieux-Port or rue St-Paul from large casement windows. Original stone walls, hardwood floors and brass headboards add to the rooms' overall appeal. The roof terrace, open to the public, is a fantastic spot to survey the Vieux-Port with a drink or meal. Eighteen large lofts that can sleep up to six are available in the buildings behind, with full kitchen and washer/dryer (⊛ www.oldmontreal apartments.com; studios $235 for two people; discounts for longer stays). Full breakfast and wine-and-cheese cocktail hour included with hotel rooms only. $205.

Casa de Matéo 438 rue St-François-Xavier ☎514/286-9589, ⊛ www.casademateo.com; Métro Place-d'Armes. The 22 rooms here are sparsely furnished but clean, and most have a mini kitchenette unit. All rooms have a/c but some are quite dark, so ask if that's a concern. Hot breakfast, included in the rates, is served with a slight Mexican twist in the ground-floor restaurant (see p.155). $92 (shared bath); $125.

Hôtel Gault 449 rue Ste-Hélène ☎514/904-1616 or 1-866/904-1616, ⊛ www.hotelgault.com; Métro Square-Victoria. Most glamorous of the recent crop of boutique hotels, the *Gault* is the place to stay – if you can afford it. The 30 individually designed loft-style rooms are a design-junkie's dream, from the Arne Jacobsen fixtures and Artemide lamps to the white-oak panelling and custom-made linens. The sleek lobby's colourful furniture contrasts nicely with the cast-iron columns that are vestiges of the 1871 former warehouse that now houses the hotel. $235.

Hôtel Nelligan 106 rue St-Paul O ☎514/788-2040 or 1-877/788-2040, ⊛ www.hotelnelligan.com;

Métro Place-d'Armes. Another of the recent spate of boutique hotels, the *Nelligan* has a cozy lobby with exposed brick wall, fireplace and leather sofas that give a hint of the similarly comfortable rooms. Down duvets keep you warm in winter while in summer windows open onto Vieux-Montréal's charming streets. The included continental breakfast and *5 à 7* cocktails are served in an atrium overlooked by wrought-iron balconies, adjacent to the hotel restaurant *Verses*, serving high-quality regional cuisine. Be sure to check out the views from the roof terrace (open to the public), though drinks are pricey. $255.

Hôtel Place d'Armes 701 Côte de la Place d'Armes ☎ 514/842-1887 or 1-888/450-1887, ⓦ www.hotelplacedarmes.com; Métro Place-d'Armes. The location of this eight-storey boutique hotel can't be beat – it's right on Place d'Armes, facing the Basilique Notre-Dame. The spacious rooms are sleekly tailored in neutral tones, and extras like in-room CD player, high-speed Internet access and cocktail hour by the lobby fireplace complete the package. Deluxe continental breakfast included. Its restaurant, *Aix Cuisine du Terroir* serves gourmet regional fare; the lounge *Suite 701* (see p.172) is a prime nightspot, and the rooftop terrace (open to the public) catches the sunset over the mountain. $225.

Hôtel St-Paul 355 rue McGill ☎ 514/380-2222 or 1-866/380-2202, ⓦ www.hotelstpaul.com; Métro Square-Victoria. This most minimalist of Vieux-Montréal's new boutique hotels is located on the district's western edge in a century-old building that was originally a bank. Its ground floor has a striking, freestanding, white marble fireplace, a very trendy restaurant, *Cube*, and a lounge where the deluxe continental breakfast is served. Upstairs, white walls and linens contrast with the dark wood floors and elegantly simple furnishings of the rooms and suites. $249.

Inter-Continental 360 rue St-Antoine O ☎ 514/987-9900 or 1-800/361-3600, ⓦ www.montreal.intercontinental.com; Métro Square-Victoria. It's plush and expensive, but worth the price. The 334 rooms and 23 suites have huge floor-to-ceiling windows overlooking either Vieux-Montréal or Downtown, and each comes equipped with marble bathrooms, bathrobes and modem hook-ups, plus free newspapers. Club floor rooms have access to their own lounge with free breakfast and drinks. $229.

Marriott SpringHill Suites 445 rue St-Jean-Baptiste ☎ 514/875-4333 or 1-866/875-4333, ⓦ www.springhillmontreal.com; Métro Place d'Armes. Tucked away down a narrow side street opposite the end of rue le Royer, this four-star chain offers reasonably priced suites with king or two double beds, kitchenettes and free Internet. Consider paying the extra $30–40 or so for an executive suite, which comes with a balcony. $189.

Pierre du Calvet 405 rue Bonsecours ☎514/282-1725 or 1-866/544-1725, ⓦ www.pierreducalvet.ca; Métro Champ-de-Mars. The *Pierre du Calvet* is housed in one of Vieux-Montréal's finest buildings (see p.77), and the accommodation is as fine as the grand exterior – guestrooms include oriental rugs, gas fireplaces and original masonry walls. The ground floor has a superb wood-panelled library and sunken dining room – a trio of mounted deer heads included – and hot breakfast is served in a plant-filled greenhouse that's home to several squawking parrots. $265.

W Montréal 901 Square Victoria ☎514/395-3100 or 1-888/627-7081, ⓦ www.whotels.com/montreal; Métro Square-Victoria. The trendy, minimalist hotel chain has taken over the old Banque du Canada building, infusing it with stylish spaces and eye-popping colours, from neon in the lobby to electric blue in the 150 guestrooms and decadent suites. All the rooms have down comforters and flat-screen TVs; the suites have terraces outside their six-metre-high windows. Absurdly trendy bar, too. $299.

Quartier Latin

For the locations, refer to the map on on pp.86–87.

Auberge Le Pomerol 819 boul de Maisonneuve E ☎514/526-5511 or 1-800/361-6896, ⓦ www .aubergelepomerol.com; Métro Berri-UQAM. The difference between the grotty hotels around the corner on rue St-Hubert and this sweet 27-room hotel is striking. The decent-size rooms are done up in beiges and taupes and kitted out with contemporary streamlined furnishings (including a desk and armchair) and abstract art. Some of the bathrooms are a bit pokey, but the more expensive rooms have whirlpool baths. $155.

Castel Saint-Denis 2099 rue St-Denis ☎514/842-9719, ⓦ www.castelsaintdenis.qc.ca; Métro Berri-UQAM or Sherbrooke. A good budget hotel right on trendy rue St-Denis in the heart of the Quartier Latin. Though the rooms are drab, they're clean and include a/c, Net access and cable TV; most have private baths. $70.

Hôtel St-Denis 1254 rue St-Denis ☎514/849-4526 or 1-800/363-3364, ⓦ www.hotel-st-denis .com; Métro Berri-UQAM. One of the city's better mid-range hotels is well located on busy rue St-Denis, and has nicely furnished rooms (though some courtyard-facing ones are a bit dark), friendly service and a downstairs café-bistro that serves a reasonably priced breakfast. $110.

Le Jardin d'Antoine 2024 rue St-Denis ☎514/843-4506 or 1-800/361-4506, ⓦ www.hotel-jardin-antoine.qc.ca; Métro Berri-UQAM. One of the nicest Quartier Latin inns, though the decor in some of the 25 rooms may be a bit too frou-frou for some, with floral bedspreads and wallpaper. Amenities include a/c, cable TV, free Wi-Fi and workspace, and you can eat your hot buffet breakfast (included) on the vine-covered patio. $105 (budget room); $125.

Maison Brunet 1035 rue St-Hubert ☎514/845-6351, ⓦ www.maisonbrunet.ca; Métro Berri-UQAM or Champ-de-Mars. Don't let the ratty reception area put you off – the main part of this budget hotel occupies a 125-year-old house with a leafy terrace out back. The furniture's old rather than antique, but the rooms are clean (if a bit cramped) and come with a/c, TVs and continental buffet breakfast; the cheaper ones have shared bath. They also rent loft studios ($129) with kitchen, living and dining areas and space for six; longer-term rates are available. Pets allowed. $70 (shared bath); $80.

Manoir des Alpes 1245 rue St-André ☎514/845-9803 or 1-800/465-2929, ⓦ www .hotelmanoirdesalpes.qc.ca; Métro Berri-UQAM. A friendly, good-value hotel in a Victorian-era building with adequate rooms that have cable TV; parking and buffet breakfast included. A couple of them feature exposed brick and whirlpool tubs as well. $78 (budget room); $90.

Manoir St-Denis 2006 rue St-Denis ☎514/843-3670 or 1-888/567-7654, ⓦ www.manoir stdenis.com; Métro Berri-UQAM. Bargain-basement lodging at the Quartier Latin's busiest intersection – the small front balcony overlooks the action on the street. Many of the rooms are dark due to the rustic pine-clad walls and ceilings, but they're reasonably clean and include private bathroom, cable TV and minifridge. Continental breakfast included. $75.

VIP Loft 329 rue Ontario E ☎514/448-4848 or 1-866/563-8847, ⓦ www.viplofthotel.com;

Métro Berri-UQAM. This 19th-century townhouse has nine rooms with architectural features like brick walls and exposed beams and queen beds that vary from futon-style to wrought iron. All have a microwave and minifridge. $126.

Plateau Mont-Royal

For the locations, refer to the map on pp.94–95.

Anne ma Soeur Anne 4119 rue St-Denis ☎514/281-3187 or 1-877/281-3187, ⓦwww.annemasoeuranne.com; Métro Mont-Royal. Situated on a prime stretch of rue St-Denis, this stylish seventeen-room hotel is a great find. The sunny, yellow rooms are clean and fresh and feature kitchenettes, large bathrooms and high-speed Internet access – some have "Eurobeds" that tuck up into a wall unit for more space during the day. Suites have their own private terraces out back. $100.

Auberge de la Fontaine 1301 rue Rachel E ☎514/597-0166 or 1-800/597-0597, ⓦwww.aubergedelafontaine.com; Métro Mont-Royal. This hotel scores high on charm and location, right across from Parc Lafontaine and close to the restaurants and shops of avenue du Mont-Royal. Its modern rooms are brightly painted and have mainly queen beds and private bathrooms. Extras like private balcony and jacuzzi are also available. Breakfast, snacks from the kitchen, Wi-Fi and limited parking are included. $166–193.

Casa Bella 264 rue Sherbrooke O ☎514/849-2777 or 1-888/453-2777, ⓦwww.hotelcasa bella.com; Métro Place-des-Arts. A surprisingly good and affordable option in a three-storey limestone townhouse a few short blocks west of boulevard St-Laurent. The rooms are basic but most have private bathrooms and the price includes continental breakfast and parking. Ask for a room in the back, as they're quieter. $70 (shared bath); $95.

Château de l'Argoat 524 rue Sherbrooke E ☎514/842-2046, ⓦwww.hotel-chateau-argoat .qc.ca; Métro Sherbrooke. A fanciful, cream-coloured fortress offering 25 spacious and attractive rooms with high ceilings, quaint chandeliers and large windows. All have private bath – in the cheaper rooms, they're quite cramped, while the more expensive have whirlpool baths. Breakfast and parking included. $95.

Doubletree Plaza Hotel 505 rue Sherbrooke E ☎514/842-8581 or 1-800/561-4644, ⓦwww .doubletreeplaza.com; Métro Sherbrooke. Despite its full name (*Doubletree Plaza Hotel Montréal Centre-Ville*), this 23-storey hotel tower is actually perched on the edge of the Plateau, overlooking the Quartier Latin. The rooms are as tastefully inoffensive as you'd expect from a four-star hotel, which is fine as you'll be goggling at the views – ask for a west-facing room for Downtown or south for the river, unless you manage to nab a larger, corner room. $169.

Hôtel Godin 10 rue Sherbrooke O ☎514/843-6000 or 1-866/744-6346, ⓦwww.hotelgodin .com; Métro St-Laurent. This boutique hotel, with an angular modern wing tacked on to a restored Art Nouveau building, is tailor-made for the flashy crowd that frequents the chic restaurants a stone's throw up the Main. Rooms are fairly minimalist, but with welcome splashes of colour, and come furnished with big LCD TVs, Egyptian cotton sheets and bathrobes. The restaurant and bar still hadn't opened at press time, but are likely to become part of the "scene". $229.

△ Hôtel Godin

Hôtel de Paris 901 Sherbrooke E ☎514/522-6861 or 1-800/567-7217, ⓦwww.hotel -montreal.com; Métro Sherbrooke. Spread across three separate properties on rue

Sherbrooke near rue St-Denis, the *Hôtel de Paris'* reception occupies a mansion with a lively ambience (and thin walls) but tiny beds in the cheaply furnished rooms. Several apartments ($155) with kitchenettes are available and there are youth hostel dorms in the basement (see p.144). $79 (budget rooms); $129.

 Kutuma 3708 rue St-Denis ☎514/844-0111 or 1-866/358-8862, ⓦwww.kutuma.com; **Métro Sherbrooke**. This delightful small hotel takes its decorating cues from downstairs restaurant *Le Nil Bleu* (see p.163), with Masai sculptures and an interesting mix of fabrics. Staying in one of the nine suites is like having your own impeccably furnished Plateau apartment, with full kitchen, large living area and jacuzzi in the bathroom. Plans are already afoot to double the number of rooms. $150.

La Résidence du Voyageur 847 rue Sherbrooke E ☎514/527-9515, ⓦwww.hotelresidence voyager.com; **Métro Sherbrooke**. A good-value hotel just east of rue St-Denis on busy rue Sherbrooke. The 28 air-conditioned rooms are clean and modern, if dull, and all have private bathrooms, telephones and cable TV. Rates include continental breakfast. $70.

Bed and breakfasts

Quebecers had been slow to take to **bed–and–breakfast** accommodation, for a long time preferring to stay in similarly priced, though characterless, motels. But B&Bs have since multiplied, having proven they can provide superior accommodation for less – many of them charge around $100 a night. In addition to highly personalized service, B&Bs are also most often found on quiet, leafy side streets, rather than the main drags and usually in interesting neighbourhoods where hotel rooms are scarce. If you have an aversion to family pets (or want to bring one or more with you), be sure to ask before booking, as many B&Bs are pet-friendly.

All bed–and–breakfast accommodation is listed in the relevant chapter maps.

Angelica Blue 1213 rue Ste-Elizabeth ☎514/844-5048 or 1-800/878-5048, ⓦwww.angelicablue.com; **Métro Berri-UQAM**. An attractive B&B in a Victorian townhouse on a pretty side street near the Quartier Latin. The five rooms have lots of character – exposed brick walls, high ceilings and original antiques – and three of the rooms are en suite. Guests can use the fridge and microwave and eat in the "bistro", where breakfast is served. An additional two-bedroom apartment with full kitchen and private entrance can sleep a family of five, and there's a sister B&B, *Jade Blue*, nearby. $115 (shared bath); $125.

B&B listings and rental agencies

Use one of these agencies below to book a B&B for you.

BBCanada.com ⓦwww.bbcanada.com. The oldest and possibly best-known Canadian B&B website covers the whole country. It takes some work, however, as even though over a hundred B&Bs turn up under its Montréal listings, many are in fact hotels and there's no narrower geographical search – accommodation in distant suburbs is indistinguishable from that on the Plateau, for example.

Downtown B&B Network in Montréal ☎514/289-9749 or 1-800/267-5180, ⓦwww.bbmontreal.ca. Dependable agency that nearly always has a vacancy either Downtown or in the Quartier Latin, starting at $75 for shared bath, $110 for private.

Gîtes et Auberges du Passant ⓦwww.inns-bb.com. An excellent service of the Fédération des Agricotours listing quality-inspected B&Bs throughout Montréal and the province, should you be moving on afterwards – you must book directly with the B&Bs, however. The service's information is also published in the annual *Inns and Bed & Breakfasts in Québec* guide ($29; most recent editions only in French), which can be ordered online or by calling ☎514/252-3138. Rates for B&Bs start at $65.

Le Beau Soleil 355 rue St-Paul E ☎514/871-0299; Métro Champ-de-Mars. A friendly owner, central Vieux-Montréal location opposite the Marché Bonsecours and four pretty, high-ceilinged rooms filled with antique Canadiana are the high points of this B&B on the top floor of an 1830s building. The drawback is that there are 52 outdoor steps to climb to reach the rooms. All have shared bath. $125.

Bienvenue Bed & Breakfast 3950 av Laval ☎514/844-5897 or 1-800/227-5897, ☻www.bienvenuebb.com; Métro Sherbrooke. Montréal's original B&B (started in 1983) is in a handsome Victorian house on a pictur-esque Plateau street. The twelve rooms don't live up to the exterior, though, as they're quite plain and the whole place has the feel of a small hotel rather than a B&B – instead of a hot breakfast, they serve a "continental-plus" buffet. Half the rooms have private bathrooms; the others have in-room sinks. $85 (shared bath); $125.

🏃 Boulanger Bassin B&B 4293 rue Brébeuf ☎514/525-0854, ☻www.bbassin.com; Métro Mont-Royal. The chatty owner of this B&B on the cycle path just north of Parc Lafontaine knows the Plateau neighbour-hood well and will offer plenty of advice over extravagant breakfasts like eggs Benedict with a smoothie starter, served next to the goldfish pond in the garden. The three bright and colourful rooms are simple but nicely furnished with a few quirky touches and all have private bath. Free computer access and long-distance calls. No credit cards; minimum two-night stay. $113.

Gîte Saint-Dominique 1074 rue St-Dominique ☎514/876-3960 or 1-866/808-3960, ☻www.gitesaintdominique.com; Métro Place-d'Armes or St-Laurent. A five-room B&B on the outskirts of Chinatown with sloped ceilings, a flower-filled terrace that's wonderful in the summer, and an indoor lounge and dining room with a cozy fireplace for the rest of the year. Shared bathrooms. $50 deposit required. $99.

À la Maison de Pierre et Dominique 271 Square St-Louis ☎514/286-0307, ☻www.pierdom.qc.ca; Métro Sherbrooke. A charming navy-blue-trimmed house facing Square St-Louis with five tastefully decorated rooms and a cheerful breakfast area. There's a small sitting area with a minifridge but none of the rooms have private bathrooms. $60 (single room); $90.

🏃 Petite Auberge les Bons Matins 1393 av Argyle ☎514/931-9167 or 1-800/588-5280, ☻www.bonsmatins.com; Métro Lucien-l'Allier. Located in adjoining townhouses on a tree-lined street near the Centre Bell, this well-appointed B&B-style inn has six spacious apartments nearby ($179) and around twenty large rooms and suites. Each has picture windows and additional details like arched ceilings and polished hardwood floors; the suites have fireplaces and whirlpool baths. Good breakfasts, too. $119 (budget rooms); $139.

🏃 Aux Portes de la Nuit 3496 av Laval ☎514/848-0833, ☻www.auxportesde lanuit.com; Métro Sherbrooke. Well-situated on one of the Plateau's most attractive streets, this Victorian house has five comfortable rooms; all with private bath, though two of these are in the corridor. One of the least expensive has a balcony overlooking Carré St-Louis; the priciest has a rooftop terrace. Breakfast includes a fruit course and hot main course. $110.

University residences and hostels

Montréal has several large **universities** scattered about the city, and from about mid–May to mid–August they open their residences to visitors. These provide excellent value if you're not picky about frills, though you will get a linen service, access to a kitchenette and a common room with cable TV. The city also has a number of youth **hostels** offering primarily dormitory–style accommoda-tion, most of which should be booked far in advance come summer.

All university residences and hostels are listed in the relevant chapter maps.

🏃 Auberge Alternative du Vieux-Montréal 358 rue St-Pierre ☎514/282-8069, ☻www.auberge-alternative.qc.ca; Métro Square-Victoria. Montréal's finest hostel is located in a refurbished 1875 Vieux-Montréal warehouse. The common room, with its exposed masonry wall and modern cooking facilities, is a great place to lounge, and the dormitories, with arched windows and wood floors, sleep from six to twenty on bunk beds. Singles and doubles also available, which include a free help-yourself breakfast (costs $4 extra if staying in a dorm). Rates include Internet access and free coffee, and coin-laundry facilities are available. $20/dorm, $55/rooms.

Auberge Chez Jean 4136 av Henri-Julien ☎514/843-8279, ⓦwww.aubergechezjean.com; **Métro Mont-Royal.** You'll either love or hate this very unofficial (and concurrently not terribly rules-oriented) youth hostel located dead-central in the Plateau. Guests bunk down all over the common rooms on its three floors, making it a great place to make new friends quickly, but forget about privacy unless you take one of the closed rooms or sleep in the van out back. Each floor has its own kitchen and there are plenty of bathrooms. The friendly, knowledgeable staff will give suggestions on where to go out and offer advice about onward travel. $20 per person.

Auberge de Jeunesse Internationale de Montréal 1030 rue Mackay ☎514/843-3317 or 1-866/843-3317, ⓦwww.hostellingmontreal.com; **Métro Lucien-l'Allier.** A well-equipped Downtown hostel with over 200 beds. Dorms sleep a maximum of ten; single and double rooms, and family quarters are also available. The lounge has a pool table, cable TV and free Wi-Fi, and reservations are advised between June and September. Foreign guests must be members of Hostelling International – if not, a day membership costs $4. $25.75/dorm, $65/rooms (with membership card); $30/dorm, $75/rooms (Canadian nonmembers).

Auberge de Paris 901 Sherbrooke E ☎514/522-6861 or 1-800/567-7217, ⓦwww.hotel-montreal.com/auberge; **Métro Sherbrooke.** The grim basements of the *Hôtel de Paris'* three properties (see p.141) on the edge of the Plateau district have dark and tiny bunk rooms with wobbly locks and sleep four to fourteen. Guests have access to cooking facilities, a café, garden and TV room. $20/dorm, $3/sheets (if needed).

Gîte Plateau Mont-Royal 185 rue Sherbrooke E ☎514/284-1276 or 1-877/350-4483, ⓦwww.hostelmontreal.com; **Métro Sherbrooke.** Bright six- to eight-bed dorms and private rooms (with shared bath), an extremely chill common room to hang out in and proximity to Plateau and Quartier Latin nightlife make this one of the city's best backpacker options. Price includes

sheets and a self-serve breakfast; Internet and laundry are extra. The main drawback is that the kitchen is only open 5–8pm. In summer, they have extra dorms and private rooms in a second house opposite Parc Lafontaine at 1250 rue Sherbrooke E (☎514/522-3910).$25/dorms,$55–80/rooms.

Hôtel Y des Femmes (YWCA) 1355 boul René-Lévesque O ☎514/866-9942, ⓦwww.ydesfemmesmtl.org; **Métro Lucien-l'Allier or Guy-Concordia.** Rooms sleep up to four and are available for men and women in this rather pricey Downtown YWCA, but only women have access to the pool and gym facilities. Other extras include kitchen and laundry facilities and Internet access. Rooms with communal bath have single beds; those with private bath have one or two double beds. $60 (shared bath) or $75 (private) per single, $70–85/double, $80–95/triple, $90–105/quad.

La Maison du Prêt d'Honneur 1 boul René-Lévesque E ☎514/982-3420 ext 5501, ⓦwww.mph.qc.ca; **Métro Place-d'Armes or St-Laurent.** Located on the edge of Chinatown, this residence of the Cégep du Vieux-Montréal junior college offers studios with one or two single beds as well as a few two-bedroom apartments. All have a kitchenette, private bath, telephone and Internet access, plus there's a café, laundry room and fifth-floor terrace. Mid-May to mid-Aug; $65–75/studio, $130/apartment; an extra cot costs $10.

McGill University New Residence Hall 3625 av du Parc ☎514/398-3471, ⓦwww.mcgill.ca/nrh; **bus #80, #129 or #535.** If this residence seems more like a hotel (and is priced that way), that's because this 422-room tower held that role until recently. Half way between McGill campus and the Main, it's also handy for treks to the mountain. The comfortable rooms have a fridge, free Internet hook-ups and private bath; rates include continental breakfast. Mid-May to mid-Aug only; $110.

McGill University Residences 3935 rue University ☎514/398-5200 or 398-6367, ⓦwww.mcgill.ca/residences/summer; **Métro McGill.** Up to 900 single rooms with shared kitchenettes, bathrooms and lounge areas are split between Royal Victoria College (near Downtown at 3425 rue University) and the four residence buildings on the mountain's slope. Sheets and towels are provided, as is breakfast (except at RVC) and free Internet access. Very popular among visiting Anglophones and, consequently, often full. Mid-May to mid-Aug only; $45–49.

Les Résidences Universitaires UQAM 303 boul René-Lévesque E ☎514/987-6669, ⓦwww.residences-uqam.qc.ca; Métro Berri-UQAM. Over a hundred clean and simply furnished studios with a double bed, kitchenette (or full kitchen) and private bath, as well as apartments with two, three or eight bedrooms (with a mix of single and double beds) in this Quartier Latin student residence. It's the same deal at their new building, located practically on top of Place des Arts at 2100 rue St-Urbain (☎514/987-7747). Price includes linen service; there's also a café and laundry facilities. Mid-May to mid-Aug; $60.50/studio, $85/studio with kitchen, $42-60.50/apartment (per room).

Vacances Canada 5155 av de Gaspé ☎514/270-4459, ⓦwww.vacancescanadamd.montrealplus .ca; Métro Laurier. Up to 250 beds are available all year at this former college residence, with up to six beds per room. The northern Plateau/Mile End location makes it very popular, and it's frequently booked-up by Francophone school groups. $15.50/dorm, $22.50/double, $39.50/single. They also offer basic studio apartments in the Plateau area for $425/month.

Cafés and restaurants

O ne of the greatest pleasures of any visit to Montréal is **eating** out; the city is easily the number three foodie destination in North America, after New York and San Francisco. On top of the expected authentic **French cuisine**, there's a huge selection of **international foods** in which to indulge. Where the city truly excels is between the extremes of speedy lunchtime fare and formal dining extravaganzas – the bewildering array of moderately priced restaurants in Montréal serve up meals of a quality you'd be hard-pressed to find elsewhere at these prices. Another bonus is that they're often clustered close together, making it easy to just walk along and see what strikes your fancy.

Montréal's European flavour is nowhere more evident than in its small **cafés**, where you can usually sit and read or talk undisturbed for hours while sipping on a drink. The majority of the cafés listed below also dish out delicious **snacks** such as *croque monsieur* and panini, and some go as far as serving light bistro fare. Montrealers tend to grab a quick fry-up **breakfast** or a croissant or muffin with their coffee on weekday mornings, but weekend **brunch** is an altogether different affair (see box, p.153).

In addition to cafés, you can seek out one of the city's many **diners** for deli-style meals, or try healthier food like soups, salads and sandwiches in smaller spots spread around the city. **Lunches** also offer the chance to try cheaper two- or three-course *spécial du midi* (lunch special) menus at the city's pricier restaurants, and a number of bars serve up grub at lunch or in the early evening (see Chapter 11, "Bars and lounges"). If quick and cheap matters more than atmosphere, there are plenty of **food courts** in the basements of Downtown's malls and loads of noodle bars towards the west end. On hot and humid days, nothing beats **ice cream** – see box, p.221, for our roundup of Montréal's best.

Montréal **restaurants** start filling up for **dinner** between 7 and 8pm and serve until around 10 or 11pm. Most offer a three-course *table d'hôte*, which works out to be cheaper than ordering an individual starter, main and dessert à la carte, and runs to about $15–25 at moderately priced restaurants, $25–40 at all but the most expensive places, not including drinks, tax or tip. Taxes come to 14 percent, and a 15 percent tip is standard (but don't be hasty, the tip is occasionally included on the bill as a service charge). While it's easy to splurge on an expensive French restaurant in Montréal, the multitude of less formal ethnic spots and local bistros can be just as satisfying and far more memorable, not to mention a good deal cheaper. Note that in French, an appetizer is called an *entrée*, while the main course is a *plat principal*. See the glossary (p.299) for more words likely to be on the menu.

If you want to grab a **late-night** bite, there are numerous places scattered along rue Ste-Catherine and in the Plateau (see box, p.154). Less conveniently, many smaller restaurants close Sunday and/or Monday, and places that cater to the business lunch crowd may not be open until dinnertime on the weekends; call ahead to avoid disappointment. It's a good idea to reserve in advance, but there are enough choices on rue St-Denis, rue Prince-Arthur, avenue Duluth, boulevard St-Laurent and avenue Laurier to stroll around and see what grabs you – although for smaller bistros, it's nonetheless a good idea to reserve, especially at weekends. Below, we've divided our listings up by neighbourhood (see box, p.150, for an overview), separated into spots that are best for a lighter meal during the day and those where you can settle down for a drawn-out evening dinner. You'll also find a complete list of restaurants cross-referenced by cuisine – see box, p.148–149.

All cafés and restaurants are listed in the relevant chapter maps throughout the Guide.

Downtown

Cafés and light meals

Basha 930 rue Ste-Catherine O ☎ 514/866-4272; Métro Peel. Mosaic floors and subdued lighting help dispel the cafeteria feel of this cheap but good second-floor Lebanese spot overlooking rue Ste-Catherine. Fill up on falafel, spit-roasted *shish taouk* (chicken) or lamb *shawarma* for around $3.50 wrapped in a pita, or $6–8 with rice, salad and hoummos. Open Sun–Thurs 11am–midnight, Fri & Sat until 1am (kitchen closes one hour prior to closing).

Ben's Delicatessen 990 boul de Maisonneuve O ☎ 514/844-1000; Métro Peel. Lithuanian Ben Kravitz opened his deli in 1908 and it's still run by his grandsons. Their tasty smoked-meat sandwiches continue to draw people in till the wee hours, and the gaudy 1930s interior and yellowing celebrity photos on the wall of this Montréal institution attest to an earlier, more prosperous time. Sun–Wed 7.30am–2am, Thurs 7.30am–3am, Fri & Sat 7.30am–4am; closes two hours earlier in winter.

△ Ben's Delicatessen

Brûlerie St-Denis Maison Alcan, 1188 rue Sherbrooke ☎ 514/985-9159; Métro Peel. If it's

sunny out, forgo the large, red-trimmed café interior and nab a seat on the glorious terrace along the garden path linking rues Drummond and Stanley. This is the nicest location of a local chain known for its terrific coffee and as a good spot for a sandwich (most are $7–8) and a pastry, if you've got room. Mon–Fri 7am–7pm. There are a number of Plateau locations, and one handy for Oratory explorations at 5252 chemin de la Côte-des-Neiges (☎ 514/731-9158).

Café Imagination 330 rue Sherbrooke O ☎ 514/985-5888; Métro Place-des-Arts. Just up the hill from Place des Arts, this sunny, modern café is divided into a lounge, to consume coffee and cakes along with newspapers and free Internet, and a bistro more amenable to the array of inventive sandwiches – try La Santé, with veggie paté, Swiss cheese, avocado and homemade mayo – salads, couscous and quiches.

Café Presto 1244 rue Stanley ☎ 514/879-5877; Métro Peel. One of the best bargains Downtown, this small, homey Italian restaurant has $3.95 specials, so its tables for two understandably fill up fast with office workers at lunch. The changing menu features simple but filling dishes like chicken cacciatore, penne *arrabbiata* and linguini with Italian sausage – and the price is the same in the less busy evenings. Open Mon–Sat 11:30am–2:30pm & 4:30–9pm, closed Sun. No credit cards.

Café République 93 rue Ste-Catherine O ☎ 514/840-0000; Métro Place-des-Arts. This relaxed café is close to Place des Arts and serves up a fine cup of coffee to go with breakfast (until 11.30am, 3pm Sat), light lunches – burgers, filled pitas and salads – and decadent cakes. The bistro/bar branch at 1429 rue Crescent (☎ 514/845-5999) has a lounge feel with a terrace overlooking the action, while the one facing Square Dorchester at 1200 rue Peel (T 514/875-1200) has a classy atmosphere with velvety red banquettes, swag lampshades and a correspondingly pricier menu.

Café Tramezzini 2125 rue de la Montagne T 514/842-5522; Métro Peel. This cool and quiet basement café feels bigger than it is thanks to a wall of mirrors reflecting the stone walls. Try the namesake *tramezzini* – small sandwiches on white bread with the crusts cut off for $4 – or panini filled with prosciutto, shaved parmesan and arugula. Great coffee, too. Closed Sun.

Ciné-Express 1926 rue Ste-Catherine O T 514/939-2463; Métro Guy-Concordia. A mix of students and Downtowners come for the cheap all-day breakfasts (served 8am–11pm, until 3pm weekends) and $7 specials (two bucks more after 5pm) like the Philly steak sandwiches, burgers and quesadillas. It's a long, casual space broken up by old sofas and tables for playing chess. The small terrace out front is a good spot to share a $10 pitcher of beer. 24hr.

CAFÉS AND RESTAURANTS | Downtown

Kafeïn 1429 rue Bishop ⊤514/904-6969; Métro Guy-Concordia. Exposed brick walls, collaged table tops and local artwork lend a cosy feel to this studenty café, which serves cakes and snacks, like panini and mini pizzas. Head to the old sofas in the candle-lit lounge downstairs to try a hookah pipe ($10) and chill to DJs spinning anything from new wave to house. Live jazz on Mondays.

Montréal Pool Room 1200 boul St-Laurent; Métro St-Laurent. A Montréal institution: nothing much but a steel counter facing the grill where steamies (hot dogs) loaded with coleslaw have been the order of the day since 1912. Two dogs, fries and a Coke will set you back $3.99. Open 9am–3am (until 4am Thurs–Sat).

Prêt à Manger 1809 rue Ste-Catherine O ⊤514/931-8889; Métro Guy-Concordia. One of the best of the noodle bars clustered at this end of Downtown, this bright, canteen-style spot serves Cantonese, Szechuan and Thai dishes starting at $6. Open until midnight (1am Fri & Sat).

 Reuben's Deli 1116 rue Ste-Catherine O ⊤514/866-1029, ⓦ www.reubensdeli.com;

⑩

CAFÉS AND RESTAURANTS | Downtown

Many of the city's priciest dining places are **Downtown**, where gastronomic French restaurants and higher-end ethnic eateries are tucked away on the side streets around rue Ste-Catherine. Here, you'll also find plenty of cheaper lunch spots and a smattering of fast-food joints. Over in **Chinatown**, rue de la Gauchetière is thronged with people seeking out not only Cantonese and Szechuan dishes, but also cheap and filling Vietnamese food. There are an increasing number of good options in **Vieux-Montréal**, with innovative bistros and top-notch hotel restaurants drawing locals who had until recently steered clear of the area and its overpriced tourist joints that don't offer much in the way of imaginative cuisine. The **Quartier Latin**'s main appeal lies in its terrace-fronted cafés – the restaurants tend to be more hit-or-miss. In the neighbouring **Village**, the gay contingent filling up before heading to the bars contributes a lively buzz to many establishments, but media types who work in the area also stick around for the casual, quality restaurants serving up a variety of international cuisines.

The best place to eat out is on the **Plateau**, where stylish restaurants serve up innovative cuisine on rue St-Denis and boulevard St-Laurent just above Sherbrooke and local bistros are dotted throughout the district. Greek-style tavernas serving brochettes (souvlaki) and a mix of other ethnic eateries vie for the tourist trade on **rue Prince-Arthur**. Better, though, to head north a few blocks to **avenue Duluth**, where more authentic cuisine from Portugal, Italy, Afghanistan and even the tiny Indian Ocean island of Réunion can be found. The majority of restaurants on both these streets aren't licensed to sell liquor – instead they invite you to *apportez votre vin* (bring your own wine), a practice quite common in Montréal; see p.206 for recommendations on where to pick up a bottle. For Greek food that's more authentic than that served at many of the tavernas mentioned above, head up to **Mile End**, where you'll also find the best bagel bakeries. Adjacent **Outremont** is full of cafés, French bistros and slightly pricier, but still good-value, ethnic joints on and around avenue Laurier, while to the north, **Little Italy** is *the* place for pizzerias, trattorias and fancier Italian cuisine.

Métro McGill or Peel. An old-school deli glammed up in black and mahogany tones that, despite management's efforts to the contrary, continues to draw diners for the wealth of smoked meats served up in a frantic atmosphere. A favourite with local business types, and thus packed at lunchtime. If you're on a budget, head to the second location a few blocks east at no. 888 (☎514/861-1255); as it's in a basement (warmed by stained-glass panels) and has a different owner, the food's often a buck or two cheaper. Main location open from 6.30am (8am weekends) until midnight (1.30am Thurs–Sat).

Sushi Shop 915 boul de Maisonneuve O ☎514/847-1188, ⓦ www.sushishop.com; Métro **Peel.** Part of a sleek chain with large back-lit images of the sushi, maki and sashimi that you can take away for a picnic on the nearby McGill campus or munch on a park bench. Boxed up and ready to go starting at $5, but it's worth the wait for them to roll you up something fresh. Closed Sun. The branch

at 1200 av McGill College is open daily and has a few window counter seats.

Restaurants

3 Amigos 1657 rue Ste-Catherine O ☎514/939-3329; Métro Guy-Concordia. The garish decor on the exterior here – Christmas lights, and red, yellow and green sombreros – extends inside and hints at the festive studenty atmosphere, where 28-ounce margaritas and piña coladas ($7) are as much of a draw as Tex-Mex staples like tacos, fajitas, *chimichangas*, and more traditional chicken in *mole* sauce. Open until midnight (1am weekends).

Bar-B-Barn 1201 rue Guy ☎514/931-3811, ⓦ www.barbbarn.ca; Métro Guy-Concordia. A fun, lively and loud restaurant on two floors serving tasty ribs ($17.50 for a half dozen) and chicken ($13.50 for half a bird) in a faux Western setting. The hundreds of business cards stuck in the log rafters attest to its popularity with the local business world, and it's always packed to the hilt.

Bâton Rouge 180 rue Ste-Catherine O
ⓣ 514/282-7444, Ⓦ www.batonrouge
restaurants.com; **Métro Place-des-Arts.** The
main draw here is the size (as opposed to
the unspectacular preparation) of their
portions of ribs – $22 for a pound of them –
burgers, fries and other American, Cajun-
tinged standards. Best enjoyed on the
terrace facing Place des Arts, as inside is a
bit claustrophobic, with low, dark-wood
ceilings over the booths and large tables
for groups.

Boccacinos 1251 av McGill College ⓣ 514/861-
5742, Ⓦ www.boccacinos.com; **Métro McGill.** A
decent spot for a bite Downtown, with loads
of tables on two floors and a good,
crowded buzz – the place is heaving at
lunchtime, spilling onto the pavement
terrace. The range of breakfasts starts at $4
and is served until 3pm or thereabouts;
otherwise choose from burgers, pasta and
salads or heftier dishes like steak and
Atlantic salmon.

Le Café des Beaux-Arts 1384 rue Sherbrooke O
ⓣ 514/843-3233; **Métro Peel or Guy-Concordia.**
Second-floor lunch spot in the Musée des
Beaux-Arts where the food – French bistro
with a regional Québécois touch – and table
service are equally good. There's a wide
range of wines by the glass and stand-out
meals on the two-course *table d'hôte*
($18–22) include lamb shank or portobello
mushroom risotto, in season. Dinner is
only available on Wednesday evenings.
Closed Mon.

Le Café du Nouveau-Monde 84 rue Ste-
Catherine O ⓣ 514/866-8669, Ⓦ www.tnm
.qc.ca; **Métro Place-des-Arts.** Located in the
Théâtre du Nouveau-Monde's lobby, this is a
place to see and be seen in, as much as to
sample the high-quality bistro fare. The food
is a bit richer in the upstairs half, where you
can dine on the likes of duck *confit*, salmon
tartare and grilled steak. There's always a
good buzz before showtime in the theatre
(see p.196), and if it's sunny out the terrace
is packed. Lunch has cheaper $12 options
like a lamb burger or chicken spinach salad.
Closed Sun; open until midnight other nights
(except Mon until 9pm).

Les Chenêts 2075 rue Bishop ⓣ 514/844-1842,
Ⓦ www.leschenets.com; **Métro Peel or Guy-
Concordia.** Superior French cuisine served up
in a warm candle-lit room adorned with
copper cookware. Highlights include wine-
soaked escargots and good game dishes,

△ Copper cookware at Les Chenêts

such as pheasant breast smothered in wild
mushrooms (both part of the four-course, $45
table d'hôte); lunch specials run from $16 to
$32. With an extensive wine list, referred to
by staff as "the bible", selecting a vintage to
accompany your meal won't be easy; there
are also some 800 varieties of cognac.

Chez Éric 1181 av Union ⓣ 514/866-1303;
Métro McGill. The rattan chairs yell bistro,
and the two-course lunch menu ($15)
delivers here, with seared *boudin noir* (black
pudding), calf's liver or tamer dishes like
poached salmon. Evening selections are
more classically French – think duck *confit*,
rack of lamb and Dover sole – and the
prices jump accordingly, though the wine list
remains reasonable. Closed Sun.

Ferreira Café Trattoria 1446 rue Peel
ⓣ 514/848-0988, Ⓦ www.ferreiracafe.com;
Métro Peel. Portuguese *azulejos* (glazed tiles)
lining the walls hint at the authenticity of the
delicious cooking here, notably fish dishes
like the grilled sardines coated in sea salt.
Mains cost $30–40 but you can save a bit
by dropping in for the two-course weekday
lunchtime special ($30–35) served up in a
lively atmosphere. Comprehensive port and
wine selection. Closed Sun; no lunch Sat.

Garçon! 1112 rue Sherbrooke O ⓣ 514/843-
4000, Ⓦ www.restaurantgarcon.com; **Métro
Peel.** The smartly furnished pavement
terrace here hints at an equally sleek interior
of leather seats and white tablecloths
waiting to receive classic French gastronomic dishes. The chef's daily inspirations
will likely include pan-seared scallops or
boudin noir (blood pudding) to start,
followed by market-fresh fish, Lac Brome
duck or veal tenderloin. Sunday brunches
are substantial two-course affairs ($14–18).

Il Cortile Passage du Musée, 1442 rue Sherbrooke O ☎514/843-8230; Métro Guy-Concordia. The name translates as "the courtyard", and that's one of this classic Italian restaurant's most winning features – it spreads into a red-brick mews decked with blooming hanging baskets. The elegant interior is also appealing, and in either space you can get carried away with the *crespella al ripieno* (crepes stuffed with ricotta and spinach) followed by scampi risotto, tagliolini with porcini mushrooms or the rich veal scaloppine. *Table d'hôte* ranges from $22–40 ($17–35 at lunch).

Katsura 2170 rue de la Montagne ☎514/849-1172; Métro Peel. Large and popular Downtown Japanese restaurant where kimono-clad servers bring sushi, sashimi and chicken or salmon teriyaki to your table (à la carte or as part of a $35 or $45 set meal). Traditional Japanese paintings add a subtle touch to the already understated decor. Weekday lunches (11.30am–3pm) include similar, though cheaper, dishes as well as Bento boxes (sushi, maki and tempura) for $10–20. No lunch on the weekend.

Le Parchemin 1333 rue University ☎514/844-1619, ⓦ www.leparchemin.com; Métro McGill. Classic French dishes with *nouvelle* touches like seared tuna or tender chicken in a honey-almond sauce are served in this light-filled former presbytery built in 1876. It's the same price for the *table d'hôte* ($18–30) at lunch but those on a budget can pick a dish from the bistro menu and a glass of wine for $13, or indulge in the four-course business lunch ($23). No lunch Sat; closed Sun.

Queue de Cheval 1221 boul René-Lévesque O ☎514/390-0090, ⓦ www.queuedecheval.com; Métro Lucien-l'Allier or Peel. Just north of the Centre Bell, this high-end steakhouse is one of the best in the city. Specials such as the arctic char – flown in fresh – cost a small fortune, but the main draw is the beef, like the juicy porterhouse steak, which they dry-age in house and also offer as retail. With two waiters to a table, service is attentive to say the least. There's also a lounge and covered terrace.

La Rotonde 185 rue Ste-Catherine O ☎514/847-6900; Métro Place-des-Arts. It can be a bit noisy here – wrapped as it is around the atrium of the Musée d'Art Contemporain – but the food is well worth it. Provençal and southern French dishes

like the roasted duck breast in a pear and honey sauce draw a busy evening crowd. Cheaper at lunch ($23 rather than $33 *table d'hôte*) when there's a similar, though toned-down, menu (*magret de canard* rather than *confit de canard* and *bavette* instead of filet mignon, for instance). Open evenings when there's a performance on at Place des Arts for pre-show sittings only.

Takara Cours Mont-Royal, 1455 rue Peel ☎514/849-9796; Métro Peel. Tucked away on the fourth level of the Cours Mont-Royal mall (there's a direct escalator from the rue Metcalfe entrance), this somewhat formal Japanese restaurant serves reasonably priced and nicely presented sushi and maki. If fish doesn't appeal, go for the sukiyaki – fat noodles and slices of beef simmering in a black cauldron. Kick your shoes off and sit around one of the lowered tables to make the most of the evening. No lunch Sat or Sun.

Zen Hôtel Omni, 1050 rue Sherbrooke O ☎514/499-0801; Métro Peel. Spicy Szechuan dishes are the order of the day in this elegantly minimalist basement restaurant, with specialities like crispy duck, beef with ginger and green onion and a particularly good General Tao chicken. Your best bet, though, is the "Zen experience" – for $32 you choose as many dishes as you want but the more you order, the smaller the portion served. The three-course lunch costs $17–25; no lunch Sat.

Chinatown

Cafés and light meals

Idée Magique 30 rue de la Gauchetière O ☎514/868-0657; Métro Place-d'Armes. Although they serve cheap Chinese food, the main draw at this café is the "bubble tea". You start with cream tea, choose one of a dozen zippy flavours (such as mango, sesame or even egg yolk) and then jellies to put on top – it's the tapioca beads that give the tea its nickname, but you can try coconut berries or green tea crystals, too. Open until midnight, 2am Fri & Sat.

Pho Bang New York 1001 boul St-Laurent ☎514/954-2032; Métro Place-d'Armes. This bright, canteen-style Vietamese restaurant is typically crowded as they don't cheat on the Tonkinoise fixings, so expect plenty of coriander, basil and mint with your noodles and beef, chicken or veg. The iced coffee, laced with condensed milk, is serious rocket fuel. If this place is full, head across the street to the similar *Pho Bac 97* at no.1016 (T 514/393-8116). Neither accepts credit cards.

Restaurants

Hong Kong 1023 boul St-Laurent T 514/861-0251; Métro Place-d'Armes. Despite the army of roasting ducks in the window, this place is best known for its seafood – try the Cantonese-style lobster, flavoured with ginger, garlic and soy sauce. The vast menu at this Chinese restaurant is one reason it's packed with Chinese-Canadians.

Jardin de Jade 67 rue de la Gauchetière O T 514/866-3127; Métro Place-d'Armes. It's a bit of a factory, but the all-you-can-eat buffet is a bargain at $8.45 for lunch, $12 for dinner ($13.30 Fri–Sun) and $10.25 for a "late dinner" (9–11pm). The wide selection gives you a chance to try a variety of Cantonese and Szechuan dishes, from dumplings to spicy stir-fried beef.

Lotté-Furama 1115 rue Clark T 514/393-3838; Métro Place-d'Armes. Two large banquet halls are crowded with Chinese-Canadian families choosing dim sum dishes from the passing trolleys (9am–3pm). The dumplings, like shrimp and coriander in a translucent rice wrapper, are wonderful. In the evenings, wedding parties take over the upper floor but you can still tuck into Peking duck ($28) and seafood ($14–18) at the large round tables on the chandelier-lit main floor.

La Maison VIP 1077 rue Clark T 514/861-1943; Métro Place-d'Armes. Just a medium-sized room with large tables, but this place draws crowds for its cheap prices (General Tao chicken for $10, salt-and-pepper squid $9, Cantonese chow mein $7), especially when the bars close as it's open until 4am daily.

Ruby Rouge 1008 rue Clark T 514/390-8828; Métro Place-d'Armes. Montréal's vast temple to dim sum is right in the heart of Chinatown. The menu is very well priced and you'll have to fight back the urge to grab spring rolls and fried seafood dumplings every time they wheel the trolley by. There are often long queues for dim sum (trolley service 9am–2.30pm) so get there early. If you go in the evening, opt for the Peking duck, Chinese fondue (winter only) or fresh lobster and crab, served Cantonese or Szechuan style.

Vieux-Montréal

In addition to the places below, gourmets may want to check out the increasing number of high quality (and rather pricey) hotel restaurants in the old town, including *Aix* at *Hôtel Place d'Armes*, *Verses* at *Hôtel Nelligan* and *Cube* at *Hôtel St-Paul* (see pp.138–139). At the other end of the scale, note that many of the cafés and lunch places here close mid-afternoon.

Brunch

In Montréal, weekend **brunch** is a long and drawn-out affair. The meal is generally used as an antidote to the previous night's partying, and most places serve until mid-afternoon – go early (before 11am) to avoid the queues. The Plateau – and Mile End's avenue Laurier in particular – has great spots to linger lazily over crepes, *pain doré* (French toast), eggs Benedict or more lunch-like dishes. For a completely different brunch experience, head to Chinatown and get stuffed on dim sum at *Lotté-Furama* (see p.153) or *Ruby Rouge* (see p.153).

Cafés and light meals

Bio Train 410 rue St-Jacques O ☎514/842-9184; Métro Square-Victoria. A counter-service health-food restaurant with tasty soups and hearty sandwiches. The muffins here – especially the tangy cranberry ones – make great snacks. Mon–Fri 6.30am–3pm.

Café du Château Château Ramezay, 280 rue Notre-Dame E ☎514/861-9948; Métro Champ-de-Mars. Enjoy a warm-weather lunch on this stone-walled château's terrace overlooking the New France–style gardens. The short menu of carpaccio, panini, salads and the like are from *Claude Postel* (see below), though the prices are higher here (mains $10–15) than at *Postel*. You'll need to reserve at peak lunch hours. Mon–Fri 10am–3pm, summer only.

Le Cartet 106 rue McGill ☎514/871-8887; Métro Square-Victoria. If the weather's decent, head here for healthy sandwiches and boxed lunches to go – it's not far from the Vieux-Port's many green spaces. Otherwise, there's plenty of space to eat in, with a number of large, family-sized tables.

Claude Postel 75 rue Notre-Dame O ☎514/844-8750, 🌐www.claudepostel.com; Métro Place-d'Armes. A real find, this classy high-ceilinged café with honey-coloured walls sells panini and sandwiches, with fillings that include *terrine de campagne* and *mousse de foie*, at decent prices. For afters, there are decadent chocolates, elegant little cakes for around $3 and mini crème brûlées for $2.20, as well as homemade ice cream.

Cluny 257 rue Prince ☎514/866-1213, 🌐www.cluny.info; Métro Square-Victoria. A trendy spot that shares digs with an art gallery in the Cité Multimédia just west of Vieux-Montréal. Best for lunch, when you can take your artfully crafted baguette sandwich or salad to one of the long wooden tables and listen in on your neighbours discussing the latest high-tech fads. Mon–Fri 8am–5pm (Thurs until 10pm).

Eggspectation 201 rue St-Jacques O ☎514/282-0119, 🌐www.eggspectation.ca; Métro Place-d'Armes. 198 av Laurier O ☎514/278-6411; Métro Laurier or bus #80. 1313 boul de Maisonneuve O ☎514/842-3447; Métro Peel or Guy-Concordia. A variety of antique objects are scattered about the Vieux-Montréal, Downtown and Mile End branches of this great local chain that's packed on weekends. Look for the cheaper "Classics" buried in the menu between the scrumptious crepes, french toast, eggs Florentine and the like. Daily 6am–5pm (Laurier branch Mon–Fri 6am–3pm, Sat & Sun 7am–4pm).

Java U 191 rue St-Paul O ☎514/849-8881; Métro Place-d'Armes. The name of this cheap, chic café is misleading – it's part of a chain that started up for the student crowd Downtown. At this particular location, the pressed-tin ceiling and ornate columns contrast with a hip design of soft modular seating. The menu offers the likes of burgers and salmon steak until 11pm, and cheaper panini and salads at lunchtime, as well as a couple of dozen kinds of martinis for when it becomes more of a lounge in the evening with DJs until 3am.

Olive et Gourmando 351 rue St-Paul O ☎514/350-1083, 🌐www.oliveetgourmando.com; Métro Square-Victoria. Delectable bakery that serves up salads and gourmet hot and cold sandwiches ($8–9) and homemade iced tea throughout the day. The menu changes regularly, but it often features items like smoked trout or toasted focaccia with goat's cheese. No credit cards. Open Tues–Sat 8am–6pm.

Scola Pasta 260 rue Notre-Dame O ☎514/842-2232, 🌐www.scolapasta.com; Métro Place-d'Armes. Warm colours can't quite dispel the cafeteria feel of this place, but it's still a good spot for a quick, cheap lunch with $5 sausage sandwiches. The main draws, though, are the build-your-own pastas and pizzas ($9–10).

Titanic 445 rue St-Pierre ☎514/849-0894, 🌐www.titanic-mtl.ca; Métro Square-Victoria. Businesspeople and tourists alike fill the large communal tables crammed into this small Italian-style deli serving antipasti, sandwiches and healthy-sized salads. Mon–Fri 7am–4.30pm. No credit cards.

Restaurants

Bonaparte 443 rue St-François-Xavier ☎514/844-4368, 🌐www.bonaparte.ca; Métro Place-d'Armes. This French restaurant's rich-red carpeting and dark-panelled wainscotting provide a perfect backdrop to dishes, like rack of lamb in port wine ($34) or lobster stew with a vanilla sauce ($32.50), though the three-course *table d'hôte* is cheaper at $25–29. If you're feeling indulgent try the six-course tasting menu ($62). No lunch on weekends.

Boris Bistro 495 rue McGill ☎514/848-9575, ⊛www.borisbistro.com; Métro Square-Victoria. Although it serves good bistro fare like duck *confit*, salmon and beef tartares and braised rabbit for around $17, the main draw here is the phenomenal tree-shaded terrace, separated from the street by the free-standing facade of an old limestone building.

Casa de Matéo 438 rue St-François-Xavier ☎514/286-9589, ⊛www.casademateo.com; Métro Place-d'Armes. A warm atmosphere pervades this busy, reasonably priced restaurant awash in terracotta and Mexican costumes. Authentic dishes from Puebla, Oaxaca and Veracruz include guacamole prepared at the table and a ceviche of white fish marinated in lime juice, followed by sizzling fajita fixings to wrap in homemade flour tortillas, duck or chicken in *mole* sauce and red snapper fried in garlic.

Chez L'Épicier 311 rue St-Paul E ☎514/878-2232, ⊛www.chezlepicier .com; Métro Champ-de-Mars. French- and Asian-influenced *cuisine de terroir* and updated comfort food – the shepherd's pie is made with snails, the quail is glazed with *mole* sauce – in a bright eighteenth-century building. There's a $75 tasting menu if you want to explore a range of flavours, and posh groceries are also on sale in the attached boutique. Lunch is a more reasonable $15–18 for two courses and there's a good selection of wines by the glass from $8. No lunch at weekends. The chef-owner opened *Version Laurent Godbout* a couple of doors down at no. 295 (☎514/871-9135, ⊛www.version -restaurant.com) as a further culinary playground for Mediterranean flavours (with a stylish garden terrace).

Le Club Chasse et Pêche 423 rue St-Claude ☎514/861-1112, ⊛www .leclubchasseetpeche.com; Métro Champ-de-Mars. One of the most talked about openings of the last couple of years, which is handy as there's no sign out front. The dark, textured earth tones and deep leather seats make it feel like dining at a members' club, and a posh one at that, with starters around $16 and mains $30. The gastro-nomic *cuisine du terroir* includes "new school surf and turf" (pan-seared sweet-breads and lobster *confit* in beurre blanc), Kobe beef tartare, roasted scallops, guinea fowl, roasted sirloin of bison and braised *kurobuta* (Japanese black pig) risotto, depending on the season. Reserve at least a week ahead. Closed Sun & Mon; no lunch Sat.

Da Emma 777 rue de la Commune O ☎514/392-1568; Métro Square-Victoria. Fantastic Italian cooking served up in a stylishly renovated basement in one of Montréal's oldest buildings. Mains run $16–23 for pasta and $18–45 for fish and meat dishes; standouts include fettucine *al funghi porcini* and succulent *abbachio* or *maialino al forno* (huge chunks of lamb or suckling pig). Save room, if you can, for the homemade sorbets and addictive tiramisu. Closed Sun; no lunch Sat.

Garde Manger 408 rue St-François-Xavier ☎514/678-5044; Métro Place-d'Armes. Opened in 2006, this small place was full before they even had their grand opening, and it's easy to see why: an enthusiastic young chef who thinks seafood should be neither precious (a rock music soundtrack) nor overly pricey (an astounding wooden trough overflowing with crab legs, whelks and other seafood works out to $35 a head; PEI mussels are $11) and funky decor (check out the confessional booth entry to the washrooms). There's also superb *bavette*, fried Mars bars for dessert and drinks until 3am. Dinner only; closed Mon.

Holder 407 rue McGill ☎514/849-0333, ⊛www.restaurantholder.com; Métro Square-Victoria. This modern bistro/brasserie buzzes with conversation bouncing off copper surfaces and plate-glass windows looking onto an attractive nineteenth-century building. Starters include marinated octopus and an indulgent foie gras on gingerbread, followed by mains such as preserved duck leg, fresh roasted cod, mussels in *pastis*, and *onglet* (hanger steak) done to a turn. No lunch at weekends. Open until 11pm (midnight Thurs–Sun).

Masala 995 rue Wellington O ☎514/287-7455; Métro Square-Victoria or Bonaventure or bus #61. Punjabi and Kashmiri dishes are prepared with style and skill in this stripped-back warehouse space – about a ten-minute walk west of rue McGill, through the Cité Multimédia district – warmed with orange and maroon walls and Indian fabrics. Start with the rich and creamy dahl before filling up on the tasty butter chicken ($14), but leave room for the lime tart or

⑩

CAFÉS AND RESTAURANTS | Vieux-Montréal

155

cardamom cake. The chef-owner also offers cooking lessons for $50, including the dishes you prepare. Open for lunch (Mon–Fri 11.30am–2.30pm) and on Friday evenings.

Le Petit Moulinsart 139 rue St-Paul O ⓣ 514/843-7432, ⓦ www.lepetitmoulinsart .com; **Métro Place-d'Armes.** If you didn't recognize the Belgian flag outside, the Tintin paraphernalia scattered about should give you an idea of the cuisine here. Top of the list is mussels, the twenty variations ranging from *marinières* to a sake with Chinese basil. For adventurous carnivores, there's beef tartare; otherwise try the *bavette* with shallots. In fine weather, sit in the courtyard terrace out back.

Stash Café 200 rue St-Paul O ⓣ 514/845-6611, ⓦ www.stashcafe.com; **Métro Place-d'Armes.** Sit on an old church pew and nosh on Polish comfort food like borscht, pierogies and meatier dishes in an equally warm atmosphere of stone walls and low lighting, with a request-taking piano player.

Toqué! 900 place Jean-Paul-Riopelle ⓣ 514/499-2084, ⓦ www.restaurant-toque .com; **Métro Sherbrooke.** World-renowned Chef Normand Laprise holds court at his new Quartier International location, and the results are still a mouthwatering fusion of styles prepared with fresh market ingredients. Definitely try the seared foie gras and perhaps the local venison with sautéed *craterelle* mushrooms, roasted scallops or guinea fowl, depending on the season. Ultra-chic, high-end and unforgettable – if you can get a seat. Dinner only; reserve at least a few weeks ahead. Closed Sun & Mon.

Quartier Latin and the Village

Cafés and light meals

La Brioche Lyonnaise 1593 rue St-Denis ⓣ 514/842-7017, ⓦ www.labriochelyonnaise .com; **Métro Berri-UQAM.** The smell of freshly baked French pastries, like flaky *mille-feuille* and chocolate éclairs, should lure you in to this café-patisserie. Try the savoury crepes filled with egg, ham and cheese, too. Daily morning to midnight (11pm on slower nights).

Croissant de Lune 1765 rue St-Denis ⓣ 514/843-8146; **Métro Berri-UQAM.** A cosy, stone-walled Quartier Latin café set a few feet below street level. There's a range of savoury and dessert crepes available, as well as omelettes, salads and sandwiches, all in the $6–7 range.

Kilo 1495 rue Ste-Catherine E ⓣ 514/596-3933, ⓦ www.kilo.ca; **Métro Beaudry.** The healthy salads and sandwiches served here are merely teasers for the wild array of killer

Late-night eats

Whether you're looking for a late bite after a show or for something to soak up the alcohol after a night on the tiles, there are plenty of places in Montréal that close around midnight (a bit later on weekends) or even well after.

desserts on offer – the cheesecake is particularly deadly. Open until 11ish, around midnight weekends. They've got another diet-buster location in Mile End at 5205 boul St-Laurent (☎514/277-5039).

La Paryse 302 rue Ontario E ☎514/842-2040; **Métro Berri-UQAM.** Delicious hamburgers for around $6 loaded with goodies – try *Le Spécial*, which is topped with cream cheese and bacon – served up in a cheery, 1950s-style diner. Vegetarians have three types of burgers to choose from – tofu, pinto bean and peanut – with toppings to complement each.

Le Resto du Village 1310 rue Wolfe ☎514/524-5404; **Métro Beaudry.** Down a side street from rue Ste-Catherine, this small diner serves filling comfort food such as *pâté chinois* (shepherd's pie) and *poutine* to a largely gay crowd. The food is so-so, but the place is open 24 hours and packs up quickly once the nearby clubs close. *Apportez votre vin.*

Starbucks 1301 rue Ste-Catherine E ☎514/904-5411, Ⓦ www.starbucks.com; **Métro Beaudry.** The Seattle monster may not have become quite as ubiquitous in Montréal as in other North American cities, but this branch is currently the cruisiest café in the Village. Popularity fades, though, and there'll likely be a different "in" café in a year's time, so keep an eye out as you walk along rue Ste-Catherine. Open until 11pm (midnight at weekends).

L'Utopik 552 rue Ste-Catherine E ☎514/844-1139; **Métro Berri-UQAM.** An unassuming door facing Place Émilie-Gamelin leads upstairs to this ramshackle studenty hangout with mismatched chairs and sofas strewn about a warren of rooms and sky-lit nooks. A nonprofit outfit, it serves organic vegetarian meals for $7–8, hosts an eclectic range of nightly musical performances and has Internet terminals for $4 per hour.

Zyng 1748 rue St-Denis ☎514/284-2016, Ⓦ www.zyng.com; **Métro Berri-UQAM.** Create your own meal by choosing a meat, shrimp or tofu base and one of a dozen seasonings, then fill your bowl from an assortment of veggies and hand it to a nearby chef who whips it all up for $10, or try a standard like pad Thai. Definitely not *haute cuisine*, but it's cheap and decent, and the tightly-packed tables ensure a good conversational buzz.

Restaurants

Area 1429 rue Amherst ☎514/890-6691, Ⓦ www.rest-area.qc.ca; **Métro Beaudry.** Well-designed restaurant with a stylish and airy atmosphere – ornamented by creamy-grey banquettes and chairs and minimalist floral arrangements against the white and exposed-brick walls – reflected in the presentation of the scallops in miso, tempura shrimp in Madras curry, roasted *coquelet* (Cornish game hen) marinated in ginger, garlic and maple syrup, and other French and Asian fusion dishes. Dinner only.

Bangkok 1201 boul de Maisonneuve E ☎514/527-9777; **Métro Beaudry.** They don't hold back on the spices for some of the unfussy authentic dishes at this simply decorated Thai restaurant. Warm up your palate with *tom yum kai* soup before trying a curry or milder chicken with cashews ($10.50) and sticky rice.

Chez Gatsé Restaurant Tibetain 317 rue Ontario E ☎514/985-2494; **Métro Berri-UQAM.** Tibetan restaurant serving bargain-priced *mômos* (dumplings stuffed with cheese, beef or veg), egg-noodle *thukpas* with beef or veg, and curry-spiced beef and chicken *shaptas* in a half-basement decorated with colourful fabrics and handicrafts. There's also a big tree-shaded courtyard out back. *Table d'hôte* $10; lunch specials $7 (but no lunch weekends).

Le Commensal 1720 rue St-Denis ☎514/845-2627; **Métro Berri-UQAM.** Choose from dozens of vegetarian dishes, including salads, couscous, stir-fried tofu and lasagne from the buffet, then pay by weight ($1.80 per 100g) and enjoy your meal in the large, glazed front room looking onto the street. A warning – it's easy to over-fill your plate and end up paying for more than you can eat. There's a Downtown branch at 1204 av McGill College (☎514/871-1480) and one near the Oratory at 5199 chemin de la Côte-des-Neiges (☎514/733-9755).

Confusion 1635 rue St-Denis ☎514/288-2225, Ⓦ www.restaurantconfusion.com; **Métro Berri-UQAM.** They have a vegetarian and a mixed grill *table d'hôte* ($39–59 for two) at this restaurant with quirky features – swingset seats and plush red banquettes downstairs, a parlour-like upstairs and a lounge bathed in red light – but most people opt for the tapas menu. The forty dishes vary from the traditional (grilled squid) to the unusual (sweetbread "popcorn" or ostrich *tataki*); three for $20 after 10pm. Open until midnight; lunch Wed–Fri only.

Élla Grill 1237 rue Amherst ⊤514/523-5553; **Métro Beaudry.** A cool, predominantly white space evokes the Greek Islands, as do the dishes of grilled market-fresh fish such as red snapper and sea bass, and marinated octopus ($14). Starters are likewise typical – *spanakopita* and *taramasalata* – and land-based mains include fried zucchini with *tzatziki* ($15) and lamb chops at $5 a pop. Dinner only; closed Sun.

Fou d'Asie 1732 rue St-Denis ⊤514/281-0077; **Métro Berri-UQAM.** More stylish than many of its Quartier Latin neighbours, this Asian fusion restaurant applies Thai and Vietnamese flavours to beef, chicken and seafood (mains $11–17), served up with noodles. The sushi bar is also a popular draw. No lunch weekends.

Ô Chalet 1393 boul René-Lévesque E ⊤514/527-7070, ⓦ www.ochalet.net; **Métro Beaudry.** The name means country shack or cottage, and the whimsical decor reflects that: there are 1970s-style plaid banquettes in one room. The casual atmosphere belies the gourmet market cuisine (though it does hint at its playfulness – try the red tuna "martini" or scallops with Campari and grapefruit). Other seasonal dishes include asparagus salad, seared foie gras with beef marrow, and mains ($24–33) such as tuna tartare with yuzu, and suckling pig served three ways. Lovely terrace, too. Dinner only; closed Sun & Mon.

O'Thym 1112 boul de Maisonneuve E ⊤514/525-3443, ⓦ www.othym.com; **Métro Berri-UQAM or Beaudry.** A bright and airy bistro with large chalkboard menus lit by dozens of simple lightbulbs suspended from the pressed-tin ceiling. The beautifully crafted dishes (mains $20–30) include fish of the day, *magret de canard* baked in sea salt, veal chops and a perfectly cooked filet mignon with wild mushrooms. No lunch Sat–Mon; two seatings Sat eve (6pm & 9pm). *Apportez votre vin* (bring your own wine).

Au Petit Extra 1690 rue Ontario E ⊤514/527-5552, ⓦ www.aupetitextra.com; **Métro Papineau.** Large, lively and affordable bistro (two-course lunch $12–16; dinner $15–24) with amazing food and an authentic French feel, reflected in the selection of sweetbreads and kidneys, in addition to the tasty duck breast and fish dishes on the weekly-changing menu. There's also a good range

of wines at affordable prices. Closed for lunch on the weekend.

Pho Viet 1663 rue Amherst ⊤514/522-4116; **Métro Beaudry.** Almost literally a hole in the wall, this tiny, barely furnished Vietnamese restaurant is nonetheless popular with those in the know, especially for its beef or chicken Tonkinoise soup ($6–7). Lunch during the week only and closed Sunday. Reservations recommended for dinner. No credit cards. *Apportez votre vin*.

Saloon 1333 rue Ste-Catherine E ⊤514/522-1333; **Métro Beaudry.** A reliable menu of pizzas, burgers, salads and brunch selections draws a mixed crowd of young and old, gay and straight to this two-level Village hangout, but it's the Thai-style grilled chicken that stands out (though the steak frites isn't bad, either). Substantial breakfasts are great for weekend recovery (Sat & Sun from 10am).

Spirite Lounge 1205 rue Ontario E ⊤514/522-5353; **Métro Beaudry or Berri-UQAM.** High-concept vegetarian dining that you'll either love or hate. The deal is that you must completely finish one course to be allowed to eat the next. The largely organic menu ($15 for three courses) is different every day and can be a bit hit-or-miss. Dinner only.

Plateau Mont-Royal: the Main and around

Cafés and light meals

Beauty's 93 av du Mont-Royal O ⊤514/849-8883, ⓦ www.beautys.ca; **Métro Mont-Royal or bus #55.** A brunch institution that's been serving meals to customers snuggled up in their booths for over sixty years. The "Beauty's Special" – bagel, lox, tomato, red onion and cream cheese – is the best such combo in the city. Be prepared to get up

△ Classic breakfast fare at Beauty's

extra early on the weekend to avoid the line-up. Mon–Fri 7am–4pm, Sat 7am–5pm, Sun 8am–5pm.

Café Santropol 3990 rue St-Urbain ☎514/842-3110, ⓦwww.santropol.com; **Métro Sherbrooke or Mont-Royal or bus #55.** This outstanding and mostly vegetarian café on the corner of avenue Duluth has a lovely "secret garden" back terrace and retains its charm in winter thanks to a cosy atrium. Massive, inventive sandwiches (the "Midnight Spread" contains honey, peanut butter, cream and cottage cheeses, nuts, raisins and bananas) on chewy dark bread are accompanied by loads of fresh fruit. Vegetarian pies, salads and soups also available. Save space for the thick, to-die-for milkshakes. No credit cards. Open daily until midnight.

Eurodeli 3619 boul St-Laurent ☎514/843-7853; **Métro Sherbrooke or bus #55.** Long a popular favourite with Plateau students, this is a great spot for a quick espresso or cheap pasta or calzone while people-watching on the Main. You can also take away a variety of deli fixings. Daily until midnight (12.30am weekends).

Laïka 4040 boul St-Laurent ☎514/842-8088, ⓦwww.laikamontreal.com; **Métro Sherbrooke or Mont-Royal or bus #55.** The sleek interior draws urbane hipsters from the Plateau for daily specials and excellent *cafés au lait*. Floor-to-ceiling windows open onto the street in summer, and a small brunch selection, including eggs Florentine, frittatas and crepes, is available on the weekends. Daily 8.30am–3am, as early as 1am on a quiet night (food served until close).

Mondo Fritz 3899 boul St-Laurent ☎514/281-6521; **Métro Sherbrooke or bus #55.** Great laid-back place for fries and a beer, as there's a wide array of dips for the former and a large, international selection of the latter. Good spot for vegetarians: both the *poutine*, served with a meat-free gravy, and the garden burgers are worth a try. Daily until midnight (around 1am weekends).

Schwartz's 3895 boul St-Laurent ☎514/842-4813, ⓦwww.schwartzsdeli .com; **Métro Sherbrooke or bus #55.** A small, narrow, ten-table deli that's been serving colossal sandwiches since 1930, *Schwartz's* consistently (and deservedly) tops the *Mirror's* annual "best smoked meat" list – choose the *gras* style for the full-fat experience. There's usually a line-up out the

door and surly service, but it's well worth it. Daily 9am–12.30am (until 1.30am Fri, 2.30am Sat).

Soupesoup 80 av Duluth E ☎514/380-0880; **Métro Sherbrooke or Mont-Royal or bus #55.** Does what it says on the tin – a daily changing menu of classic soups such as ratatouille and concoctions like the lemony squash, mussels and fennel combo are served in a small space with colourful ceramic-tile tabletops and walls panelled with old doors. Sandwiches, too. Daily 8am–6pm. Also at 174 rue St-Viateur O (☎514/271-2004; Mon–Fri 11am–4pm).

Restaurants

Amelio's 201 rue Milton ☎514/845-8396; **Métro Place-des-Arts or bus #24.** Hearty pastas and pizzas – including their unusual five-cheese "white pizza" – are served in this tiny restaurant tucked away in the heart of the McGill University student ghetto. The service is friendly and the raspberry cheesecake heavenly. Closed Sun & Mon; no lunch Sat. No credit cards. *Apportez votre vin.*

Globe 3455 boul St-Laurent ☎514/284-3823, ⓦwww.restaurantglobe.com; **Métro Sherbrooke or St-Laurent or bus #55.** Best of the flashy restaurants on this block of the Main, *Globe* scores high for food as well as for its sleek, simple decor. The seasonal produce – fiddleheads in late spring, kale in winter, for instance – are locally sourced and simply but expertly combined with a variety of fish, seafood and meats like roasted chicken and braised rabbit (mains $25–35). It stays open for drinks until 3am after the kitchen closes (11pm except Thurs–Sat, when there's a $12 midnight menu until 2am).

△ Sleek dining at Globe

Jano 3883 boul St-Laurent ☎ **514/849-0646; Métro Sherbrooke or bus #55.** The gaily decorated rooster on the facade seems blissfully unaware of its cousins – along with sardines, sole, rabbit and lamb chops – visible grilling away through the front window of this longtime Plateau restaurant. Other Portuguese dishes like *chouriço* and squid are available, but the focus is very much on the grilled meats. Open until 11.30pm.

Laloux 250 av des Pins E ☎ **514/287-9127,** Ⓦ **www.laloux.com; Métro Sherbrooke.** Creamy yellow walls lined with mirrors add an elegant touch to this Parisian-style bistro serving exquisite *nouvelle cuisine*. The chef likes to contrast flavours, serving, for instance, foie gras with grapes or rhubarb. Follow it up with the marvellous sweetbreads with white port and morels, but make sure to try the chocolate cake with tarragon and Pernod ice cream, a memorably sweet/zesty/bitter medley. The *table d'hôte* runs $18–20 at lunch, $24–29 at dinner, but many appetizers and desserts cost extra. No lunch weekends. Sixties Danish teak furniture gives adjacent wine-bar *Pop!* an altogether different feel.

Maestro SVP 3615 boul St-Laurent ☎ **514/842-6447,** Ⓦ **www.maestrosvp .com; Métro Sherbrooke or bus #55.** If you're in the mood for oysters, this is the place – some fifteen species are served up in a myriad of ways. Try them Rockefeller (pesto, cheese and white sauce), raw with lemon one-by-one ($2–8) or in a shooter with vodka and horseradish sauce. The $72 "Maestro Platter" for two is another sure bet, loaded with clams, mussels, calamari, shrimp, king crab and lobster.

Moishe's 3961 boul St-Laurent ☎ **514/845-3509,** Ⓦ **www.moishes.ca; Métro Sherbrooke or bus #55.** This steakhouse with dark panelled walls has been a favourite haunt of Montréal's business community since 1938. Excellent (and huge) charcoal-broiled steaks, but very expensive, with notoriously bad-tempered service. No lunch at weekends; reservations recommended.

Na Brasa 121 av Duluth E ☎ **514/287-9096; Métro Sherbrooke or Mont-Royal.** This casual and friendly spot is as good a place for a drink on the terrace as for the inexpensive but good meals served until 2am. It's

changed flavour in recent years, dropping its old name (Bistro Duluth) for one that means "on the grill" in Portuguese and adding fishy tapas, grilled fish and mixed-grilled platters to the standby burgers and bowls of mussels ($16.50 all-you-can-eat Sun–Wed). The $9–14 lunch specials include a drink.

Pintxo 256 rue Roy E ☎ **514/844-0222; Métro Sherbrooke.** Named after the tapas-like Basque dishes, this restaurant, enlivened by brightly coloured paintings, delivers small mouthfuls of lovingly presented pan-fried calamari, mushrooms stuffed with duck *confit*, Galician-style poached octopus and more ($3–6). Although less fun, there are also Spanish mains such as lamb shank on a bed of couscous and cassoulet for around $20, though the best deal is $28 for four *pintxo* and a main. The wine list is, of course, all Spanish. Closed Sun; lunch Wed–Fri only.

Red Thai 3550 boul St-Laurent ☎ **514/289-0998; Métro Sherbrooke or Saint-Laurent.** This restaurant serves up delightful Thai in a decor straight out of *Anna and the King*. They've got chicken satay starters ($8) and a sizzling seafood plate and Mekong scampi (both $28). You can opt for cheaper curries ($16) or sample "Bangkok lunch" specials ($9–14) until 3pm (Wed–Fri only).

Tasca 172 av Duluth E ☎ **514/987-1530; Métro Sherbrooke or Mont-Royal.** Authentic tapas restaurant filled with Portuguese families, especially at weekends when an accordionist plays. Pick a few dishes from the wide range of charcoal-grilled fish and seafood to share – try the octopus, either grilled or marinated in a herb and onion sauce – or go whole hog on a seafood platter or paella.

Time Boutique Café 3509 boul St-Laurent ☎ **514/842-2626,** Ⓦ **www.timeboutiquecafe .com; Métro Sherbrooke or St-Laurent or bus #55.** This trendy restaurant is cheaper than its equally flashy neighbours, though the wide tables and loud DJ music on weekends make conversation a challenge. The fusion menu varies from starters like *saganaki* (fried Greek cheese) to mains like duck *confit* crepes, and citrus and chilli shrimps (both $22). It becomes more of a lounge later on, especially the terrace, an *Arabian Nights* fantasy with gauzy white curtains. Open 9am–3am (weekends from 10am).

Cafés and light meals

La Banquise 994 rue Rachel E ☎514/525-2415; **Métro Mont-Royal.** Colourful restaurant near Parc Lafontaine that specializes in *poutine* – there are around two dozen varieties, from traditional (just fries, gravy and cheese curds), to more extravagant combinations such as the "B.O.M." – piled with bacon, onions and *merguez* sausages. Open 24hrs and packed when the bars close.

La Binerie Mont-Royal 367 av du Mont-Royal E ☎514/285-9078; **Métro Mont-Royal.** Just four tables and a long counter in this hole-in-the-wall diner, which prides itself on the traditional Québécois cuisine served here since 1938. The house specialty is *fèves au lard* (baked beans), and other worthwhile dishes include *tourtière* and *pouding au chômeur* ("unemployed pudding") – a variation on bread pudding. Cheap, filling breakfasts served all day. Mon–Fri 6am–8pm, Sat & Sun 7.30am–3pm.

Le Café Cherrier 3635 rue St-Denis ☎514/843-4308; **Métro Sherbrooke.** An older Francophone crowd congregates here for guilt-free brunches – the buttery eggs Benedict oozes calories – often making it hard to find a table. *Croques* and quiches fill the afternoon gap before the fuller bistro menu becomes available in the evening.

Caffé ArtJava 837 av du Mont-Royal E ☎514/527-9990, ⓦwww.caffeartjava .com; **Métro Mont-Royal.** They serve sublime coffee – arguably the city's best – at this sleek café opened wide to the passing parade along avenue du Mont-Royal; it's certainly the prettiest, since they swirl hearts and other designs in the foam topping New York's Gimme! coffee. Choose a pastry to accompany your brew or one of the big brunches or creative sandwiches, wraps and salads. Free Wi-Fi keeps the laptop brigade happy.

Aux Deux Marie 4329 rue St-Denis ☎514/844-7246; **Métro Mont-Royal.** One of the better of the many rue St-Denis cafés, *Aux Deux Marie* roast their own coffee beans (stacked in burlap sacks by the entrance) and serve cheap cakes to go with the finished brew. You can also have sandwiches, quiches, *croques* or salads on the street-front terrace or at one of the wooden tables alongside the exposed brick walls.

Folies 701 rue Mont-Royal E ☎514/528-4343, ⓦwww.folies.tv; **Métro Mont-Royal.** A hip café-lounge perfect for an excellent breakfast (and wider-ranging brunches on the weekends) on the umbrella-shaded terrace or in the retro-space-age interior full of sleek curves. Later on, choose from pastas, burgers and bistro dishes or nibble away at tapas and drinks while the DJ spins electronic beats. Daily 9am–midnight or a bit later.

Les Gâteries 3443 rue St-Denis ☎514/843-6235; **Métro Sherbrooke.** Opposite Square St-Louis, the warm ochre-and-cream interior of this café makes for a quiet spot to indulge in one of the excellent cakes on offer – a big slice of dark chocolate mousse *royale* goes for $5.50. If you want something less sweet, the typical standbys – sandwiches, quiches and inventive *croques* – are also available.

St Viateur Bagel & Café 1127 av du Mont-Royal E☎514/528-6361, ⓦwww.stviateurbagel.com; **Métro Mont-Royal.** If you want to actually sit down to enjoy the products of the famous bagel bakery (see p.207), you can try them with breakfasty or sandwich fillings along with a salad at this Plateau café.

Restaurants

L'Avenue 922 av du Mont-Royal E ☎514/523-8780; **Métro Mont-Royal.** Extremely popular among the hip Plateau set for its stylish, ever-evolving decor and great prices for the quality and quantity of food on offer. Sit at one of the sparkly gold booths and tuck into huge portions of thoughtfully prepared updates on classic diner food – like goat's cheese and wild-mushroom-topped hamburgers – which share the menu with salads, pastas and really good *bavette*. Long queues for weekend brunch – *Café El Dorado*, opposite, is a reasonable alternative if you're too hungry to wait.

△ See and be seen at L'Avenue

Bières & Compagnie 4350 rue St-Denis
T 514/844-0394, W www.bieresetcompagnie
.ca; Métro Mont-Royal. A stylish restaurant/bar
with large booths and dim lighting, serving
up $18 all-you-can-eat platters of mussels
(Mon–Wed), beer-soaked sausages and a
range of burgers made with exotic meats –
try the rich buffalo burger served with
homemade mayonnaise for dipping the
great fries into. It should also rank high on
any beer fanatic's list as there are more than
a hundred types of brews to choose from,
including a wide Belgian selection.

Brunoise 3807 rue St-André T 514/523-
3885, W www.brunoise.ca; Métro
Sherbrooke. This low-lit restaurant should be
high on any foodie's wishlist. The *cuisine de
marché* menu ($42–52 for three courses) is
a great deal for the quality of sculptural
dishes such as Parma ham-wrapped rabbit
loin, seared salmon and combinations like
seared scallops and braised beef short-rib,
all with creative sauces. Extensive and
reasonable wine list, too. Evenings only;
closed Sun & Mon.

ChuChai 4088 rue St-Denis T 514/843-
4194; Métro Mont-Royal or Sherbrooke.
Terrific and fresh vegetarian Thai food
featuring a wide array of tasty mock meats,
including a delicious crispy "duck". Get the
divine deep-fried spinach as an accompani-
ment. The adjoining *Chuch Express* is more
casual and lively and serves the same food
as well as cheaper ready-prepared dishes to
eat in or take away; the $7 lunch special
includes soup, two dishes and rice.

La Colombe 554 av Duluth E T 514/849-8844;
Métro Sherbrooke or Mont-Royal. Open for
dinner only, this small, stylish bistro attracts
a well-heeled Francophone crowd and
serves a higher level of cuisine than the
average BYO restaurant. Fresh seasonal
ingredients accompany mains like venison
or *jarret d'agneau* (lamb shank) served *au
jus*. *Table d'hôte* $38–48. Closed Sun &
Mon. *Apportez votre vin*.

Le Continental 4169 rue St-Denis
T 514/845-6842, W www.lecontinental
.ca; Métro Mont-Royal. An always-packed
French bistro that has a few Italian dishes
thrown in to the moderately priced à-la-carte-
only menu – the carpaccio, fish bisque, lamb
medallions and steak frites are tops. The Art
Deco–influenced retro decor attracts an artsy
crowd, and those eating at the bar add to
the talkative buzz. Finish off with the

decadent chocolate-mousse cake. Open for
dinner only, until midnight Sun & Mon, until
1am other nights. Reservations advised.

Côté Soleil 3979 rue St-Denis T 514/282-8037;
Métro Sherbrooke or Mont-Royal. Light,
Mediterranean-influenced bistro fare (*table
d'hôte* $13–17), including a delicious
roasted goat's-cheese salad, served in a
welcoming space with exposed-brick walls.
Great terrace for surveying the St-Denis
scene, especially when lingering over one of
the gorgeous brunches (Thurs–Sun) – try
the "Ibiza" eggs accompanied by a zesty
tomato salsa.

Crêperie Bretonne Ty-Breiz 933 rue Rachel E
T 514/521-1444; Métro Mont-Royal. Despite
the incredibly tacky decor with pictures of
Brittany and traditional costumes, this
family-style creperie has drawn a local
following for over four decades. Their large
crepes are the real thing, filled with ingredients like sausage, apples or asparagus in
béchamel sauce ($4.50–14). Tues–Sun from
11.30am.

Eduardo 404 av Duluth E T 514/843-3330;
Métro Sherbrooke or Mont-Royal. Cheap,
crowded Italian restaurant featuring huge
$12 portions of veal dishes and *tuto mare*
(linguini with shrimp, clams and scallops in a
rosé sauce) and cheap pasta ($6.50–8.50)
served in a dark and cosy space with back-
lit stained-glass windows. No lunch on the
weekend. *Apportez votre vin*.

L'Express 3927 rue St-Denis T 514/845-
5333; Métro Sherbrooke. Fashionable
Parisian-style bistro whose hectic but
attentive service adds to the atmosphere.
Try the steak tartare if you're feeling adventurous; otherwise opt for the safer steak
frites or *canard confit* (slow-roasted duck);
all cost around $20. Table reservations are
essential – though you might be able to
squeeze in at the bar unannounced. Mon–
Fri from 8am (Sat & Sun from 10am) until
2am (1am Sun).

Fonduementale 4325 rue St-Denis
T 514/499-1446, W www.fonduementale
.com; Métro Mont-Royal. Set in a red-brick
Victorian two-storey house, *Fonduementale*'s main living room is fitted with late
nineteenth-century lights and mouldings and
warmed by a fireplace in winter, and there's
a blooming outdoor terrace in summer. The
fondue here is exquisite – especially *Le
Mental*, which features chunks of venison
and caribou among the options. Be sure to

CAFÉS AND RESTAURANTS | Plateau Mont-Royal: rue St-Denis and east leave room for the chocolate fondues for dessert. *Table d'hôte* $31–45.

Le Jardin de Panos 521 av Duluth E
☎ 514/521-4206, Ⓦ www.lejardindepanos.com;
Métro Sherbrooke or Mont-Royal. Popular *brochetterie* serving heavy meals – the standard is chicken or beef shish-kebabs with fried potatoes accompanied by Greek salad, though the grilled salmon filet is a lighter option (either is $16) – in a warren of rooms. The food's better than similar spots on rue Prince-Arthur and it has a garden terrace to boot. *Apportez votre vin.*

Khyber Pass 506 av Duluth E ☎ 514/844-7131;
Métro Sherbrooke or Mont-Royal. The cosy furnishings and music here feel as authentic as the menu of Afghan specialties, including kebabs, *kofta* and *korma*. The *sabzi chalaw* – lamb shank with spinach and three kinds of basmati rice – is the stand-out. Dinner only. *Apportez votre vin.*

Mañana 3605 rue St-Denis ☎ 514/847-1050,
Ⓦ www.restaurantmanana.com; **Métro Sherbrooke.** Tuck into inexpensive (mains $11–17) and tasty beef fajitas and vegetarian quesadillas in this small stone-walled spot opposite Square St-Louis, surrounded by Mexican masks, sombreros and colourful woven tablecloths.

🏃 **La Montée de Lait 371 rue Villeneuve E**
☎ 514/289-9921; **Métro Laurier or Mont-Royal.** The clean lines and pale woods are the first hint that this isn't the tiny neighbourhood bistro it first appears to be. Among the twists are the menu – divided into categories from which you choose four or seven plates ($40 or $60) in the order you prefer – to the name: *lait* means milk, and dairy originally featured in every dish. It still makes an appearance – notably in the gorgeous cheese plate – but the precisely presented dishes now include venison tartare, seared scallops and lobster bisque, in addition to the goat's-cheese tart and *crème brûlée*. Lunch Wed–Fri only (two plates $18); closed Mon.

Le Nil Bleu 3706 rue St-Denis ☎ 514/285-4628;
Métro Sherbrooke. Walls of water, grass wreath sculptures and candlelight give this Ethiopian restaurant a dark and close feel. It's a perfect atmosphere for the spicy *doro wat* stew with beef, chicken, lamb or vegetables that's served on top of spongy *injera* bread. Dinner only.

Ouzeri 4960 rue St-Denis ☎ 514/845-1336;
Métro Mont-Royal or Laurier. Jutting out on a

triangular street corner, this sunny yellow restaurant fills with a noisy crowd at packed tables and along the long bar backed by a wall of wine bottles. Reasonably priced Greek and other Mediterranean dishes, such as seafood and grilled meats, keep them coming back, as do nice touches like the free sampling dish of *mezes* when you sit down.

🏃 **Au Pied de Cochon 536 av Duluth E**
☎ 514/281-1114, Ⓦ www.restaurant aupieddecochon.ca; **Métro Mont-Royal or Sherbrooke.** Crowded and noisy bistro that's carnivore heaven, from deep-fried pork rinds and heavenly pork chops to venison ribs and bison steak, supplemented by seafood in summer. The highlight is the foie gras, served a number of different ways – most unusually with *poutine*. Evenings only; closed Mon.

La Piton de la Fournaise 835 av Duluth E
☎ 514/526-3936, Ⓦ www.restolepiton.com;
Métro Mont-Royal or Sherbrooke. This cute little restaurant features the cuisine of Réunion – the French island colony in the Indian Ocean – and the mix of the three cuisines is flavoured with turmeric, ginger, garlic and Thai pepper, applied to dishes like the shark curry or octopus stew. Evenings only; two seatings Fri & Sat (6pm & 9pm); closed Mon. *Apportez votre vin.*

Pizzédélic 1250 av du Mont-Royal E ☎ 514/522-2286 Ⓦ www.pizzedelic.net; **Métro Mont-Royal.** The signature square pizzas at this great local chain come with adventurous toppings like goat's cheese, walnuts and black olives, or smoked salmon, capers, cream cheese, red onion and ginger. The curvy ceiling painted in primary colours adds to the fun atmosphere, while the garage-door front opens up to the street on balmier days. The decor is more sober in the branches at 3467 boul St-Laurent (☎ 514/845-0404, Ⓦ www.pizzedelic-montreal.com), 39 rue Notre-Dame O in Vieux-Montréal (☎ 514/286-1200) and 5153 chemin de la Côte-des-Neiges (☎ 514/739-2446), but the pizza's equally good.

Au P'tit Lyonnais 1279 rue Marie-Anne E
☎ 514/523-2424, Ⓦ www.auptitlyonnais.com;
Métro Mont-Royal. A number of Lyonnais specialities like frog's legs, *andouillette* (tripe sausage) and *quenelles de brochet* (pike dumplings) feature on the menu alongside lambchops and scallops at this small French bistro decked out with sunny yellow walls

⑩

and glazed-tile floor. The five-course *table d'hôte* runs $28–38, and there's no mark-up on the wines. Evenings only; closed Mon.

Le P'tit Plateau 330 rue Marie-Anne E ☎514/282-6342; Métro Mont-Royal. A moderately expensive (*table d'hôte* $28–38) but worth it French bistro whose warm interior bubbles with conversation in between courses of foie gras, smoked pork terrine or cassoulet, and mains of duck, lamb, pork or salmon but hushes when the golden *crème brûlée* arrives. Evenings only – two seatings, at 6.30pm and 8.30pm; closed Sun & Mon. Reservations are a very good idea. *Apportez votre vin.*

La Selva 862 rue Marie-Anne E ☎514/525-1798; Métro Mont-Royal. Simple, hearty Peruvian dishes fill you up for a pittance at this family-run place that draws a steady local clientele to this quiet corner of the Plateau. Go for the popular grilled fresh fish of the day or try the chicken in a rich and mild peanut sauce. No credit cards. Dinner only; closed Sun & Mon. *Apportez votre vin.*

Mile End and Outremont

Cafés and light meals

La Croissanterie Figaro 5200 rue Hutchison ☎514/278-6567, ⓦwww .lacroissanteriefigaro.com; bus #80. Delightful café that everyone just calls *La Croissanterie*. Marble-topped tables and dark wood fixtures lend it an Old World feel perfect for coffee and pastries – the almond croissants alone make the trip here worthwhile. You can also settle in for light meals and rich cakes on the wraparound terrace. Daily 7am–1am.

Dusty's 4510 av du Parc ☎514/276-8525; bus #80. A good spot to fill up before tackling the mountain, this old-school diner with its vinyl booths and counter stools has been around since 1949, though the sign outside has been missing for years. The basic fry-up – eggs, bacon, fried potatoes, toast and coffee – will only set you back $3.95. Daily 7am–7pm. *Pines Pizza* (☎514/277-3178), next door, is another good bet and is open 24hr.

La Petite Ardoise 222 av Laurier O ☎514/495-4961; Métro Laurier or bus #80. The *ardoise* (blackboard) in question is reflected in the intellectual make-up of the Francophone Outremont regulars, who come for rich breakfasts, salads, quiches and cheap bistro plates (like $14 *bavette*) in this cheery yellow-and-blue café. The secluded garden terrace is an idyllic spot to sip your *café au lait*. Daily 8am–midnight.

La Pharmacie Esperanza 5490 boul St-Laurent ☎514/948-3303; bus #55. A laid-back, funky café with mismatched charity-shop furniture and changing art installations that draws local artists and musicians, who hang around for $5 pints in the evening and listen to bands (often free). During the day, there's a basic selection of soups, panini and burritos to accompany the organic coffee. Tues–Sun 9am–1am.

Wilensky's Light Lunch 34 av Fairmount O ☎514/271-0247; Métro Laurier or bus #55. A lunch counter whose decor hasn't changed since 1932, and that includes the till, the grill and the drinks machine – you can still get an old-fashioned cherry coke. The $3.50 Wilensky Special includes bologna and three types of salami on a kaiser roll. Mon–Fri 9am–4pm.

Restaurants

Anise 104 av Laurier O ☎514/276-6999, ⓦwww.anise.ca; Métro Laurier or bus #55. High-end fusion of French and Middle Eastern cuisine served in a simple, elegant decor. The seasonal menu might include grilled scallops or seared foie-gras "french toast" as starters, followed by market-fresh fish or lamb *shawarma* (two courses $45). For a real blowout, try the six- or nine-course menus ($70–95, $115–150 with wine pairings). Evenings only; closed Sun & Mon.

Arahova Souvlaki 256 rue St-Viateur O ☎514/274-7828; bus #80. Superb choice for authentic Greek cuisine at very reasonable prices. The basic dishes are the best, such as the souvlaki and fried calamari, all of which are served up in a taverna-style restaurant with pictures of the old country hung about. Open until 5am Fri & Sat, 2am other nights.

Chao Phraya 50 av Laurier O ☎514/272-5339, ⓦwww.chao-phraya.com; Métro Laurier or bus #55. One of the city's top Thai restaurants, with an elegant but unfussy decor. Start with the *tom yum gai* (hot and sour chicken soup) to loosen your tastebuds for the fish and seafood highlights ($15–17) – choose either the *pad ped ta-lay* (a spicy combo of crab claws, scallops, shrimp, squid and fish) or the sautéed shrimp in various spicy sauces. Dinner only.

Il Piatto Della Nonna 5171 boul St-Laurent ☎514/843-6069; Métro Laurier. A family-run restaurant serving well-prepared Italian specialities from Calabria like roast rabbit and lamb for $15–27 for three courses. Between the pressed-copper ceilings and wide-plank pine floors, you can also tuck into charcoal-grilled veal sausage or wolf down a pasta fagiola for lunch (two courses $9–12; weekdays only).

Le Jardin du Cari 21 rue St-Viateur O ☎514/495-0565; bus #55. A simply furnished and friendly spot to sample Caribbean specialities like goat curry and curried chicken or shrimp wrapped in a roti, as well as Guyanese-style chow mein and fried rice dishes. Mains are a cheap $7–9. Closed Mon; no lunch on weekends.

Laurier BBQ 381 av Laurier O ☎514/273-3671; bus #80. Great hunks of typical Québec-style rotisserie chicken ($12–14), served drizzled with the delicious house barbecue sauce, have made this comfortable family-run restaurant a favourite for over half a century. If you're after comfort food, the homemade macaroni and cheese with meat sauce is hard to beat (ditto the $9 price tag).

Leméac 1045 av Laurier O ☎514/270-0999, ⓦ www.restaurantlemeac.com; bus #80. Large windows look onto a vine-shaded terrace at this bustling, ever-popular bistro, whose seasonally changing menu includes delights like veal liver in a herb crust, Icelandic roast cod, beef tartare, seared scallops and the old standby steak frites for $20–30, accompanied by one of 400 wines. The two-course weekday lunch is a good deal at around $20, as is the after-10pm $22 menu (until midnight). Lovely weekend brunches, too.

Mikado 368 av Laurier O ☎514/279-4809, ⓦ www.mikadomontreal.com; bus #80. Excellent sushi, sashimi and maki served in a smashing modern Japanese setting that draws a fun but dressy crowd. The grilled salmon and chicken teriyaki are tasty alternatives if you prefer your food cooked. They have a second restaurant at 1731 rue St-Denis (☎514/844-5705) in the Quartier Latin. Three-course lunch (Tues–Fri; Thurs & Fri only at St-Denis location) costs around $12.

Milos 5357 av du Parc ☎514/272-3522, ⓦ www.milos.ca; bus #80. *Milos* is the finest Greek restaurant in the city. The seafood is exceptionally fresh and dishes are prepared simply and skilfully – try the grilled Mediterranean sea bass or delicately seasoned grilled lobster; the lamb chops are a tasty terrestrial alternative. A cheaper but more limited four-course menu served 5.30–6.30pm and on Sundays costs $35; otherwise bank on close to $75 (including wine). Reservations are essential. No lunch weekends.

Senzala 177 rue Bernard O ☎514/274-1464, ⓦ www.senzala.com; bus #55 or #80. The colourful tablecloths and easy-going staff create a great atmosphere to enjoy Brazilian specialities at this locals' haunt. Start with a *ceviche* (cocktail of fresh fish, shrimp and squid in lime juice for $8), follow with a $15 main such as traditional *feijoada* (beef, sausage and pork simmered with black beans and garlic) or salmon in spicy mango sauce, and wash it down with a *caipirinha*. The cute blue terrace is a perfect spot to sample inventive brunches like poached eggs in a scooped-out mango or avocado ($9). Open for brunch Thurs–Sun (9am–3pm) and dinner daily. There's another branch near Parc Lafontaine at 4218 rue de la Roche (☎514/521-1266).

Terrasse Lafayette 250 rue Villeneuve O ☎514/288-3915; bus #80. A great little neighbourhood restaurant, popular for its wrap-around terrace, where you can tuck into *pikilia* (Greek hors d'oeuvre platter), fried calamari and tender pita bread stuffed with chicken or souvlaki. The Greek specialities are best, though the spinach, shallot and feta pizza is really good as well. No credit cards. *Apportez votre vin.*

Little Italy

Cafés and light meals

Café Italia 6840 boul St-Laurent ☎514/495-0059; bus #55. Boisterous Italian debates and mismatched tables await at this atmospheric café that froths up cappuccino with a potency nearing jet-fuel. They've got biscotti and *panettone* to go with it, as well as grilled panini if you need something a bit more substantial. Daily from 6am (7am Sun) to 11pm.

Aux Derniers Humains 6950 rue St-Denis ☎514/272-8521; Métro Jean-Talon or Beaubien. At the southeastern edge of Little Italy, this artsy café (works of a different artist are displayed each month) serves up great breakfasts and a cheap but good

CAFÉS AND RESTAURANTS | Little Italy

array of international dishes like pizzas, risottos, crepes and *confit canard*. Closed Mon. No credit cards.

Motta 303 rue Mozart E ℡ 514/270-5952; **Métro Jean-Talon.** A speciality Italian food emporium selling gourmet goodies, cold cuts and pastries that's also a great spot to sit down for a quick bite off the menu. Order one of the really good spinach or seafood pies from the deli counter, or try one of the authentic one-person pizzas or more substantial pasta meals. Daily 9am–7pm (until 9pm Wed–Fri).

Restaurants

You'll need to reserve ahead at pretty much all of the restaurants here, especially at weekends.

Casa Napoli 6728 boul St-Laurent ℡ 514/274-4351/2; **bus #55.** A warren of rooms divided by faux stone walls and classical statues gives a taste of home to the many Italian families that descend here, though it's the lively street-front terrace that fills first in summer. Classic Italian risottos and pastas – like *linguini alla pescatore*, loaded with clams, mussels and calamari – range from $16–21. Seafood and veal specialities start at around $25, but there's a cheaper menu of pasta, pizza and panini available next door until 11pm. You can also opt for the three-course lunch ($15–23). Closed Mon (Jan–May).

🏃 **Lucca 12 rue Dante** ℡ 514/278-6502; **bus #55.** This contemporary trattoria, where the daily menu is chalked on the board, emphasizes refreshing antipasto combinations, delicious grilled meats and light seafood. The deep-fried calamari on a bed of red pepper *aïoli* and the grilled veal chop on creamy polenta with wilted spinach and roasted red peppers make frequent appearances (starters around $13, mains $20–35). The three-course lunch is more affordable (pasta $15–25, meat and fish $18–25). No lunch Sat; closed Sun.

🏃 **Pizzeria Napoletana 189 rue Dante** ℡ 514/276-8226, ⓦ www.napoletana .com; **bus #55.** A casual restaurant with a lively outdoor terrace in the summer and hearty pizzas – try the sausage and mushrooms *tutta bella* – and pastas like canelloni, *pennine all' arrabbiata* and tortellini in rosé sauce on the menu (mains around $13). Save space for the decadent tiramisu or tartufo. *Apportez votre vin.*

Tre Marie 6934 rue Clark ℡ 514/277-9859; **bus #55.** If you don't like veal, there's not much point visiting this family-run trattoria decked out with homey paintings, antiques and checked tablecloths, as they've been serving veal Milanese (schnitzel), *osso bucco* and veal kidneys ($18–25) since 1967. That said, you can still get pasta ($12–15) or the catch of the day. Closed Sun & Mon; no lunch Sat.

Côte-des-Neiges

In addition to the places listed below, you can grab a bite at branches of local chains *Brûlerie St-Denis* (p.147), *Le Commensal* (p.157) and *Pizzédélic* (p.163) on chemin de la Côte-des-Neiges between the Métro and chemin Queen Mary.

Cafés and light meals

Duc de Lorraine 5002 chemin de la Côte-des-Neiges ℡ 514/731-4128, ⓦ www.ducdelorraine .com; **Métro Côte-des-Neiges or bus #51, #165 or #166.** For a sinful pastry or homemade ice cream after visiting the Oratory, veer right before the last set of steps down and head through the gate posts to reach this half-century-old patisserie and tea salon. You can also fill up on quiche Lorraine or filled croissants in the bright conservatory if you're feeling virtuous. Fine groceries, cheeses and cakes are available to take away. Open 8.30am–6pm (weekends until 5pm).

Pho Lien 5703b chemin de la Côte-des-Neiges ℡ 514/735-6949; **Métro Côte-des-Neiges or bus #165.** Brightly coloured walls and simple furnishings are as no-nonsense as the ingredients in the Tokinoise soup at this good and cheap Vietnamese restaurant located 10–15 minutes' walk from the Oratory – though pay close attention to the menu if you prefer it without tendon or tripe. They also have pork, beef and chicken dishes for around $8, a few bucks more for a full meal (remarkably, the prices include taxes). Closed Tues.

Westmount and the Lachine Canal

Cafés and light meals

Calories 4114 rue Ste-Catherine O ℡ 514/933-8186; **Métro Atwater.** In contrast to the imposing Square Westmount opposite, the dark wood wainscoting and ochre walls give this café a hidden-away feel. The food is dead cheap – panini, salad and homemade iced tea for $6.30 – and the cakes are divine. Choose one of the imaginative cheesecakes (mango or Baileys) or go whole hog on the goopy chocolate-fudge Typhoon. Open until 1am (2am Fri, 3am Sat).

Quoi de N'Oeuf 2745 rue Notre-Dame O Ⓣ 514/931-3999; **Métro Lionel-Groulx.** Lively breakfast joint whose exposed-brick walls and wood floors invite lingering over crepes, omelettes and eggs Benedict (with the option of bacon or sausage) before you head to the nearby shops on "antiques row". They also serve light lunches during the week. Open daily 7am–2.45pm (Sun from 8am).

Restaurants

Joe Beef 2491 rue Notre-Dame O Ⓣ 514/935-6504; **Métro Lionel-Groulx.** Despite the name, seafood predominates on the blackboard at this tiny restaurant around the corner from the Marché Atwater. The chef has a playful touch, for instance mixing scallops, bacon, beer and barley in one dish. Mains range from around $26 for trout to $48 for lobster. And, yes, there is usually some beef on the menu, including a rather good *onglet* (hanger steak). Dinner only; closed Sun & Mon.

Kaizen 4075 rue Ste-Catherine O Ⓣ 514/707-8744, Ⓦ www.70sushi.com; **Métro Atwater.** It's worth the trip out to Westmount for what is arguably the city's best sushi. There's an extensive list of sushi, sashimi and maki (notably the tuna tartare),

with set menus starting at $55 and rising to $120 for variations on Kobe beef. Cheaper mains à la carte range from udon noodles with shrimp ($14) to Alaska black cod ($22) and steak teriyaki ($29) – or try the $20 Kobe beef burger at lunch. There's a lovely terrace in front, fishtail-shaped seats at the sushi bar and live jazz most nights.

Magnan 2602 rue St-Patrick Ⓣ 514/935-9647, Ⓦ www.magnanresto.com; **Métro Charlevoix.** Mention the name "Magnan", and most Montrealers go dreamy-eyed thinking about the excellent steaks that have been served at this restaurant-tavern since the Thirties. From around mid-May to mid-June – about the time the terrace opens – it becomes a pilgrimage destination for the "festival du homard" (lobster festival). Fortunately, the Lachine Canal is nearby so you can work off those extra pounds.

Taverne sur le Square 1 Westmount Square Ⓣ 514/989-9779; **Métro Atwater.** Hardly a tavern, this restaurant at the corner of rues Ste-Catherine and Wood has a clean, modern look, done up in creams and earth tones, with art for sale on the walls and a nice terrace out front. The food is equally posh, with grilled calamari salad a popular starter, and pan-roasted salmon and occasionally lamb shank on a bed of lentils among the mains on the $25–30 *table d'hôte*. It's all accompanied by a long wine list writ large in the freestanding wine cellar. Closed Sun; no lunch Sat.

Bars and lounges

W ith its 3am closing time and minimum drinking age of 18, Montréal's vibrant **bar scene** has earned it a reputation as the party capital of Canada. The majority of bars start serving at lunchtime, though many don't open until mid-afternoon, especially in the colder months. Things really tend to kick off with the bustling *5 à 7* happy hour (see box, p.171), and many bars remain packed well into the early hours, especially on the weekend – which for many here begins on Thursdays. Quite a few bars, however, only tend to get going around 11pm.

Several of the places listed below are part café or restaurant (but best for drinking) and may have a small dance floor or host bands on some nights. Similarly, many clubs and live music venues keep things well lubricated with cocktails and pitchers of beer (see Chapter 12, "Clubs and live music"). And anywhere with a decent terrace will be packed with drinkers for the *5 à 7*. For quieter spots to quaff a few, see our café and restaurant reviews in Chapter 10, "Cafés and restaurants", though with the increasing trend for eating spots to heat up as suave lounges after the kitchen closes, these so-called "supper clubs" get progressively louder after midnight. Since smoking indoors is banned, bars are now easy to spot by the huddles of smokers puffing away outside, and, conversely, places that look dead may have a heaving scene on the terrace out back.

Without a doubt, the best spot to bar hop is the **Plateau**, where on weekends it feels like the whole city has come to party. There's a great mixing of Franco-phones and Anglophones, although the smaller bars on and around **rue St-Denis** tend to have a more Gallic flair. **Boulevard St-Laurent** has every-thing from flashy resto-bars to grungy student watering-holes, with some fabulously hip lounges sprinkled in between.

The **Downtown** scene is also reliable, if (not surprisingly) less exciting, with bars catering to businesspeople and McGill and Concordia students dotted about. The action here centres on **rue Crescent**, where the block north of rue Ste-Catherine is choked with bars and pick-up joints, but there's less testo-sterone and a more neighbourly feel in a couple of the watering holes on parallel **rue Bishop**.

The **Quartier Latin**'s terrace-fronted bars on **rue St-Denis** draw a rollicking crowd; nearby bars in the **Village** are covered in Chapter 13, "Gay Montréal". **Vieux-Montréal** is starting to show up on the drinking radar; in addition to the terraces lining **Place Jacques-Cartier**, which often have a festive vibe, a happening lounge scene is evolving in hotel bars and rooftop terraces. In **Outremont**, you're better off having a glass of wine in a café or restaurant on **avenue Laurier**, whereas adjacent **Mile End** has more and more cool alterna-tive places along boulevard St Laurent and on cross streets like rue St-Viateur and avenue Bernard.

Note that you should tip the bar staff fifteen percent (usually a buck a beer, a little more for cocktails) – the perks constitute the main whack of their wages. Even so, don't ever expect to see your pint filled to the brim – and stick to local brews (around $5–5.50) if you're on a budget as imports are usually a couple of dollars more. If you're planning on a long night, leave the car behind; **drinking and driving** penalties are harsh and taxis are cheap and plentiful. Be forewarned that beer tends to be stronger here than in the US or the UK – five percent is standard, dry beers and the like are around six percent and some of the local brews are even more lethal. For more on regional beers and the city's brewpubs, see "Les bières" in the Food & Drink colour section.

All bars and lounges are listed in the relevant chapter maps throughout the Guide.

Downtown

Alexandre et Fils 1454 rue Peel ☎514/288-5105, ⓦwww.chezalexandre.com; **Métro Peel.** A Parisian café, bistro and brasserie rolled into one, replete with marble-topped tables and rattan chairs facing the street. Pose with the rest of the *beau monde* while quaffing one of the dozen wines by the glass.

Altitude 737 1 Place Ville-Marie, level PH2 ☎514/397-0737, ⓦwww.altitude737.com; **Métro McGill or Bonaventure.** The bar itself here is surprisingly drab, but that's no matter as it's all about the view: a pair of large terraces occupy two arms of Place Ville-Marie's cross, where you can enjoy a drink surrounded on three sides with nothing but the tops of Downtown skyscrapers and the city spread out below.

Benelux 245 rue Sherbrooke O ☎514/543-9750, ⓦwww.brasseriebenelux.com; **Métro Place-des-Arts.** Given its location in a bland apartment tower, the dark, chic interior of this new brewpub comes as a surprise, with its stainless counters lined by swivel chairs. Witbier (a cloudy white beer), stout, blonde Belgian abbey beer and other varieties ferment in the vats appearing through the window behind the bar. The bare walls and terrazzo floor make for a lot of echo – if you want to chat, lounge on one of the modular sofas inside the old bank vault in back.

Brutopia 1219 rue Crescent ☎514/393-9277, ⓦwww.brutopia.net; **Métro Peel or Guy-Concordia.** A cosy yet occasionally boisterous three-floor pub with exposed-brick walls serving up tapas and pub grub to accompany a great selection of tasty ales, porters and stouts that are brewed in the vats next to where customers chat or play board games. Live music most nights, but no cover charge.

Cock 'n' Bull Pub 1944 rue Ste-Catherine O ☎514/933-4556; **Métro Guy-Concordia.** There's a good mix of old, crusty regulars and fresh-faced Concordia students at this unpretentious watering hole at the western end of Downtown. The cheap tap beers keep many of them rooted until closing. Pop by the Monday arts-and-crafts night for something different.

Hurley's Irish Pub 1225 rue Crescent ☎514/861-4111, ⓦwww.hurleysirishpub.com; **Métro Peel or Guy-Concordia.** Located a little south of the rue Crescent carnival, *Hurley's* is one of the city's best Irish pubs, its warren of stone-walled rooms and back terrace filled with friendly regulars downing pints of Guinness in the hope that it'll improve their dart-tossing skills. There's a nice selection of single malts and good pub food served from 11am until just after the live bands start up at 9.30pm nightly.

Jimbo's Pub 1238 rue Bishop ☎514/398-9661; **Métro Guy-Concordia.** A dark and smoky local favourite with a friendly Anglophone crowd that surges before and after the comedy and improv shows at *Comedyworks* upstairs (see box, p.196). There's karaoke on the main floor whenever the owner is in the mood.

Madhatter Saloon 1220 rue Crescent ☎514/987-9988, ⓦwww.madhattersaloon.com; **Métro Peel or Guy-Concordia.** Although popular with students from nearby Concordia, the main studies in this rumpled campus pub involve who can down a pint of *rousse* or other microbrew the fastest. Nightly drink specials. If it looks empty, it may be because everyone heads to the rooftop terrace first.

Magnétic Terrasse Hôtel de la Montagne, 1430 rue de la Montagne ☎514/288-5656; **Métro Peel.** Like a little piece of Miami perched twenty stoeys up, this rooftop terrace lets you sip on a cocktail by the pool while gazing out over Downtown and the St Lawrence. Busiest for the *5 à 7*, but also popular with Downtown workers looking for a quick lunchtime dip in the pool and with strippers working on their tans. Open mid-May to early Sept (11.30am–3am), whenever the sun is shining.

McKibbin's Irish Pub 1426 rue Bishop ☎514/288-1580, ⓦwww .mckibbinsirishpub.com; Métro Guy-Concordia. Wood timbers, floors and tables give this relaxed pub a cosy feel conducive to conversations fuelled by quality pub grub and pints of Guinness, Harp, Kilkenny, Hoegaarden and the like – but stick to the basement level if you don't want to be interrupted by the cover bands that play most nights from around 10pm. There's also a dance club upstairs and a terrace out back.

McLean's Pub 1210 rue Peel ☎514/392-7770, ⓦwww.mcleanspub.com; Métro Peel. Centrally located near the Centre Infotouriste and facing Square Dorchester, this attitude-free tavern lacks a cohesive identity – TVs beaming sports matches contrast with the ornate beamed ceiling, and the crowd is equally varied with businessmen at lunch and for the *4 à 8*, and students in the evenings. There are also a couple of pool tables upstairs.

Nyks 1250 rue de Bleury ☎514/866-1787, ⓦwww.nyks.ca; Métro Place-des-Arts. A handy escape from the festival crowds at nearby Place des Arts, this spot has an almost rustic feel with scuffed wooden floors and tables nearly crowding out the garage-door windows. There are some interesting options on the short menu, from tapas and veggie burgers to *onglet de bison*, though most come for cheap shooters ($3) or a pint of Belle Gueule. Live music some nights, with a regular jazz slot on Tuesdays.

Peel Pub 1196 rue Peel ☎514/871-5930, ⓦwww.peelpub.com; Métro Peel. A pilgrimage spot for first-year McGill students – and sports fans who come for the cheap pitchers of draft and largely forgettable food (try the cheap rib steak, if pressed) – in an air-conditioned, mess-hall atmosphere spread over two floors. You can come back to pay for your sins the next morning – $3.99 fry-ups are available from 8am.

Sharx 1606 rue Ste-Catherine O ☎514/934-3105; Métro Guy-Concordia. A cavernous, dimly lit pool hall with loud music in the basement of the Faubourg Ste-Catherine that draws a mix of young Downtown workers to its 36 tables ($12/hr; $20 deposit). You can also give one of the ten black-lit bowling lanes a try ($6 per person per game).

Sir Winston Churchill Pub 1459 rue Crescent ☎514/288-3814; Métro Peel or Guy-Concordia. A prime pick-up joint, this sprawling English-style pub, also known as "Winnie's", attracts an older crowd of local and visiting Anglophone professionals. Though there are pool tables, a small dance floor downstairs and a club upstairs, the real action is on the double-decker front terrace, *the* place to be seen on the Crescent strip.

Stogies 2015 rue Crescent ☎514/848-0069; Métro Peel or Guy-Concordia. Swanky cigar lounge, popular with businessmen, where you can still puff away on a *cubano* from the humidor while sipping a martini ($8.50 and up); it's one of the few places to have an exemption from the smoking ban, though cigarettes are not allowed except on the wraparound terrace. A DJ spins jazz and R&B on weekends. It's sandwiched between the small and friendly ground-floor *London Pub* and the chilled *Ice* bar-lounge (weekends only) up top.

Les 3 Brasseurs 1356 rue Ste Catherine O ☎514/788-9788, ⓦwww.les3brasseurs.ca; Métro Peel or Guy-Concordia. The French brewpub chain brings its welcome mix of artisanal beers and light meals – including Alsatian *flamms*, an ultra-thin, pizza-like dish – to a lively mezzanine-wrapped space with copper vats suspended over tall pew-style seating. There's another Downtown branch at 732 rue Ste Catherine O (☎514/788-6333), a Quartier Latin locale at 1658 rue St-Denis (☎514/845-1660) and a handy spot for thirst-quenching in Vieux-Montréal at 105 rue St-Paul E (☎514/788-6100).

Le Vieux Dublin Pub & Restaurant 1219a rue University ☎514/861-4448; Métro McGill. Don't let the windowless facade put you off – the inside of the *Old Dublin* (as it's better known) has a warm glow furnished by back-lit stained-glass panels, polished wood and the best pint of Guinness in town. Irish bands create a rollicking mood by cramming onto the corner stage nightly at 10pm. It's also a popular lunch spot for burgers and curries.

11

Vinyl 2109 rue de Bleury ☎514/588-0846;
Métro Place-des-Arts. Chilled-out lounge near
Place des Arts that attracts a twenty- and
thirty-something set. Occasional live bands
play in the early evenings against a backdrop
of cushy old sofas and tables draped with
red tablecloths. Later on, DJs get things
moving with anything from oldies to jungle
and reggae depending on the night.

Vieux-Montréal

In addition to the places listed below,
there's a branch of *Les 3 Brasseurs* (see
p.170); café/bistro *Java U* (see p.154)
becomes a hip lounge as the evening
wears on; and *Garde Manger* (see
p.155) continues to serve drinks after
the kitchen closes.

Café des Éclusiers 400 rue de la
Commune O (at rue McGill) ☎514/496-
0109; Métro Square-Victoria. The striking

wedge-shaped pavilion housing the café
provides a terrific backdrop for the canal-side
terrace, which always fills up first. Nab one of
the moulded seats on the raised promenade
for views of the Vieux-Port. Clever salads and
pastas appear on the lunch *table d'hôte*,
while the *5 à 7* crowds nibble on tapas.
Open May to Sept daily until 11pm.

La Cage aux Sports 395 rue Le Moyne
☎514/288-1115, ⊕www.cage.ca; Métro
Square-Victoria. If there's a big game on,
then head to this branch of a province-wide
sports bar chain for a pitcher of beer and
some popcorn while watching one of the
dozens of TVs surrounded by baseball
pennants and portraits of hockey players.
Don't come hungry, though – the food is
mediocre at best. Closed Sun.

Le Cigare du Pharaon 139 rue St-Paul O
☎514/843-4779; Métro Place-d'Armes. The
hints of Tintin at the adjacent *Le Petit
Moulinsart* (see p.155) run riot in this fun

5 à 7

Thanks in part to Montréal's continued economic health, there are still plenty of bars
throughout the city offering **happy-hour specials**, like two-for-one beers, once the
workday is done. Rather than referring to "happy hour", you're more likely to hear
Montrealers say such-and-such bar has a great *5 à 7* (*cinq à sept*) – literally 5 to 7pm,
the standard time for cheap booze – though many bars are stretching things to *4 à
8*. Unlike in many other North American cities, however, this deal rarely extends to
food, though a few places may offer cheap nibbles. This keeps the focus on drinking,
with the best spots (including almost anywhere with a terrace on a sunny day – see
below) usually packed full of boisterous people.

Numerous Downtown bars entice the after-work crowd, notably on and around rue
Crescent; elsewhere, you could start at *Pub Quartier Latin* (p.172), *Sky* (p.188) in the
Village, *Réservoir* (p.174) on the Plateau or *Dieu du Ciel* (p.175) in Mile End.

Top terraces

After months of huddling indoors, Montrealers take full advantage of the warm
weather by heading in droves to anywhere with a **terrasse** – pavement tables, patios
or garden or courtyard seating – even more so now that smoking is banned indoors.
The few places that aren't lucky enough to catch the al fresco trade will usually at
least have a few tables that are next to windows opened wide to the street. For a
brew with a view, a number of Vieux-Montréal hotels have rooftop terraces – *Auberge
du Vieux-Port*, *Hôtel Nelligan* and *Hôtel Place d'Armes* (see pp.138–139) – and the
major gay complexes (see pp.187–189), but you can't get higher than *Altitude 737*
(see p.169). Other choice terraces for a drink are:

B Side	p.173	Réservoir	p.174
Café des Éclusiers	p.171	Le Saint-Sulpice	p.172
Club Social	p.175	Le Ste-Élisabeth	p.173
Folies	p.161	Sir Winston Churchill Pub	p.170
Le Jardin Nelson	p.172	Terrasse Les Remparts	p.172
Madhatter Saloon	p.169	Vol de Nuit	p.175
Magnétic Terrasse	p.169		

bar, named after his *Cigars of the Pharaoh* adventures. You can rent one of the small coffins painted with mummified Tintin characters to store a bottle of your favourite tipple; otherwise, if the weather's warm, settle down in the loungey front bit or the courtyard terrace (given over to diners in the evening). Jazz acts and the like on various evenings may be free or cost $10–15 at the door.

Cobalt 312 rue St-Paul O ☎514/842-2960, ⊛www.cobalt-montreal.com; **Métro Square-Victoria or Place-d'Armes.** Stone walls give this small bar-restaurant a dark and cosy feel, perfect for indulging in a drink with a live-jazz chaser (Wed–Sat 8.30pm). You can also catch classical or jazz combos at the weekend musical brunches.

Le Jardin Nelson 407 Place Jacques-Cartier ☎514/861-5731, ⊛www .jardinnelson.com; **Métro Champ-de-Mars.** Most come here to enjoy a glass of wine on one of the finest terraces facing Place Jacques-Cartier, or in the large, romantic garden, but there are decent crepes and light meals as well. A jazz band plays throughout the day (joined by a vocalist for evening sets on weekends). Closed in winter.

Modavie 1 rue St-Paul O ☎514/287-9582, ⊛www.modavie.com; **Métro Place-d'Armes.** Although they serve pasta, steaks and grilled fish, the focal point of this bistro is the huge bar at its centre, popular with bureaucrats from nearby city hall who come to sip Scotch or port. Live jazz every evening from 7pm.

Pub St-Paul 124 rue St-Paul E ☎514/874-0485, ⊛www.pubstpaul.com; **Métro Place-d'Armes.** A large and friendly pub with passable grub and a good range of suds on tap. Its atmospheric location amid the stone buildings of one of Vieux-Montréal's prettiest cobblestone streets and its portside views ensure that it's packed. Rock and alternative bands play Fri & Sat ($5 after 9.30pm).

Suite 701 Hôtel Place d'Armes, 701 Côte de la Place d'Armes ☎514/904-1201, ⊛www.aixcuisine.com; **Métro Place-d'Armes.** A flashy crowd of models and rich young men descend for weekend cocktails and dancing to house in this long, high-ceilinged space where ornate cornices and pilasters contrast with a slick bar with back-lit shelves showcasing the quality booze. Earlier on, it's a quiet spot to lounge on the cubic sofas; as is the eighth-floor terrace,

where you can watch sunsets over the mountain or chill in the "ice bar" in winter. The short menu is top-notch, too, with tuna tartare and spicy rabbit wings from the same kitchen as hotel restaurant *Aix*.

Terrasse Les Remparts 97 rue de la Commune E ☎514/392-1649; **Métro Place-d'Armes.** For the best view of the Vieux-Port you can get with a drink in hand, head to this unnamed rooftop terrace on the top of the *Auberge du Vieux-Port* (take the lift to the fifth floor, then the stairs). It's run by the ground-floor *Les Remparts* restaurant, who provide good but pricey light meals on the rooftop – stick to drinking unless you're feeling flush. Open in decent weather from mid-May to mid-Sept (noon–10pm).

Quartier Latin

Le Cheval Blanc 809 rue Ontario E ☎514/522-0211, ⊛www.lechevalblanc.ca; **Métro Berri-UQAM.** Old-style Montréal pub, with the same Art Deco decor as when it opened in the 1940s; popular with a fun Francophone crowd. They brew their own beer, which is quite good – try one of the seasonal varieties or from the regular cast of amber, *rousse*, dark, bitter and wheat varieties. Occasional live music on Mondays.

L'Île Noire 342 rue Ontario E ☎514/982-0866, ⊛www.ilenoire.com; **Métro Berri-UQAM.** Named after the Tintin book in which he travels to Scotland (*The Black Island*, in English), this pub with cushy, dark-green booths attempts to help their clientele do the same. It certainly succeeds on the Scotch front, with an amazing selection of single-malt whiskeys, which you can chase with a pint of Tartan, bitter or stout.

Pub Quartier Latin 318 rue Ontario E ☎514/845-3301, ⊛www.pubquartierlatin.com; **Métro Berri-UQAM.** Stylish pub that attracts thirty-something professionals for the *5 à 7* on the terrace or at the large island bar, followed by students chilling out later in the evening in the sofa-like booths. DJs spin a mix of deep house, Eighties and funk.

Le Saint-Sulpice 1680 rue St-Denis ☎514/844-9458, ⊛www.lesaint-sulpice.com; **Métro Berri-UQAM.** A bar complex comprising paired three-storey grey-stone houses that's as active outside as inside. The lively terrace in front is a good place to watch the human traffic on rue St-Denis, but it's even more fun out back in the massive, boisterous garden. Inside is a warren of often-crowded rooms, with atmospheres conducive to chilling out, energetic dancing, or catching a rock or world music gig (Thurs–Sat).

Le Ste-Élisabeth 1412 rue Ste-Élisabeth ☎514/286-4302, ⓦwww.ste-elisabeth .com; Métro Berri-UQAM. Boxed in by high brick walls, the ivy-covered courtyard terrace is one of Montréal's finest – but if it's full (and it likely will be), a window seat on the upper floor is the next best thing. In winter, an open fire keeps things cosy for knocking back a Scotch or imported beer along with the casual but boisterous crowd of UQAM students and slightly older regulars.

Plateau Mont-Royal

L'Barouf 4171 rue St-Denis ☎514/844-0119, ⓦwww.barouf.qc.ca; Métro Mont-Royal. Though the fug of Gauloises smoke is now a memory, the rattan bistro chairs crowded about round tables still evoke a bit of the Parisian atmosphere that draws French expats for a glass of Stella and occasionally *le football*. The dark wood-panelled walls, beamed ceilings and bar bathed in red all create a warm glow below the curious louver-fans, and the window opened wide to the street makes a great place to people-watch.

Barraca 1134 av du Mont-Royal E ☎514/525-7741; Métro Mont-Royal. The glam but somehow unpretentious crowd creates a great vibe in this long, narrow tapas bar that glows with light from parchment-shaded lamps and spills into a cosy garden terrace. They may stop serving the $4–6 tapas dishes at 11pm, but the bar still offers a dozen Spanish wines by the glass, rums from all over the Caribbean and also happens to make a mean *mojito*. A DJ spins funky, jazzy beats most nights, though there's live jazz on Sundays (8pm).

Bifteck St-Laurent 3702 boul St-Laurent ☎514/844-6211; Métro Sherbrooke or Saint-Laurent. A loyal crowd of students and ex-students frequent this tavern to drink cheap pitchers of Boréale Rousse ($9, $10.50 weekend evenings) between sets of pool. The stereo blasts anything from hip-hop to hard rock, and band members occasionally drop in (Melissa Auf der Maur, who played bass for both Hole and Smashing Pumpkins, once worked here).

Bily Kun 354 av du Mont-Royal E ☎514/845-5392, ⓦwww.bilykun.com; Métro Mont-Royal. Tiled floors lend an Eastern European feel to this hopping Plateau bar, where stuffed ostrich heads look down on a mixed Anglo/Franco crowd. The music's too loud to really worry what language someone's speaking anyway, and the range of microbrews from mother bar *Le Cheval Blanc* (see p.172) provide more than adequate distraction. Live bands play everything from Francophone folk-pop to jazz and electronica early evenings (Tues–Sun 6–8pm) as well as in the *O Patro Vys* hall upstairs. If it's full, opt for *Plan B* (☎514/845-6060, ⓦwww.barplanb.ca), which opened across the street at no. 327 to handle the overflow – it's a groovy little bar in its own right.

△ Live music at Bily Kun

Blizzarts 3956a boul St-Laurent ☎514/843-4860; Métro Sherbrooke or Mont-Royal or bus #55. Funked-out lounge with retro bucket-chairs, semicircular booths, exhibitions by local artists on the walls and a dozen varieties of beer on tap. The tiny dance floor gets packed every night – there's a $4 cover charge for the dub and reggae on Wednesdays and scratch break and hip-hop Thursday nights. It's a buck more for the grooving afrofunk and hip-hop vibe on Fridays and the great electro set with a mash-up of styles on Saturdays. Opens at 9pm.

B-Side 3616 boul St-Laurent ☎514/973-5968; Métro Sherbrooke or Saint-Laurent. Give the downstairs club of the same name a miss and head up the external stairs on the right to one of the city's coolest terraces – the roof's been removed from the second floor to allow for drinking under the stars. They fire up the heat lamps on cooler nights. **Copacabana 3910 boul St-Laurent ☎514/982-0880; Métro Sherbrooke or Mont-Royal or bus #55.** Despite the truly awful decor – fake palm trees and beach-scene murals – the *Copa* attracts a loyal following of Anglo hipsters for a game of pool and lots of cheap beer ($12 for a large pitcher of Boréale Rousse). If happy hour seems to go on all night, it does – prices are low all the time.

Else's 156 rue Roy E ☎514/286-6689; Métro Sherbrooke. A great neighbourhood bar where you can hang out and play board games at the collage-covered tables while quaffing pints of local brews amid a good-natured buzz. There's also a choice selection of imported beers and scotches – the only downside is that to keep your table you need to order food (starting at only $2.50 for bar snacks, fortunately).

El Zaz Bar 4297 rue St-Denis ☎514/288-9798; Métro Mont-Royal. The garish piñata-coloured stairs and solarium of this second-floor bar create a festive feel perfect for knocking back margaritas and sangría. The rest of the bar is dark and tight, with a dance floor beneath a low ceiling cluttered with giant vines. There's a nightly $2–5 cover charge after 9.30pm for DJ sets and live bands (Thurs & Sun) playing anything from Québec pop to reggae or hip-hop.

△ À Gogo Lounge

À Gogo Lounge 3682 boul St-Laurent ☎514/286-0882; Métro Sherbrooke or Saint-Laurent. A long and narrow bar with psychedelic paintings on the walls and a great vibe on the weekends. There are loungey areas at the front and back where you can listen to the funky Sixties to Eighties tunes playing on the stereo and sip a martini while sitting in the palm of a giant, red plastic hand.

Laïka 4040 boul St-Laurent ☎514/842-8088, ⓦwww.laikamontreal.com; bus #55 or Métro Sherbrooke or Mont-Royal. Hip café by day, trendy lounge by night, *Laïka*'s urbane decor looks like it was torn from the pages of *Wallpaper* magazine, with designer fibreglass chairs set against the large tiles on the wall. In summer, the windows slide open, letting the sounds of the DJ sets spill onto the street.

Miami 3831 boul St-Laurent ☎514/845-2300; Métro Sherbrooke or bus #55. A total dive, but this dingy watering hole for Plateau nihilists and eternal students has cheap beer ($4 a pint) and $2.75 shots of Jägermeister and Jameson's that allow for some serious drinking. The rooftop terrace in back makes for a great escape from the crowded Main. Free pool, too.

Le P'tit Bar 3451 rue St-Denis ☎514/281-9124; Métro Sherbrooke. Though technically on the Plateau (it's just north of rue Sherbrooke), this small *boîte à chanson*, with its regular customers and Francophone appeal, has more in common with the Quartier Latin scene. French singers perform nightly (around 9.30pm onwards); during the day, content yourself with checking out the cartoon-strewn walls. Shows are free but they pass a hat around for the musicians.

Le Quincaillerie 980 rue Rachel E ☎514/524-3000; Métro Mont-Royal. Twenty-foot ceilings create a dramatic sense of space here, which the designers have taken advantage of with twin rows of chunky wooden tables precisely aligned under domed aluminium lamps and alongside photo-like murals. Nonetheless, it's still a *bar de quartier*, with locals drawn by a no-nonsense mix of French and English indie on the iPod and $3.75 pints during the *4 à 9* happy hour.

Réservoir 9 av Duluth E ☎514/849-7779; bus #55. Trendier than your typical brewpub, *Réservoir* serves up fancy bar snacks like fried cod balls or smoked mackerel (until 11pm) to accompany the ales and bitters brewed on the premises (a reasonable $5.50 a pint). If the stripped-back decor isn't to your liking, head upstairs and grab a seat on the terrace overlooking Duluth – if you can find a seat. Good weekend brunches, too.

Sofa 451 rue Rachel E ☎514/285-1011, ⓦwww.sofa-bar.com; Métro Mont-Royal. A wonderful little port and cigar lounge filled with low-slung banquettes tucked into cosy nooks. The dark-blue and burgundy interior is a bit gloomy in the day but at night it feels just fine for chilling or listening to bands playing soul, funk and R&B (Sat & other nights; $7).

Vol de Nuit 14 rue Prince-Arthur E ☎514/845-6243; Métro Sherbrooke or Saint-Laurent. Forgo the unremarkable interior here and nab a table on the pavement. In the summer, *Vol de Nuit*'s location at one of the busiest spots on rue Prince-Arthur's pedestrian strip makes it a mighty fine spot to share a big pitcher of sangría on a nice evening.

Mile End and Outremont

L'Assommoir 112 rue Bernard O ☎514/272-0777; bus #55. The back-lit bar at this trendy Mile-End lounge provides a backdrop for bottle-throwing acrobatics, a reflection of the skill that goes into the 350-strong cocktail list, including inventive martinis based on the likes of basil or red pepper. The DJs set-lists are similarly intriguing, running from *chanson* to house. You'll need to order a bite, though: there's a variety of tapas (starting at $5 but mostly around $10) and *ceviches*, tartares and grills ($15–$20) served until midnight (Thurs–Sat until 1.30am).

Baldwin Barmacie 115 av Laurier O ☎514/276-4282, ⓦwww.baldwinbarmacie.com; Métro Laurier or bus #55. A sleek bar to match the fancy restaurants on this strip; the split levels, adorned mainly in pale cream tones, pivot around a central bar where beer and cocktails are served up below funky light fixtures. A fashionable twenty- to thirty-something crowd grooves to DJs playing a wide mix running from rock to electro.

🏃 **Club Social 180 rue St-Viateur O ☎514/495-0114; bus #55 or #80.** The tree-shaded corner terrace at this Italian café-bar is a perfect spot to watch the goings-on along Mile End's hippest street,

with a beer or cappuccino in hand. Inside, old Italian men watch the soccer, ignoring the scenesters who've infiltrated their long-time haunt. There's a similar mix at *Café Olimpico* (also known as "Open Da Night"), a block to the east. Open 7am until around 11pm (midnight on weekends).

Dieu du Ciel 29 av Laurier O ☎514/490-9555, ⓦwww.dieuduciel.com; Métro Laurier or bus #55. Comfortable neighbourhood pub that fills up for the *3 à 7* when the tasty ales and lagers (brewed on the premises) go for $4.50 a pint. There's a constantly changing beer menu with some seven or eight brews (of the thirty or so house recipes, which include some potent abbey beers) – on tap at any given time.

The Green Room 5386 boul St-Laurent ☎514/495-4448, ⓦwww.mileend.ca; bus #55. There's a good vibe at this no-nonsense spot that attracts a young, energetic crowd and local musicians for DJ sessions of indie pop, which inevitably lead to dancing. The chunky wooden bar supports taps of Belle Gueule and St-Ambroise to keep things flowing. You can catch bands in the upstairs *Main Hall* show venue.

Mile End Bar 5322 boul St-Laurent ☎514/279-0200, ⓦwww.mileendbar.com; bus #55. A sleek spot with pale woods, varnished concrete bar and semicircular booths that won an award for its design – something that may or may not impress the stylish pretty-young-things who head straight upstairs for the techno-funk remixes on the dance floor ($8 cover upstairs Fri & Sat).

Sergent Recruteur 4801 boul St-Laurent ☎514/287-1412, ⓦwww.sergent-recruteur .com; Métro Laurier or bus #55. Now more of a restaurant, this local's haunt is still worth dropping into just for the British-style ales brewed, which include a rich cream ale, as well as a stout and hand-pumped bitter. They go well with original pizzas such as escargot and Portobello mushroom, or the even more exotic "Natashquan" pizza topped with *bourgot* (sea snails) and a creamy aubergine base. If you want to practice your French come on Sunday for storytelling night (Sept–May).

Whisky Café 5800 boul St-Laurent ☎514/278-2646, ⓦwww.whiskycafe.ca; Métro Outremont or bus #55. Way up at the corner of avenue Bernard, this elegantly decorated bar draws a wealthy clientele of all ages – the prices aren't cheap, but then the liquor's purely top shelf. The design-conscious approach even extends to the toilets, with water cascading down a zinc wall in the boys' room, and featuring the only girls' urinal in Montréal.

Côte-des-Neiges

McCarold 5400 chemin de la Côte-des-Neiges ☏**514/344-9009; Métro Côte-des-Neiges.** In summer, the umbrella-shaded front terraces of this friendly neighbourhood pub fill up quickly with a crowd of locals and Université de Montréal students. Inside the well-worn interior, taps for a dozen brands of local and imported beer as well as a locally produced cider line the bar, though if you're in a group you can nab a table in the back room with its own tap (Belle Gueule for 25¢ an ounce). A decent menu of burgers, *moules frites* and fish and chips is available until midnight. Live bands on Saturdays. Open from 11.30am (3pm on weekends).

Clubs and live music

O n weekend nights, Montréal's main drags are an endless parade of glamorous fashionistas ready to cruise the city's spectacular **nightlife** scene. The city has long been considered Canada's nightlife capital, and with good reason – dozens of **clubs** pulsate until the wee hours, pumping out music that ranges from Madonna remixes to thumping drum'n'bass, with a roster of home-grown and international DJs manning the turntables.

Filling out the city's nightlife possibilities is a wide range of **live music** venues, from large concert halls where you may luck out and catch one of Montréal's latest **indie-rock** darlings – like Arcade Fire, Wolf Parade, Stars or The Stills – on a rare hometown tour (see box, p.180), to intimate jazz joints that prove the city's **jazz** roots remain strong. Indeed, Louis Armstrong, Ella Fitzgerald, Dizzy Gillespie and Billie Holiday all played to sold-out crowds here during the Roaring Forties. Charlie Parker recorded *Montréal 1953*, and the city produced its own jazz star in Oscar Peterson. But traditional **rock**, **punk** and **ska** bands also take their share of the limelight and a small **folk** and **spoken-word** scene adds a pleasantly low-key vibe. When heading out to catch a show, keep in mind that bands usually get off-stage no later than 1am, and some end as early as 11pm. Accordingly, Montrealers treat seeing a band as an evening's primer – not its climax.

Though some live venues close once the show is over, Montréal's clubs serve alcohol until 3am, and even then the party goes on. Heavy-hitting DJs keep the dance floors packed well past dawn at the large (and legal) **after-hours clubs**, which serve up juice and caffeine-laced drinks rather than alcohol; it's not hard to figure out how the denizens of the nightlife scene stay up.

Clubs

Montréal's **clubs** are easy to find – just look for the jostling line-ups spilling out onto the sidewalks either Downtown or in the Plateau, along the stretch of the Main between rue Milton and avenue des Pins. **Dance clubs** in the latter neighbourhood tend to groove to house and techno, with some R&B and funk also clambering on deck, drawing young and up-for-it Francophones and Anglophones. Top 40 and retro pop generally rule Downtown, especially among the clubs catering to a slightly older and mainly Anglophone crowd on and around rue Crescent. Downtown's clubs also offer the most in the way of "Ladies' Nights" – decide for yourself whether the free entry and drinks outweigh the meat-market atmosphere.

Most clubs open around 10pm but only get really busy at about 1am, and usually apply a cover charge ranging from $5–15, with fees towards the higher end on weekends (and even higher at after-hours venues). Still, the weekend starts as early as Thursday night for club kids (especially as some venues only open Thursday to Saturday or Sunday). The city's best **gay clubs**, often the most happening spots in town, are listed on p.187. The popular trend towards **DJ bars and cafés** continues unabated in Montréal, offering a more relaxed environment in which to still hear great music; we cover some of the best in Chapter 11, "Bars and lounges".

If you're off to one of the larger clubs, it's a good idea to **dress up** – you likely won't be refused entrance, but you may still feel a tad out of place. At most lounges, and the clubs in the Village, though, dress codes are virtually nonexistent. Note that some clubs have a 21-and-over policy on some nights.

The evening doesn't have to end when the clubs call it a night at 3am, however, as two excellent **after-hours spots** pick up the slack on weekends, getting started only when the others close shop. To suss out the latest club happenings, you'll find plenty of **flyers** at the Plateau's record shops or clubwear boutiques. You can also check online; two of the best sites are: ⓦwww.nightlifemontreal.ca, a French site (with listings under "agendas") and ⓦwww.montreal-clubs.com, a relatively up-to-date English site.

Dance clubs

Central Station 4432 boul St-Laurent ☎514/842-2836, ⓦwww.clubcentralstation.com; Métro Mont-Royal. This Plateau hotspot draws a big late-twenties crowd to its large main dance floor grooving to house. The a/c and sleek Miami-style decor keep things feeling and looking cool, though the hip-hop room in back gets packed to capacity fast. Fri–Sun only.

Club 6/49 1112 rue Ste-Catherine O ☎514/868-1649; Métro Peel. Long-running Latin dance club with plenty of tables to sit at if you don't have the spirit for salsa and merengue. If you do have the urge but don't know how, drop by for free salsa lessons on Monday and Thursday nights. Friendly crowd, but can be a bit cruisey on the weekends, which also feature live bands.

Club Vatican 1432 rue Crescent ☎514/845-3922, ⓦwww.clubvatican.com; Métro Peel or Guy-Concordia. The pope certainly didn't sanctify this rue Crescent club, notable for its Gothic-lounge decor of white brick walls and stained-glass windows. The irreverent name doesn't seem to bother the hordes of Anglophone twenty-somethings who strut their stuff to R&B, hip-hop and house on the dance floor. Fri & Sat 9pm–3am.

Exit 3553 boul St-Laurent ☎514/285-2223, ⓦwww.exit3553.com; Métro Sherbrooke or bus #55. The decor in this long and narrow two-storey club is minimal, stripped back to the steel beams, leaving the focus firmly on dancing. The hip-hop sessions from Thursday to Saturday attract a mostly under-25 crowd.

Jet 1003 rue Ste-Catherine E ☎514/842-2582, ⓦwww.jetnightclub.com; Métro Beaudry. One of the city's top spots for danceable R&B, with a dash of old school, house and club anthems. Make sure to dress up as the door turns away clubbers wearing baggy trousers, jeans, hats or running shoes. Fri & Sat 10pm–3am.

Living 4521 boul St-Laurent ☎514/286-9986, ⓦwww.livingnightclub.com; Métro Mont-Royal or bus #55. *Living* took an old Plateau bank building, kept its classical facade, and turned the interior into a three-floor club frequented by under-35 yuppies and musically ruled by urban beats ranging from R&B to deep house. The ground-storey bar, with its lofty ceiling and snug sitting areas, is the best spot to scope out the action. Thurs–Sun; open bar for women all-night Sun.

Newtown 1476 rue Crescent ☎514/284-6555, ⓦwww.newtown.ca; Métro Peel or Guy-Concordia. The streamlined, horizontal louvers on the facade hint at the sleek design inside F1-racer Jacques Villeneuve's nightlife complex. The bright and beautiful head to the rooftop terrace, stopping off at the club's own restaurant for pricey Mediterranean food or a drink in the lounge before bopping to disco, house and R&B grooves in the basement club.

Orchid 3556 boul St-Laurent ☎514/848-6398, ⓦwww.orchidnightclub.com; Métro Sherbrooke or bus #55. A swanky second-storey nightclub with five bars and comfy lounge areas overlooking the Main and the heaving dance floor; it's very popular with fashionable young things on the make who dance to a mix of commercial house, hip-hop or R&B on any night of the week. Thurs–Sat from 10pm; Sat 21 and over.

Passeport 4156 rue St-Denis ☎514/842-6063; **Métro Sherbrooke or Mont-Royal.** An intimate bar-club that evokes the polished 1980s – spot lighting cuts through the black-painted decor, booze is served from a burnished wood-and-steel bar and the smallish dance floor gleams with stainless steel. Not surprisingly, Eighties music is the norm. Dress stylishly in black, and you'll fit right in.

🏃 **Société des Arts Technologiques (SAT) 1195 boul St-Laurent** ☎514/844-2033, ⓦwww.sat.qc.ca; **Métro St-Laurent.** A large, stripped-down warehouse-like space where you can catch some of the most cutting-edge electronic sound and video in North America, as part of an evolving digital culture centre that promotes the development of local DJs and VJs. On summer weekends, *SAT* also organizes frequent outdoor performances at the facing Place de la Paix.

Time Supper Club 997 rue St-Jacques O ☎514/392-9292, ⓦwww.timesupperclub.com; **Métro Bonaventure.** Tucked away in an industrial area just east of Old Montreal, this sophisticated brainchild of trend-setter David McMillan (the man responsible for *Globe*; see p.159) takes its cues from New York and South Beach hotspots; the sleek 7500-square-foot space combines 1940s Art Deco furnishings with warm orange hues and glamorous denizens, who descend on the place for dinner (from 7pm) and stay for drinking and dancing (from 11pm) Wednesday to Saturday. Be sure to dress the part.

🏃 **Tokyo 3709 boul St-Laurent** ☎514/842-6838, ⓦwww.tokyobar.com; **Métro Sherbrooke or bus #55.** A busy club in the thick of the Main that attracts a mixed ethnic crowd to its main room decked out with Japanese lanterns, plush and intimate booths, and R&B and Top 40 tunes. A smaller room off to the left, known as the *Blue Room*, spins house and techno to scenesters lounging on sunken oval sofas. There's a smashing rooftop deck in summer. Wed–Sun 10pm–3am.

△ The scene at Tokyo

Montréal has boasted a thriving **music scene** for quite a while – the combination of a vibrant cultural mix and abundant cheap venues creating the ideal conditions for musical expression – but it wasn't until 2005 that the international media took note and proclaimed it the next big, post-Seattle, post-Brooklyn city to watch. And all because of a little band named Arcade Fire whose **indie-rock** sound was winning praise from rock icons David Bowie and David Byrne and rave reviews from music critics around the globe. While locals were none too fussed by the new attention, and many even rejected it outright, there was no denying that this French-Canadian city, once known primarily for exporting Leonard Cohen, Oscar Peterson and, to some extent, Céline Dion (who's actually from Charlemagne, some 30km from Montréal) had set a new musical standard.

That said, Montréal lacks the single, unifying sound of a Seattle or a Brooklyn. While Arcade Fire and other local bands like Stars are working with an indie-rock sound, other big-name acts like Wolf Parade are known for **art rock**, and The Stills for **post-punk**. At the same time, the city has established itself as a global pioneer of **electronica**, thanks to homegrown DJs like Tiga, Kid Koala, Mateo Murphy and A-Trak (who now plays with Kanye). The *SAT* (see p.179) not only cultivates these talents, but MUTEK, a cutting-edge electronica festival that debuted in 1999, now attracts 70 local and international turntablists and audiovisualists to the city for a week of DJ sessions, workshops and video experimentation every year (see p.224).

The **French music** scene adds its own distinctive strains to the mix, too, even influencing the names of local bands; the post-punk Les Georges Leningrad and industrial Et Sans are not, in fact, French bands at all, but English ones. Bona fide French artists like Les Cowboys Fringants (The Frisky Cowboys) and Dan Bigras, meanwhile, tend to be more political than their Anglophone counterparts; the former, for instance, reappropriates traditional **Québécois folk music** and loads it with slangy, sovereignist lyrics.

One event that brings it all together is **Pop Montréal** – a five-day music festival showcasing major Montréal and international talent; past acts have included international heavy-hitters Beck and Interpol, plus local names like Tiga, Arcade Fire and The Dears (see p.227). It's also one of the only times you're likely to see a major Montréal band at home, since, in order to maintain their newfound success, most of them are usually on the road.

After-hours clubs

Aria 1280 rue St-Denis ☎514/987-6712, ⊛www.arianightclub.com; Métro Berri-UQAM. From 2am until 10am, Montréal's club kids dance the night and morning away in this former cinema to house music, with occasional detours into techno and trance, all of it pumping from a massive sound system. Big-name guest DJs keep the main room going while residents energize the urban room. Fri & Sat only; $10–25.

Stereo 858 rue Ste-Catherine E ☎514/286-0325, ⊛www.stereo -nightclub.com; Métro Beaudry. Founded by local hotshot DJ Mark Anthony and New York's DJ David Morales, and outfitted with a stellar sound system, this Quartier Latin club is consistently ranked one of the best of its kind in the world. Techno and house are on deck from 2am to 10am (there's also a bar to get primed in from 11pm to 3am). The guest DJ roster includes local talent and brilliant out-of-towners too; a host of UK and US DJs like Danny Tenaglia, as well as Dutch superstars Armin Van Buuren and Tiesto have headlined here. Fri & Sat only; $25, $30 for big-name guests.

Partied late and don't want to call it quits just yet? DJs keep the music going well into day – and evening – every Sunday from early May to late September, as part of an outdoor event known as **Piknic Electronik** (Electronic Picnic) held on **Parc Jean-Drapeau** (see p.117), around Calder's *Man* stabile on Île Ste-Hélène (and occasionally in the Jardins des Floralies, on Île Notre-Dame). The event goes from 1–9pm and features anywhere from three to five DJs on its weekly roster, with local, Canadian and international talent laying down tracks – Richie Hawtin, Luc Raymond, Magda and Mateo Murphy have all made appearances at the outdoor fest.

You're as likely to be sharing the grass with families as you are with club kids – which is part of its appeal – and, considering it only costs $5–7 to attend, it's a lot more affordable than hitting *Stereo* or *Aria*. Plus, you may luck out and get to hear the previous night's headliner doing a bit of a post-show on the wheels of steel. No matter who's on the decks, it's the perfect way to chill out at the end of a weekend – all you have to do is bring your own blanket and picnic supplies. Check ⓦwww .piknicelectronik.com for the weekly line-up.

Live music venues

Unlike dance clubs, Montréal's **live music** venues are pretty well dispersed throughout the city. **Jazz** spots have the highest profile, and there's quite a bit of **worldbeat**, but **folk**, **rock**, **punk** and **ska** also have a good hold on the performance scene. Going to a gig in Montréal is nowhere near as much of a regular night out as it is in Toronto and similarly sized US cities, however. Many of the locales do double duty as watering holes or dance clubs, but when there is a performance on, it typically begins around 9pm, with headliners taking the stage around 11pm. Big-ticket bands play in the city's **large venues**, most of which are located in or around the Quartier Latin, though some marquee names headline open-air shows at Parc Jean-Drapeau. None of the major venues has a favourite genre, and instead book whoever can fill the place.

Covers range from $3 at smaller clubs on weekdays to upwards of $25 at the larger music halls on the weekends, with freebie shows occasionally thrown in during the week. Your best bet for free shows, though, are the city's Irish and brew pubs, reviewed in Chapter 11, "Bars and lounges". For up-to-the-minute show listings, consult the *Mirror* (ⓦwww.montrealmirror.com) and *Hour* (ⓦwww.afterhour.com), two free English-language weeklies available in stores and on newspaper stands. The *Montreal Gazette* (ⓦwww.montrealgazette.com), the English-language daily, also carries comprehensive listings; its Friday weekend guide is best. Tickets for big shows are available through the Admission network (☏514/790-1245 or 800/361-4595, ⓦwww.admission.com), which adds a hefty service charge ($6.99–9.75 per ticket, depending on the venue), and at each venue's box office.

Jazz and blues

Bistro à Jojo 1627 rue St-Denis ☏514/843-5015, ⓦwww.bistroajojo.com; Métro Berri-UQAM. A step below sidewalk level, the low ceilings and stone walls give this blues cave an intimate feel, as do the wooden chairs and tables at close quarters. It's been an

unpretentious spot for a pitcher of beer and an earful of blues since 1975. Shows nightly from 10 or 10.30pm.
House of Jazz 2060 rue Aylmer ☏514/842-8656, ⓦwww.houseofjazz.ca; Métro Peel. Known as *Biddles* until the eponymous Charlie Biddle passed away in 2003, this Downtown jazz joint offers up a sampling of

jazz with a side order of ribs. But, for a mere $5 cover charge, you can skip the meat and savour a pint at the bar while being serenaded by the in-house band from 8pm–midnight.

Jello Bar 151 rue Ontario E ☎514/285-2621, ⓦwww.jellobar.com; Métro St-Laurent. Live acid jazz, blues and funk acts frequently take to the tiny stage at this Quartier Latin bar-cum-lounge furnished with 1960s and 1970s novelties like lava lamps and loveseats. They serve superb martinis, too.

Upstairs 1254 rue Mackay ☎514/931-6808, ⓦwww.upstairsjazz.com; Métro Guy-Concordia. *Upstairs* is actually downstairs in a half-basement ensconced between walls of exposed rock and wood. It's certainly the city's most easy-going jazz spot, with fresh jazz and blues on tap nightly in a wonder-fully attitude-free atmosphere. There's also a pleasant outdoor terrace come summer-time. Admission charges on Friday to Sunday are between $10 and $20 – more if it's an exceptional act.

Worldbeat and folk

Balattou 4372 boul St-Laurent ☎514/845-5447; bus #55. The city's main nightclub for African music (with forays into Latin and worldbeat) has been around so long – since 1986 – that it's achieved institution status. The dark and smoky establishment attracts a mostly older crowd out to the Plateau for weekends of African, Caribbean and Latin American music – think salsa, souk and lambada. Tuesdays and Wednesdays usually showcase live worldbeat acts from just about anywhere.

Barfly 4062a boul St-Laurent ☎514/284-6665; bus #55. This Plateau hole-in-the-wall is the city's least pretentious showcase for local folksy and alternative bands. The beer is cheap, there's a pool table to while away the hours, and the odd time a cover applies, it's usually next to nothing.

Casa del Popolo 4873 boul St-Laurent ☎514/284-3804, ⓦwww.casadelpopolo.com; Métro Laurier bus or #55. "The House of the People" is a sofa-strewn, low-key Plateau spot where high-calibre spoken-word evenings and folk and other bands perform for a marginal fee. A good spot to mingle with the locals any time from noon until 3am. Some similar shows take place at *La*

Sala Rossa down the block at no. 4848, which is owned by the same people.

Les Deux Pierrots 104 rue St-Paul E ☎514/861-1686 or 861-1270, ⓦwww.lespierrots.com; Métro Champ-de-Mars. Québécois folk singers are the mainstay of this Vieux-Montréal club where everyone sings along. There's usually a good crowd, but don't expect to understand a word unless your French is excellent. There's an outside terrace in the summer.

Rock, electropop, punk and ska

Café Campus 57 rue Prince-Arthur E ☎514/844-1010; Métro St-Laurent. A low-frills venue with two stages showcasing local bands that run the gamut from rock to electropop and a DJ that keeps things humming when there's no band in the house.

Café Chaos 2031 rue St-Denis ☎514/844-0738, ⓦwww.cafechaos.qc.ca; Métro Berri-UQAM. Punk, metal and alt-rock bands play upstairs at this Quartier Latin co-operative; DJs take over when the stage is quiet. The ground-floor bar, lined with bright blue walls and wood panelling, is a laid-back, student hangout. Hosts occasional art shows and theatre happenings as well.

Divan Orange 4234 boul St-Laurent ☎514/840-9090, ⓦwww.ledivanorange.org; bus #55. An intimate live-music venue that showcases everything from reggae and R&B to electropop and jazz fusion, this worker's co-op has something on tap five nights a week. Shows start at 9.30 or 10pm most days of the week (except Monday); a pay-as-you-wish cover goes to the band. Food is served, too.

Foufounes Électriques 87 rue Ste-Catherine E ☎514/844-5539, ⓦwww.foufounes.qc.ca; Métro St-Laurent. Don't let the bizarre name ("The Electric Buttocks") throw you; this graffiti-strewn complex on the Quartier Latin's western outskirts is the best place in Québec to catch punk and ska acts – and has been for two decades. In addition to punk outfits like Ripcordz, Ab Irato and Hands of Death, you might also catch groups from across the alt spectrum, from hardcore to stoner rock. A huge outside terrace is perfect for summer evenings, while downstairs there's usually one or two people involved in some form of body painting in the ground-floor bar, crowded

△ Revellers line up outside Foufounes Électriques

with young Francophones knocking back cheap pitchers of beer. Admission to the bar is free; if you want to catch an act on one of the two stages upstairs, you're looking at $5–21 or more, depending on how massive the band is. Club nights (in the second room or after the band has packed up) take a different theme each night (eg Wednesday is skater night) and vary from $3 early in the week to $8 on Saturday.

Large venues

Centre Bell 1260 rue de la Gauchetière O ☎514/932-2582, ⓦwww.centrebell.ca; Métro Bonaventure. The Canadiens' ice rink is covered over for mainstream stadium rock and pop acts in Montréal's 21,000-seat main arena.

🏃 **Club Soda** 1225 boul St-Laurent ☎514/286-1010, ⓦwww.clubsoda.ca; Métro St-Laurent. Small enough to remain intimate, but still large enough to attract quality acts like French DJ Laurent Garnier and the Thievery Corporation. It's especially popular during the Jazz Festival.

Métropolis 59 rue Ste-Catherine E ☎514/844-3500 or 861-5851, ⓦwww.metropolismontreal .ca; Métro St-Laurent. Hosts acts with fairly large followings like Björk, The White Stripes and The Flaming Lips in a 2200-capacity venue that started off as a vaude-ville theatre. With recent renovations, they've improved the sightlines throughout the large main floor space and from the balconies.

🏃 **Spectrum** 318 rue Ste-Catherine O ☎514/861-5851, ⓦwww.spectrum demontreal.ca; Métro Place-des-Arts. Excellent acoustics, hundreds of candlelit tables and an upstairs balcony with great views of the stage. You should get there early to get a seat. Drum'n'bass star Roni Size has played here as has Brazil's Bebel Gilberto. Note that there has been talk of building a new performance hall and perhaps closing *Spectrum* down; call ahead to confirm.

La Tulipe 4530 rue Papineau ☎514/529-5000, ⓦwww.latulipe.ca; Métro Papineau and bus #45. Indie rock, jazz and contemporary French singers are the buzz words at this attractive live-music newcomer set in a grand 1913 movie house on the western fringes of the Plateau. Tickets range from $5–32.50 depending on the act. The same company also manages *Le National* (1220 rue Ste-Catherine E; Métro Beaudry).

Gay Montréal

ontréal is rightly considered to be one of the most open and tolerant cities in the world. The province of Québec was one of the first jurisdictions anywhere to begin recognizing the rights of same-sex couples; a year after the Parti Québécois rolled into office, they introduced Bill 88 in December 1977, which included "sexual orientation" in the province's charter of rights two decades before the federal government followed suit. Subsequent provincial bills gave further rights and allowed same-sex civil unions that approached parity with marriage. But Québec was trumped by the Ontario Court of Appeal's declaration that marriage should no longer be restricted to opposite-sex couples, and after further lawsuits throughout Canada, the federal government finally sanctioned same-sex marriages in 2005, making Canada one of only a few countries in the world to legalise gay marriage (a state of affairs that the Conservative government elected in 2006 intends to rescind, or at least weaken).

Things haven't always been so welcoming, though. The attitudes of police lagged behind those of provincial politicians and the rest of society, with landmark raids on the *Truxx* bar in 1977 and the Sex Garage loft party in 1990, both resulting in large demonstrations. Nor were local authorities tolerant: until the mid-1970s, the city's gay district was located around rue Stanley, but in an effort to present a "cleaner" image of Montréal for the Olympic Games, gay businesses faced increased harassment. Partly due to this pressure, and for economic reasons, they subsequently relocated to the then-run-down Centre-Sud neighbourhood, where the **Village** (see p.89) has since developed along the dozen or so blocks of rue Ste-Catherine between rues Amherst and Papineau, and you'll find the majority of the city's gay services, **accommodation** and **nightlife** here as well as an open, often cruisey attitude.

Matters steadily improved for the gay community, thanks in part to a joint police-community committee, as well as the province's progressive politics. The Village continued to diversify, with the bars being joined by shops and restaurants that catered to both the gay community and workers in the nearby media institutions. And with prices rising in the Plateau, the streets surrounding rue Ste-Catherine are becoming an increasingly desirable place to live, regardless of one's sexual orientation.

The city tourist board heavily promotes Montréal as a top gay destination (notably in the run-up to the first World Outgames in 2006) and with good reason. From the extravagant **circuit parties** and huge **pride celebrations** to the city's wealth of cafés, restaurants, shops, saunas, bars and nightclubs that are hopping throughout the year, there is a wealth of possibilities here for gay visitors, be they leather boys, drag queens and even sedate, long-term partners.

Information and resources

It's pretty hard to find English-language **information** about gay and lesbian life in Montréal – such publications tend to come and go, *to be* (Ⓦwww.tobe.ca) being the latest – although the English weeklies *Mirror* and *Hour* (see p.30) may also have some info to get you started. As long as you know just a smattering of French you should be able to decipher the **listings** in the free French-language magazines found in bars and cafés. Of these, the monthly *Fugues* (Ⓦwww .fugues.com) is best, with a comprehensive directory of gay resources and event listings – their bilingual *Rainbow Guide*, published in May and October, is especially useful. Even without speaking French, you can enjoy the glossy images in the city's gay lifestyle monthly, *La Voix du Village*. On the **radio**, catch the weekly *Queercorps* show of gay news and features on CKUT 90.3FM (Mon 6–7pm), immediately followed by *Dykes on Mykes* every other week; for a variety of French music and talk, try Internet station Ⓦwww.gayradiobec.com. Still, your best bet may be the **Internet**: Tourisme Montréal has a number of pages on gay and lesbian Montréal and links to other sites at Ⓦwww.tourism -montreal.org/gay. And, of course, the various gay dating websites are a good way to hook up with locals before you arrive – or at least get some advice on the latest happenings on the scene.

On the western edge of the Village, the **tourist information centre** opposite Place Émilie-Gamelin, on the second floor of 576 rue Ste-Catherine E (Mon–Fri 10am–6pm, weekends during major events; ℡514/522-1885 or 1-888/595-8110, Ⓦwww.infogayvillage.com), can help with queries about accommodation, services and entertainment. The city's main queer **resource centre** is the Centre Communautaire des Gais et Lesbiennes de Montréal, 2075 rue Plessis, Suite 110 (Mon–Fri 10am–noon & 1–5pm; ℡ 514/528-8424, Ⓦwww.ccglm .org), which has information about community groups and a well-stocked library (Wed & Fri 1–8pm). Bulletin boards and event information can be found at the store Priape (see p.209), which also sells event tickets. Montréal

Major gay events

Montréal is a major stop on the gay party circuit, with a number of large events that tend to attract the gym-toned, clubbing crowd (though in 2006 it attracted the gym-toned, athletic crowd to the inaugural World Outgames – Ⓦwww.montreal2006.org). More inclusive are the annual Pride Week celebration, Divers/Cité, and the gay and lesbian film festival, image+nation; for details on these, as well as the Black & Blue party, see Chapter 18, "Festivals and events". Info about the other circuit parties is available at Ⓦwww.bbcm.org, except for Ⓦwww.balenblanc.com. Major events include:

Events calendar

Mid-Feb Red Weekend (circuit party)

Easter Bal en Blanc (White Party)

Late May Hot & Dry / Fresh (circuit party)

Early July Festival des Arts du Village (LGBT art festival; Ⓦwww.festivaldesarts.org)

Late July to early Aug Divers/Cité (LGBT pride celebration), see p.226

Early Aug Twist Weekend (circuit party)

Late Sept La Récolte (Harvest; LGBT theatre festival; Ⓦwww.villagescene.com)

Early to mid-Oct Black & Blue (circuit party, fundraiser and cultural week), see p.227

Mid- to late Nov image+nation (film festival), see p.227

New Year's Eve Bal des Boys (circuit party)

once again has a gay and lesbian bookshop, *SergetRéal Librairies*, at 1455 rue Amherst (☎ 514/527-7759, ⓦ www.sergetreal.com), although the big chain bookshops (see p.200) also carry a decent selection of gay and lesbian books.

General **information and help lines** are Gay Line (daily 7–11pm; ☎ 514/866-5090, ⓦ www.gayline.qc.ca), the McGill student-run Queer Line (Sept–April Mon–Sat 8–11pm; ☎ 514/398-6822, ⓦ www.queermcgill.ca) and the French-language Gai Écoute (daily 8am–3am; ☎ 514/866-0103, ⓦ www .gaiecoute.org).

Accommodation

Although you shouldn't have a problem staying in any of the accommodations listed in Chapter 9 "Accommodation", there is a decent range of options for visitors wanting to stay in a specifically gay **hotel**, **guesthouse** or **B&B**. If you're arriving in the summer or for one of the major annual events, it's best to book way ahead, and prices are likely to be higher than those listed here, which include the lowest-priced rooms for two people staying in the general high season. If the accommodation choices listed here are filled, try the resources listed above or a gay accommodation site like ⓦ www.purpleroofs.com. Note that most Village establishments offer only a continental breakfast to get you started, rather than a large, cooked breakfast to fill you up.

Alexandre Logan (1870) B&B 1631 rue Alexandre-DeSève ☎ 514/598-0555 or 1-866/895-0555, ⓦ www.alexandrelogan.com; Métro Beaudry or Papineau. Lovingly restored, this B&B on a residential street not far from rue Ste-Catherine features five bright rooms trimmed with ornate mouldings. Two of the rooms (one quite small) share a bath; the other three have nicely designed shower or bath, plus individual features like balcony or sitting room. Prices vary from $90–145 and include a full breakfast of scrambled eggs, pancakes or similar.

Auberge Cosy 1274 rue Ste-Catherine E ☎ 514/525-2151, ⓦ www.aubergecosy.com; Métro Beaudry. A tastefully furnished hotel in the heart of the Village, whose fourteen simple rooms come with a/c and TV. There's a jacuzzi for relaxing in as well. The $95 price includes continental breakfast.

Bed & Breakfast du Village 1279 rue Montcalm ☎ 514/522-4771 or 1-888/228-8455, ⓦ www .bbv.qc.ca; Métro Beaudry. Clean and cosy B&B in the Village spread over two floors and equipped with a hot tub for summer. Its four rooms have a shared bath and cost $75–95; the two-bed suite is $150 for two, $190 for four. You can have the included continental breakfast on a secluded terrace. Indoor parking is $10/day extra.

La Conciergerie Guest House 1019 rue St-Hubert ☎ 514/289-9297, ⓦ www.laconciergerie.ca; Métro Berri-UQAM. A Victorian townhouse with duvet-covered queen-sized beds in seventeen comfortable air-conditioned rooms, around half of which have a private bath. There's also a rooftop terrace, indoor jacuzzi and an exercise room. Continental buffet breakfast included. $99 shared bath; $117 private bath; $200 suite for four.

Hotel Bourbon 1578 rue Ste-Catherine E ☎ 514/523-4679 or 1-800/268-4679; Métro Beaudry. The ever-expanding *Complexe Bourbon* includes restaurants, bars and the *Tools* nightclub (see p.188), which is good if you want to be in the centre of things. The hotel itself has 27 rooms with one or two beds ($95–125), three junior suites ($140) and two suites ($195), each with two bedrooms, a lounge and a jacuzzi.

Le House Boy 1281 rue Beaudry ☎ 514/525-1459 or 1-866/525-1459, ⓦ www.lehouseboy .com; Métro Beaudry. A friendly B&B with a quiet garden and large cooked breakfasts that might include French toast, crepes or omelettes. The six brightly painted rooms have contemporary IKEA-style furnishings, and the bathrooms are shared (as is the hot tub on the terrace). Men only. $80–120.

Lindsey's B&B for Women 3974 av Laval ☎ 514/843-4869 or 1-888/655-8655, ⓦ www.lindseys.ca; Métro Sherbrooke. A Plateau B&B in an 1887 Victorian house

Montréal's cruisey reputation is no doubt helped by the dozen or so saunas (bathhouses), around half in the Village and the rest scattered about town. Prices and clientele at each establishment tend to differ depending on the time of day, but most are open 24 hours and busiest for *5 à 7* and late at night when the clubs close. All offer rooms and lockers, and most include a steam room, jacuzzi and sauna, as well as secluded corners and somewhere to watch videos. The saunas with the best reputations are Oasis Spa, 1390 rue Ste-Catherine E (℡514/521-0785), for the young and fit; Le 456, 456 rue de la Gauchetière O (℡514/871-8341, ⓦwww.le456.ca), which also has a gym and is handy to Downtown; and Le 5018, 5018 boul St-Laurent (℡514/277-3555, ⓦwww.le5018.com), which has a varied clientele, student specials and a roof deck. A complete list of the city's saunas is available in *Fugues* (see p.185). The summer of 2006 saw a new twist to the scene with the opening of the city's first gay sex club, *Backroom* (ⓦwww.backroommontreal.com), in the cavernous Station C building at 1452 rue Ste-Catherine E, once home to the fabled *K.O.X.*

that caters to lesbians only. Two attractively furnished rooms share a bathroom with four-poster tub while the suite has a private bath and fireplace. Decadent breakfasts are served in a light-filled conservatory. $95–145.

Nightlife

Montréal's energetic and varied **bar** and **club** scene for gay men is almost entirely concentrated in the Village. The venues here have remained somewhat static for the past few years, but with various theme nights. To find out which venue is the hotspot for a particular night, it's best to ask around or check one of the listings magazines (see p.30) for the latest hotspot. The city is notoriously fickle when it comes to entertainment for **lesbians** – bars and clubs open every year just to close down again after a few months – and at press time, no venue catered primarily for women, though *Le Drugstore* is a popular mixed hangout and *Metro Lounge* has a women's night on Fridays. The larger dance clubs usually have a **cover charge** of around $6 at the weekend, but cost only a couple of dollars or are even free on quieter nights. There are plenty of cafés and restaurants in the Village, which draw a mix of straight and gay customers - see p.156. More drinking spots outside the Village – many of them gay-friendly – are covered in Chapter 11, "Bars and lounges". After-hours clubs – notably *Stereo* (see p.180) – attract a sizeable gay contingent.

Aigle Noir (Black Eagle) 1315 rue Ste-Catherine ℡514/529-0040, ⓦwww.aiglenoir.com; **Métro Beaudry.** A favourite haunt of leathermen, this dark and narrow bar is appropriately decked out in industrial decor and lots of chains. The "donjon" in back is an even darker, cruisey space. 8am–3am. Men only.

🏃 **Cabaret Mado 1115 rue Ste-Catherine E** ℡514/525-7566, ⓦwww.mado.qc.ca; **Métro Beaudry.** Local drag celebrity Mado and her cohorts put on shows attracting a large number of straight people as well as a

△ Cabaret Mado in the Village

loud and appreciative gay contingent. There are also live cabaret-type or jazz-style bands on some nights.

Campus 1111 rue Ste-Catherine E ☎514/526-3616, ⓦwww.campusmtl.com; **Métro Beaudry.** One of the best known of the Village's handful of strip joints, it's as cheesy as you'd expect with mirrored walls and young men baring it on the stage or at your table. Women allowed on Sundays after 9pm.

Club Bolo 960 rue Amherst ☎514/849-4777, ⓦwww.clubbolo.com; **Métro Beaudry.** Don your cowboy hat and boots for two-step, line and country dancing at this friendly gay and lesbian Western club. You can either take lessons ($10; call for schedules), come to dance on Friday or occasional Saturday nights (10pm–2am; $5) or try the Sunday T-dance (4–9pm; $14 including dinner, $8 without).

Club Date 1218 rue Ste-Catherine E ☎514/521-1242; **Métro Beaudry.** Most younger gay men walk right past this piano bar, though the karaoke (every night from 11pm) can be a lot of fun if you're able to leave your attitude at the door. Open from 8am.

Complexe Bourbon 1560–1594 rue Ste-Catherine E ☎514/523-4679, ⓦwww.tools-club .com; **Métro Papineau or Beaudry.** If a Las Vegas casino were designed for gay men, it might look something like this complex of bars, restaurants, nightclub and hotel decked out with hundreds of light bulbs. The street-corner pavement tables of the *Café Européen* are a good place to check out the passing traffic, while around back there's a parody of a pedestrianized European street – complete with water-wheel. The pastiche continues inside, with the café blending in to an Irish pub, an *Orient Express* restaurant-cum-railcar and the long-standing 1950s-style *Club Sandwich* diner. Tucked away in the basement, *Tools* is a dance club (open Wed–Sun) that draws a mainly male crowd for free sessions of house and retro tunes in an industrial decor, and it has a cruisey "play space".

Le Drugstore 1366 rue Ste-Catherine E ☎514/524-1960; **Métro Beaudry.** A central stairwell lit up like Times Square connects the many levels of this gay and lesbian entertainment complex. If you don't fancy drinking or dancing, you can shoot some pool (there are half a dozen tables) or even get your hair cut here. In summer, the roof terrace overlooking the action on rue Ste-Catherine is the place to be.

Gotha 1641 rue Amherst ☎514/526-1270, ⓦwww.aubergell.com/gotha; **Métro Beaudry.** This lounge bar, slightly removed from the rue Ste-Catherine hubbub, both geographically and in spirit, is a good spot to chill out in a retro Sixties chair and have an audible conversation. A piano and a fireplace add to the relaxed ambience.

Metro Lounge 1285 rue Amherst ☎514/282-1199, ⓦwww.metrolounge.ca; **Métro Beaudry.** The Village has been lacking in intimate, hip lounges, and this place from the *Parking* team aims to fill the gap. Opened in summer 2006, it was still finding its feet as this guide went to press, but its "Femme Fridays" look promising, and the cubic seats by the sliding front window are handy for surveying the street scene. Closed Mon & Tues.

Parking 1296 rue Amherst ☎514/282-1199, ⓦwww.parkingbar.com; **Métro Beaudry.** Bilevel club, with an alternative bent on the hot and sweaty dance floor upstairs, and a smaller, often packed space for grooving to R&B and other urban sounds downstairs. Mixed nights (Thurs & Sun) here have become more and more popular with heterosexual clubbers – perhaps one reason why the club recently opened up *Garage*, a men-only area downstairs. The back terrace gets quite busy with people of all persuasions (and nicotine habits). Cover of $3–5 after 11pm.

Sky 1474 rue Ste-Catherine E ☎514/529-6969, ⓦwww.complexesky.com; **Métro Beaudry.** Back in the day, this was *the* place to go, and almost annual facelifts over the past decade or so keep people coming back (though they tend to be fickle about which night is "good"). The ground-floor bar opens onto the street and attracts an after-work and pre-clubbing crowd, but is busiest for the Friday *5 à 7*, Saturday's Latino night and the Sunday T-dance. The next floor up is divided into a hip-hop room and a cabaret playing retro pop hits and chart dance music when there isn't a drag show, while the third-level club spins mainly house (club levels Fri & Sat only). The rooftop terrace gets packed whenever the weather's fine.

Station 1160 1160 rue Mackay ☎514/934-1428; **Métro Guy-Concordia.** Downtown bar frequented by businessmen complemented by a few students from nearby Concordia

University. A horseshoe-shaped bar takes up most of the small space downstairs, the high stools giving a good vantage-point to watch the nightly karaoke singers (from 10pm). If you can't bear to watch, there are a couple of cushy sofas for chilling upstairs (but they're still within earshot).

Stud 1812 rue Ste-Catherine E ☏514/598-8243, ⓦwww.studbar.com; Métro Papineau. As the name suggests, you're more likely to find beefy boys than precious young things here, but the atmosphere is more friendly than intimidating. You can dance to a mix ranging from Eighties tunes to techno on the dance floor or just chat or cruise in the quieter side-bar or shoot pool in back. Men only, except Wednesday nights.

Unity 1171 rue Ste-Catherine E ☏514/523-2777, ⓦwww.clubunitymontreal.com; Métro Beaudry. A young and outgoing crowd fill the large dance floor here, though the smaller *Bamboo Bar* upstairs tends to get more packed and sweaty – head to the rooftop terrace to cool off (also a great spot to catch the fireworks). Music varies by the night – if there's hip-hop and R&B upstairs, it'll be pop or house downstairs (and vice versa). Wed–Sat 10pm–3am. Below the club, on the ground floor, you'll find the beefiest strippers in the city at *Stock Bar*.

Performing arts and film

D rawing on both its French and English cultural heritages, Montréal's richly varied performing arts scene ranges from highbrow **classical music** – led by the world-renowned Orchestre Symphonique de Montréal (OSM) – to excellent avant-garde **dance** companies, like the explosive La La La Human Steps. Still, the city's best-known cultural attraction is undoubtedly the **Cirque du Soleil**, who've wowed audiences with their kaleidoscopic performances in more than one hundred cities around the world (see box, p.194).

The city is blessed with a major performing-arts complex right Downtown: **Place des Arts** is home to the OSM and Les Grands Ballets Canadiens as well as opera and theatre troupes and a host of chamber-music ensembles. Along with the host of theatres and music venues in the surrounding area, it's part of what city authorities are promoting as the "Quartier des Spectacles" (Entertainment District) and is also centre stage for the city's big **festivals** – notably the Festival International de Jazz de Montréal and Les FrancoFolies festival of French music – with stages festooned about the large plaza and the closed-off streets nearby. For more on these and other major festivals, see Chapter 18, "Festivals and events", and the Summer Festivals colour section.

Compared to Montréal's rich array of classical and dance offerings, English **theatre** is a bit of a letdown, and it especially pales next to the rewarding variety of French theatre on offer, from Molière to contemporary works by Québécois playwrights. You won't have as much of a problem finding decent English-language **film**, though – in addition to a couple of mainstream movie megaplexes Downtown (and more in the suburbs) there's a clutch of repertory cinemas showing fairly diverse programmes, and the city hosts more than a dozen film festivals year-round. Likewise, there is humour aplenty in English during the Just for Laughs festival, as well as year-round at the city's **comedy** clubs.

Information on cultural events is available from the main concourse of Place des Arts, as well as in Friday's *Montreal Gazette* and the free alternative weekly papers, *Hour* and the *Mirror*. You can also pick up a quarterly booklet listing special events and festivals from the Infotouriste office. Most companies and venues sell **tickets** directly, as well as through the Admission Network (☎514/790-1245 or 1-800/361-4595, ⊛www.admission.com), which adds service and handling charges of around $7–11.

Multidisciplinary spaces

A number of Montréal's larger performance spaces don't stick to a single genre – instead they provide a range of programming choices throughout the year. The major companies performing at these spots are detailed individually elsewhere in this chapter, but these are the multipurpose venues where you're likely to catch them:

Venues

Place des Arts ☎514/285-4200, 514/842-2112 (tickets), ⓦ www.pdarts.com; Métro Place-des-Arts. Montréal's premier performing arts showcase is home to the city's flagship orchestra, opera and ballet companies. The two largest halls are the Salle Wilfrid-Pelletier, which seats 3000, and the Théâtre Maisonneuve, about half that size. Tickets for events here can also be purchased from the main concourse box office (Mon–Sat noon–9pm; Sun one hour before showtime only).

Salles du Gesù 1200 rue de Bleury ☎514/861-4036, ⓦ www.gesu.net; Métro Place-des-Arts. Located below the Église du Gesù (Jesuit Church), the Salle du Gesù's 425 seats arc around the front of the main stage, which hosts theatre, comedy and classical music, as well as jazz acts during the festival. Events are also sometimes held in the centre's smaller spaces.

Le Théâtre de Verdure ☎514/872-2644. The open-air theatre in Parc Lafontaine has the most eclectic scheduling in the city, with Shakespeare, contemporary dance, world music and cinema interspersed with appearances by the city's major ballet, symphony and chamber companies. Best of all, the performances are free.

Théâtre St-Denis 1594 rue St-Denis ☎514/849-4211, ⓦ www.theatrestdenis.com; Métro Berri-UQAM. The biggest names in comedy play here during the Just for Laughs festival (see p.226), while concerts and touring Broadway-style productions fill it up the rest of the year.

Classical music and opera

Montréal's main **symphony** and **chamber** groups perform in the various halls at Place des Arts throughout the autumn–spring season, spreading out to other venues like the outdoor Théâtre de Verdure and the Basilique Notre-Dame in the summer. Other ensembles play at a number of smaller concert halls, particularly at the universities. **Opera** productions are staged at Place des Arts, while the Université de Montréal's Faculté de Musique shows opera films Fridays (and some Tuesdays) throughout the year: their Opéramania screenings, some subtitled in English, take place in the Salle Jean-Papineau Couture, 200 av Vincent-d'Indy (☎514/343-6479; $7).

During the summer, there are also frequent lunchtime concerts in Montréal's churches (often free, though a donation is appreciated), as well as in city parks. St James United Church, 463 rue Ste-Catherine O (☎514/288-9245), and Christ Church Cathedral, 635 rue Ste-Catherine O (☎514/843-6577), both offer weekly concerts, while the Oratoire St-Joseph, 3800 chemin Queen-Mary, provides a suitably grand setting for the annual **Organ Festival** held on Wednesdays throughout the summer (☎514/733-8211). Check out *The Gazette*'s entertainment listings for a full list of concerts and recitals or *La Scena Musicale*, a free monthly magazine distributed around town and on the Web at ⓦ www.scena.org.

Companies and venues

Chants Libres ☎514/841-2642, ⓦ www.chantslibres.org. Although they only perform one or two operas a year, this company is known for pushing the genre's boundaries, with lyrical singers accompanied by anything from techno music to multimedia spectacles.

I Musici de Montréal ☎ 514/982-6038, ⊛ www
.imusici.com. From September to May, this
celebrated chamber orchestra performs
from a varied repertoire – Baroque classics
to present-day compositions – under the
direction of cellist Yuli Turovsky for two
decades. Although you can catch them at
McGill's Pollack Concert Hall or the Théâtre
Maisonneuve for $36, the morning and
afternoon "rush-hour" concerts in the Tudor
Hall on the fifth floor of the Ogilvy department store (see p.205) are much more
intimate and will only set you back $23.
Musica Camerata ☎ 514/489-8713, ⊛ www
.camerata.ca. For more than three decades,
this chamber ensemble has been promoting
the works of Canadian composers, as well
as works from the classical canon, ranging
from Beethoven to Sibelius. The $27
concerts are held mainly at Redpath Hall.
**Orchestre Métropolitain du Grand Montréal
Théâtre Maisonneuve, Place des Arts**
☎ 514/598-0870, ⊛ www.orchestre
metropolitain.com; Métro Place-des-Arts.
Though overshadowed somewhat by the
OSM, the Orchestre Métropolitain still turns
out a decent range of concerts at, no
surprise, the Place des Arts, along with
other performance spaces across the city.
Tickets for the PdA shows start at $21, and
the best seats cost a mere $37.
**L'Opéra de Montréal Salle Wilfrid-Pelletier, Place
des Arts** ☎ 514/985-2222 or 985-2258 (box office),
⊛ www.operademontreal.com; Métro Place-des-
Arts. L'Opéra de Montréal has fallen into a
precarious position, with large budget deficits
forcing them to reduce their annual output to
four shows, and after a number of sackings in
summer 2006, there was not an artistic
director in sight at press time. The backbone
of the schedule is chosen from the European
lyrical repertory, but twentieth-century
composers like Debussy and Janácek might
appear on the programme. English and
French surtitles are projected above the
stage. Tickets range from $40–132.
**Orchestre Symphonique de Montréal (OSM) Salle
Wilfrid-Pelletier, Place des Arts** ☎ 514/842-9951,
⊛ www.osm.ca; Métro Place-des-Arts. Founded
in 1934 and the granddaddy of the city's
classical scene, the OSM was led by the
energetic Charles Dutoit for a quarter of a
century until 2002. His successor, Kent
Nagano, who officially took over the reins in
September 2006, has his work cut out for
him – Dutoit ran a gruelling schedule of

concert series built around guest artists,
composers and nations, as well as crossover
and contemporary performances. The
symphony also manages to squeeze in
Sunday afternoon shows and Wednesday
morning matinees, summer concerts in city
parks and at the Festival de Lanaudière, and
sell-out Christmas and Easter performances
in the Basilique Notre-Dame. Tickets for most
shows start at $15 for balcony seats; regular
seating varies from $30–75 for evening
concerts to $23–40 for matinees, and you
can pay $100 or more for the best box seats.
If not sold out, rush tickets are available ninety
minutes before concerts begin.
Pollack Concert Hall 555 rue Sherbrooke O, McGill
University ☎ 514/398-4547 or 398-5145,
⊛ www.mcgill.ca/music/events; Métro McGill.
Located in McGill's Faculty of Music building,
this modern concert hall offers the up-and-
coming generation of musicians a chance to
perform. Everything from recitals and
chamber groups to symphonies and opera
companies are heard here, oftentimes for
free. With the completion of the adjacent New
Music Building, performances also spill over
into the 200-seat Tanna Schulich Recital Hall.
Pro Musica Place des Arts ☎ 514/845-0532 or
1-877/445-0532, ⊛ www.promusica.qc.ca;
Métro Place-des-Arts. Every year, the nonprofit
Pro Musica society lines up a strong international selection of small chamber groups to
perform in either the Théâtre Maisonneuve or
Cinquième Salle at Place des Arts during the
October to March season. They also offer
musical workshops ($3) that engage kids
ages 5 to 10 while their parents attend a
concert. Tickets are normally $25–35,
around half that for students.
Redpath Hall 861 rue Sherbrooke O, McGill
University Main Campus ☎ 514/398-4547 or 398-
5145, ⊛ www.mcgill.ca/music/events; Métro
Peel. The more traditional of McGill's two main
classical music venues, Redpath Hall likewise
gives students a chance to shine as brightly
as professional chamber ensembles. The
warm wood of its interior adds to the
ambience of the many chamber and early-
music concerts performed here, several of
which are taped for broadcast by CBC Radio.
Tudor Hall Ogilvy, 1307 rue Ste-Catherine O
☎ 514/842-7711; Métro Peel. Tucked away on
the fifth floor of a swank department store,
this intimate Old World space is well suited to
regular daytime chamber recitals, including
those organized by I Musici (see above).

△ Cirque du Soleil's striped tent on Quai Jacques-Cartier

Dance

Montréal has a justifiably strong reputation in the world of **dance**, based not just on its well-regarded **ballet** and **jazz dance** companies – Les Grands Ballets Canadiens de Montréal and Les Ballets Jazz de Montréal – but on the huge variety of **experimental and contemporary dance** companies and performers. Dancers and choreographers like Marie Chouinard, Margie Gillis, and Édouard Lock and (formerly) Louise Lecavalier of La La La Human Steps have blazed an international reputation for the city – though unfortunately this means they're often out of town. Other companies to look out for are Montréal Danse, O Vertigo and PPS Danse. In addition to the local talent, some of the city's globe-trotting companies also come home for the Montréal High Lights Festival in February (see p.224) and Festival TransAmériques in early summer (see p.224). Cheaper and often wackier are the dance performances at the Fringe Festival (see p.225). Besides newspaper listings of performances, the French-language *Dfdanse* magazine (⑩www.dfdanse.com) covers the city's contemporary dance scene. For background info on local choreographers, dancers and companies, consult the ⑩www.choreme.ca website.

Dance troupes and venues

L'Agora de la Danse 840 rue Cherrier ⓣ514/525-1500, ⑩ www.agoradanse.com; **Métro Sherbrooke.** This four-storey building is ground-zero for contemporary dance in Montréal – it's not only the city's main dance centre but a number of companies have their studios here. Performances cost $26 in the 260-seat Studio.

BJM Danse ⓣ514/982-6771, ⑩www .bjmdanse.ca. For more than three decades, the recently renamed Ballets Jazz de Montréal has been touring the world and showing off a brilliant fusion of dance and

jazz. You might be able to catch them at the Montréal High Lights Festival in spring or for free at the Théâtre de Verdure (see p.191) in summer, if you're lucky.

Compagnie Marie Chouinard ⓣ514/843-9036, ⑩ www.mariechouinard.com. Since Marie Chouinard founded her dance company in 1990, she has staged some brilliant works combining classical scores, like Stravinsky's *The Rite of Spring*, with outrageous costumes, though lately the focus has been more on solo works.

Danse-Cité ⓣ514/525-3595, ⑩www.danse -cite.org. For more than two decades, Daniel Soulières has been co-producing performances with various dance companies at venues around town. Tickets for the four or so works staged annually cost $25.

Danse Danse ⊤ 514/848-0623, ⓦ www .dansedanse.net. Danse Danse produces half a dozen or more shows from October to April, inviting guest choreographers from Québec (such as dancers Margie Gillis and Louise Lacavalier) and abroad. Tickets for the shows, performed at various spaces around town, run about $45.

Les Grands Ballets Canadiens de Montréal Théâtre Maisonneuve and Salle Wilfrid-Pelletier, Place des Arts ⊤ 514/849-0269 (information and subscriptions) or 842-2112 (PdA box office), ⓦ www.grandsballets.com; Métro Place-des-Arts. Under the tutelage of Gradimir Pankov, Les Grands Ballets presents a season of classical ballet combined with more contemporary works, collaborating with some of the biggest names in the dance world, such as Alvin Ailey in 2007, marking the Grands Ballet's 50th anniversary. Tickets are normally in the $60–80 range, but go for as cheap as $30 in the furthest balcony. From mid- to late December every year, not surprisingly, seats are snapped up quickly for seasonal favourite, *The Nutcracker*.

La La La Human Steps ⊤ 514/277-9090, ⓦ www.lalalahumansteps.com. Since 1980, choreographer Édouard Lock's highly gestural and energetic works have been blazing a trail across Montréal's dance scene. Lock's production *Amelia* had a multi-year world tour and DVD produced of the performance; book well ahead if you want to catch the Montréal dates at Place des Arts.

O Vertigo 175 rue Ste-Catherine O ⊤ 514/251-9177, ⓦ www.overtigo.com. Artistic director and choreographer Ginette Laurin's gymnast training is evident in O Vertigo's lively works. This is one more Montréal dance company that you're more likely to catch abroad, though you'll find them at venues ranging from local cultural centres to Place des Arts, as well for public rehearsals, workshops and "creation labs" at the O Vertigo Creation Centre.

Tangente 840 rue Cherrier ⊤ 514/525-5584 or 525-1500 (box office), ⓦ www.tangente.qc.ca; Métro Sherbrooke. In the same building as L'Agora de la Danse (see p.193), this dance organization supports and produces pieces by up-and-coming choreographers and dancers in a smaller performance space, Éspace Tangente ($16).

Theatre

Montréal may be largely bilingual on the streets, but that rarely carries over to **theatre** productions, as most troupes perform in either French or English only

Cirque du Soleil

Started by a group of young street performers in 1984, the **Cirque du Soleil** (⊤ 514/722-2324 or 1-800/678-2119, ⓦ www.cirquedusoleil.com) has grown into Montréal's most famous cultural export. With a mix of street-theatre whimsy and big-top drama – without the animals – this human circus relies on acrobatic performers, colourful costumes and atmospheric lighting and music to keep your attention. And they do, as evidenced by sell-out shows throughout the world, including permanent residencies in Las Vegas and Orlando.

Not only were each of the Cirque's dozen-plus different productions created and produced in Montréal, but each new touring show premieres in the city and often returns between tours. When in town, they usually perform under the bright blue and yellow tent erected on Quai Jacques-Cartier in the Vieux-Port (see p.81).

Next to the Cirque du Soleil's headquarters in the northern suburb of St-Michel, the **École Nationale de Cirque** (National Circus School) has also set up shop. You can catch their annual show, as well as performances by international contemporary circus troupes and free outdoor shows on Summer Sundays, at the nearby **Pavillon de la TOHU**, 2345 rue Jarry E (⊤ 514/376-8648 or 1-888/376-8648, ⓦ www.tohu.ca; bus #193 from Métro Jarry or #94 from Métro D'Iberville).

– although when *Les Misérables* came to town, the same actors performed in English one night and French the next. While on the whole the finest theatres perform in **French** (as might be expected in a predominantly Francophone city), there are a few noteworthy **English** options in the city and a number of fledgling independents; the rest are scattered about the Anglophone bastion of the Eastern Townships (see p.247 & p.251).

We've included a few of the finest Francophone theatres below also, but note that they're only worthwhile if your language skills are up to the task. Expect to pay around $25–45 at established theatres for a regular-price ticket regardless of the language spoken.

In addition to the local theatre productions, bigger Broadway-style shows play at Place des Arts and Théâtre St-Denis. Festivals also supplement the regular September to May theatre season – the annual **Festival TransAmériques** is the best of the lot.

English-language theatre

Black Theatre Workshop MAI, 3680 rue Jeanne-Mance ⓣ 514/932-1104 ext 226, ⓦ www.blacktheatreworkshop.ca; bus #80 or #129. This long-running company presents theatre and other events that promote directors and playwrights of African descent from Québec and across Canada in their performance space at the MAI cultural centre. Tickets cost $21.50.

Centaur Theatre 453 rue St-François-Xavier ⓣ 514/288-3161, ⓦ www.centaurtheatre.com; **Métro Place-d'Armes.** The old Stock Exchange Building that houses the Centaur's two stages is a grand and fitting setting for Montréal's most established English-language theatre company. Both modern and contemporary plays make up the half-dozen productions in the season, which runs from late September to early June. Regular tickets cost $38–42 ($20 for

△ Centaur Theatre

students); matinees and previews go for $30. Cheaper rush tickets are available ninety minutes before the show (if it isn't sold out).

Mainline Theatre 3997 boul St-Laurent ⊤514/849-3378, ⓦwww.montrealfringe.ca; **bus #55.** The Fringe Festival (see p.225) now has a year-round performance space, with a capacity of up to 150, where you can catch a variety of up-and-coming theatre companies.

Monument National 1182 boul St-Laurent ⊤514/871-2224, ⓦwww.monument-national .qc.ca; **Métro St-Laurent.** Renovated by the top-calibre National Theatre School, this venue has three stages and still features plays put on by the students, at least a couple of which are in English. The rest of the year, smaller theatre companies and individual performers rent out the space.

Players' Theatre 3480 rue McTavish ⊤514/398-6813, ⓦwww.ssmu.mcgill.ca/players; **Métro Peel.** Hidden up on the third floor of the William Shatner University Centre (named after the famous McGill alumnus following a student referendum), this small black-box theatre sees half a dozen low-budget productions a year, put on by the entirely student-run resident company, with an emphasis on contemporary Canadian plays. Tickets are a snip at $8.

Saidye Bronfman Centre for the Arts 5170 chemin de la Côte Ste-Catherine ⊤514/739-2301 or box office: 739-7944, ⓦwww .saidyebronfman.org; **Métro Côte-Ste-Catherine.**

This multimedia centre's Leanor and Alvin Segal Theatre is home to the Yiddish Theatre, the only one of its kind in North America (translation in English is available); plays (including translations of pieces like *Fiddler on the Roof*) and dramatizations of Yiddish texts reflect the Jewish experience internationally as well as life in Montréal. The centre's English Theatre also stages three productions a year, and guest companies occasionally appear. Tickets range from $30–47 depending on the play and time of performance.

French-language theatre

Théâtre d'Aujourd'hui 3900 rue St-Denis ⊤514/282-3900, ⓦwww.theatredaujourdhui .qc.ca; **Métro Sherbrooke.** As the name suggests, "today's theatre" is the focus, and this company has been *au courant* for three decades now. Théâtre d'Aujourd'hui specializes in the work of Québécois playwrights and often stages premieres of their plays. Tickets cost $30.75.

Théâtre du Nouveau Monde 84 rue Ste-Catherine O ⊤514/866-8668, ⓦwww.tnm .qc.ca; **Métro St-Laurent.** At the time this French theatre company was formed in 1951, the theatre it now occupies was the Gayety Burlesque Theatre (where the famous stripper Lili St Cyr performed – see p.51). Renovations have since brought the building up to date, but the company itself focuses on large-scale mainstream fare,

Comedy clubs

The city has made a name for itself on the comedy circuit with its stellar Just for Laughs festival (see p.226), but you're just as likely to catch an international headliner or emerging comedian at a couple of mainstay Downtown clubs the rest of the year – and even try out your own material at an open-mike night.

Comedy Nest Forum Pepsi, 2313 rue Ste-Catherine O ⊤514/932-6378, ⓦwww .comedynest.com; Métro Atwater. A comedy club with acts Wednesday through Saturday starting at 8.30pm, with a 10.30pm late show on Friday and Saturday nights. Wednesday nights feature local comedians for free; out-of-town headliners take the stage starting Thursday for $12.

Comedyworks 1238 rue Bishop ⊤514/398-9661, ⓦwww.comedyworksmontreal .com; Métro Guy-Concordia. Montréal's best comedy club is a dark, low-ceilinged den that stages stand-up every night but Sunday starting at 9pm, with late shows on Fridays and Saturdays at 11.15pm. Monday is open-mike night, Tuesdays and Wednesdays belong to the club's in-house improv troupe and weekends showcase out-of-town talent. Sit further back to avoid becoming part of the act. Tickets range from $3 on Mondays to $12 on Saturdays.

staging French repertory standards like Molière as well as translations of Shakespeare and European works.

Théâtre Espace GO 4890 boul St-Laurent ☏ 514/845-5455 or 845-4890 (tickets), ⓦ www.espacego.com; bus #55 or Métro Laurier. Innovative and contemporary still, despite having been around long enough to be considered an established theatre, they cram in at least half a dozen shows (mostly modern French theatre, with some dance) between early September and April, though half are outdoor productions. Regular price for tickets is $28.

Usine C 1345 av Lalonde ☏ 514/521-4493, ⓦ www.usine-c.com; Métro Beaudry. This former factory was converted into a superb multidisciplinary performance space by Carbone 14, a company known for pushing the bounds of theatre with their innovative, multimedia productions (their show *Le Dortoir* toured internationally and the filmed version of it won an Emmy Award). The space is also used by a number of emerging and experimental theatre and dance companies. There's a funky café open for weekday lunch and from 6pm on performance nights. Most shows are $26, but prices can go up to $40.

Film

Like any large North American city, Montréal has a glut of **multiplex cinemas** showing the latest Hollywood releases and the odd independent or foreign film. Though only a few of the cinemas that show films in English are Downtown, they share thirty odd screens between them and offer plenty of choices. The multiplexes are supplemented by several quality **repertory theatres** – in addition to those listed below, cultural centres such as the Goethe-Institut at 418 rue Sherbrooke E (☏ 514/499-0159, ⓦ www.goethe.de/ins/ca/mon/enindex .htm) and the Centre Canadien d'Architecture at 1920 rue Baile (☏ 514/939-7026, ⓦ www.cca.qc.ca) screen special series of films and provide venues for festivals. For a bigger than big screen experience, you can lose yourself in one of two **IMAX** cinemas.

To find out what's playing, listings are readily available in daily newspapers as well as the free weekly papers *Hour* (ⓦ www.hour.ca) and the *Mirror* (ⓦ www .montrealmirror.com), and on the Cinéma Montréal website (ⓦ www .cinemamontreal.com). Cinemas show either French or English versions, rarely both; unless noted otherwise, the cinemas listed below screen English films (versions of French and foreign-language films tend to be subtitled, unlike French versions of Hollywood blockbusters, which are more likely to be dubbed). If in doubt, ask before you make your purchase. The average movie ticket is $10–13, though matinees and Tuesday-night screenings are cheaper.

Multiplexes and IMAX

AMC Forum 22 Forum Pepsi, 2313 rue Ste-Catherine 0 ☏ 514/904-1250, ⓦ www .amctheatres.com; Métro Atwater. Part of the entertainment complex carved out of the old Forum arena – there's a mock-up of "centre ice" with a section of seating as a reminder – the 22 cinemas here tend to be on the small side, but the seating is comfy enough. There's plenty of other money-draining activities for teenagers, including an arcade and bowling alley. Tickets are $13, $8 Tues, $10 afternoons, $6 before noon (Fri–Sun).

Cinéma IMAX du Centre des Sciences de Montréal Quai King-Edward (opposite boul St-Laurent) ☏ 514/496-4724, ⓦ www .montrealsciencecentre.com; Métro Place-d'Armes. The big screen on Quai King-Edward offers the usual eye-popping 2D and 3D IMAX fare, but its location provides a welcome escape if you are touring the Vieux-Port and the weather turns ugly. There are only a couple of English screenings throughout the day, so check schedules beforehand. The 45-minute films will set you back $10–12.

Famous Players Paramount Montréal 977 rue Ste-Catherine 0 ☏ 514/866-0111,

Taking up a good chunk of the old Simpson department store, the Paramount was the first cinema in Montréal to offer stadium-style tiered seating. It's got the best "event" feel of the Downtown cinemas, with throngs of people in the lobbies – there's nearly four thousand seats shared among a dozen large floor-to-ceiling screens, along with an IMAX cinema.

Repertory and specialty cinemas

Centre Cinéma Impérial 1430 rue Bleury ☏ 514/848-7187, ⓦ www.ffm-montreal.org; Métro Place-des-Arts. The grandest of Montréal's film palaces began life as a vaudeville theatre, and after its most recent restoration, the 819-seat cinema is again a great place to indulge in a movie, either in the balcony or the sweeping main floor. Unfortunately, it's rarely open to the public except during festivals.

Cinéma du Parc 3575 av du Parc; bus #80 or #129. This student standby, in the mall under the intersection of rue Prince-Arthur and avenue du Parc, staged week-long runs of worthy independents and a repertory programme of second-run and classic films on the other two screens, until its closing in summer 2006. As this guide went to press, plans were already under way for reopening under new management. Consult the local papers for the latest news.

Cinémathèque Québécoise 335 boul de Maisonneuve E ☏ 514/842-9768, ⓦ www .cinematheque.qc.ca; Métro Berri-UQAM. Founded over forty years ago to preserve and promote film and television, the Cinémathèque now has a collection of over 50,000 predominantly French films and videos. Their programme features everything from retrospectives to a diverse series of festivals, by Québécois as well as international auteurs. Facilities include the "médiathèque" documentation centre (Tues–Fri 1–8pm), exhibition galleries (Tues–Fri noon–9pm, Sat & Sun 4–9pm; free; a boutique and bar with terrace. Films cost $7.

Ex-Centris 3536 boul St-Laurent ☏ 514/847-3536 or 847-2206 (box office), ⓦ www .ex-centris.com; Métro St-Laurent or Sherbrooke or bus #55. This sleek art-house theatre has three screens and one very trendy café, *Café Méliès* (open until 2am). A mix of thoughtfully chosen independent films are shown in either English or French (but mostly the latter), supplemented by experimental works – the Festival du Nouveau Cinéma (see p.227) is held here annually. Purchasing the $10 tickets ($7.50 Mondays and weekday matinees) at the high-tech kiosks is an experience in itself.

NFB Cinema (Cinéma ONF) 1564 rue St-Denis ☏ 514/496-6887, ⓦ www.nfb.ca/cinerobotheque; Métro Berri-UQAM. The National Film Board of Canada showcases their own films here, as well as other Canadian productions in English and/or French. There are comfortable seats in the cinema and video-screening theatre, but for a novel experience try the individual "CinéScopes" ($3/hr; Tues–Sun noon–9pm), where viewers can select films and freeze the frame or fast-forward as the whim strikes. These gadgets are run by the unique "CinéRobothèque", a central robot that dishes out one of the 8200 available videodiscs like a twenty-first-century jukebox. Film prices vary: usually $7–10, but some screenings and events are free.

15

Shopping

W hile Montréal has its share of chain stores, the city's reputation as a stylish **shopping** centre stems from its trove of smart **boutiques**, most of which are clustered in neighbourhoods outside of Downtown. The city's real strength is its selection of designer and streetwear threads – and politically incorrect furs, too. Clothing aside, Montréal is also a hotspot for music collectors and aficionados of twentieth-century design.

  The best part of shopping in Montréal is the atmosphere on the streets themselves, as some of the best boutiques are wedged in beside terrace-fronted cafés perfect for a breather and to eye up the passing fashion parade for further inspiration. Nowhere blends shopping and drinking better than the Plateau's two main drags: rue St-Denis' forte is Québec-designer boutiques along with sleek home-decor shops and funky accessory outlets. In contrast, affordable clubby-chic is the mainstay of boulevard St-Laurent, or "The Main", which also has the city's most concentrated selection of techno-driven record shops, especially between rue Sherbrooke and avenue Duluth. The tone changes around avenue Mont-Royal, where designer furniture showrooms target the Plateau's yuppie residents, and again north of rue Laurier, where a new league of upscale, local fashion designers are opening their own shops and colonizing the street.

  On the Village's western border, rue Amherst is tops for retro twentieth-century furniture and collectibles (mostly from the Thirties to the Seventies), while more traditional antiques can be found along rue Notre-Dame ouest in St-Henri. Near the western end of this "antiques row", a different sort of feast awaits at the Marché Atwater, where farmers sell their wares outside and some of the city's best butchers and fromageries ply their trade along the interior arcade.

  Otherwise, most of the action is concentrated Downtown along rue Ste-Catherine. Most chains have their Montréal flagship stores here, but the real standout is Simons, a Québec City original with highly affordable contemporary garb and upmarket designer threads to boot. There are also several shopping malls, the best being the Cours Mont-Royal, a former hotel that now hosts dozens of fashionable boutiques in a swanky setting. Many of these are also connected underground via the 32km Underground City (RÉSO) (see p.49), a subterranean shopping and restaurant network that provides a welcome respite from summer heat and winter cold. For art dealing, the nexus of rue Sherbrooke and rue Crescent, near the Musée des Beaux-Arts, finds the city's finest commercial galleries.

  Unless otherwise specified, the shops listed here keep standard opening hours: Mon–Wed 10am–6pm, Thurs–Fri 10am–9pm, Sat 11am–5pm, Sun noon–5pm.

Antiques and twentieth-century design

Montréal's greatest concentration of **antique dealers** ply their trade along rue Notre-Dame ouest between rue Guy and avenue Atwater, a stretch known as the **rue des antiquaires** (antiques row). Annoyingly, almost none are open for a Sunday browse and, during the rest of the week, tend to keep shorter hours than most other shops (Mon–Fri 10 or 11am until 5pm, Sat 11am or noon until 4pm). The plenitude of **twentieth-century design** shops on rue Amherst likewise open later during the week and there are no late closings as the area gets a bit dodgy later on. Typical hours are: Mon–Fri 11am–6pm, Sat 11am–5pm, Sun 1–4pm.

Boutique Jack's 1036 rue Ontario E ☎514/596-0060; Métro Beaudry. The eponymous Jack's tastes range from chrome retro Sputnik lamps and moulded plastic housewares in bright reds and yellows to contempory teak and rosewood Scandinavian furniture. Enter through 1860 rue Amherst.

Cité Déco 1761 rue Amherst ☎514/528-0659; Métro Beaudry. As its name suggests, this smart shop is an excellent stop for Art Deco accessories, like armchairs with sleek curved sides trimmed in aluminium. Other top finds include 1960s Danish sofas, teak or rosewood sideboards and tables, and chrome-accented dining sets.

🏃 **Couleurs Meubles & Objets du 20ème Siècle 3901 rue St-Denis** ☎514/282-4141; Métro Sherbrooke. A twentieth-century design boutique tucked in a half-basement

and full of pristine early-1960s Scandinavian teak tables and chairs and exotic 1930s pottery pieces. Some knick-knacks cost as little as $7.

Grand Central 2448 rue Notre-Dame O ☎514/935-1467; Métro Lionel-Groulx. The classiest shop on the rue Notre-Dame strip, Grand Central stocks first-rate eighteenth- and nineteenth-century antiques. Superbly crafted chandeliers sway over a collection of dining tables, sculptures and gleaming gold-leaf candelabras.

Milord 1870 rue Notre-Dame O ☎514/933-2433, ⊕www.milordantiques.com; Métro Lionel-Groulx. The emphasis at this attractive shop is on European arts and furniture, and its showroom floor is laden with ornately carved writing desks, marble busts and Rococo gilt mirrors.

Books

Despite the city's Francophone majority, the presence of so many Anglophone university students ensures a decent trade in **English-language books**. Your best bet for mega-bookshops with hefty stock lists is Downtown around rue Ste-Catherine, while specialist and used booksellers are on Downtown's western fringes or the Plateau. **French bookstores** are all over, with the best selection of shelves on rue St-Denis. In sunny weather, a row of bookstalls in the Vieux-Port is a pleasant spot to browse French titles.

New books

Chapters 1171 rue Ste-Catherine O ☎514/849-8825, ⓦwww.chapters.ca; **Métro Peel.** Montréal's biggest English-language bookstore (with a fair-sized French selection), where people tend to linger a while in the comfortable armchairs scattered amidst the four and a half floors. There's also a café, regular readings and book-signings, with up to thirty percent off bestsellers. Mon–Thurs 9am–10pm, Fri and Sat until 11pm, Sun 10am–9pm.

Indigo Books, Music and Café Place Montréal Trust, 1500 av McGill College ☎514/281-5549, ⓦwww.indigo.ca; **Métro McGill.** This bright and airy two-storey bookstore stocks titles on fashion, cooking, architecture, art, fiction, travel and music on the second floor, where the discount bins frequently turn up great finds for under $10. There's a pleasant café on the second floor, as well. New English and some French texts and, surprisingly, housewares are found on the main floor. Daily 9am–11pm.

Nicholas Hoare 1366 av Greene ☎514/933-4201, ⓦwww.nicholashoare.com; **Métro Atwater.** A superb array of books – ranging from fiction to children's to travel, with a strong emphasis on British titles – adorn the shelves in an atmosphere reminiscent of an old boys' club, wood-panelled walls included. The top floor also stocks a selection of CDs, mostly classical and jazz. There's a second outlet in Ogilvy (see p.205).

Paragraphe 2220 av McGill-College ☎514/845-5811, ⓦwww .paragraphbooks.com; **Métro McGill.** Though it was bought out a few years back by chain conglomerate Québecor, this bookshop has maintained an independent attitude and boasts well-chosen stock that's especially good for fiction, philosophy and art. Frequent readings, too. Mon–Fri 7am–11pm, Sat & Sun 9am–11pm.

Renaud-Bray Champigny 4380 rue St-Denis ☎514/844-2587 or 1-800/817-2587, ⓦwww .renaud-bray.com; **Métro Mont-Royal.** One of the finest French bookstores in town, located in a lofty, wood-toned space, this Renaud-Bray branch stocks everything from CDs to cookbooks in addition to large kids' and literature sections. Daily 9am–10pm.

Secondhand bookstores

Footnotes 1454 rue Mackay ☎514/938-0859; **Métro Guy-Concordia.** A hole-in-the-wall spot whose shelves are filled by nearby Concordia University students trading in their texts. The fiction is hit-and-miss, but there are plenty of good finds in philosophy and history.

Sam Welch 3878 boul St-Laurent ☎514/848-9358; **bus #55.** On sunny days there's a bargain bin out in front, while inside there's always a good selection of modern fiction, sci-fi and art books, all guarded by the requisite bookstore cat.

The Word 469 rue Milton ☎514/845-5640; **Métro McGill.** Aside from being the text-book dumping ground for nearby McGill University students, there's also a respect-able collection of out-of-date publications bought from estate sales and a decent lit section.

Travel books and maps

Aux Quatre Points Cardinaux 551 rue Ontario E ☎514/843-8116 or 1-888/843-8116, ⓦwww .aqpc.com; **Métro Berri-UQAM.** Although they carry travel guides and accessories, this store's real strength is globes and maps, including 1:50,000 topographic maps of Québec.

Librairie du Voyage Ulysse 4176 rue St-Denis ☎514/843-9447; **Métro Sherbrooke or Mont-Royal.** The city's main shop devoted to selling travel guides and travel-related accessories also has a great selection of items like neck pillows, money belts and voltage converters, along with plenty of French and English guidebooks. Also at 560 av du Président-Kennedy (☎514/843-7222).

⑮

SHOPPING | Books

Clothing

Designer boutiques

Boutique Reborn 231 rue St-Paul O ☎514/499-8549, Ⓦwww.reborn.ws; **Métro Place d'Armes.** Old Montreal's top designer boutique stocks cutting-edge clothes for men and women from an international roster of young labels from New York, Berlin, São Paulo and Montréal (including Denis Gagnon; see below). A small collection of arty CDs and magazines will keep you occupied while you wait for a changing room.

△ The chic Boutique Reborn in Vieux-Montréal

Denis Gagnon 5392a boul St-Laurent ☎514/272-1719, Ⓦwww.denisgagnon.ca; **bus #55.** One of the newest and brightest stars of the Québec fashion scene, Gagnon's edgy-yet-feminine collections are rife with Japanese and Rococo influences, with results that are both spare and decadent at once. His namesake boutique, in a whitewashed loft space in Mile End, is a suitably minimalist affair that oozes exclusivity.

Marie St-Pierre 2081 av de la Montagne ☎514/281-5547, Ⓦwww.mariesaintpierre.com; **Métro Peel.** Quebecers in the know can spot this designer's works from a mile away. The items here are completely original, made out of exquisite hand-painted silks, crinkly chiffon and high-tech fabrics like polyamide, in innovative cuts that easily pass for *haute couture*.

Philippe Dubuc 4451-4453 rue St-Denis ☎514/282-1465, Ⓦwww.dubucstyle.com; **Métro Mont-Royal.** Philippe Dubuc's flair for finely cut suits, ties and shirts produces sharp, sexy and *très chic* men's attire – a trend he's carried over to his women's line.

Revenge 3852 rue St-Denis ☎514/843-4379; **Métro Sherbrooke.** Although heavily accented towards Québécois designers, this smart boutique also stocks a decent collection of niche Canadian labels, as well as their own men's line. The selection caters mostly to an older, moneyed crowd, but the occasional trendy outfit for the younger set can be found.

Rudsak 1400 rue Ste-Catherine O, ☎514/399-9925, Ⓦwww.rudsak.ca; **Métro Guy-Concordia.** This downtown label's modern take on leather everything – pants, jackets, skirts and especially handbags and wallets – in fashionable colours and exceedingly soft material, appeals to both men and women. Also in-house are handsome travel bags and stylish (animal-free) clothes.

Scandale 3639 boul St-Laurent ☎514/842-4707; **Métro Sherbrooke or bus #55.** Designer Georges Lévesque's fashion sense matches fluid retro-styled knits and jersey fabrics with wild and bright colour combinations. Not the place to pick up the perfect little black dress, but an excellent stop for something no one else will have back home.

u&i 3650 & 3652 boul St-Laurent ☎514/844-8788, Ⓦwww.boutiqueuandi.com; **Métro Sherbrooke or bus #55.** By far the chicest store on the Main, the sleek u&i has made a name for itself by introducing contemporary prêt-à-porter to the Plateau. Look for foreign labels like Comme des Garçons, Vivienne Westwood, Acne and APC, and homegrown talents like Denis Gagnon (see above).

L'UOMO 1452 rue Peel ☎514/844-1008, Ⓦwww.luomo-montreal.com; **Métro Peel.** The clothes here ooze quiet elegance – sedate grey and black tints abound – in labels like Kiton, Nino Cerruti, Giorgio Armani and Prada. The service is exceptional – no wonder Mick Jagger, Eric Clapton and Michael Jackson shop here when in town. Suits start around $1500, making the mid-July and late December sales – when stock is 30–50 percent off – very popular.

Chain stores

Club Monaco Cours Mont-Royal, 1455 rue Peel ☎514/499-0959, Ⓦwww.clubmonaco.com;

Métro Peel. Once designed by Toronto-born Alfred Sung, the clothes have lost some of their spark after this chain was bought out by Ralph Lauren several years ago. But while the line is decidedly more beige and conservative than it once was, it's still exemplary for its clean lines and modernist look – and you might find the odd funky piece.

Harry Rosen Cours Mont-Royal, 1455 rue Peel ⊕514/284-3315, ⊛www.harryrosen.com; **Métro Peel.** Making and tailoring fine clothes for the white-collar professional – read high-powered, high-salaried CEO – is Harry Rosen's mantra. His annual Boxing Day sale, where everything is marked down a minimum of 50 percent, has men lined up outside the front doors well before they open.

Parasuco Santana Jeans 1414 rue Crescent ⊕514/284-2288, ⊛www.parasuco.com; **Métro Guy-Concordia.** The jeans in this brand's name are some of the sexiest denim on the market, made to hug every curve and then some. The stock also includes slinky sweaters, halter tops and some Italian imports. The men's collection is equally hot (if less curvy). Open until 9pm summer weekdays.

Roots 1035 rue Ste-Catherine O ⊕514/845-7995, ⊛www.roots.com; **Métro Peel.** Although founded by two Americans, Roots is treated by Canadians as a made-in-Canada phenomenon. The chain's hallmark leather jackets, bags and cotton sweatshirts have a classically preppy sense about them that never goes out of style.

Furs and winter coats

🏃 **Harricana 3000 rue St-Antoine O** ⊕514/287-6517, ⊛www.harricana.qc.ca; **Métro Lionel-Groulx.** Local designer Mariouche Gagné takes old fur coats and recycles them into new, fashion-forward threads and accessories – boot covers, sleeveless vests, handbags and pillow cases are among the standouts. Handbags start around $150, while pillow cases range from $200 to $600. She does coats, too – they'll set you back a grand. Closed Sun.

Kanuk 485 rue Rachel E ⊕514/284-4494, ⊛www.kanuk.com; **Métro Mont-Royal.** The massive ranks of winter jackets made and sold here are warm but pricey ($250–800), and you can even get the sleeve length

adjusted – something that's well-nigh impossible at most places. There's also a stock of outdoorsy clothes and a few sleeping bags and knapsacks.

Clubwear and street fashions

Fly 1970 rue Ste-Catherine O ⊕514/846-6888; **Métro Guy-Concordia.** The coolest clubwear store in the city, with local independent labels Umsteigen, Castle Dream and Betty Blush displayed alongside imports from New York and Italy, trendy trainers and funky bags and jewellery. There's also a small selection of dance music on CD and vinyl – a DJ sets the pace on weekends.

Lola and Emily 3475 boul St Laurent ⊕514/288-7598, ⊛www.lolaandemily.com; **Métro Sherbrooke or bus #55.** It's hard to walk out of here empty-handed, especially since almost everything is for sale. It feels a bit like someone's loft, with antique Indian furniture and fun knick-knacks – though it's mainly about the clothes, with some unusual styles, fun labels like Juicy Couture and Paul Frank, and creations by Montréal designers.

space fb Cours Mont-Royal, 1455 rue Peel ⊕514/848-6494, ⊛www.spacefb.com; **Métro Peel.** The fb stands for François Beauregard, a Montréal designer whose highly affordable collection of colourful sweats, Ts, dresses and shirts earns raves from his young, hip clientele. A second outlet is at 3632 boul St-Laurent (⊕514/282-1991).

Three Monkeys Cours Mont-Royal, 1455 rue Peel ⊕514/284-1333, ⊛www.threemonkeys.com; **Métro Peel.** For street couture no one will have back home, it's hard to beat Three Monkeys, where a roster of Montréal-based talent, including Roadkill, Umsteigen, Travis Taddeo and Sugarmilk, rule the racks. Look for the original men's T-shirts featuring silkscreens of off-the-path Montréal landmarks like Habitat and the Milk Bottle.

Zara Place Montréal Trust, 1500 av McGill-College ⊕514/281-2001, ⊛www.zara.com; **Métro McGill.** Decent-quality knock-offs of Euro fashions arrive here before the original pieces they're modeled on even hit stores. The stock is hip and unbelievably cheap – and produced so quickly you'll be lucky if it lasts an entire season. But by then it will likely have gone out of style anyway.

⑮

SHOPPING | Clothing

Vintage, consignment and discount shops

Boutique Encore 2165 rue Crescent ☎514/849-0092; **Métro Peel.** Tucked away in this second-floor shop is a gold mine of designer names at cut-rate prices – you'll find Helmut Lang and Costume Nationale skirts for $200 and Christian Lacroix coats at $1200, some of which have never been worn. Tues–Fri 10am–6pm, Sat 10am–5pm, closed Sun & Mon.

Eva B 2013 boul St-Laurent ☎514/849-8246; **Métro St-Laurent.** A 20-year-old mainstay on the Montréal thrift-store scene, this funky loft-like boutique carries an impressive collection of retro clothes for men and women – costume designers and photographers often make this their first stop when looking for clothing for shoots. Just browsing here is an experience.

J Schreter 4358 boul St-Laurent ☎514/845-4231 or 1-877/745-4231, ⊛www.schreter.com; **Métro Mont-Royal or bus #55.** Schreter's (as it's better known) has been a fixture on the Main since 1928 (but only moved to its present location in the 1950s). Still family-run, it's a great spot for deep discounts on name-brand basics – especially jeans, socks and underwear – as well as sportswear and running shoes. There's a stronger selection for men than for women.

local 23 23 rue Bernard O ☎514/270-9333; **bus #55.** You're apt to feel like you're browsing for clothes and accessories in a friend's apartment – and trying them on in her bathroom – at this charming Mile End shop that mixes cut-rate vintage shoes, clothes and handbags with new and unworn designs by local fashionistas. Mon–Wed noon–6pm, Thurs & Fri noon–8pm, Sat & Sun 11am–6pm.

Mémento 3678 rue St-Denis ☎514/843-8391; **Métro Sherbrooke.** A recent newcomer to the vintage scene, this stellar boutique is just as strong on men's fashions as it is on women's, with suits and dresses from the 1920s to the 1980s, and chic accessories like fedoras and costume jewellery to boot.

Twist Encore 3972 boul St-Laurent ☎514/842-1308; **bus #55.** Good retro shoes, original jewellery and a wicked used-coat selection are the hallmarks here, although there's also a fairly good in-house clothing line, Jong.

Village des Valeurs 2033 boul Pie-IX ☎514/528-8604, ⊛www.villagedesvaleurs.com; **Métro Pie-IX.** When out by the Stade Olympique (see p.111), drop into this massive store to browse among dozens of racks crammed to the hilt with bargain-basement used threads. Of the five Value Villages in Montréal, this outlet is the best for decorative scarves, shoes and fur coats that often go for as low as $35.

Street sales

Just about anything provides an excuse for outdoor festivities in Montréal, and street sales are no exception. While a number of sidewalk sales take place throughout the summer, two in particular – the **Nuit Blanche sur Tableau Noir** and **Main Madness** – are more like fairs than markets. In addition to racks of cheap clothing and piles of household goods, bars and restaurants extend their terraces onto the street for al fresco drinking and dining, and several outdoor stages set the tune with free musical acts.

Things kick off in early June with the Nuit Blanche sur Tableau Noir on **avenue du Mont-Royal** (⊛www.tableaunoir.com), between rues St-Hubert and de Lorimier, where locals work into the wee hours painting murals on the road, setting a colourful stage for a weekend of shopping and entertainment. The following weekend, Main Madness turns **boulevard St-Laurent** (☎514/286-0334, ⊛www.boulevardsaintlaurent.com) into a massive four-day street party, with the blocks between rue Sherbrooke and avenue du Mont-Royal packed with people browsing and nibbling by day, and drinking and carrying on well into the night. Main Madness usually coincides with part of the Fringe Festival (see p.225), for some soberer evening fun. If you miss the June event, don't fret: the Main shuts down again for a final summer sidewalk splurge over the second-last weekend in August.

Accessories

Agatha 1054 av Laurier O ☎514/272-9313, ⓦwww.agatha.fr; bus #80. Québec women's fashion magazines favour this jewellery shop over all others when it comes to accessorizing their models. Hundreds of spectacular pieces of costume, silver and gold jewellery, mostly imported from home base in France, are crammed into a shoebox-sized space.

Henry Birks and Sons 1240 Square Phillips ☎514/397-2511, ⓦwww.birks.com; Métro McGill. Birks' turquoise blue boxes are as eagerly received as those from Tiffany & Co – largely because they contain the same expensive types of goodies: Murano crystal, Breitling and Cartier watches, pearls and diamond rings. Birks also designs their own lines of watches and jewellery in platinum or white gold.

Kamikaze Curiosités 4156 rue St-Denis ☎514/848-0728; Métro Sherbrooke or Mont-Royal. By night, this eclectic shop transforms into the retro nightclub *Passeport* (see p.179). You'd never know it by day, though, when they somehow clear out the space and cover the walls and floor with hair accessories, hats, leggings, socks and nylons of all stripes and shades.

Voyeur 3844 rue St-Denis ☎514/288-6556; Métro Sherbrooke. An impressive collection of handcrafted silver jewellery for both men and women, as well as some imported pieces like Storm, Skagen and Boccia titanium watches. Closed Sun & Mon.

Department stores and malls

If the weather's too unpleasant to hit the generally more interesting street-front shops, Downtown Montréal has plenty of warm and dry malls and department stores for browsing. Except for Holts and Ogilvy, all of the following are integrated into the Underground City (RÉSO – see box, p.49).

Department stores

La Baie 585 rue Ste-Catherine O ☎514/281-4422, ⓦwww.hbc.com; Métro McGill or Place-des-Arts. With Eaton's downturn in fortunes, The Bay has regained its status as Canada's flagship department store. Though it's shortened its name from the Hudson's Bay Company, it still stocks the trademark striped blankets that began as bartering fodder in the fur-trading days and now go for $300–450 (though you can get a cozy throw for $125). The rest of the selection is quite contemporary – mid-priced name-brand clothing, electronics, housewares and so forth.

Holt Renfrew 1300 rue Sherbrooke O ☎514/842-5111, ⓦwww.holtrenfrew.com; Métro Guy-Concordia. Head here for your Chanel, Prada, Gucci and Calvin Klein fix. The in-house line, found on the third floor, offers similarly chic styles at more affordable prices.

🏃 **La Maison Simons 977 rue Ste-Catherine O** ☎514/282-1840; Métro Peel. Simons' house lines Twik and Trente-et-Un promise good-quality clothing for both men and women at very reasonable prices, and fashion snobs will be happy here as well; designer labels like Gaultier, Dolce & Gabbana, Calvin Klein and Tommy Hilfiger are on hand, occasionally at reduced prices.

Ogilvy 1307 rue Ste-Catherine O ☎514/842-7711, ⓦwww.ogilvycanada.com; Métro Peel. Stocks upscale fashions, including a Louis Vuitton boutique, in an atmosphere true to the original department-store concept. Chandeliers hang overhead as you browse along oak counters and a bagpiper serenades the place during the lunch hour.

Malls

Centre Eaton 705 rue Ste-Catherine O ☎514/288-3708, ⓦwww.centreeatonde montreal.com; Métro McGill. This large mall covers an area roughly the size of a city block, with some 175 shops on four floors. It's the best place to shop if you're short on time since virtually every major chain store has an outlet here – in addition to The Gap and Levi's, you'll find Canadian chains like Jacob, Pegabo and Tristan and America. The high-end shops are on the second floor; mid-range gear is on the main floor; and cheapie togs and accessories dominate the lower levels. The basement has a food court; the top level has cinemas. Mon–Fri 10am–9pm, Sat 10am–5pm, Sun noon–5pm.

Complexe Les Ailes 677 rue Ste-Catherine O ☎514/285-1080, ⊛www.complexelesailes.com; Métro McGill. Wrapped around a dramatic oval atrium carved out of the centre of the old Eaton's department store are sixty mid-to upper-end shops, including large Guess? and Tommy Hilfiger stores, Archambault (see p.208), the flagship SAQ outlet (see below) and some good lingerie and acces-sories boutiques. The main anchor, though, is Les Ailes de la Mode, a department store with four floors of high-end men's and women's fashions and housewares.

Cours Mont-Royal 1455 rue Peel ☎514/842-7777; Métro Peel. Three

floors of high fashion – the dozen odd shops on the mall's second floor cater to the young, hip, clubby set, while the third floor goes way upmarket with Donna Karan and Giorgio Armani. The basement level is oriented towards budget shoppers.

Place Montréal Trust 1500 av McGill-College ☎514/843-8000, ⊛www.placemontrealtrust .com; Métro McGill. Perhaps the most conservative mall in the city, Place Montréal Trust does boast an excellent bookstore, Indigo (see p.201), and the high-street fashion vixen, Zara (see p.203), as part of its ground-floor offerings.

Food and drink

Gourmet food and wine shops

Au Festin de Babette 4118 rue St-Denis ☎514/849-0214; Métro Sherbrooke. A small gourmet shop selling rich delicacies like glazed duck gizzards, foie gras and truffles, along with sweets like dark chocolates, alcohol-preserved fruits and rich, creamy ice cream.

Première Moisson 1490 rue Sherbrooke O ☎514/931-6540; Métro Guy-Concordia. A mouthwatering gourmet shop selling delec-table patés, cheeses and pastries – to take away or eat in the cozy attached café. If you're on a diet, stay far away. You'll find other branches in the Marché Atwater (see opposite) and Marché Maisonneuve (see opposite).

SAQ Express 4053 rue St-Denis ☎514/845-5200, ⊛www.saq.com; Métro Sherbrooke. Good for grabbing a bottle before heading to an *apportez votre vin* joint, this liquor outlet is conveniently located right at the corner of avenue Duluth and the busiest BYO restaurant strip in town. Appropriately, they keep a wide range of whites and rosés perpetually chilled. Open until 9pm weeknights, 7pm weekends.

SAQ Signature Complexe Les Ailes, 677 rue Ste-Catherine O ☎514/282-9445 or 1-888/454-7007, ⊛www.saq.com; Métro McGill. There's no cheap *plonk* at this liquor store – instead you'll find an exemplary port, spirit and rare-wine selection. Keep an eye out for local specialities, like *pomme de glace*, a cider

version of ice wine, and the incredibly smooth maple-syrup whiskey.

Yannick Fromagerie d'Exception 1218 rue Bernard O ☎514/279-9376; Métro Outremont. Though off the beaten path in the northwest corner of Outremont, this shop is undoubtedly one of the best fromageries in the entire province, with superb cheeses from across Québec, as well as from Portugal, Spain and France. It's particularly strong on Roquefort and Vacherin cheeses, as well as a triple-cream Riopelle, with a replica of one of the artist's works on its label. As an extra bonus, you don't buy without getting a taste first.

Bakeries and sweets

Chocolats Geneviève Grandbois 162 rue St-Viateur O ☎514/394-1000, ⊛www.chocolatsgg .com. They ought to put up warning signs at this stylish little boutique – the smells from the adjoining chocolate factory may drive you insane. The Chuao chocolates are outrageously expensive ($3.25 for a small cube), but the ones made with 25-year-old balsamic vinegar are especially exquisite – and the taste lingers for a while after. Closed Sun & Mon; open until 10pm the rest of the week. They also have a stand in the Marché Atwater.

Fairmount Bagel Bakery 74 av Fairmount O ☎514/272-0667; Métro Laurier. The granddaddy of Montréal bagel shops, opened in 1951, produces nearly 2000 bagels an hour (the most popular are poppy and sesame seed, best when still warm).

The lines on the weekend stretch outside the door, even in the middle of winter. 24hr.

Pâtisserie de Gascogne 237 av Laurier O ☎514/490-0235; Métro Laurier or bus #80. The French term for window-shopping is *lèche vitrine* (window licking), which is exactly what you'll want to do before the array of rich cakes and sweet tarts displayed behind the glass. For once, though, heed your parents' orders and allow yourself first to sample the savoury cheeses, patés, quiches and fresh-baked breads, before jumping right to dessert.

St-Viateur Bagel 263 rue St-Viateur O ☎514/276-8044, ⓦ www.stviateurbagel.com; bus #80. In business nearly as long as Fairmount Bagel (see opposite), this 24-hour bakery produces a product with little discernible difference – except to Montrealers, who will invariably swear that one or the other is better.

Health-food stores

Rachelle-Béry 4660 boul St-Laurent ☎514/849-4118, ⓦ www.rachellebery.com; bus #55. This chain of health-food shops is run by top-notch consultants and features superb organic foodstuffs and supplements. Another branch is at 505 rue Rachel E (☎514/524-0725). Mon–Tues 9am–7pm, Wed–Fri 9am–9pm, Sat 9am–6pm, Sun 10am–6pm.

Tau 4238 rue St-Denis ☎514/843-4420; Métro Mont-Royal or Sherbrooke. If you're looking for vitamin-enriched fruit juices, herbal medicines, soy milk and other organic foodstuffs, this small and helpful Plateau shop is bound to have it.

Markets

Marché Atwater 138 av Atwater ☎514/937-7754, ⓦ www.marchespublics-mtl.com; Métro Lionel-Groulx. A wonderfully atmospheric, 1930s Art Deco market with an interior arcade that's home to forty-odd gourmet butchers, bakers and cheese-makers who often proffer bite-sized samples to passing customers. It's a riot of colour and

movement in summer with blooming flowers and tempting produce spilling out of the stalls.

🏃 **Marché Jean-Talon** 7075 rue Casgrain ☎514/277-1588, ⓦ www.marchespublics-mtl.com; Métro Jean-Talon. Little Italy's market buzzes with shoppers year-round as dozens of stalls display superb fresh produce, flowers and baked goods in a plaza lined with gourmet cheese and meat shops; worth checking out for the palette of colours alone, but great for loading up on snacks or picnic supplies, too.

△ Marché Jean-Talon

Marché Maisonneuve 4375 rue Ontario E, ☎514/872 6211, ⓦ www.marchespublics-mtl .com; Métro Pie-IX. The smallest of the lot, this historic Beaux-Arts market near the Stade Olympique (see p.111) nonetheless makes a good stop if you're out that way and need a bite. Your best bet is the *Première Moisson* outlet here (see opposite), which has both indoor seating and a covered outside terrace (in summer).

Galleries

If money is no object when searching for that perfect *objet*, the galleries evoking the wealth of the Golden Square Mile era on rue Sherbrooke ouest should be your first stop. Otherwise, your best bet for contemporary works are the loft spaces on rue Ste-Catherine near rue St-Alexandre, with more than a dozen galleries to browse (see p.54). Diverse styles can be found in galleries scattered throughout the Plateau, as well as along rue St-Paul in Vieux-Montréal where the selection runs the gamut from cheesy landscapes to avant-garde pieces.

Espace Pepin 350 rue St-Paul 0 ☎514/844-0114, ⓦ www.pepinart.com; **Métro Place d'Armes.** Artist Lysanne Pepin prefers "art seen in the proper context" – by which she means in a liveable apartment space rather than a stale gallery showroom. It's a concept she achieves admirably in her bright Old Montreal loft full of fluid portraits, still lifes and handmade creations. Mon–Sat 10am–6pm, Sun noon–6pm.

Galerie Claude Lafitte 2160 rue Crescent ☎514/842-1270, ⓦ www.lafitte.com; **Métro Peel.** The ritziest gallery in the city, Lafitte deals heavily in European, Canadian and American masters; works by Chagall, Picasso and Renoir have all made appearances here, as have those by the Group of Seven, Borduas and Riopelle. Mon–Sat 10.30am–5pm, Sun noon–5pm.

Guilde Canadienne des Métiers d'Art 1460 rue Sherbrooke 0 ☎514/849-6091, ⓦ www.canadianguild.com; **Métro Peel.** This nonprofit gallery sells a wide selection of native crafts, including sterling Inuit soapstone and West Coast Haida prints and carvings. The top floor has a free permanent exhibition of predominantly Inuit artworks supplemented by temporary displays. The shop is closed Sun & Mon; the exhibition is open Tues–Fri 10am–6pm, Sat 10am–5pm.

Oboro 4001 rue Berri ☎514/844-3250, ⓦ www.oboro.net; **Métro Sherbrooke.** This happening Plateau gallery has a penchant for multidisciplinary works from local artists. Installations commonly showcase video, radio and Internet projects. Tues–Sat noon–5pm.

Zeke's 3955 boul St-Laurent ☎514/288-2233; **bus #55.** A quirky upstairs Plateau gallery devoted exclusively to showcasing first-time artists' works, a bent that gets some

innovative output like former *Montreal Mirror* restaurant critic Spanky Horowitz's photographs of what he ate for six months. The concept extends to music – acoustic bands play a couple of times a week (you can buy CDs of the recorded sessions) – and other one-off cultural events like poetry readings. Sun–Thurs 3–8pm. Closed during baseball games (the owner's a big fan); may be open at other times – either try the door or call ahead.

△ Inuit artwork at Guilde Canadienne des Métiers d'Art

Music

Archambault 500 rue Ste-Catherine E ☎514/849-6201, ⓦ www.archambault.ca; **Métro Berri-UQAM.** This music superstore seemingly has every French artist who ever recorded. It also features one of the best electronica sections in town. As an extra

bonus, you can listen to any of the CDs before buying. Other Downtown outlets are in Complexe Les Ailes and in the concourse of Place des Arts.

Cheap Thrills 2044 rue Metcalfe ☎514/844-8988, ⓦ www.cheapthrills.ca; **Métro Peel.** The

Summer festivals

As soon as the warm weather hits, Montrealers come out of hibernation in a mood to party. With the international flavour of the city's summer festivals – many of them free – visitors are more than welcome to join in the merriment. Just about anything provides an excuse to shut down city-centre streets and throw up stages – you'll find buzzing festivals celebrating everything from jazz, beer and comedy to cycling, film and ethnic cultures. For dates and contact information on festivals and major events, see Chapter 18.

▲ Montrealers take to the streets in summer

▲ King Changó perform at Jazz Fest

Sounds of summer

The soundtrack to Montréal's summers is an eclectic mix, from classical to experimental electronica, but it's fitting that in the city that played such a key role during the jazz age, the biggest event is the ten-day **Festival International de Jazz de Montréal**, from late June to early July. First held in 1980, with Chick Corea, Ray Charles and others performing before 12,000 fans on Île Ste-Hélène, it has evolved over the decades into the world's premier jazz fest and now presents 350 free shows on ten stages around Place des Arts and over a hundred more concerts in halls dotted about the area – drawing well over a million spectators. Most any jazz luminary you can think of has performed here, from legends such as Cab Calloway, Etta James, Dave Brubeck, Wynton Marsalis, Tony Bennett and hometown hero Oscar Peterson to Diana Krall, BB King, Buddy Guy, Cassandra Wilson and even Zakir Hussain and Elvis Costello.

The highlight is a giant outdoor show with often tangentially jazz-related acts – past performers have included the Spanish Harlem Orchestra, Cirque du Soleil, *nuevo*

Thunder and lightning

The roar of Formula One engines are deafening on Île Notre-Dame during the **Canadian Grand Prix** in late June. All of the attendant hoopla of one of Montréal's biggest draws creates a great sense of occasion, with concert stages, racing-car displays and other events on rue Crescent and elsewhere Downtown.

During the **Montréal International Fireworks Competition**, it's the splashes of dazzling colour over Île Ste-Hélène that catches everyone's attention – and the thousands of spectators along the quays of the Vieux-Port provide a uniquely festive atmosphere. The series of half-hour shows takes place once or twice a week from mid-June until the end of July.

◀ International Fireworks Competition

latino combos and tributes to Louis Armstrong and Paul Simon.

The other major musical event around Place des Arts is **Les FrancoFolies de Montréal**, an August celebration of Francophone music that runs the gamut from traditional folk to the latest DJs. It was here that singer Patricia Kaas made her North American debut during the inaugural 1989 festival, and since then it has showcased Québec

▲ Place des Arts as an open-air concert arena

rockers Beau Dommage and Les Cowboys Fringants, chanteuse Diane Dufresne and international artists as varied as MC Solaar and Angélique Kidjo. Later on that month, Montréal's own outdoor indie-rock fest, **Osheaga**, takes over Île Ste-Hélène. The inaugural 2006 weekend featured local bands making it big (Wolf Parade, Islands), up-and-comers (Think About Life) and big names (The Flaming Lips, Sonic Youth) on the fifty-strong roster.

For those looking for easier listening, Montréal offers a couple of classical sessions each June with the **Festival Musique de Chambre Montréal** and the **Festival de Musique Baroque de Montréal**.

Stage and screen

Like everything else in a city that's gone completely stir crazy by winter's end, the performing arts spill out onto Montréal's streets for an array of free performances to accompany paying events. The **Just for Laughs** (*Juste pour Rire*) festival in mid-July attracts the hottest comedic acts from around the world to its gala premiers at Théâtre St-Denis and annual club shows such as Queer Comics and Britcom. Out on the streets near Place des Arts, you'll see mimes, clowns and a variety of physical comedy, as well as just plain silly events like the Twins' Parade.

A similar silliness pervades the mid-June **Festival Fringe de Montréal** and the antics of the shows' promoters, who compete with gimmicks and occasional gratuitous nudity to drum up interest in a host of affordable, experimental and sometimes hit-or-miss theatre and dance performances. The gaiety peaks at the beer tent and stage in the Main's Parc des Amériques.

While various festivals present films, the most interesting screenings you'll likely see are at the **Festival des Films du Monde Montréal** (World Film Festival), which unveils a broad scope of international cinema. More esoteric is the genre-specific **FanTasia**, where thousands of cinemagoers head for dark spaces to watch zombie horror flicks and Japanese animé. Both festivals are in August.

▼ Just for Laughs

Gay pride

The biggest date on the calendar for the city's queer community – and for thousands of out-of-towners – is the LGBT Pride Parade, capstone of a week of celebrations known as **Divers/Cité**. Over the course of a dozen years or so, the parade has built up a huge audience of gay

▲ Band of drummers during Gay Pride

and straight people who came in support or simply to groove to the club-sponsored floats or ogle the more outrageous costumes. Recently the organizers began to hold the parade at night and at the beginning of the week, but it's still good fun, and sets the tone for circuit parties, concerts, cabaret, gay cruises, a blocks-long street party and the ever-popular Mascara outdoor drag show hosted by local cabaret queen Mado.

Cultural celebrations

Montréal's many cultures celebrate with festivals throughout the year but the biggest outdoor events, naturally enough, take place in the hottest months. It'd certainly be hard to imagine the dancers in colourful and elaborate costumes and the calypso-playing *mas* bands of **Carifiesta** slogging through inches of snow along boulevard René-Lévesque in February. And the big party with Caribbean food, drink and dancing on Champ de Mars wouldn't be much fun at ten below either.

The warm days are perfect for a pow-wow and other Native Canadian revelry during the **First Peoples' Festival** in June. The main event takes place around the summer solstice and National Aboriginal Day (June 21), with a long weekend of traditional music, dance and handicrafts on Place Émilie-Gamelin. Three weeks later, the square resounds with the beats of African nations for the **Festival International Nuits d'Afrique**, which tops off a week of concerts across the city.

▲ Cherokee Nation dance troupe visit the First Peoples' Festival

The entire province of Québec gets decked out in blue and white to mark **La Fête Nationale**, the provincial holiday also referred to as St-Jean-Baptiste Day. A big parade trundles through Downtown on June 24, though the atmosphere is even more raucous at block parties all over the city on the preceding evening. A week later, festivities for the lower-key **Canada Day** take place mainly in the Vieux-Port.

stock is dictated by the musical tastes of local university students. You'll find an eclectic mix of used jazz, rock, world, soul, reggae and electronica on vinyl and CD here as well as a reasonable collection of used books. **HMV** 1020 rue Ste-Catherine O ☎514/875-0765, ⓦwww.hmv.com; Métro Peel. Sure it's mammoth and impersonal, but it's also practical. Listening booths abound, and with three floors packed with all musical styles, HMV is sure to have what you're looking for.

🏃 **Inbeat Record Store** 3814 boul St-Laurent ☎514/499-2063, ⓦwww.inbeatmusic .com; bus #55. Owned by DJ Christian Pronovost, a veteran of the electronica

scene, the focus here is mainly on house. You can listen to the 12" singles that make up most of the stock (along with a few CD mixes and compilations) on one of the eight available decks. **Pop Shop** 4081 boul St-Laurent ☎514/848-6300; bus #55. World music, Francophone, club music and rock show up used on vinyl and CD alongside small jazz and techno sections that deal more in new imports. **Primitive** 3828 rue St-Denis ☎514/845-6017; Métro Sherbrooke. A good stop for used rock, psychobilly, punk, garage and Francophone vinyl, as well as some disco, jazz and soul.

Specialty shops

Bella Pella 3933 rue St-Denis ☎514/845-7328, ⓦwww.bellapella.com; Métro Sherbrooke. You can find a gorgeous array of handcrafted beauty products here which are made from natural ingredients that smell good enough to eat: goat's-milk soap, cranberry bubble-bath and lavender shampoo bars are just the start. **Curio Cité** 3870 rue St-Denis ☎514/286-0737; Métro Sherbrooke. A great find, this little shop is tucked under a set of stairs and packed to the hilt with knick-knacks of a predominantly Asian influence. The sushi plates, posters, cushions and handbags are all exquisite and, best of all, affordable. **Essence du Papier** 4160 rue St-Denis ☎514/288-9691; Métro Sherbrooke. A stationery store with everything related to the pleasures of writing – elegant gift cards, notepaper and pens are on offer, along with luxurious wrapping paper.

🏃 **Joy Toyz** 4200 boul St-Laurent, suite 415 ☎514/845-8697 or 877/569-8699, ⓦwww.joytoyz.com; bus #55. This popular woman-owned sex emporium not only sells the expected toys and accoutrements, but also runs excellent weekly workshops like "stiptease and burlesque" and "groovin' with your gal" ($25+ per person). Mon & Tues noon–6pm, Wed–Fri noon–8pm, Sat noon–5pm. Closed Sun. **Priape** 1311 rue Ste-Catherine E ☎514/521-8451, ⓦwww.priape.com; Métro Beaudry. This has been Montréal's unofficial gay department store since 1974, with all sorts of gifts, clothing, calendars, magazines, books and videos and a more hard-core collection of leather gear and accessories downstairs. It's also a good spot to pick up event tickets and community info.

Sporting goods

Whether it's for heading out into the woods or onto the slopes, Montréal naturally has a wide selection of sporting goods shops. In addition to the all-rounders listed below, check out Kanuk for fine winter wear (see p.203) and Chapter 16, "Sports and outdoor activities", for cycle and in-line skate shops.

Altitude Sports Plein-Air 4140 rue St-Denis ☎514/847-1515 or 1-800/729-0322, ⓦwww .altitude-sports.com; Métro Mont-Royal. A small but friendly boutique to get geared up for the outdoors. They sell and also rent sleeping bags, tents, backpacks and stoves (about $30 per day altogether), along with shoes, boots, clothes and other camping gear.

🏃 **Mountain Equipment Co-op** Marché Central, 8989 boul de l'Acadie ☎514/788.5878, ⓦwww.mec.ca; bus #100, 179 or 460. Outdoorsy Canadians are often fanatical about MEC – and with good reason: most of the clothes and accessories are their own brand and, though they can be expensive, they're top-notch. The staff

SHOPPING | Specialty shops • Sporting goods

tend to be avid adventure-seekers who've road-tested much of what's on offer. MEC also has a wide range of gear to rent but charge more than the others listed here. As it's a co-op, you need to purchase a membership ($5 for life). The store is located out near the junction of highways 40 and 15, so you're best to drive there.

Sports Experts 930 rue Ste-Catherine O ☎514/866-1914, ⓦwww.sportsexperts.ca; **Métro McGill.** A one-stop, all-season sporting-goods superstore – if you can't find what you're looking for here, then it probably doesn't exist. Also does ski and snowboard tune-ups for around $20 and $30, respectively.

16

Sports and outdoor activities

M ontrealers are among the continent's most fickle **sports** fans, and in recent years their attitudes towards their **major league teams** could best be described as dejected. In the city where Jackie Robinson first played for the Montréal Royals in 1946, the rumours of baseball's financially strapped **Expos** leaving town finally came true at the end of 2004, the result of poor ticket sales and the lack of a suitable downtown stadium. Meanwhile, the one-time pride of this hockey-worshipping nation, the **Canadiens**, appear to have left their glory days well behind them. Indeed, the only professional sport that gets a passionate response nowadays is Canadian football – the **Alouettes** are one of the league's best teams and their games consistently sell out – though the first-division soccer team, the **Impact**, is increasingly popular (and successful). Tickets to sporting events can be purchased through the Admission network (☎514/790-1245 or 1-800/361-4595, ⓦ www.admission.com) or at individual stadium box offices.

Though professional sports may be on a downturn, Montrealers continue to indulge in **recreational sporting activities**, especially during the winter months when **cross-country skiing**, **ice-skating** and even **snowshoeing** provide excellent antidotes to the winter blues, as do the many downhill **ski slopes** within striking distance. But the city is also blessed with warm summers and residents take full advantage of them by **bicycling** and **in-line skating** along the many bike paths at their disposal. The waterways also get full use come summer as **boating** and **whitewater rafting** outfits cast off for wet and thrilling excursions. To find any public recreational facility and enquire about opening hours and fees, call **Accès Montréal**, the city's telephone information service (Mon–Fri 9am–5pm; ☎514/872-1111 or the 24-hour automated line ☎514/872-2237, ⓦ www.ville.montreal.qc.ca /outdoors).

Hockey

The **Montréal Canadiens** are the most fabled **hockey** team in the National Hockey League (NHL). Some of the league's greatest stars – Ken Dryden, Guy Lafleur and Maurice "Rocket" Richard (subject of recent film *The Rocket*) –

have donned the team's classic red- and- blue uniforms, helping them win an astounding total of 24 Stanley Cups, professional hockey's ultimate trophy. Still, even with their storied history – which will be the focus of a documentary planned for release during their 2009 centenary – *Les Habitants* (or the Habs, as they're familiarly known), have lost some polish in recent years: the team hasn't won a Stanley Cup since 1993 and their losses pile up year after year. Some claim the move from the hallowed Forum – the Habs' former digs – into the Centre Bell in 1996 put a curse on the team's game.

A perhaps even more damaging blow to the team's aura came in January 2001 when American businessman George Gillett, Jr, bought a controlling interest in the Canadiens. However, the resulting influx of cash has resulted in some solid acquisitions, though the team still hasn't made it past the conference semifinals. Perhaps Guy Carbonneau, the former Habs captain (1989–94) who was appointed head coach in 2006, will see another cup under his watch, after sharing in the 1986 and 1993 Stanley Cup wins. Though GM Bob Gainey (another veteran of the Habs' glory days and Carbonneau's predecessor as captain) hasn't managed to recreate any of the magic of his five cup wins.

The NHL's regular season runs from October to April, and the playoffs can carry on into June. Home-game schedules are posted on ⓦ www.canadiens .com; **tickets** range between $22 and $192.

Football

Canadian football, though lacking the panache of its American counterpart, is still good fun: it's played on a longer and wider field than its southern

version, with twelve rather than eleven players on each team and three rather than four downs to advance the ball in ten-yard increments. The result is a faster-paced, arguably more dramatic game; and it's one that Montréal's team, the **Alouettes**, excel at. The Als won the league title – the Grey Cup – in 2002 and were runners-up twice since then.

You'll need to buy tickets well in advance if you want to see the Alouettes play. The season runs from August to November, culminating with the Grey Cup playoffs, and the games are played at McGill University's Molson Stadium, at 475 av des Pins O; catch bus #144 from either Sherbrooke or Atwater Métro stations or the free shuttle from Square Victoria or

△ Montréal Alouettes quarterback Anthony Calvillo

McGill stations. **Tickets** cost $21 to $125; home-game schedules are posted on
ⓦ www.montrealalouettes.com.

Motorsports

For decades, **motorsports** meant one thing in Montréal – the **Canadian
Grand Prix** (ⓣ 514/350-0000, ⓦ www.grandprix.ca). For nearly three
decades, the Circuit Gilles-Villeneuve on Île Notre-Dame has been a spectacle
of roaring engines and whizzing blurs of colours with the Formula One
racecars speeding around the track. The city's biggest tourist draw, it's accompanied by a host of events on rue Crescent and boulevard St-Laurent, from
parties and displays of race cars to a fashion show for the less enthusiastic
partners of speed freaks.

The track is named after Gilles Villeneuve, who won his first Grand Prix race
here during the track's 1978 debut and died when his Ferrari flipped during
qualifying at the Belgian Grand Prix four years later. His son, Jacques, carried
on the family tradition, winning the Indianapolis 500 and CART championships in 1995 before moving to the F1 circuit, winning the 1997 world
championship for Williams. His luck failed after joining the fledgling BAR
(British American Racing) team in 1999, and at the end of 2003 his contract
wasn't renewed. Things didn't look much better for the Grand Prix itself, due
to the clash between government laws banning tobacco advertising and the
cigarette logos emblazoned on many of the cars, but after differences were
resolved, the city's biggest tourist draw is assured for the foreseeable future.
Unfortunately, Villeneuve's F1 future seems finished: after BAR and a brief stint
with Renault, he raced with Sauber BMW for most of the next two years,
parting company mid-season in August 2006.

As an added bonus for motorsports fans, Montréal was added to the Champ
Car circuit in 2002, though at press time the **Grand Prix de Montréal**
(ⓣ 514/394-9000, ⓦ www.champcarmontreal.com) looked likely to be dropped
in favour of adding Montréal to the **NASCAR Busch Series** (ⓦ www.nascar
.com) stock-car racing circuit – the only non-US stop other than Mexico. As
with the Grand Prix, tickets are likely to go quickly – reserve well in advance.

Soccer

Though it's nowhere near as popular as elsewhere in the world, **soccer** is
increasingly drawing crowds in Montréal. Indeed, the **Impact** (ⓣ 514/328-
3668, ⓦ www.impactmontreal.com) have been averaging over 11,000 spectators
per game at the Complexe Sportif Claude-Robillard in northern Montréal, and
the last games of the 2006 season were sold out. Despite the Expos' difficulties
attracting fans to the east-end Stade Olympique, there are plans for a new soccer
stadium at the northeast corner of the Olympic site; though the Stade Saputo
won't be constructed in time for the city's stint as one of the hosts for the 2007
FIFA U-20 World Cup.

The Impact debuted in the American Professional Soccer League (APSL) in
1993, winning the championships the following year and again winning the
A-League title in 2004. Now playing in the United Soccer Leagues, the
Impact finished top of the First Division (the tier below Major League Soccer,
North America's premier league) in 2005 and 2006. Tickets for games run
from $10 to $20.

Skiing

After a heavy snowfall, city residents often treat main streets as **cross–country ski** trails. Throughout the winter season, they tote their skis to the numerous **trails** located around town, though by far the most popular are the 20km of well-groomed paths winding around Mont Royal (the same paths that make great jogging trails in warmer months). Other hotspots for cross-country skiing are the Lachine Canal path and Île Ste-Hélène, which aren't groomed, but are far more serene than the heavily used mountain paths. Otherwise, the wintry flora and fauna of the Jardin Botanique can also be cruised on skis. Information on additional trails on the city's fringes and ski conditions is available through the **Parcs Nature** network (℡514/280-7272, ⓦwww.ville.montreal.qc.ca /parcs-nature); your best option for ski **rentals** is Mont Royal's Pavillon du Lac aux Castors ($8/hr, $15/2hr; ℡514/843-8240, ⓦwww.lemontroyal.com), which also rents **snowshoes** for stomping the trails ($6/hr, $10/2hr).

Although Montrealers may call it a mountain, Mont Royal is no place for **downhill skiing**. Instead, city-dwellers head out of town in droves for the ski hills in the Laurentides (Laurentian Mountains). The region begins with Mont St-Sauveur, which has good night-skiing and a trendy après-ski scene, and heads as far north as all-inclusive Mont Tremblant, the biggest resort in the province. To the east, the spread-out hills in the Cantons-de-l'Est (Eastern Townships) have the most interesting terrain and gladed areas for expert skiers. The province's other main ski district is the Québec City area, with mountains close enough that you can base yourself in the country's most romantic city. For details, see the appropriate "Out of the City" chapters.

Ice-skating

A mind-boggling 166 public **skating rinks** are open from late December to late February in Montréal's parks, used for figure skating, "shinny" (informal hockey matches) and just plain goofing off. The best of the lot are Mont Royal's Lac aux Castors (where rentals are available for $7/2hr) and Parc Lafontaine's ponds (rentals $6; $40 deposit), though a much less crowded option is the Olympic Rowing Basin on Île Notre-Dame. The city-run sports and recreational service keeps daily tabs on rink conditions (Mon–Fri 9am–noon & 1–5pm; ℡514/872-2644), which vary greatly as nearly all are naturally frozen and exist at the whim of the temperature. Montréal's only artificial outdoor rink is the privately run one on Bassin Bonsecours down in the Vieux-Port (early Nov to mid-March depending on the weather: Mon–Wed 11am–9pm, Thurs & Fri

---

Snow fun

For a quick blast of winter fun, head to the slides at the top of Mont Royal, which are frozen over for **inner-tubing**, weather permitting (mid-Dec to mid-March Mon–Thurs 9am–5pm, Fri 9am–6pm, Sat 9am–8.30pm, Sun 10am–6pm) If snow conditions are good, you can have as much fun simply **sliding** down the mountain's gentler slopes – Montrealers often just bring carpets and sleds to the corner of the park near the intersection of avenues du Parc and du Mont-Royal.

To experience the full range of ways locals have made the cold climate more enjoyable, plan your visit to coincide with the Fête des Neiges (see p.224) or the more extravagant Carnaval de Québec (see p.271).

11am–10pm, Sat & Sun 10am–10pm; $4; rentals $10, deposit $25; ☎514/496-7678, 🆆www.quaysoftheoldport.com) and it's always kept in smooth, polished shape by Zamboni machines. If you're looking to go indoors, head downtown to the year-round rink in the Atrium Le 1000, 1000 rue de la Gauchetière O (Easter to mid-Oct Sun & Tues–Fri 11.30am–6pm, Sat 11.30am–7pm; mid-Oct to Easter Sun–Thurs 11.30am–9pm, Fri & Sat 11.30am–7pm; $5.50; ☎514/395-0555, 🆆www.le1000.com); there's also a DJ night for the over-16 crowd on Saturday nights from 7–10pm in summer, Friday and Saturday 7pm–midnight in winter.

Cycling

Montréal gets high marks for its **bicycle**-friendly attitude, boasting 400km of paths throughout the city streets and parklands. You'll find bike stands on most major streets, and some thoroughfares also have two-way lanes and traffic lights specifically for cyclists – look for the sections marked off by waist-high metal posts. Still, the most popular routes are those totally immune to car traffic, the path through the former industrial heartland along the Lachine Canal being among the most picturesque. The circuitous roads that traverse Île Notre-Dame and Île Ste-Hélène are also well travelled, and the former's 2.4km Circuit Gilles-Villeneuve teems with cyclists when it's not in use by Formula One drivers. Further afield, the P'tit Train du Nord is an excellent 200km cycle trail on an old rail bed through spectacular Laurentian scenery (see Chapter 20, "The Laurentians"), part of the projected 4300km (3600km of which is complete) *La Route Verte* system of cycle paths and trails that crisscross the province (🆆www.routeverte.com).

Note that, in Montréal, bicycles are subject to the same rules of the road as cars, though there's no equivalent to the seatbelt law (the city doesn't mandate that cyclists wear protective helmets). Bikes are allowed in the Métro when it's not rush hour, but only in the first car (Mon–Fri 10am–3pm & 7pm–close; all day Sat, Sun & holidays). Rentals are available from various outfits across the city (including those listed below), with those in Vieux-Montréal being the handiest for most visitors.

Ça Roule 27 rue de la Commune E ☎514/866-0633, 🆆www.caroulemontreal.com; Métro **Place-d'Armes.** Facing Quai King-Edward, this reliable outfit rents bikes for $7–$7.50/hr, $22–$25/day and $30/24hrs (higher prices are for weekends), as well as tandems at roughly twice the price. They also have in-line skates ($8.50–$9 for the first hour, then $4–$4.50/hr, up to $25–$30/day or $30/24hr), electric bikes ($20 for the first hour, then $10/hr, up to $50/day) and, upon reservation, offer blading lessons (1hr; $25–$30) and various cycling tours (2–4hr; $25–$40 includes rental). May to early Sept 9am–8pm daily; shorter hours in cooler months.
Cycle Pop 1000 rue Rachel E ☎514/526-2525, 🆆www.cyclepop.ca; Métro Mont-Royal. You can pick up a hybrid bike at this established Plateau location for $15/4hr, $25/24hr or

$70/wk. In addition, they offer out-of-city tours, including a long day each way to Québec City and back for $279. May to mid-Sept Mon–Wed 10am–7pm, Thurs & Fri 10am–9pm, Sat & Sun 9am–5pm; mid-Sept to May Thurs–Tues 9am–5pm.
Cycle Technique 2733 rue Notre-Dame O ☎514/937-3626; Métro Lionel-Groulx. A couple of blocks north of the Marché Atwater this shop is handy if you want to head out west along the Lachine Canal bike path, avoiding the most heavily used section towards the Vieux-Port. Rentals cost $15/2hr, $22/4hr, $34/24hr and $120/wk, roughly double that for a tandem. Mon–Wed 10am–6pm, Thurs & Fri 10am–8pm, Sat 10am–4pm, Sun noon–4pm.
Guidavélo ☎514/844-4021, 🆆www.guidatour.qc.ca.** The cycling arm of walking-tour

company Guidatour has a 15km, three-hour city tour that covers the main sights from the mountain to the old port (late May to early Oct Sat & Sun 9am; late June to early Sept also Thurs & Fri 9am). Rates are $25 with your own wheels, $40 including a full day's rental. Other tours are available for groups. Departures from Ça Roule (see above). **Maison des Cyclistes 1251 rue Rachel E** T 514/521-8356, W www.velo.qc.ca; Métro **Mont-Royal.** The city's best cycling resource sells books, maps and gear and organizes the annual Féria du Vélo races (see p.224) and guided bike tours in the countryside.

They also publish *Cycling in Québec*, a detailed cycling guide with maps. **Vélo Aventure Quai des Convoyeurs (100m west of Quai King-Edward); Métro Place-d'Armes.** Under new management, this kiosk on the promenade offers bike and blade rentals for $9.50/hr or $30/day, as well as tandems and electric bikes. You can learn to in-line skate for $20/hr (plus rental) or join a bike or blade tour (2hr 30min–5hr; from $25 plus rental). May to mid-Sept daily 9am–9pm; mid-Sept to mid-Oct Sat & Sun 9am–9pm; T 514/847-0666, W www.veloaventure2005 .com.

Skateboarding and in-line skating

Most Montrealers show no regard whatsoever for the law banning **in-line skates** and **skateboards** from the streets of the city – though there are perfectly legal ways to partake of both activities. As with biking and cross-country skiing, the Lachine Canal and the Formula One racetrack get most of the action, but Parc Lafontaine draws its share of bladers too. Several shops **rent** in-line skates (along with wrist and kneepads) for around $9/hr or $25/day in the Vieux-Port area (see "Cycling", p.215).

Though the city's public squares get high traffic from boarders, especially after nightfall, neither the authorities nor the locals look favourably on the activity. There is a good outlet for skateboarders, however, in the **outdoor skate-park** of Parc Jarry. It's a bit out of the way, northwest of Little Italy, but it's equipped with brilliant ramps and half-pipes and, best of all, is free (daily until dusk; T 514/872-5107). The popular nonprofit **TAZ** (T 514/284-0051, W www.taz .ca), an indoor skate park and blading centre, has been in limbo for years but is due to reopen once a new location in north Montréal is settled; until then, the

△ Rollerblading along the Vieux-Port

SPORTS AND OUTDOOR ACTIVITIES | Skateboarding

16

island's only indoor venue is **Orkus Skatepark** (schedule varies; ☎514/789-6758, ⓦwww.orkus.ca; Métro De la Savane), a 30,000-square-foot site that charges $15/day or $25 for a block of five hours over a number of days. There are also plans to build a "skate plaza" underneath the Pont Jacques-Cartier, at the corner of boulevard de Maisonneuve and avenue de Lorimier. As plans keep changing, check online skateboarding forums for the latest news.

Watersports

The Lachine Rapids that once prohibited ships from travelling between Montréal and Lachine get ample **boating** action nowadays in the form of inflatable zodiacs and jet-boats that **raft** the current. Two quality outfits (listed below) run trips down the choppy waters; you're guaranteed to get wet, so bring along a change of clothing. For a more direct experience of the river, you can **surf** on a standing wave just behind Habitat, where local surfer Corran Addison gives lessons for $200 for two days, including gear; contact the 2Imagine (☎514/583-3386, ⓦwww.2imagine.net) or Surf 66 (☎514/697-0366, ⓦwww.surf66.com) boardshops for details.

Less demanding, but a nevertheless great way to see the city, are the meandering river **cruises** on glassed-in boats that depart from the Vieux-Port; more unusual is the amphibious **Amphi-bus** that sails on water and also drives along the streets of Vieux-Montréal (for both types of cruises, see box, p.84). For cruises and boat rentals on the **Lachine Canal**, see box, p.125. You can also rent watercraft on Île Notre-Dame (p.121) or take a turn on pedal-boats in the placid Bassin Bonsecours (p.82) and the ponds at Parc Lafontaine (p.96).

Les Descentes sur le St-Laurent ☎514/767-2230 or 1-800/324-7238, ⓦwww.rafting montreal.com. Located further afield than their competitor Saute-Moutons, Les Descantes cast off from 8912 boul LaSalle (May–Sept daily 9am–6pm, times vary) and offer the option of jet-boating (1hr 15min; $55) or rafting the frothy Lachine Rapids (2hr 15min; $46). The best way to get there is via the shuttle-bus service provided from the Centre Infotouriste at 1001 Square Dorchester. Reservations required.

Saute-Moutons ☎514/284-9607, ⓦwww .jetboatingmontreal.com. Jet-boats depart from the Vieux-Port's Quai de l'Horloge (May to mid-Oct every two hours 10am–6pm; $60) for a wild and woolly 1hr ride through the Lachine Rapids. The company also runs twenty-minute speedboat rides (every 30min 10am–6pm; $25), whipping around and doing 360s not far from the Quai Jacques-Cartier departure point. Reservations recommended; arrive 45 minutes prior to departure.

Kids' Montréal

ontréal may not appear to be a child's city, with so much focus on the grown-up pursuits of shopping, dining and nightlife, but those with tots in tow can rest assured that there are plenty of activities tailor-made to keep kids engaged. The many **outdoor parks**, notably Mont Royal, Parc Lafontaine and Parc Jean-Drapeau – where you can picnic and ride pedal-boats along the waterways – are ideal for spending an afternoon simply playing and lounging about. **Boat trips** on the St Lawrence (see box, p.84) are another favourite pastime and a fun way to see the city – the same goes for the **funicular** ride up the leaning tower above the Stade Olympique (see p.111). There are also a number of exceptionally kid-friendly museums, listed and cross-referenced below. Be sure to ask about family rates before purchasing tickets for any of the attractions listed in this chapter.

Museums and sights

The **Biosphère**, where exciting exhibits on water ecology include squirt-guns and ship-sinking (see p.118), stress the fun side of learning. The **Jardin Botanique de Montréal**'s lush gardens, especially the Chinese and Japanese pavilions, are equally captivating (see p.112). For animal spotting, head to the **Biodôme**, where monkeys frolic amidst the greenery (see p.111). The **Insectarium** (see p.115), with its creepy-crawly bugs, and the **Centre des Sciences de Montréal** (see p.82), filled with interactive science displays, are obvious places to let the kids loose; both appeal to the curious-minded, not to mention the always important gross-out factor. For creative activities, the **Musée des Beaux-Arts** (see p.102), **Musée d'Art Contemporain** (see p.55) and **Musée McCord** (see p.59) have supervised art classes and activities, including summer day camps, for kids who might be too young to appreciate the main exhibitions.

Though further afield, both the **Centre-de-Commerce-de-la-Fourrure-à-Lachine** (see p.131) and the **Maison St-Gabriel** (see p.127) historical sites provide good Sunday diversions with costumed performances, demonstrations and activities that bring the city's past to life.

Activities

If the weather turns bad, or if you've got serious bookworms to feed, an hour or two in the library might be a welcome respite. Though it provides a good opportunity to learn a bit of French, there are plenty of picture books in English at the large "Espace Jeunes" kids' section in the basement of the **Grande**

Bibliothèque (see p.87), which also has a bilingual selection of music and stories at listening booths and films and cartoons at video posts. The collection at the **Bibliothèque Centrale–Jeunes**, the municipal children's library facing Parc Lafontaine at 2225 rue Montcalm (Tues 10am–8pm, Wed 10am–6pm, Thurs 10am–5pm, Fri & Sat noon–5pm, Sun 1–5pm; closed Sun late June to early Sept; ℡514/872-1633), is predominantly in French.

For a less informative, but likely more fun, kind of entertainment, you can visit one of the **arcades** along rue Ste-Catherine ouest, though your best bet for one-stop recreation are the big **movie complexes** (see p.197). In addition to video games and movie theatres decked out with comfy armchairs, the Paramount has an IMAX screen while the Forum has a bowling alley with UV-lighting, fluorescent pins, pounding music and video screens (and a bar nearby for over-stimulated parents). For sheer thrills, the city's **amusement park** (see p.120) can't be beat, though it will probably sap a great deal of energy (and dollars) on your part. For a more relaxed day, bring a picnic lunch and wander about the rest of the islands, perhaps taking a pedal-boat through the canals of the Jardins des Floralies (see p.122). Between the Plateau and the mountain, **Parc Jeanne–Mance** has a playground and paddling pool (opposite the Georges-Étienne Cartier monument – see p.76) for cooling down after wandering around, as well as playing fields and picnic tables for a relaxing afternoon *en famille*.

There's also plenty to do at the array of outdoor festivals (see Chapter 18, "Festivals and events") – including the city-run kids' weekend, La Fête des Enfants, at Parc Maisonneuve in mid- to late August (℡514/872-0060, ⓦwww .ville.montreal.qc.ca/fetedesenfants) – and more **active pursuits** to partake in (see Chapter 16, "Sports and outdoor activities"), notably along the Vieux-Port's promenade and along the Lachine Canal. Likewise, there's an array of family-friendly activities a short drive from Montréal – both the Laurentians and Eastern Townships have beginners' ski runs in winter and water parks and a host of other activities come summer – see the "Out of the City" chapters of this

The kid-friendly Polar zone at the Biodôme

book. Otherwise, any of the options listed below should prove to be worthwhile distractions. Your best resource for additional activities is the "Family" section in the *Montreal Gazette*'s Friday events listings; the *Mirror* also has a "Kids' Stuff" section in its Open City listings.

Céramic Café Studio 4201b rue St-Denis. Mon–Wed 11am–11pm, Thurs 11am–midnight, Fri 11am–1am, Sat 10am–1am, Sun 10am–10pm. ☎514/848-1119, ⊛www.ceramiccafestudio .com; Métro Sherbrooke or Mont-Royal. Children explore their creative sides by painting on ceramic mugs, bowls and plates. Just note that you'll need to go back and pick up the piece a week later ($5 for a two- to three-day rush). Prices start at $8 for a mug, with hourly fees added to the total to cover the paint and glazing: $8 adults first hour, $6 per hour thereafter; $6/$4 under-17s.

Complexe Aquatique de Île Ste-Hélène Mid-May to mid-Sept Sat & Sun 11am–4pm; mid-June to late Aug daily 10am–8pm; $5 adults & teens; $2.50 6- to 13-year-olds; free under-6s. ☎514/872-6120, ⊛www.parcjeandrapeau.com; Métro Jean-Drapeau. A large, shallow pool and a children's water-play area draw hordes of families to this aquatic centre right near the Métro on Île Ste-Hélène to escape the summer heat. Don't worry – the nearby diving towers are off-limits to non-competitors.

Labyrinthe du Hangar 16 Quai de l'Horloge, Vieux-Port. Mid-May to mid-June & Sept Sat & Sun 11.30am–5.30pm; mid-June to Aug daily 11am–9pm (late Aug until 5.30pm); Oct Sat 11.30am–9pm, Sun 11.30am–5.30pm; $12 adults, $11 teens, $9.50 children; ☎514/499-0099, ⊛www.labyrintheduhangar16.com; Métro Champ-de-Mars. It might come as a shock to kids raised on computer games, but they will actually have to navigate corridors and overcome obstacles in person to solve the mystery of this maze.

Laser Quest 1226 rue Ste-Catherine O. Late June to early Sept Mon–Thurs 2–10pm, Fri 2–11pm, Sat noon–11pm, Sun noon–5pm; early Sept to late June Wed & Thurs 5–9pm, Fri 4–11pm, Sat noon–11pm, Sun noon–7pm. ☎514/393-3000, ⊛www.laserquest.com; Métro Peel. A video game brought to life as players armed with lasers chase each other through a dark maze, along catwalks and up various ramps while sound effects echo around them. Each game lasts twenty minutes and costs $8; three games for $18 in summer.

Planétarium de Montréal 1000 rue St-Jacques O. Late June to early Sept Mon 12.30–5pm, Tues–Thurs 9.30am–5pm, Fri 9.30am–4.30pm, Sat & Sun 12.30–4.30pm, also Fri–Sun 7–9.30pm; early Sept to late June Tues–Fri 9.30am–5pm, Sat & Sun 10am–5pm, also Fri–Sun 6.45–9.30pm; $8 adults, $4 under-18s; ☎514/872-4530, ⊛www.planetarium.montreal .qc.ca; Métro Bonaventure. Documentaries about the solar system are projected onto the Planétarium's domed ceiling while you lie back in reclined chairs; the stars and planets swooshing above produce a fun out-of-body experience and sneak in some education, too. The above times are for the box office and gift shop; English and French show times are staggered, with shows aimed at younger audiences taking place earlier in the day. Contact the Planétarium for schedules.

Shops

When the kids get tired of pushing buttons – both yours and the exhibits' – you can always get lost in one of Montréal's malls (see p.205). You won't find the best children's stores in the malls, though; they tend to be a bit more scattered about, with a particular concentration along the blocks of avenue Laurier to either side of avenue du Parc. We've listed a few of the best below.

Atelier Toutou 503 place d'Armes ☎514/288-2599, ⊛www.ateliertoutou.com; Métro Place-d'Armes. Facing the basilica, this shop will hold much more appeal for younger kids. They get to choose an animal and stuff it themselves – giving it a "hug test" to check for optimal softness/firmness – apply for a photo passport and take their new friend home in a cardboard suitcase, for $21–$27. There are also clothes for those who don't want a bare bear. A Québec City branch is at 28 côte de la Fabrique (☎418/692-2599).

Chez Farfelu 843 av du Mont-Royal E
Ⓣ514/528-6251; Métro Mont-Royal. The name
means "scatterbrained" – and it's intended
in the best way possible. The shop's shelves
are chock-full of amusing gimmicks and
squishy toys. A second location across the
street, at no. 838, brims with kid-friendly
accessories like cartoon-decorated cups
and saucers and colourful shower curtains.
Citrouille 206 rue Laurier O Ⓣ514/948-0555,
Ⓦwww.boutiquecitrouille.com; Métro Laurier or
bus #80. This small Mile End boutique is the
place to shop for unique, creative wooden
toys like trains, building blocks and string
puppets. Most are imported from Europe
and are of excellent quality.

Franc Jeu 4152 rue St-Denis Ⓣ514/849-9253;
Métro Mont-Royal or Sherbrooke. Franc Jeu's
shelves stock everything from Meccano and
wooden toys to dolls and princess dresses.
Be sure to check the language of board
games though – they come in both French
and English at this Plateau store.
Friperie Peek A Boo! 807 rue Rachel E
Ⓣ514/890-1222, Ⓦwww.friperiepeekaboo.ca;
Métro Mont-Royal. One of the few used-
children's-clothing stores in Montréal, this
shop focuses mainly on kids up to 6 years
old and sells everything from sun hats to
snowsuits. The store also sells some new
items, including Canadian-made Coccoli
sleepers and Robeez booties.

Crème de la crème glacée

During Montréal's icy winters, the last thing you'd want is something cold to lick, but
on warmer days people flock to the city's **ice cream parlours**. Here's a sampling of
the city's best:

Ben and Jerry's 1316 boul de Maisonneuve O Ⓣ514/286-6073; Métro Peel or Guy-
Concordia. The former Vermont independent still dishes up favourites like Cherry
Garcia and Chunky Monkey as the Jersey cows painted on the walls look patiently
on. Daily 11am–10pm, except summer Sun–Wed 10am–1am, Thurs–Sat 10am–3am.
There are a number of other outlets, including one on Place Jacques-Cartier in
Vieux-Montréal.

Bilboquet 1311 av Bernard O Ⓣ514/276-0414; Métro Outremont. Delectable
homemade ice-cream is the reason to visit this popular spot, where people line up
until midnight on summer nights. The banana ice cream is loaded with real chunks,
and the seasonal specialities, like the Maple Taffy flavour, are brilliantly original.
Numerous Downtown cafés also stock Bilboquet's products. Closed Jan to
mid-March.

Havre aux Glaces 7070 av Henri-Julien Ⓣ514/278-8696; Métro Jean-Talon. Made
on-site at the shop in the east building of the Marché Jean-Talon, the seasonal
flavours of these delectable artisanal sorbets and ice creams reflect what's on sale at
the market, from blood orange to *marron* (chestnut). A second outlet, at Marché
Atwater (Ⓣ514/592-8696), is delightfully situated on a terrace overlooking the canal
but closes mid-October to April and is only open weekends in May and September.

Meu Meu 4458 rue St-Denis Ⓣ514/288-5889; Métro Mont-Royal. They pack a lot of
flavours into this tiny Plateau parlour, applied to tasty and well-crafted sorbets, frozen
yoghurt and ice cream (including a number of soya varieties) – even the ice cream
sandwiches are homemade. The potent rum-and-raisin is for over-18s only, though.
Closed mid-October to mid-April.

Ripples 3880 boul St-Laurent Ⓣ514/842-1697; bus #55. Nowhere's cooler on the
Main come summertime – they do an ace job on vanilla and chocolate standards, as
well as zestier sensations like the ginger ice cream. Open until midnight (until 10pm
on colder days). Closed mid-October to April.

Roberto 2221 rue Bélanger, corner of rue des Érables Ⓣ514/374-9844; Métro
D'Iberville. Miles from anywhere, but they serve the best *gelato* in town. The *nocciola*
has a heavenly creamy hazelnut flavour, but the *baci* takes it a step further by mixing
it with chocolate.

17

KIDS' MONTRÉAL | Shops

Il Était une Fois... 1089 rue Laurier O ℡514/227-4741, ⓦwww.iletaitunefois.com; bus #51, #80 or #129. This small toy shop specializes in French cartoons such as Asterix and Marsupilami, though the widest selection of collectibles features Tintin – everything from books and figurines to watches and bedsheets. For gender balance, there are Groovy Girls dolls, stuffed animals and Hello Kitty stationery.

Oink Oink 1343 av Greene ℡514/939-2634; Métro Atwater. The ground floor of this Westmount boutique is devoted to selling Hello Kitty gear alongside girly accessories like rhinestone headbands, fanciful make-up and feathery boas. Although the focus is much less on boys, they can have fun, too, with model building sets, plastic figurines and board games upstairs. There's also a good selection of kids' clothing and some original novelty gifts, like old trading cards and squirting cameras, that'll appeal to nostalgic parents. Closed Sun in summer.

Uni Foods 1029 boul St-Laurent ℡514/866-9889; Métro Place-d'Armes. Don't let the bland name put you off; this small souvenir and grocery shop has the most original candy selection in town. Its Chinatown location gives it an exotic edge, reflected in a bewildering variety of Asian sweets, as well as chocolate-coated Pocky breadsticks and Hello Kitty–branded candies.

Le Valet d'Coeur 4408 rue St-Denis ℡514/499-9970, ⓦwww.levalet.com; Métro Mont-Royal. A great spot for older kids (especially boys), as there's a wide selection of role-playing games, figurines and cards here, in addition to board games, jigsaw puzzles, kites and a few toys like plastic dinosaurs.

Theatre and puppet shows

While there are several children's theatre troupes in Montréal, none of them have their own stages. Your best chance of seeing one perform is at the **Centaur**, in Vieux-Montréal at 453 rue St-François-Xavier (℡514/288-3161, ⓦwww .centaurtheatre.com), which hosts the Saturday Morning Children's Series from mid-October until early May, with a midwinter break (show time is 10.30am; $6 adults, $4 children). Their children's classics performances are generally of high quality (they sell out fast), and a few educational pieces are thrown into the programme, too. **La Maison Théâtre** at 245 rue Ontario E (℡514/288-7211, ⓦwww.maisontheatre.qc.ca) stages mostly Francophone plays, but occasionally puts on silent puppet shows. The curtain rises Saturday and Sunday afternoons (with other performances at various times) during the October to May season, and tickets cost $18.50 adults, $14.50 children.

Festivals and events

Perhaps as a reaction to the long harsh winters, Montréal's social calendar is booked solid throughout the warmer months, with one or more big **festivals** happening nearly every week. Folks take to the blocked-off streets in the thousands for huge international events like the jazz and comedy festivals, where a wonderfully exuberant atmosphere pervades. Even street sales take on a festive vibe, with concert stages and other events (see box, p.204). In the cooler months the regular performing arts season is supplemented by a host of smaller film festivals, and there's a variety of ethnic celebrations on offer all year long. Québec City's main festivals – including the famous Carnaval – are described on p.271.

While the selection of events below can give you a general idea of what's going on, it's worth asking for the quarterly calendar of events put out by local **tourist offices** (see p.40).

△ Wintry fun at La Fête des Neiges

January

La Fête des Neiges (late Jan to early Feb)
☏ 514/872-6120, ⊛ www.fetedesneiges.com/en.
Île Ste-Hélène is transformed into a winter
playground for three straight weekends
during the chilliest time of the year. There's a
massive snow-castle to explore, ice-skating
trails and toboggan-friendly hills to romp
around on, as well as horse-sleigh and
dogsled rides.

February

**Festival Montréal en Lumière (late Feb to early
March)** ☏ 514/288-9955 or 1-888/477-9955,
⊛ www.montrealhighlights.com. The Montréal
High Lights Festival brightens up Place
Jacques-Cartier and surroundings with
video and pyrotechnic performances – with
frequently spectacular results. DJ sets,
gastronomic events, and theatre, music and
dance performances by some of the city's
top companies round out the ten-day
festival.

March

**Festival International du Film sur l'Art (mid-
month)** ☏ 514/874-1637, ⊛ www.artfifa.com.
There are some fascinating subjects among
the hundreds of documentaries shown at
Downtown cinemas during the ten-day
International Festival of Films on Art. Profiles
of architects, composers and writers run
alongside screenings of creative output
such as ballet performances.

St Patrick's Day Parade (mid-month)
☏ 514/932-0512, ⊛ www.montrealirishparade
.com. Regardless of their own ethnic
heritage, most everyone in Montréal sports
green for one of the largest and longest-
running (the first parade was in 1824)
celebrations of all things Irish. The parade is
always on the Sunday closest to March 17
and rolls down rue Ste-Catherine.

April

Metropolis Bleu (late April) ☏ 514/932-1112,
⊛ www.blue-met-bleu.com. The five-day Blue
Metropolis literary festival brings Québécois
and international writers (such as Margaret
Drabble and Norman Mailer) together for
multilingual readings, signings, panel discus-
sions and a "translation slam".

May

**La Féria du Vélo de Montréal (late May to early
June)** ☏ 514/521-8687 or 1-800/567-8356,
⊛ www.velo.qc.ca/feria. The Tour de l'Île de
Montréal is billed as the world's largest
bicycle race – the 48km spin around the
island attracts over 30,000 participants
annually. It caps off a week of cycling
events, including nighttime and kids' rides,
under the Montréal Bike Fest banner.
Advance registration required.
Mutek (late May) ☏ 514/392-9251, ⊛ www
.mutek.ca. A five-day festival of underground electronic music and digital culture,
with acts like ModeSelektor, Pole and
German techno experimenter Thomas
Brinkmann.
**Festival TransAmériques (late May to early
June)** ☏ 514/842-0704, ⊛ www.fta.qc.ca. A fair
share of the dozen or so plays staged at
Montréal's largest theatre festival are in
English, performed by companies – often
young and experimental – from throughout
the Americas and beyond. Formerly the
Festival de Théâtre des Amériques, the
event was renamed for the 2007 edition as
contemporary dance was added to the mix.

June

Mondial de la Bière (early June) ☎514/722-9640, 🌐www.festivalmondialbiere.qc.ca. Once a year, for the better part of a week, Gare Windsor turns into a giant booze can, with well over 300 varieties of beer, Scotch and whiskey on offer. There are various forms of entertainment, but testing one's limits of inebriation seems to be the main draw. Wed–Sun.

Le Festival Fringe de Montréal (mid-month) ☎514/849-3378, 🌐www.montrealfringe.ca. With tickets priced at $9 or less, the Fringe Festival brings affordable theatre and dance to venues around the Main for ten days. The quality of the productions varies wildly, so head first to the beer tent at Parc des Amériques to catch the buzz on what the must-see shows are (and listen to the free rock concerts).

First People's Festival (late June) ☎514/278-4040, 🌐www.nativelynx.qc.ca. A celebration of Québec's First Nations takes over Place Émilie-Gamelin for a weekend of concerts, traditional dance and exhibitions of aboriginal sculpture and painting in the second half of this two-part festival. It follows exhibitions and a mini film festival at the NFB and the Cinémathèque Québécoise from late May to early June.

Montreal International Fireworks Competition (mid-June through July) ☎514/397-2000, 🌐www.internationaldesfeuxloto-quebec.com. Fantastic half-hour fireworks displays light up the sky over the St Lawrence starting at 10pm. Although you can pay to hear an orchestra accompany the pyrotechnics at La Ronde ($38–48; includes ride pass), most Montrealers watch from the Pont Jacques-Cartier, the Vieux-Port or whatever rooftop terrace they can find. Wed & Sat (occasionally Sun) evenings.

Grand Prix (late June) ☎514/350-0000, 🌐www.grandprix.ca. For one weekend every June, Formula One cars battle it out on the Circuit Gilles-Villeneuve on Île Notre-Dame. If you don't want to shell out the steep ticket prices (starting at $65 for general admission), at least check out the entertainment (including car and fashion shows) on rues Crescent and Peel, and boul St-Laurent. For further details, see p.213.

Fête Nationale du Québec (June 24) ☎514/849-2560, 🌐www.cfn.org or www.fetenationale.qc.ca. The provincial holiday – St-Jean-Baptiste Day – sees thousands parading down the street on June 24, proudly waving the blue-and-white *fleur-de-lis* of the Québec flag. Many events take place the evening before, with fireworks, concerts and loads of neighbourhood block parties throughout the city.

Festival Montréal Baroque (late June) ☎514/845-7171, 🌐www.montrealbaroque.com. Vieux-Montréal venues like the Chapelle Notre-Dame-de-Bon-Secours provide the appropriate ambience for the music of Bach and his contemporaries. There are also free concerts, dance classes and other events at the Baroque Fair site alongside the Château Ramezay.

Festival International de Jazz de Montréal (late June to early July) ☎514/871-1881 or 1-888/515-0515, 🌐www.montrealjazzfest.com. During the world's best jazz festival, the streets around Place des Arts are shut down for hundreds of free concerts on a dozen or so stages; the major show, held the middle of the festival's second week, draws an audience of up to 200,000 good-humoured revellers. There's always a range of other genres to check out, from salsa to hip-hop, if jazz isn't your bag – a state of affairs that led to the creation of an off-festival (☎514/570-0722, 🌐www.lofffestivaldejazz.com) at small venues for serious aficionados.

July

Canada Day (July 1) ☎514/866-9164, 🌐www.celafete.ca. While there's a parade and fireworks, and festivities in the Vieux-Port promoted as *Célafête*, Canada Day is better known to most Montrealers as "moving day". A large percentage of leases end on July 1, and it's hilarious to watch the scramble as thousands try to move house on the same day.

Carifiesta (early July) ☎514/735-2232, 🌐www.carifiesta.ca. It's too cold in February for a Caribbean-style Carnival, so the colourful parade along boul René-Lévesque takes place in summer instead. The calypso music and dancers of the *mas* bands move on to the big party at Champ de Mars afterwards, where you can, of course, tuck into some spicy Caribbean cooking.

FanTasia (early to late July) Ⓦ www .fantasiafestival.com. A great chance to see genre films, from Japanese animé fantasies to zombie gore-fests, that you won't otherwise catch on the big screen.

Festival International Nuits d'Afrique (mid-month) ☎ 514/499-3462, Ⓦ www.festivalnuits dafrique.com. Ten-day African and Caribbean music festival best attended during the long weekend of outdoor concerts in Place Émilie-Gamelin.

Just for Laughs (mid-month) ☎ 514/790-4242, Ⓦ www.hahaha.com. Over a thousand free shows (including street theatre and concerts) along boulevard de Maisonneuve and hundreds more at venues around the city comprise the *Juste pour Rire* festival, one of the world's largest comedy festivals. The best acts are always at the sell-out "Gala" shows at Théâtre St-Denis, hosted by the likes of John Cleese and Jason Alexander.

Les FrancoFolies de Montréal (late July to early Aug) ☎ 514/876-8989 or 1-888/444-9114, Ⓦ www.francofolies.com. Hot on the heels of the jazz festival, rue Ste-Catherine is again closed for ten days for this celebration of French song and music from around the world. Indoor shows at various city venues supplement more than a hundred free outdoor shows ranging from traditional *chansons* to electronic.

△ Rogers Cup

Divers/Cité (late July to early Aug) ☎ 514/285-4011, Ⓦ www.diverscite.org. On the last Sunday in July, the biggest event of the year for Montréal's LGBT community takes place with a massive nighttime parade near the Village, full of colourful and outrageous costumes, cheered on by hundreds of thousands of spectators. A week-long series of parties, concerts and events in celebration of gay and lesbian pride follows the main event.

August

Rogers Cup (early or mid-Aug) ☎ 514/273-1515 or 1-877/283-6647, Ⓦ www.tenniscanada.com. The brightest stars in the tennis universe descend on Parc Jarry (northwest of Little Italy) for an international tournament, with women playing even-numbered years and men the odd. The best seats are usually sold out half a year in advance.

L'International de Montgolfières (mid-month) ☎ 450/347-9555, Ⓦ www.montgolfieres.com. A great treat for the kids, the nine-day International Balloon Festival in St-Jean-sur-Richelieu (a twenty-minute drive east of Montréal) features over a hundred colourful hot-air balloons in all sorts of wacky designs that are lit up at night like giant Chinese lanterns. Concerts and events help keep those on the ground (and unprepared to pay for a $175–200 flight) entertained.

Festival des Films du Monde Montréal (late Aug to early Sept) ☎ 514/848-3883, Ⓦ www .ffm-montreal.org. Although Toronto's higher-profile festival tends to nab more premieres, the financially troubled Montréal World Film Festival has more of an international focus. There's plenty happening, including films on the outdoor screen in front of Place des Arts. Screenings at the Cinéma Impérial and other Downtown cinemas cost $10 – cheaper if you buy in bulk.

September

Osheaga (early Sept) Ⓦ www.osheaga.com. The inaugural 2006 edition of this outdoor weekend festival on Île Ste-Hélène saw fifty rock bands on four stages, with headliners Ben Harper, Sonic Youth and the Flaming Lips joining local heroes like Wolf Parade and the Stills.

Le Mois de la Photo (early Sept to early Oct) ☏ 514/390-0383, Ⓦ www.moisdelaphoto.com. For over a month every odd-numbered year, Montréal becomes a giant photo gallery, with over a dozen simultaneous photography exhibitions scattered about town.

October

POP Montréal (early Oct) Ⓦ www.popmontreal .com. A good chance to catch local bands on their way up, this five-day grassroots festival slots independent musicians into interesting venues, with a few loft parties and cinema events as a bonus.
Black & Blue Festival (early Oct) ☏ 514/875-7026, Ⓦ www.bbcm.org. www.popmontreal .com. A festival of cultural events, sports and club nights fills the week leading up to the Canadian Thanksgiving weekend, when the Black & Blue, a huge gay circuit-party and

AIDS fundraiser, fills the Olympic Stadium with some 18,000 all-night revellers.
Festival du Nouveau Cinéma (mid- to late Oct) ☏ 514/282-0004 or 844-2172 (tickets), Ⓦ www .nouveaucinema.ca. Given the strength of the city's multimedia industry, it's fitting that the Festival of New Cinema, showcasing cutting-edge works in cinema, video and digital media is held in the Plateau's suitably high-tech Ex-Centris cinema, among other venues.

November

Cinemania (early to mid-Nov) ☏ 514/878-0082, Ⓦ www.cinemaniafilmfestival.com. Ten days of screenings of independent French-language films – all with English subtitles – at the Cinéma Impérial.
Image + Nation (mid- to late Nov) Ⓦ www .image-nation.org. The largest of its kind in Canada, Montreal's festival of gay, lesbian, bisexual and transgendered films offers thought-provoking and occasionally silly

glimpses of the lives and fantasies of the queer community.
Santa Claus Parade (late Nov) The big guy in red draws over a quarter of a million spectators to rue Ste-Catherine, though for many Montrealers it's the unveiling of the Christmas display in the Ogilvy department-store window that truly marks the start of the holiday season.

December

Salon des métiers d'art du Québec (early to mid-Dec) ☏ 514/861-2787, Ⓦ www.salondes metiersdart.com. Hundreds of mostly Québécois artisans display their creations for sale in the lead-up to Christmas at Place Bonaventure.

New Year's Eve (Dec 31) ☏ 1-877/266-5687. In addition to the wide array of parties thrown in the city's clubs and bars, you can ring in the new year under the stars with thousands of revellers at the free ball on Place Jacques-Cartier, complete with bands and fireworks.

19

Directory

Airport Aéroport International Pierre-Elliott-Trudeau de Montréal ☎514/394-7377 or 1-800/465-1213, 🌐 www.admtl.com. Renamed at the beginning of 2004, the old Dorval airport is referred to as Montréal-Trudeau. See p.25 for details.

Car rental Downtown branches include: Avis, 1225 rue Metcalfe ☎514/866-7906; Budget, 1240 rue Guy ☎514/938-1000; Discount, 607 boul de Maisonneuve O ☎514/286-1554; Hertz Canada, 1073 rue Drummond ☎514/938-1717; Thrifty, 845 rue Ste-Catherine E ☎514/845-5954; and Via Route, 1255 rue Mackay ☎514/871-1166, which charges a bit less than the majors. See p.29 for toll-free reservation numbers and websites.

City information Accès Montréal (☎514/872-1111 or 872-2237 recorded info, 🌐 www .ville.montreal.qc.ca) has recorded information on all manner of municipal services, from tennis courts to parking tickets.

Consulates France, 1 Place Ville Marie ☎514/878-4385, 🌐 www.consulfrance -montreal.org; **Germany**, 1250 boul René-Lévesque O ☎514/931-2277, 🌐 www .montreal.diplo.de; **Italy**, 3489 rue Drummond ☎514/849-8351, 🌐 www .italconsul.montreal.qc.ca; **Japan**, 600 rue de la Gauchetière O ☎514/866-3429, 🌐 www.montreal.ca.emb-japan.go.jp; **UK**, 1000 rue de la Gauchetière O ☎514/866-5863, 🌐 www.britainincanada.org; **US**, 1155 rue St-Alexandre ☎514/398-9695, 🌐 http://montreal.usconsulate.gov. For the following countries, contact the embassy in Ottawa: **Australia** ☎613/236-0841, 🌐 www .ahc-ottawa.org; **Ireland** ☎613/233-6281; **New Zealand** ☎613/238-5991, 🌐 www .nzembassy.com/canada.

Currency exchange Most large Downtown banks will change currency and travellers'

cheques, or you can try the following: Calforex, 1250 rue Peel ☎514/392-9100; Thomas Cook, Centre Eaton, 705 rue Ste-Catherine O ☎514/284-7388.

Dentists Centre Dentaire, 3546 av Van-Horne (24-hour dental clinic; ☎514/342-4444); Walk-in Clinic, 3rd floor, Montréal General Hospital, 1650 av Cedar (Mon–Fri 8.30am–4.30pm, but go as early as possible; ☎514/934-8397; after-hours call ☎514/934-8075).

Emergencies ☎911 for fire, police and ambulance.

Helplines Tel-Aide (☎514/935-1101, 🌐 www.telaide.org) is a 24-hour anonymous and confidential service for people who are feeling suicidal or just need to talk. For gay and lesbian concerns, see p.185. If you have been the victim of sexual assault, see "Rape crisis", opposite.

Hospitals Central English-language hospitals that are part of the McGill University Health Centre "superhospital" (☎514/934-1934) are the Montréal General Hospital, 1650 av Cedar, on the mountain's slope northwest of downtown, and Royal Victoria Hospital, 687 av des Pins O, up the hill from McGill University.

Laundry Net-Net, 310 av Duluth E (☎514/844-8511; 8.30am–10pm, until 9pm weekends), will wash, dry and fold your clothes in neat bags for you within 24 hours for 89¢/pound (delivery costs $7 and is available on orders of $25 or more – equivalent to a large garbage bag); doing it yourself works out to around $5/load. Buanderie du Village, 1499 rue Amherst (☎514/526-4084; Mon–Fri 9am–9pm, Sat 9am–7pm, Sun 11am–7pm), will wash your clothes in a few hours for $8.50/load, around $5 if you do it yourself. Brainwash Café, 3565 av Lorne (☎514/282-3344), serves drinks and snacks, and you can play chess, watch DVDs or surf the Internet for free while you wait for the rinse cycle (9am–midnight; from 10am Sat; from noon Sun). Most hotels have laundry service as well.

Left luggage There are $3 lockers at the main bus terminal (24hr maximum), as well as left-luggage storage (open 7am–7pm; $5 and up, with hefty late charges). The train station has left-luggage facilities for passengers only ($3/24hr, $6 oversized); open until 7.15pm.

Pharmacies Jean Coutu (ⓦ www.jeancoutu .com) and Pharmaprix (ⓦ www.pharmaprix .ca) are the major chains with branches all over the city. The Pharmaprix near the Oratoire St-Joseph at 5122 chemin de la Côte-des-Neiges (ⓣ 514/738-8464) is open 24 hours. Closer to the centre and open until midnight are its branches at 901 rue Ste-Catherine E (ⓣ 514/842-4915) and 1500 rue Ste-Catherine O (ⓣ 514/933-4744). Late-opening Jean Coutu outlets include 501 av du Mont-Royal E (ⓣ 514/521-3481; daily until 11pm) and 1675 rue Ste-Catherine O (ⓣ 514/933-4221; daily until midnight).

Police For emergencies, call ⓣ 911. Dial ⓣ 514/280-2222 for non-emergency situations.

Post offices The main downtown branch is at 1250 rue University (Mon–Fri 8am–5.45pm). Many smaller outlets can be found at counters in shops and pharmacies – contact Canada Post (ⓣ 1-866/607-6301, ⓦ www.canadapost.ca) for your nearest branch.

Public toilets Your best bets are attractions such as museums, as well as shopping malls (usually near the food court). If pressed, you can always make a small purchase (eg a cup of coffee) in a bar or restaurant if they won't let you use the facilities otherwise.

Rape crisis Bilingual rape crisis line ⓣ 514/934-4504.

Ski/snow reports ⓦ www.quebecskisurf.com, as well as regular radio reports.

Tax Two taxes are applied to just about every purchase: the 6 percent GST (TPS in French) and the 7.5 percent QST (TVQ in French).

Taxis Taxi Diamond (ⓣ 514/273-6331) and Taxi Co-op (ⓣ 514/725-9885) are two reputable firms.

Telephones You must dial ⓣ 514 the area code for local calls, which cost 25¢ at a payphone and more if you pay by credit card. Prepaid cards (see p.39) are available from Bell-Canada outlets, newsagents, the airport and the Centre Infotouriste. Dial ⓣ 411 for information, 0 to reach the operator. Toll-free (freephone) numbers begin with 1-800, 1-866, 1-877 or 1-888.

Tickets The Admission network sells tickets for almost everything (ⓣ 514/790-1245 or 1-800/361-4595, ⓦ www.admission.com).

Tipping It's customary to tip 15 percent of the total before taxes to waiters and bar staff (usually "a buck a beer"). Note that "TPS" or "GST" which appear on the bill are not abbreviations for "tips" or "Good Service Tip" – these are taxes. Taxi drivers and hairdressers also expect a 15 percent tip; for porters, doormen and bellhops, tip $1 per bag.

Travel agents Tourisme Jeunesse Boutique, 205 av du Mont-Royal E (ⓣ 514/844-0287, ⓦ www.tourismejeunesse.org), and Club Voyages Tourbec St-Denis, 3419 rue St-Denis (ⓣ 514/288-4455), are both excellent sources for budget travellers; the former has a branch in Québec City at 94 boul René-Lévesque O (ⓣ 418/522-2552 or 1-866/461-8585). Voyages Campus (Travel Cuts; ⓣ 1-866/246-9762, ⓦ www .travelcuts.com), with branches at 1455 boul de Maisonneuve O (ⓣ 514/288-1130), 3480 rue McTavish (ⓣ 514/398-0647), 225 av du Président-Kennedy (ⓣ 514/281-6662) and 1613 rue St-Denis (ⓣ 514/843-8511) books travel primarily for students with an International Student Identification Card (ISIC).

Weather and road conditions Environment Canada (ⓣ 514/283-3010, ⓦ www .weatheroffice.ec.gc.ca) for info on weather and winter road conditions; Transports Québec (ⓣ 1-888/355-0511, ⓦ www.mtq .gouv.qc.ca) for roadworks. Up-to-the-minute traffic reports are also on radio stations such as CJAD 800 AM.

⑲

DIRECTORY

Out of
the City

Out of the City

20

Les Laurentides

E asily reached from Montréal, and a good choice if you want to stretch out a bit in the outdoors and perhaps do some skiing, the **Lauren-tides** (Laurentians) combines acres of farmland dotted with relaxed, historic towns and a few splendid resorts in its mountainous upper reaches. Immediately north of Montréal and separated from it by the Lac des Deux-Montagnes and suburban island-city of Laval, are the **Basses-Laurentides** (Lower Laurentians). Once home to the region's main farmlands (some of which are still in operation), its flat and quiet landscapes are graced by centuries-old whitewashed cottages and manor houses. Here, two laid-back destinations make for pleasant afternoon detours: **St-Eustache**, along the Rivière des Milles-Îles, is notable for its battle-scarred historic centre, while on the shores of Lac des Deux-Montagnes lies **Oka**, home to one of North America's oldest monasteries, bordering on an attractive provincial park.

For more active pursuits, most visitors head straight for the Laurentian heartland beginning north of St-Jérôme – the area most Montrealers have in mind when they talk about the Laurentians. Here, the mountains begin to climb higher into the sky, affording great hiking in their forested glades and all manner of watersports in the lakes and rivers dotted about. Don't expect dramatic, jagged peaks, though – 500 million years of erosion have moulded one of the world's oldest ranges into a rippling landscape of rounded peaks and smooth valleys. The area boasts one of the largest concentrations of **ski** resorts in North America – come winter, skiers conquer dozens of hills, with those around the town of **St-Sauveur-des-Monts** being among the most accessible and popular. In contrast to the yuppified ski resorts found around here, artsy **Val-David** is better for cross-country skiing and snowshoeing – though it has its pistes too, along with a host of summertime pursuits. Continuing north, the mountains reach an altitude of nearly 1000m, with the famous **Mont-Tremblant** the biggest draw of all; as it is 130km north of Montréal, you pretty much need to make a weekend of it or longer – there are plenty of full-week ski packages available.

St-Eustache

After passing through the monotonous suburbs of Laval and crossing the Rivière des Milles-Îles to sprawling **St-Eustache** (forty minutes northwest of Montréal along Hwy-13 or 15 north to Hwy-640 west), the town's tiny historic core, **Vieux-St-Eustache**, comes as a bit of a surprise. The riverside old-town dates from the eighteenth century and its historic sites are clustered along two narrow streets: rues St-Louis and St-Eustache. The silver twin-bell-towered **Église de St-Eustache** at 123 rue St-Louis looms over the whole district,

Access to the Laurentian heartland by **bus** is provided by Galland Laurentides (☎514/842-2281, ⓦwww.galland-bus.com), which stops at St-Sauveur (6 daily, 1hr 30min), Val-David (3 daily, 2hr), the St-Jovite sector of Mont-Tremblant (6 daily, 2hr 25min) and the Tremblant resort (in season; 3 daily, 2hr 45min); there are additional runs on the weekend. Within the Laurentians, there are also regional buses stopping at main towns between St-Jérôme and Mont-Tremblant (4 daily; ☎819/425-9979 or 1-800/717-9737, ⓦwww.tcil.qc.ca).

Only the Basses Laurentides is accessible from Montréal by **public transit**: the Oka Express local bus (☎450/479-1625, ⓦwww.okatransport.qc.ca) runs a couple of times a day between Oka and Deux-Montagnes commuter rail station (☎514/287-8726, ⓦwww.amt.qc.ca), stopping at the park on summer weekends. A number of local buses (CIT Laurentides; ☎450/433-7873, ⓦwww.surf.amt.qc.ca) aimed mainly at commuters also run between the train station and St-Eustache. More frequent are the Société de Transport de Laval (STL; ☎450/688-6520, ⓦwww.stl.laval.qc.ca) local buses, which run at least hourly between St-Eustache and Métro Henri-Bourassa (#46; 55min) and Métro Montmorency (#53; 45min).

The main regional **tourist information** office for the Basses Laurentides is located off exit 14 from Hwy-640, a short drive north of Vieux St-Eustache (daily: late June to late Aug 8.30am–6.30pm; late Aug to late June 9am–4pm; ☎450/491-4444, ⓦwww.basseslaurentides.com). For the rest of the Laurentides, the main tourist office is at exit 51 off Hwy-15 (late June to early Sept Sun–Thurs 8am–6pm, Fri & Sat 8am–7pm; early Sept to late June Sun–Thurs 8.30am–5pm, Fri & Sat 8.30am–7pm; ☎450/224-7007, 514/990-5625 or 1-800/561-6673, ⓦwww.laurentides.com) or you can stop by one of the smaller local offices described in this chapter.

and it was here that a faction of the Patriotes rebels, protesting oppression of the Francophones under British rule, was put down by military detachments in 1837. A third of the 150 men who took refuge in the church were killed after it was blasted by cannon fire, and the church still bears a few scars on its recently cleaned-up stone facade. The interior vault was rebuilt following the battle, with gold rosettes alternating with cream-coloured beams above an altar shimmering with gold leaf. British troops went on to raze much of the town, leaving a dozen-odd fieldstone buildings intact, most of which today are simply marked with heritage signs and form the core of Vieux-St-Eustache. The **Manoir Globensky** at 235 rue St-Eustache postdates the battle and is worth a quick visit if you're interested in the rebellion. It houses the **Maison de la Culture et du Patrimoine** (mid-June to mid-Oct 11am–6pm; $5; ☎450/974-5170 for schedules), where guided tours take in temporary exhibitions on local history and displays of various tools and weapons; most are reproductions, though the cannon ball and British rifle are legitimate articles. Also of historical interest, and included in the tour, is the **Moulin Légaré** (☎450/974-5400, ⓦwww.moulinlegare.com), the oldest continually operating water-powered flour mill in North America, directly opposite; you can pick up fresh bread here, as well. If you want to stop to **eat**, *Ristorante Da Dario*, a block back towards the church at 198 rue St-Eustache (☎819/623-8094; no lunch Sat–Mon), is a good spot for ciabatta sandwiches and Italian dishes in a house dating from 1812.

Oka

Some 20km southwest of St-Eustache on Hwy-344 lies the lakeside municipality of **Oka**, site of the controversial 78-day armed stand-off between the

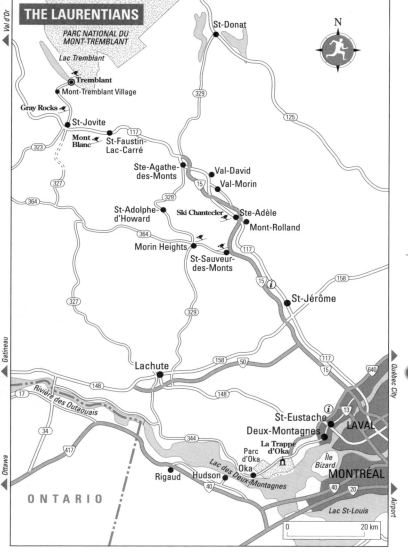

THE LAURENTIANS

PARC NATIONAL DU
MONT-TREMBLANT

Lac Tremblant

Tremblant
Mont-Tremblant Village

Gray Rocks

St-Jovite

Mont
Blanc

St-Faustin-
Lac-Carré

St-Donat

Ste-Agathe-
des-Monts

Val-David
Val-Morin

St-Adolphe-
d'Howard

Ski Chantecler

Ste-Adèle
Mont-Rolland

Morin Heights

St-Sauveur-
des-Monts

St-Jérôme

Lachute

St-Eustache
Deux-Montagnes

LAVAL

La Trappe
d'Oka

Parc
d'Oka

Oka

Île
Bizard

MONTRÉAL

Rigaud

Hudson

Lac des Deux-Montagnes

Lac St-Louis

ONTARIO

Rivière des Outaouais

N

Gatineau

Ottawa

Val d'Or

Québec City

Airport

0   20 km

LES LAURENTIDES | Oka

20

Mohawks and provincial police in the summer of 1990, triggered when the town's council decided to expand its golf course onto the tribe's sacred burial ground (a territory for which they had been trying to settle a claim for decades). The tiny village itself is a sleepy spot – the areas of interest are located in the nearby countryside, which is dotted with apple orchards and dominated by the impressive **Abbaye Cistercienne d'Oka**, 1600 chemin d'Oka (daily 4am–8pm;

🕾 450/479-8361, 🌐 www.abbayeoka.com). Some thirty Trappist monks live in the abbey, built to house two hundred, and notable for its century-old bell tower rising amidst the enveloping hills. Given its diminishing numbers, the abbey is building a new, smaller monastery in the Lanaudière region and will be moving sometime in 2008 or 2009. The bright **church** inside has arched ceilings warmly offset by wood panelling on the lower walls, and the nearby monastery shop (closed Sun) sells organic Trappist products, including their trademark Oka cheese, a smooth and creamy semi-soft ripened cheese similar to Port Salut.

Pick up a wedge before heading to the splendid **Parc National d'Oka** (open year-round; $3.50 plus $6.25 beach parking; 🕾 450/479-8365 or 1-800/665-6527, 🌐 www.sepaq.com), which stretches south of the abbey to the shores of **Lac des Deux–Montagnes** (the main entrance is five-minutes' drive west of the abbey on Hwy-344). The park is laced with 45km of biking and hiking trails: the best of these is the scenic 5.5km **Calvaire d'Oka** trek that ascends to the top of a spectacular viewpoint, passing a grouping of seven deserted stone chapels built around 1740 by the Sulpicians (see box, p.72). In winter, cross-country skiers and snowshoers take over the same trails ($8.50 including park entry) – notably the Pinède, a 4km trail lit up for evening skiing; rentals are available (from $19.50 for a full set of gear). One of the park's main draws is the long stretch of sandy **beach** along the shores of Lac des Deux-Montagnes (which faces across to the west end of the island of Montréal); bicycles and various watercraft can be rented at its western end (starting at $11/hr), while far along the eastern end is Québec's most popular

---

Hitting the slopes

The rounded and forested hills of the Laurentians that make up Montréal's winter playground are dotted with over a dozen **ski hills** served by **resort towns** that come alive at night with energized skiers. The ski resorts start under an hour's drive north of Montréal with the mountains surrounding the St-Sauveur valley. Tickets for **Mont St-Sauveur** (see opposite) are also valid at four associated resorts – of these, **Morin Heights** (🌐 www.skimorinheights.com) is mainly intermediate and has a number of night runs, while **Mont-Olympia** (🌐 www.montolympia.com) is geared more to beginners, as is independent **Mont-Habitant** (see opposite). Further north, near Ste-Adèle, the upscale resort of **Le Chantecler** (🌐 www.skichantecler.com) has 23 runs split between beginner and intermediate levels, many lit at night.

Surrounding **Val-David** (see p.238), a number of smaller hills depend on a good snowfall. In addition to the all-inclusive **Tremblant** operation further north (see p.240), nearby **Gray Rocks** (🌐 www.grayrocks.com) is a smaller, family-oriented resort with varied terrain. Its lift tickets are interchangeable with those at **Mont Blanc** (🌐 www.ski-mont-blanc.com), just off Hwy-117, 10km closer to Montréal than Tremblant; it has a 300m vertical, a challenging intermediate tree run and the best-maintained half-pipe in the area.

As many of the region's towns are little more than bases for the ski hills, accommodation tends to be of the pricey resort variety, though a smattering of B&Bs, motels and a couple of hostels offer cheaper options. Check with travel agents in Montréal (see p.229) before heading out as weekend packages can be a bargain, or try the region's free accommodation service (🕾 450/224-7007, 514/990-5625 or 1-800/561-6673, 🌐 www.laurentides.com). Keep in mind, though, that staying overnight need not be a priority if you're willing to leave early and come back late the same day. For up-to-date ski conditions visit 🌐 www.quebecskisurf.com or listen out for regular updates on the radio.

nude beach. There are nearly 900 serviced **campsites** ($31) and more rustic spots to pitch a tent (from $16.30); you can rent all the gear you need from $52/night for a minimum of two nights (includes pitch rental; $217 deposit) – enquire at the entry kiosk. There's also a lodge with basic rooms ($53) if you'd rather not rough it.

St-Sauveur-des-Monts

Most visitors skip the Basses-Laurentides and head directly for the mountainous terrain of the Laurentian heartland. **St-Sauveur-des-Monts**, 60km north of Montréal, marks the beginning of the region and is its ritziest resort town. During the peak skiing season, the town's resident population of 7000 quadruples, and the main drag, rue Principale, boasts every type of restaurant, designer boutique and craft shop imaginable (and there are outlet stores in a nearby mall complex). Come nightfall, flash clubs and discos fill quickly with tired skiers in trendy outfits. Rue Principale spreads out to either side of the **Église St-Sauveur**, a century-old grey-stone building typical of the province's massive parish churches with its tin-clad steeple and flanking cupolas; the vaulted interior is disappointingly plain. Even without snow, the town's still a pleasant spot to wander around, especially during the Festival des Arts de St-Sauveur (℡450/227-9935, ⓦwww.artssaintsauveur.com) – ten days of dance, chamber music and jazz concerts in early August.

Information on shopping and skiing is available from the **tourist bureau**, near exit 60 from Hwy-15, at 605 chemin des Frênes (daily 9am–5pm, late May to early Sept 8.30am–7pm; ℡450/227-3417 or 1-800/898-2127, ⓦwww .saint-sauveur.net or www.tourismepdh.org); there's also a kiosk in front of the church on rue Principale in the warmer months.

Of the six separate nearby ski mountains, the best are **Mont St-Sauveur** and **Mont-Habitant**. The former features the most extensive night-skiing in the province and some decent expert runs and glades; it often has enough snow to keep the ski season going until June ($38–46/adults, $26–30/6–12 years; ℡450/227-4671 or 514/871-0101, ⓦwww.montsaintsauveur.com). The latter is a great spot for families with kids just starting out, with ten gentle slopes and a good ski school ($28–35/adults, $22–24/6–12 years; ℡450/227-2637 or 1-866/887-2637, ⓦwww.monthabitant.com). In summer, the area continues to be a good destination for families thanks to a number of **water parks** – the most popular is the Parc Aquatique Mont St-Sauveur (full day: $30, $26 for kids under 1.39m; ℡450/227-4671, ⓦwww.mssi.ca), with a giant wave pool and slides you can race down in a raft, on a tube or on your butt.

Accommodation

Le Bonnet d'Or 405 rue Principale ℡450/227-9669 or 1-877/277-9669, ⓦwww.bbcanada.com/bonnetdor. A quaint B&B in an 1888 house with five handsome rooms, some of which feature amenities, like an in-room fireplace, that raise the price; all have private bathrooms, as well as wood floors, quilts and antique furnishings. Breakfasts include a fruit course, hot dish (omelette, soufflé, crepes) and dessert. $115.

Manoir St-Sauveur 246 chemin du Lac Millette ℡450/227-1811 or 1-800/361-0505, ⓦwww.manoir-saint-sauveur.com. A massive complex with 300 well-appointed rooms and suites; the best are on the top floor, nestled in the eaves. $149–199.

Aux Petits Oiseaux 342 rue Principale ℡450/227-6116 or 1-877/227-6116, ⓦwww .bbcanada.com/auxpetitsoiseaux. A countrified B&B with four glossy wood-panelled rooms (two with private bathrooms) and a cheaper basement room ($70). Guests also have access to a garden and pool. $85 (shared bath); $110.

Eating and drinking

The range of **dining options** runs the gamut from fast-food joints nearer the highway to expensive restaurants of both the posh and trendy varieties. For mid-range choices, there are local branches of a number of Montréal outfits such as *Pizzédélic*, 16 rue de la Gare. Or try one of the good local spots listed below.

Allégria 22 rue Lafleur N ☎450/227-9979, ⓦ www.allegriarestaurant.ca. The fresh take on regional Italian dishes incorporates fresh, organic ingredients and *nouvelle* presentation at this chic newcomer. The four-course *table d'hôte* (around $70) highlights the chef's inventiveness.
La Bohème 251 rue Principale ☎450/227-6644, ⓦ www.restoboheme.com. French bistro food in a rustic ambience with specialities like frog's legs *provençale* and *bœuf Bourguignon*, with pasta and couscous as alternatives. Most mains cost $16–18.

Brûlerie des Monts 197 rue Principale ☎450/227-6157, ⓦ www.bruleriedesmonts.ca. A trendy but cosy café next to the church with the aroma of freshly roasting coffee and offering *croques*, panini and breakfast fare. Open 6.30am–8pm (until 10pm Fri & Sat).
Papa Luigi 155 rue Principale ☎450/227-5311, ⓦ www.papa-luigi.com. A lively restaurant in a handsome nineteenth-century house serving Italian veal and pasta dishes, though the main draw is the sizzling Angus beef steaks ($21–35 for 8–16oz). Reservations strongly recommended. Open for dinner only.

Val-David

Some 16km further north along Hwy-117 lies bohemian **Val–David**, the most laid-back of the Laurentians' towns, chosen by artists and artisans as a haven from the yuppie developments elsewhere. Its progressive credentials suffered a setback in 2003, however, when the municipal authorities bulldozed half a dozen low-rent homes to make way for a car park for the regional park; protesters, including one who shackled herself to the roof of her house, tried in vain to stop the move.

Le P'tit Train du Nord

The bed of **Le P'tit Train du Nord**, a railway line that once ferried Montrealers to the Laurentians' resorts, now sees brisk business as a major **bicycle trail** as thousands of cyclists pedal their way among the mountains throughout the summer. The former stations have been renovated as well, now often housing tourist-information centres, some with facilities such as showers and snack bars for cyclists taking a break. Access to the 200km trail, which runs north from St-Jérôme to Mont-Laurier, costs $5/day, $15 for the whole May to October season.

In winter, the snow-covered route is equally in demand by **cross-country skiers** ($7/day, $35 for the whole December to March season), who can explore numerous side-trails branching off into the hills between St-Jérôme and Val-David, and to **snowmobilers** – the Ste-Agathe to Mont-Laurier stretch is part of the network of thousands of kilometres of trails that crisscross the province. **Information**, as well as a guide with maps and lists of services (including cycle repair, baggage transport and accommodation) along the route, is available from the Association Touristique des Laurentides (see p.234).

For a combination of land and water fun, Les Excursions Rivière du Nord (☎450/229-1889 or 1-866/342-2668, ⓦ www.riviere-du-nord.ca) gives you the chance to **canoe, kayak or raft** downriver for a couple of hours from Mont Rolland station (near Ste-Adèle) to Piedmont (just east of St-Sauveur) starting at $22 and then cycle ($14/2hr) the 7km back north. Similar trips are available for the four-hour return trip from Val-David to Mont Rolland via Lac Raymond (see opposite).

The main street, rue de l'Église, reflects the town's cultural bent with several galleries and craft shops that make for a pleasant afternoon of browsing, interspersed with the majority of the town's cafés, restaurants and bars. Also on rue de l'Église, at no. 2501, is the **tourist information** office (late June to mid-Oct daily 9am–5pm; mid-Nov to mid-March Mon–Fri 10am–5pm, Sat & Sun 9am–5pm; other times as per winter hours Wed–Sun only; ☎819/322-2900 or 1-888/322-7030 ext 235, ⓦ www.valdavid.com).

Though surrounded by three small mountains – **Mont-Alta** has the most pistes at 22 (☎819/322-3206, ⓦ www.mont-alta.com; $20/adults, $15/6–12 years) – the town sets itself apart with non-ski-related attractions come summertime. In addition to the artistic sights, Val-David is a great base for exploring the Laurentian scenery as there are a number of **hiking** trails within a short distance and the relatively flat Le P'tit Train du Nord **bicycle trail** extends for miles to the north and south (see box opposite). If you want to explore the trail, or just tool around the surrounding countryside, Pause Plein Air, 1381 chemin de la Sapinière (☎819/322-6880 or 1-877/422-6880, ⓦ www.pause-plein-air .com), rents bikes for $7/hr or $20/day (including trail permit) and **canoes and kayaks**; a downstream trip and return by bicycle costs $30. Aventure Nouveau Continent, 2301 rue de l'Église (☎819/322-7336 or 1-866/922-7336, ⓦ www .aventurenouveaucontinent.com), offers similar deals.

The area is popular for **rock climbing** as well, with half a dozen well-developed sites: Passe Montagne (☎819/322-2123 or 1-800/465-2123, ⓦ www .passemontagne.com) offers beginners' courses on summer Saturdays for $75. If you're an experienced climber, contact the Fédération Québécoise de la Montagne et de l'Escalade (FQME), the provincial mountain-climbing association (☎514/252-3004, ⓦ www.fqme.qc.ca), for details of more challenging climbs.

Accommodation

In contrast to some of the flashier resort towns, Val-David offers cheaper and generally laid-back accommodation in small **inns** and **B&Bs**, as well as a great, if sometimes noisy, **youth hostel**.

Auberge Le Creux du Vent 1430 rue de l'Academie ☎819/322-2280 or 1-888/522-2280, ⓦ www.lecreuxduvent.com. A woodsy inn with six subtly themed rooms complete with slanted ceilings, cable TV and private shower. Price includes choice of full breakfast. The wood-beamed restaurant has an evening *table d'hôte* for $30–39 (three or four courses), with a range of gourmet dishes using locally sourced game and fowl like wapiti (elk) and pheasant. Or opt for cheaper grilled sausage or *bavette* ($9–12.50) on the terrace overlooking the rapids. $105.

Le Chalet Beaumont 1451 rue Beaumont ☎819/322-1972, ⓦ www.chaletbeaumont.com. Youth hostel in a massive chalet with roaring fires in the winter and a pub with terrace in the summer. Accommodation in dormitory, double and single rooms can be noisy at times, though. Call from the bus station,

and they'll come pick you up. Family rates available. $24/dorm ($20 nonmembers); $60/$55 (shared bath) or $75/$65 (private) per room.

La Maison de Bavière 1470 chemin de la Rivière ☎819/322-3528 or 1-866/322-3528, ⓦ www.maisondebaviere.com. Pretty house painted in a Bavarian folk style and backing onto river rapids, which you can see from the fireplace-warmed sitting room and some of the bedrooms, all of which have private bath. The two studios ($140) have kitchen and sofabed, but only the four B&B rooms get to share in the extravagant breakfasts with gourmet teas, a fruit course and hot dishes such as french toast with maple and walnut mousse. $95 (river view); $78.

La Sapinière 1244 chemin de la Sapinière ☎819/322-2020 or 1-800/567-6635, ⓦ www .sapiniere.com. An upscale ski-lodge of log and stone offering 70 well-appointed rooms with cable TV and a/c, some with fireplace, and a host of outdoor activities on the property. Its gastronomic restaurant serves a five-course *table d'hôte* ($54) with a good range of meat, fish (they smoke their own salmon) and vegetarian options on the menu. $350.

Eating and drinking

In addition to the dining rooms in the hotels mentioned above, most of Val-David's eating spots are concentrated on and around rue de l'Église.

L'Express 1337 chemin de la Sapinière ☎819/322-3090. A café-bistro on the corner of rue de l'Église serving soup and hot and cold sandwiches, as well as good daily specials like *tourtière* and flavourful couscous. Buckwheat pancakes and egg dishes make it a great spot for breakfast; open 7am–3pm, until 4pm weekends.
Le Grand Pa 2481 rue de l'Église ☎819/322-3104. A friendly restaurant serving simple and affordable French food that turns into a rollicking *boîte à chanson* on weekend evenings. There's a range of salads and croissants topped with melted cheese at lunch, as well as a fixed menu for around $14. Evening *table d'hôte* contains the likes of smoked trout filet and lamb-shank *confit* for around $22–25.

Mont-Tremblant

Situated some 50km north of Val-David, **Mont–Tremblant** is the Laurentians' oldest and most renowned ski area, focused on the range's highest peak (915m). In 1997, the company that developed British Columbia's Whistler ski-resort pumped some $50 million into the region's main resort, **Tremblant**, and the resulting European–style village has made it one of Canada's premier ski destinations. The accolades abound for the slopes themselves, since Tremblant boasts

△ Skiers at Mont-Tremblant

94 ski runs in all ranges and is particularly notable for its challenging expert runs and gladed areas; it also has the longest run in Québec (6km). **Ski passes** cost around $58 per day, with savings on multi-day tickets.

The municipality of Mont-Tremblant comprises three separate sectors separated by a forested and lake-dotted countryside and linked by an at-least hourly bus service ($1.25). Each sector has its own atmosphere: the merged town of **St-Jovite** (now sometimes referred to as "centre-ville", or "downtown"), nearest Hwy-117, has the most in the way of services along its pleasant commercial strip of boutiques and eating and drinking spots. The main **tourist information** office is just off Hwy-117 as you enter Ste-Jovite, at 48 chemin de Brébeuf (June–Sept daily 8am–8pm; Oct–May Sun–Fri 9am–5pm, Sat 9am–7pm; ☎819/425-3300 or 1-877/425-2434, ⓦwww.tourismemont tremblant.com). A second tourist office is located further north at 5080 montée Ryan (☎819/425-2434), en route to **Mont-Tremblant Village**, which is just as quiet as its name suggests and is best used for its accommodations. The resort of **Tremblant** itself (ⓦwww.tremblant.ca), centred around its Disney-esque pedestrian village with a gondola (*Le Cabriolet*) running above the middle of it, is the liveliest spot in the whole area come winter (though there are plenty of hiking, cycling, boating and golfing activities in warmer months). If you're planning to take advantage of the outdoors, contact the resort for details of bike and other equipment rentals and for what activities are on offer. It's worth checking out the Centre d'Activités Tremblant (☎819/681-4848, ⓦwww .tremblantactivities.com) on Place St-Bernard, around the corner from the top of *Le Cabriolet*; they can arrange horseback riding and whitewater-rafting trips, and spa treatments for afterwards.

Accommodation

Accommodation, scattered throughout the area, includes more than a dozen **B&Bs** (many listed with BB Tremblant ☎1-866/660-4635, ⓦwww .bbtremblant.com), as well as rustic **chalets** and ritzy **inns and resorts**; the tourist office can provide more information, or phone ☎1-866/274-7731 for reservations. Although St-Jovite has some cheap motels, the second sector, Mont-Tremblant Village, 10km to the north, has better places to sleep, including a **youth hostel**. The third sector is the aforementioned *Tremblant* resort itself, located another 3km east of the village between Lac Tremblant and the ski slopes. Hotels and chalets are pricier here – the *Fairmont Tremblant* (☎819/681-7000 or 1-800/257-7544, ⓦwww.fairmont.com) is the most glamorous of the lot – but in many cases you can ski right up to your front door, and with around 3500 beds, getting a place should be no problem. If skiing is your main focus, check out the ski-and-accommodation **packages** offered by the resort itself – their website, ⓦwww.tremblant.ca, lists everything in the area and includes photos, rates and ski packages – as well as what's being promoted by the Laurentides tourist board (see box, p.234). You could also try one of the package tour operators listed in the "Getting there" section of Basics near the front of this book (see p.23), or book in person at Tremblant Sunstar (☎819/681-4717 or 1-866/311-2167) at the entrance to the pedestrian village.

Auberge de Jeunesse Internationale de Mont-Tremblant 2213 chemin du Village ☎819/425-6008 or 1-866/425-6008, ⓦwww .hostellingtremblant.com. Hostelling International's youth hostel can sleep 70 in dormitories and in private rooms with double and bunk beds. In addition to amenities like laundry facilities, Internet station ($3/hr), pool table and a teepee for campfires, they offer plenty of organized activities, free canoeing and rentals (bikes $20/day, snowshoes $12/day). $23.75/dorm ($27.75

nonmembers); $59.50/room ($67.50 nonmembers).

Country Inn & Suites by Carlson 160 chemin Curé-Deslauriers ☎819/681-5555 or 1-800-456-4000, ⓦ www.countryinns.com. This nicely furnished, but not overly fussy, four-star is one of the cheaper of the numerous hotels surrounding the pedestrian village. The rooms are large enough to relax in, with sofa and chairs, plus microwave and mini-fridge; extras include free continental-plus breakfast and parking. Like most of the accommodation nearest the ski hill, prices vary greatly: a $139 room in August jumps to $239 in February.

Hôtel Mont-Tremblant 1900 chemin du Village ☎819/425-3232 or 1-888/887-1111, ⓦ www .hotelmonttremblant.com. Bright colours enliven the simply furnished rooms at this old

inn, but it's worth paying the extra $20 for a superior room with sofabed. The rates include full breakfast, and you can also take lunch ($13) or dinner ($16–30 for two courses) in the hotel restaurant, *Le Bernardin*, which serves fine bistro dishes and steaks and has a wide terrace for chilling out. $88.

Tremblant Onwego 112 chemin Plouffe ☎819/429-5522 or 1-866/429-5522, ⓦ www .tremblantonwego.com. Located right where the P'tit Train du Nord bike path passes Lac Mercier, this friendly B&B is well-equipped for active visitors – it even has its own stretch of lakefront beach and watercraft you can use. Some of the rooms have fanciful themes and others shared bath; except for the apartments ($175), a full breakfast is included. $110 (shared bath); $140.

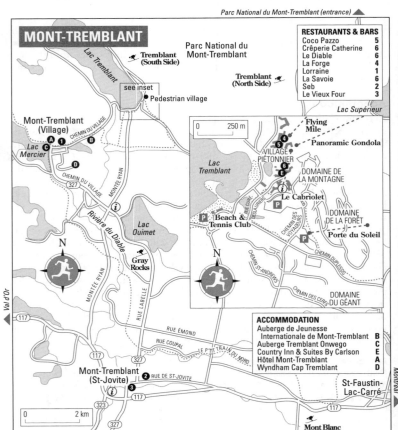

Parc National du Mont-Tremblant (entrance)

MONT-TREMBLANT

Parc National du Mont-Tremblant

RESTAURANTS & BARS
Coco Pazzo	5
Crêperie Catherine	6
Le Diable	6
La Forge	4
Lorraine	1
La Savoie	6
Seb	2
Le Vieux Four	3

ACCOMMODATION
Auberge de Jeunesse Internationale de Mont-Tremblant	B
Auberge Tremblant Onwego	C
Country Inn & Suites By Carlson	E
Hôtel Mont-Tremblant	A
Wyndham Cap Tremblant	D

Wyndham Cap Tremblant 205 rue du Mont-Plaisant ☎819/681-8043 or 1-800/996-3426, ⓦ www.wyndham.com. A good option if you want a more secluded retreat away from the mountain, the condos in this mixed owner/rental development tend to be larger for less money than at the resort itself – even the one-bedroom units have a living/dining area and full kitchen, and the five-bedroom apartments ($589) can sleep a dozen. Amenities include waterslides and hot tubs at the indoor-outdoor swimming pools, a shuttle to the slopes, and a restaurant at the central "country club" with panoramic views along the valley. $139–159.

Eating and drinking

You'll find good-value **restaurants and bars** clustered on **St-Jovite**'s main drag, rue de St-Jovite, and along the main road of Mont-Tremblant Village (including *Le Bernardin* – see opposite), but the largest concentration (and some of the priciest) is at the resort's pedestrian village, which has all manner of **après–ski** spots to eat and drink.

Coco Pazzo Promenade Deslauriers (pedestrian village) ☎819/681-4774, ⓦ www.coco-pazzo.ca. Chef-owner Luigi is passionate about using local, organic produce to craft Italian classics like linguini *pescatore* ($29) and *osso bucco* ($35) in this stylish restaurant tucked away to the side below Place St-Bernard. Pasta and pizza feature among the two-course lunch specials for $11–12.

Crêperie Catherine Vieux-Tremblant (pedestrian village) ☎819/681-4888, ⓦ www.creperie catherine.ca. There's often a wait to get into this jaunty red-and-cream-coloured cottage for all-day breakfast crepes and traditional savoury and dessert crepes, but it's worth it. Open 7.30am–9pm (until 10pm weekends).

La Diable Vieux-Tremblant (pedestrian village) ☎819/681-4546. This micro-brewery with its barn-board vaulted ceiling and scuffed wooden floors is not only a great spot to sample home-brewed pints of Le Blizzard blanche and Septième Ciel blonde beers, but also has reasonably priced burgers and European sausages ($11–13). It attracts a slightly older crowd – younger and more raucous drinkers head to the nearby *P'tit Caribou* (☎819/681-4500, ⓦ www.ptitcaribou.com).

La Forge Bar & Grill Place St-Bernard (pedestrian village) ☎819/681-4900, ⓦ www .laforgetremblant.com. With a wraparound terrace at the foot of the Flying Mile lift and loud rock music, the rustic main-floor bistro attracts a lively crowd for decent salads, pastas and burgers (around $12). The upstairs bar and grill's high-backed leather chairs suggest a more refined ambience, evident in pricier dishes from fourteen-ounce sirloin steak ($35) to the Henry IV filet mignon with foie gras ($42) and a lengthy international wine list. No lunch upstairs.

Lorraine 2000 chemin du Village ☎819/425-5566. This no-nonsense family restaurant draws plenty of locals for cheap breakfasts,

---

Parc National du Mont-Tremblant

Mont-Tremblant ski resort is but a small part of the **Parc National du Mont-Tremblant** ($3.50; ☎819/688-2281 or 1-800/665-6527, ⓦ www.sepaq.com), a mammoth provincial park that sprawls out north of the mountain for almost 1500 square kilometres. Marked by undulating hills and hundreds of lakes, the park is a natural habitat for moose, white-tailed deer and beaver, and one of the best ways to spot them is by canoe, though determined landlubbers can head out on the plentiful hiking trails and bike paths that cut through the park. You can rent bicycles, canoes, row-boats, kayaks and pedal-boats in summer, and cross-country skis and snowshoes once the snow's arrived. **Camping** is available (mid-May to early Oct $16.30–31) and there are also huts ($22/person) and cabins ($35–51/person) if you'd rather have a solid roof over your head. The park has several entry points, the nearest accesses the Diable sector of the park, east of the Tremblant resort along chemin Duplessis; if you're heading there directly, exit Hwy-117 at St-Faustin-Lac-Carré.

smoked meat and club sandwiches, and mains such as chicken and ribs or fish and chips. Open 6am–11pm (until 10pm low season).

La Savoie Vieux-Tremblant (pedestrian village) ☏819/681-4573. This cosy restaurant serves typical alpine treats from Savoy ($32–40), including fondues, *pierrades* (meat or seafood grilled on a hot stone) and their signature *raclette*, for which you melt a half-round of cheese onto your plate. Reservations recommended; dinner only.

Seb 444 rue St-Georges (St-Jovite) ☏819/429-6991, ⊛www.resto-seb.com. Subtitled "L'Artisan Culinaire", this small bistro has a casual ambience that belies the fine *cuisine du terroir*, that includes braised meats, imaginative variations on familiar dishes (shepherd's pie with duck *confit* and cauli-flower purée) and plenty of fish – tuna might come seared, tataki or tartare. Try the $15 lunch special if the four-course $45 *table d'hôte* is out of range. Closed Mon & Tues; no lunch at weekends.

Le Vieux Four 973 rue de St-Jovite ☏819/425-5992. The wood-burning brick oven gets plenty of use at this large Italian restaurant, pumping out plenty of pizzas ($10–13). There's also a range of pastas for around the same price and a range of veal scaloppini ($17–18).

Les Cantons-de-l'Est

B eginning 80km east of Montréal and extending south to the US border, the scenic **Cantons-de-l'Est** (Eastern Townships) was once Québec's best-kept secret, but its nineteenth-century villages are fast gaining popularity with shoppers seeking out antiques and discounted labels at outlet stores. A burgeoning service industry caters to summer cyclists and hikers, while the ski slopes and hiking trails of Mont-Orford and other resorts make it a great outdoorsy destination year-round. However, the region's charm still outweighs its ever-increasing commercialization, with plenty of picture-postcard villages, their white-clapboard or tin-steepled limestone churches and handsome Victorian manors clustered around glistening lake-shores.

The land, once home to scattered groups of Algonquin peoples known as the Abenaki, was later settled by Loyalists hounded out of the US after the American Revolution. Their loyalty to the Crown resulted in freehold land grants from the British (as opposed to the tenanted *seigneuries* commonplace elsewhere), and settlements with very English names like Farnham and Bedford were soon founded. In the mid-nineteenth century the townships opened up to industry, which attracted an influx of French Canadians seeking work: today, nearly 95 percent of the Eastern Townships' 400,000 population are Francophone. For the most part, relations between the linguistic groups have been amicable, though pockets like the towns and villages around Knowlton and North Hatley remain staunchly tied to their Anglophone heritage, and the English-language cultural scene is much stronger than the size of the population would suggest.

Practicalities

Magog is the only town covered here that is accessible by **bus** from Montréal's Station Centrale d'Autobus (up to ten trips daily; 1hr 30min on the express; call ☎514/842-2281 for schedules and fares; ⊛www.limocar.ca). To stop at Knowlton or North Hatley, you'll have to rent a car (see p.29 & p.228). From Montréal, the Auto-route des Cantons-de-l'Est (Hwy-10) flies across the top of the region, but the slower Hwy-112 or Hwy-104 (the latter only as far east as Knowlton) are more picturesque as they wind through the towns and villages at the heart of Loyalist country. If you've got time, detour onto the secondary roads nearer the US border that pass rustic barns, duck under covered bridges and wind through the province's fledgling vineyards (see p.247). The region's main **information centre** is located off exit 68 on Hwy-10, south-west of Granby (June–Aug daily 8.30am–7pm; Sept–May Mon–Fri 8.30am–4.30pm, Sat & Sun 9am–5pm; ☎819/820-2020 or 1-800/355-5755, ⊛www.easterntownships .org). For background info, historic photos and thematic itineraries, check out the *Townships Heritage WebMagazine* (⊛www.townshipsheritage.com).

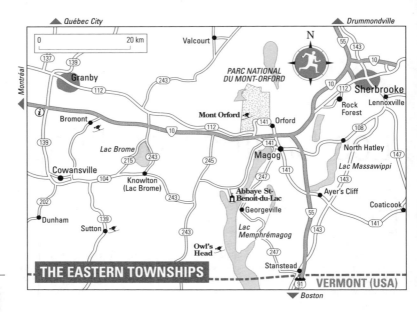

The trek from Montréal to the Cantons-de-l'Est is worth it for the scenery alone, as the northern range of the Appalachian Mountains cuts through the region, especially majestic come autumn when the slopes explode with yellows, oranges and reds. The dull city of Granby, 85km east of Montréal, marks the beginning of the Townships region, which extends all the way east past the university city of Sherbrooke, but it's the picturesque villages nestled in the valleys between them that brim with character. Quaint **Knowlton** exudes Victoriana and boasts terrific antique shops, while **North Hatley**'s breathtaking collection of mansions lends the town a refined air. Between these two lies the town of **Magog**, whose primary appeal is the wide selection of excellent year-round outdoor activities afforded by the impressive Lac Memphrémagog and the rugged **Mont Orford**, laced with hiking trails and ski runs.

Knowlton

The peaceful township of **Lac Brome**, named for the twenty-kilometre-long shimmering lake at its centre, is home to seven sleepy communities, the most handsome of which is pocket-sized **Knowlton**. Settled at the lake's southern end, the town's Loyalist flavour is still strongly felt along its two main drags – chemin Lakeside (Hwy-243) and, perpendicular to that, chemin Knowlton (Hwy-104/243) – which boast an eye-catching combination of red-brick and clapboard houses decorated in a palette of colours and fronted by verandas and wooden benches. At the centre of town, the small **Parc Coldbrook** sits at the edge of a quaint waterfall and stream. Lac Brome is renowned for the quality of its duck, celebrated during the annual **Duck Festival**, a jamboree of music and gastronomy in late September and early October (☎514/242-2870, ⓦ www.knowltonquebec.ca). At other times, you can pick up a duck meal, duck foie gras or a package of "hot ducks" (a pun on hot dogs) at Canards Lac Brome, 40 chemin Centre (☎450/242-3825, ⓦ www.bromelakeducks.com).

The town's only museum, the cluttered **Musée Historique du Comté de Brome**, occupies a complex of buildings at 130 chemin Lakeside (mid-May to mid-Sept Mon–Sat 10am–4.30pm, Sun 11am–4.30pm; $5; ☎450/243-6782), including an easy-to-spot, white-clapboard fire tower. A county history museum with a focus on local heritage, it is surprisingly strong on military arte-facts – the show-stopper is an original Fokker DVII airplane, the type flown by the Red Baron. Further down the street at Arts Knowlton, 9 chemin du Mont-Écho, the **Théâtre Lac Brome** (☎450/242-2270, ⓦ www.theatrelacbrome.ca) offers light-hearted fare during its late-June to mid-August season (other troupes stage short runs throughout the year); tickets are in the $23–26 range and there's a pub next door.

Most visitors overlook these cultural attractions in favour of shopping. **Antique shops** are clustered along chemin Knowlton, while discount designer **clothing outlets** selling the likes of Jones of New York and various European labels are found more on chemin Lakeside. The annual **antique show and sale** held in late May (☎450/243-6782) is the biggest such event, though the museum hosts smaller antique sales on its grounds on a couple of summer Sundays.

Knowlton also marks the eastern end of the 132km **Route des Vins** (Wine Route; ⓦ www.brome-missisquoi.ca), which wends its way through the south-west corner of the Townships towards the US border and then back north to Hwy-10 near Farnham; detailed maps are available from the tourist office (see box, p.245). If you only have time to visit one of the dozen or so wineries – notable for their ice wine – your best bet is the **Vignoble de L'Orpailleur** (mid-April to Dec daily 9am–5pm, Jan to mid-April Sat & Sun 11am–5pm; ☎450/295-2763, ⓦ www.orpailleur.ca), a twenty-minute drive southwest of Knowlton via highways 104 and 202, just past the Loyalist-founded town of Dunham. It operates as an "economuseum", combining its artisanal trade with guided tours and exhibits relating to grape-growing and wine-making, and has a restaurant too.

Practicalities

Just off the *autoroute*, there's a seasonal **tourist office** near the intersection of highways 243 and 215 (late June to early Sept daily 9am–5pm; ☎450/242-2870 year-round). Knowlton is easily handled as an afternoon jaunt out of Montréal – it's just over an hour from the Pont Champlain – so there's no real need to stay the night. If the town's charm does grab you, however, there are a handful of country **inns and B&Bs** to choose from. The most centrally located B&B is *La Venise Verte*, a veranda-wrapped 1884 house at 58 rue Victoria (☎450/243-1844 or 1-888/443-1844, ⓦ www.laveniseverte.com) with four simple, coun-try-style rooms ($110; $90 shared bath), breakfasts made with local and/or organic products and a swimming pool. Right at the town's main intersection, at 286 chemin Knowlton, the modernized *Auberge Knowlton* (☎450/242-6886, ⓦ www.aubergeknowlton.ca) has been operating as an inn for a century and a half (rooms $110); the bustling downstairs restaurant, *Le Relais*, is popular for its Brome Lake duck ($17–24; from $12 at lunch) and weekend breakfasts. Lighter **food** options include nearby *Frostys Bistro Pub*, 51 chemin Lakeside (☎450/242-2929, ⓦ www.frostysbistro.ca), which serves pub grub on a terrace overlooking a stream, while *Café Inn*, in the Woolrich outlet mini-mall at 264 chemin Knowlton (☎450/243-0069), offers scrumptious *tartines* (open-faced sandwiches) and funky pizzas as well as a mountain view.

Magog and around

The resort town of **Magog**, about thirty minutes east of Knowlton along Hwy-10 or Hwy-112, combines some of the best swimming and cycling in the Eastern Townships. Magog fans out around one of the townships' largest lakes, **Lac Memphrémagog** – reputedly home to Memphré, a local variant of the Loch Ness Monster (see Ⓦ www.memphre.com for a list of some of the 200-odd reported sightings since the mid-nineteenth century). Strangely enough, there's greater controversy at the moment over who owns the rights to the name – a Vermont woman has threatened to sue anyone who cashes in on "her" monster – than whether Memphré in fact exists.

Magog is a lively spot fairly teeming with bars and restaurants along its main street, rue Principale. Magog's north–south artery, rue Merry (Hwy-141) hosts much of the town's accommodation and also allows access to most of the area's outdoor activities since it both runs down the eastern shore of the lake and crests **Parc National du Mont-Orford**, passing through the uninteresting village of Orford's scattered houses and businesses along the highway.

The **tourist office** is located at 55 rue Cabana, just off Hwy-112 on the way into Magog from the west (late June to early Sept daily 8.30am–8pm; early Sept to late June 9am–5pm; ℡ 1-800/267-2744, Ⓦ www.tourisme-memphremagog .com). **Buses** from Montréal stop at 768 rue Sherbrooke (℡ 819/843-4617), near the intersection of rue Principale. There is also a local tram-style bus service (daily July, Aug and ski season; weekends-only most other months; ℡ 819/678-7888, Ⓦ www.trolleymagogorford.com) linking Magog and Mont-Orford for $2 each way.

Accommodation

Hotels tend to be expensive in Magog – if you want to stay in town, your best bet is one of the two dozen or so **B&Bs**, clustered mainly around rues Merry Nord and Abbot. Mont-Orford is better for budget options, with lodgings at a woodsy arts centre and camping in the park (see p.250).

Auberge du Centre d'Arts Orford 3165 chemin du Parc (Hwy-141) ℡ 819/843-3981 or 1-800/567-6155, Ⓦ www.arts-orford.org/en/ auberge. Right in the Parc du Mont-Orford, this music academy and arts centre has clean, simple rooms in four large pavilions on an expansive wooded property. $54–64.
La Belle Échappée 145 rue Abbott ℡ 819/843-8061 or 1-877/843-8061, Ⓦ www.labelleechappee .com. A gabled 1880 house with five colourful rooms, wicker chairs on the veranda, and free use of bicycles – a good deal at this price. $58 (single); $75 (shared bath); $95.

La Belle Victorienne 142 rue Merry N ℡ 819/847-0476 or 1-888/440-0476, Ⓦ www .bellevic.com. An attractive B&B in a Victorian home featuring beautiful gardens, an ivy-covered terrace and five tastefully decorated rooms, all with private bathroom. $92.
Au Coeur du Magog 120 rue Merry Nord ℡ 819/868-2511 or 1-877/668-2511, Ⓦ www .aucoeurdemagog.com. A fine old house with individually themed rooms, some with private bath. There's a jacuzzi out back near the deck where a hot breakfast is served on sunny days. $70 (shared); $85.

The Town

Much of Magog's activity centres on the **waterfront**, which is heaving on summer weekends and especially during **La Traversée Internationale du Lac Memphrémagog**, a 40km swim across the lake that provides the excuse for ten days of festivities and free concerts (late July to early Aug; ℡ 819/847-3007, Ⓦ www.traversee-memphremagog.com). Strollers, bladers and cyclists roam the paths along the shore heading west from the centre of town, but swimmers skip the beach here for one further west (see opposite). Idyllic **boat cruises** ply

21

Hitting the slopes

Although not as numerous as their Laurentian cousins, the Eastern Townships' four main **ski resorts** are generally larger and feature more interesting terrain, particularly on the expert runs and gladed areas. Independent **Bromont** (Ⓦ www.skibromont.com) is the nearest to Montréal – making it possible to do some night skiing and still drive the 45 minutes back to the city well before the bars close – and offers well-groomed cruisers for intermediate skiers as well as a separate peak, Mont Soleil, for beginners. Due south, towards the Vermont border, **Sutton** (Ⓦ www.montsutton.com) is suited to a range of abilities on its gladed runs. Further east, **Orford**'s three peaks (see p.250) also cater to all skill levels and the attractively forested slopes usually have the best snow conditions. South past Magog, **Owl's Head** (Ⓦ www.owlshead.com) offers terrific vistas over Lac Memphrémagog from its varied beginner and intermediate trails. You can get an interchangeable lift ticket (four days or more) for the latter three resorts: contact the resorts themselves or visit Ⓦ www.easterntownships.org/ski.

Although it can make for a rather tiring excursion if you're heading to one of the further resorts, it's possible to get in a full skiing session as a day-trip from Montréal. Plenty of cozy B&Bs and charming (and sometimes pricey) inns supplement the resorts' slope-side accommodation, but other than at Bromont, you'll need to head to one of the nearby towns for any après-ski nightlife. As when travelling to the Laurentians, check with Montréal travel agents before heading out, as weekend packages can be a bargain, or try the tourist office's free accommodation service for the region (☎ 1-800/355-5755). For up-to-date ski conditions, visit Ⓦ www.quebecskisurf.com or listen for regular updates on the radio.

Lac Memphrémagog daily during the summer and on weekends in September and October (1hr 45min tour $20; 2hr 30min tour $25); unless you need a visa to visit the US (see box, p.34), you can also opt for a day-long cruise south to Newport, Vermont ($75.75; ☎ 819/843-8068 or 1-888/842-8068, Ⓦ www.croisiere-memphremagog.com); a tower marks the dock, located a third of the way along the promenade from rue Merry.

You'll want a bicycle or car to reach the sheltered Plage des Cantons, a sandy **beach** for swimming that fringes the lake further west. At a nearby kiosk, Club de Voile Memphrémagog rents out water transport ranging from pedal-boats to sailboats (June to mid-Sept daily 9am–6pm; ☎ 819/847-3181, Ⓦ www.voilememphremagog.com; $12–110); lessons are available. If you'd rather stay dry, there's a pricey **labyrinth** made up of chain-link fences that you can navigate on rollerblades or on foot (May to mid-Oct daily 10am–dusk; $7.75, $5 extra to rent in-line skates). You can also rent **in-line skates and bicycles** from Loca-Roule ($9/hr; T819/847-4377), at Le Rigolfeur mini-golf near the tourist office; in town, Ski-Vélo Vincent Renaud, set back from the main drag at 395 rue Principale O (☎ 819/843-4277, Ⓦ www.skivelo.com), rents bicycles ($15/half-day) and snowboards ($25/day) in season.

Eating and drinking

There are loads of **places to eat** along rue Principale in Magog and a few fun **bars** on rue Merry Sud. We've listed some of the best below.

🏃 **L'Actuel Bar & Grill 677 rue Hatley O**
☎ 819/847-1991, Ⓦ www.lactuelbargrill
.ca. There's a warren of romantic candle-lit rooms inside this big old house on the corner of rue Merry, as well as a

terrace facing the lake. In addition to standards like mussels and fries (served nine ways; $16–20), the fine French cuisine has a few surprises, from lamb filet with maple sauce to the chef's

②

signature kangaroo medallions. Three courses $24–36. Dinner only.

Bistro Lady of the Lake 125 chemin de la Plage des Cantons ☎819/868-2004, ⓦ www.bistrolady .com. Laid-back bar-bistro that feels like a Mediterranean beach house, complete with terrace overlooking the beach. They also brew their own beer on-site. The French and Italian fare is a bit pricey at $25–30 for three courses, but there's a cheaper daytime terrace menu in summer (from 2pm Mon–Wed, noon Thurs–Sun). Dinner only and closed Sun–Wed in winter.

Caffuccino 219 rue Principale O ☎819/868-2225, ⓦ www.caffuccino.com. A trendy café serving up a variety of breakfast fare, lunch (salads, panini, wraps and pizza bagels), sinfully sweet desserts and good coffee. Open 8am–midnight.

La Memphré 12 rue Merry S ☎819/843-3405. A pleasant bar in a charming house with views of the lake from the veranda; they serve quality pub food such as pasta, panini, salads and burgers (spicy lamb with a slab of goat's cheese, bison with local blue cheese) for $10–14. The main draw, though, is the extremely tasty local beer named after the sea serpent that allegedly lives in the nearby lake.

La Petite Place 108 place du Commerce ☎819/847-3067, ⓦ www.lapetiteplacecafe .com. A nondescript little place just off rue Principale that serves cheap vegetarian meals such as melted brie with pesto salad, veggie-paté or hummos tortillas and panini stuffed with feta. They have Internet access to boot ($2/15min or $6/hr). There's a second entrance at 280 rue St-Patrice O. Open 8.30am–3pm weekdays, until 2pm Sat; closed Sun.

Parc National du Mont-Orford

A mature sugar-maple forest blankets three-quarters of the 58-square-kilometre **Parc National du Mont-Orford** ($3.50 plus $6.25 beach parking; ☎819/843-9855 or reservations 1-800/665-6527, ⓦ www.sepaq.com), interspersed with stands of birch and conifers and laced with small lakes and rivers. Plans to privatize part of the park and allow slope-side accommodation were at the centre of a political storm in 2006, and the issue had yet to be resolved as this guide went to press. The park's frontier is ten minutes' drive north of Magog, along rue Merry Nord (Hwy-141) via the blink-and-you've-missed-it village of Orford, and actually comprises three mountain peaks, of which Mont Orford is the tallest at 853m. In **summer**, the grassy slopes are a nature-lover's paradise with 80km of hiking trails, cycle paths, golfing, boating and supervised swimming. You can rent gear for most activities from park offices (see above for contact details). You can also **camp** at one of the sites dotted about or off in the woods (rustic $16.30 in summer, $21.80 in winter; unserviced $21–22, serviced $24–32).

The park is equally lively in **winter**, when 52 downhill ski runs, a snow park with half-pipe and challenging jumps, 70km of groomed cross-country ski trails and 10km of snowshoeing trails all open. The chair lifts operate year-round. The ski hill and golf course are administered separately from the rest of the park ($45/adults, $35/students, $26/6–13 years; ☎819/843-6548 or 1-866/673-6731, ⓦ www.orford.com).

If that all sounds too active, time your visit for one of the **classical music concerts** during the Orford Festival (late June to mid-Aug; $15–50; ☎819/843-3981 or 1-800/567-6155, ⓦ www.arts-orford.org) at the Centre d'Arts Orford, 3165 chemin du Parc (Hwy-141).

Abbaye St-Benoît-du-Lac

The Eastern Townships' most unique attraction, the **Abbaye St-Benoît-du-Lac** (☎819/843-4080, ⓦ www.st-benoit-du-lac.com), looms over Lac Memphrémagog 25km southwest of Magog, a fantastical, castle-like building colourfully trimmed with pinks, yellows and greens. To get here, take Hwy-245 south from the western edge of Magog and follow the signs to St-Benoît-du-Lac.

Fifty-some Benedictine monks, renowned for their **Gregorian chants**, reside in the abbey and perform three times daily in the lofty modern church at its western end (daily 5am–8.30pm; sung services daily 7.30 & 11am, Fri–Wed 5pm and Thurs 7pm). They also make some of the region's best cheese – their light **Ermite blue cheese** started the abbey's tradition of making high-quality regional produce and is sold at the on-site shop (Mon–Sat 9–10.45am & 11.50am–4.30pm, until 6pm in summer) along with cider and other goodies. In keeping with St Benedict's rule on hospitality, the monastery accepts men as guests (accommodation for women is available at the Villa Ste-Scholastique, ☎819/843-2340); a donation of $45 is all that you'll be asked for a night's stay

△ Abbaye St-Benoît-du-Lac

and three meals but you'll need to reserve months in advance to secure a bed.

North Hatley

The region east of Magog is one of the few areas in Québec where you'll encounter vestiges of the snobbish Anglophone attitudes that once pervaded the whole province. No town epitomizes this more than picturesque **North Hatley**, thirty-minutes' drive east from Magog along Hwy-108, where boutiques sell English teas and biscuits to a resident population that steadfastly refuses to change the town's name to "Hatley Nord". Grand manors, many of which house hotels and B&Bs, curve in a U-shape around the pleasant **Lac Massawippi** that extends south from the village centre. Parking ($2/hr, $10/day) is tucked just behind the main strip, rue Principale, along with a small tourist information office (summer only; hours vary).

Just about the only organized activity here is theatre, as the province's longest-running English-language playhouse, **The Piggery**, stages several quality productions throughout the summer (tickets $22.50–25; mid-June to mid-Sept; ☎819/842-2431, ⓦwww.piggery.com). Theatre aside, North Hatley is a quiet town with little to do but hang out with a good book and absorb the scenery. There's a public **beach** on the lake's western shores, and several small **art galleries** and **antique shops** clustered along rue Principale make for a pleasant afternoon of shopping. If you fancy a spot of **fly-fishing** for trout and bass, contact the owner of the *Serendipity Bed & Breakfast* (see p.252) – a four-hour trip costs $175 per couple and lessons are available. Motorboat **cruises** are also available from Roger Ross ($25; 1hr 15min; ☎819/842-2279).

Accommodation

North Hatley's rarefied air extends to its accommodation – some of the best inns in the province are here (including *Manoir Hovey*; see below), but you'll pay for the privilege of spending the night. Likewise, the B&Bs are generally pricier than those in Magog.

Auberge La Raveaudière 11 chemin Hatley Centre ☎819/842-2554 or 1-866/272-2554, ⓦwww.laraveaudiere.com. An elegant nineteenth-century inn with seven spacious, well-appointed en-suite rooms; the included breakfasts are excellent. $125.

Le Cœur d'Or 85 rue School ☎819/842-4363, ⓦwww.aubergelecoeurdor.com. A kitschy and cluttered inn occupying an old New England–style house, with six comfortable, frilly rooms with private bath and two chalets ($165). Large breakfasts included in the price; dinner available for $30 extra. $95.

Manoir Le Tricorne 50 chemin Gosselin ☎819/842-4522, ⓦwww.manoirletricorne.com. The six-kilometre drive from town is worth it for the spectacular views over the lake and countryside from the 92-acre estate of this 145-year-old pink house. Converted to an inn, most of its seventeen large and nicely furnished rooms and suites have fireplaces. Rates include full breakfast and access to the swimming pool. $135.

Serendipity Bed & Breakfast 340 chemin de la Rivière ☎819/842-2970, ⓦwww.serendipitybb .qc.ca. A century-old house done up with country-style furnishings in the three rooms, one of which has private bath. The owner runs fly-fishing trips (see p.251) on Lake Massawippi, visible from the veranda, and serves a hot breakfast to get you started. $80 (shared bath); $95.

Eating and drinking

There isn't much of a drinking scene in this staid village – you'll most likely pass the evening lingering over a meal.

Café Massawippi 3050 rue Capelton ☎819/842-4528, ⓦwww.cafemassawippi.com. A cosy restaurant offering original remakes of international classics like smoked-duck carpaccio, venison tartare, and seared scallops with fava bean and sausage stew. Delightful seasonal cuisine, but it's expensive (*table d'hôte* $42–50). Open for dinner only.

Manoir Hovey 575 chemin Hovey ☎819/842-2421, ⓦwww.hoveymanor.com. Award-winning, regional cuisine – a game-heavy menu on which duck figures strongly, enhanced with delectable flavours like ginger and chokecherry – and an extensive wine list at this posh inn. Reserve a table overlooking the lake (or near the fireplace in winter). The three-course *table d'hôte* costs $60; it's included (along with breakfast) in the room rate ($290 and up).

Pilsen 55 rue Principale ☎819/842-2971, ⓦwww.pilsen.ca. Gastronomic pub whose eclectic menu includes mussels, seared duck, fondues and terrific grilled salmon, as well as cheaper pub grub, best washed down with one of the local Massawippi ales while seated at the waterside terrace.

21

Québec City

f Montréal is French-speaking Canada at its most dynamic, New France's religious and colonial legacy is more evocatively captured by **Québec City**, some 250km northeast. Spread over Cap Diamant and the banks of the St Lawrence, Québec City is Canada's most beautifully situated and historic city. At its centre stands **Vieux-Québec**, the only walled city in North America, a fact that prompted UNESCO to classify it as a World Heritage Site in 1985. In both parts of the old city – Haute- and Basse-Ville (Upper and Lower Town) – the winding and sometimes cobbled streets are flanked by seventeenth- and eighteenth-century stone houses and churches, graceful parks and squares, and countless monuments.

This is an authentically and profoundly French city: 95 percent of its half-million inhabitants (over 700,000 in the metropolitan area) are French-speaking. Though not as bilingual as Montrealers, the people of Québec City are generally friendlier and most speak some English. While Montréal feels international, Québec City is more than a shade provincial, often seeming too bound up with its religious and military past – a residue of the days when the city was not only the bastion of the Catholic Church in Canada, but also its strategic linchpin. The Church was responsible for the creation and preservation of the city's finest buildings, from the quaint Église Notre-Dame-des-Victoires to the opulent Basilique-Cathédrale Notre-Dame de Québec and the vast Séminaire. Austere and awe-inspiring defensive structures, like the massive Citadelle, reveal the military pedigree of a city dubbed by Churchill as the "Gibraltar of North America".

Some history

For centuries, the clifftop site on which Québec City sits was occupied by the Iroquois village of **Stadacona**. Permanent European settlement did not begin until 1608, when **Samuel de Champlain** established a fur-trading post in what is now Place Royale. To protect the rapidly developing inland trade gateway, the main settlement shifted to the clifftop in 1620 when Fort St-Louis was built. Québec's steady expansion was noted in London, and in 1629 Champlain was starved out of the fort by the British, an occupation that lasted just three years. Before the century was out, the long-brewing struggles between England and France spilled over into the colony again, prompting the Comte de Frontenac, known as the "fighting governor", to replace Champlain's Fort St-Louis with Château St-Louis, and begin work on the fortifications that ring Vieux-Québec.

During the Seven Years' War (1756–63), the most significant battle in Canada's history took place here, between the British under General James

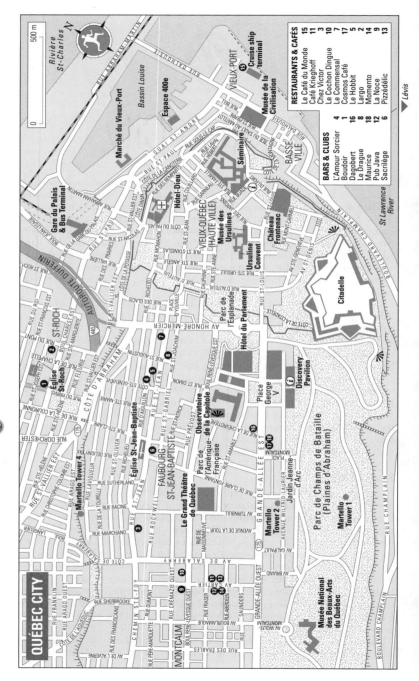

QUÉBEC CITY

Rivière St-Charles

RUE ABRAHAM MARTIN

500 m

0

Bassin Louise

Espace 400e

Marché du Vieux-Port

Vieux-Port

Gare du Palais & Bus Terminal

AUTOROUTE DUFFERIN

ST-ROCH

Musée de la Civilisation

Cruise ship terminal

VIEUX-PORT

Séminaire

Hôtel-Dieu

VIEUX-QUÉBEC (HAUTE VILLE)

Musée des Ursulines

BASSE VILLE

Château Frontenac

St Lawrence River

Lévis

Ursuline Convent

Parc de l'Esplanade

Hôtel du Parlement

Citadelle

Église St-Roch

Observatoire de la Capitole

Place George V

Discovery Pavilion

FAUBOURG ST-JEAN-BAPTISTE

Église St-Jean-Baptiste

Le Grand Théâtre de Québec

Parc de l'Amérique-Française

Martello Tower 4

Martello Tower 2

Jardin Jeanne d'Arc

Parc de Champs de Bataille (Plaines d'Abraham)

Martello Tower 1

MONTCALM

Musée National des Beaux-Arts du Québec

RESTAURANTS & CAFÉS

Le Café du Monde	15
Café Krieghoff	11
Chez Victor	3
Le Cochon Dingue	10
Cosmos Café	7
Le Commensal	17
Le Hobbit	5
Largo	2
Momento	14
La Noce	9
Pizzédélic	13

BARS & CLUBS

L'Amour Sorcier	4
Boudoir	1
Dagobert	16
Le Drague	8
Maurice	18
Pub Java	12
Sacriège	6

Wolfe and the French army, led by Louis Joseph, Marquis de Montcalm. The city had already been under siege from British forces on the opposite shore for three months, during which time Montcalm had carefully protected the city from any approach by water. Finally, in September 1759, Wolfe and his 4500 troops heard of an unguarded track, scaled the cliff of Cap Diamant and crept up on the unprepared French regiment. The twenty-minute **Battle of the Plaines d'Abraham** left both leaders mortally wounded and the city of Québec in the hands of the British, a state of affairs ultimately confirmed by the Treaty of Paris in 1763.

In 1775, the town was attacked again, this time by the Americans, who had already captured Montréal but were unable to take Québec City. For the next century the city quietly earned its livelihood as the centre of Canada's timber trade and shipbuilding industry. By the time it was declared the provincial capital of Lower Canada in 1840, though, the accessible supplies of timber had run out. Ceasing to be a busy seaport, the city quietly declined, its way of life still largely determined by the Catholic Church until the Quiet Revolution in the 1960s and the rise of Québec nationalism (see p.285). Québec City has since grown with the upsurge in the economy, developing a suburban belt of shopping malls and convention centres as slick as any in the country. And with the waning influence of the once all-pervasive Church, many of the city's less historic religious structures are now being converted into condos.

Arrival

Québec City is easy enough to get to from Montréal, with excellent air, rail and road links. You won't save much time by flying once you've tacked transport and airport formalities onto the fifty-minute flight time; flights arrive at **Aéroport Jean-Lesage** (Ⓦ www.aeroportdequebec.com), 20km west of the city and the twenty-minute trip by taxi to the city centre is a fixed rate of $30.

VIA Rail **trains** from Montréal take three hours to reach the central Gare du Palais (☏ 1-888/842-7245) in Basse-Ville. **Buses** are cheaper, and the regular express buses just as fast as the train, arriving at the main bus terminal, 320 rue Abraham-Martin (☏ 418/525-3000), adjoining the Gare du Palais. A **ridesharing** service between Montréal and Québec City is available through Allô-Stop – see p.28 for details.

If you come by **car**, there's a choice of two *autoroutes* for the two-and-a-half-hour journey from Montréal: Hwy-40 follows the north shore of the St Lawrence (if you have the time, switch over to the picturesque and much slower Hwy-138 – the old Chemin du Roy, or King's Highway – east of Trois-Rivières) and Hwy-20 the south, the latter being a marginally more interesting drive if you don't have time for the Chemin du Roy. On-street **parking** within the city walls can be a pain and, although there are car parks there (beneath the Hôtel de Ville, for instance), it's best to leave your vehicle outside the centre. Try the car park near the tourist office on avenue Wilfrid-Laurier outside Porte St-Louis or along the river in front of rue Dalhousie (but expect traffic jams during rush hour); the long-term car park is opposite the bus terminal. Note that motorcycles are not permitted in Vieux-Québec.

Information and city transport

Québec City's main **information centre**, which also offers an accommodation service, is located beside the Voltigeurs de Québec armoury at 835 av Wilfrid-Laurier (late June to early Sept daily 8.30am–7.30pm; early Sept to mid-Oct daily 8.30am–6.30pm; mid-Oct to late June Mon–Thurs & Sat 9am–5pm, Fri 9am–6pm, Sun 10am–4pm; ☎418/641-6290, ⓦwww.quebecregion.com). More information is available at the province-run **Centre Infotouriste** on the opposite side of Place d'Armes from the *Château Frontenac* at 12 rue Ste-Anne (daily: late June to early Sept 8.30am–7.30pm; early Sept to late June 9am–5pm; ☎514/873-2015 or 1-877/266-5687, ⓦwww.bonjourquebec.com). It also has an accommodation service and counters for the various tour companies. Grab the free booklet *Québec City and Area* from either for a detailed map.

If you plan to squeeze in a number of museums, it's worth investigating the Québec City Museum Card, a **pass** that allows entry to 23 museums over three days, plus two days' public transport for $40. It's available at the main tourist office and at participating museums (see ⓦwww. museocapitale.qc.ca/cartema .htm for a list).

Québec City's sights and hotels are packed into a small area, so **walking** is the most practical and pleasurable way to get around. A funicular and staircase near the *Château Frontenac* provide easy access down to Basse-Ville. For sights further out, like the Musée National des Beaux-Arts du Québec, RTC **local buses** (☎418/627-2511, ⓦwww.rtcquebec.ca) are efficient and run from around 6am to 1am (certain routes run until 3am Fri & Sat). Fares are $2.25 per journey by prepaid ticket, available at newsstands and grocery stores across town, as are one-day passes ($5.80; valid for two people Sat & Sun); the cash fare per journey is $2.50, exact fare only. **Taxis** are available from Taxi Coop (☎418/525-5191) and Taxi Québec (☎418/525-8123).

Accommodation

There's a wealth of **accommodation** in Québec City, with dozens of **hotels** and **bed and breakfasts** in Vieux-Québec alone. Many of these are smaller, family-run affairs and generally do not offer parking (although they may be able to sell you a voucher for one of the car parks for around $10–12 a day). Because they are often in converted houses, the rooms may have various quirks – don't be afraid to ask to see a couple of rooms as they can vary greatly within a hotel (and may have one or two beds of various sizes). Generally, the cheaper rooms will be darker, smaller, and have one double bed and/or shared bath; see p.135 for pricing information. There are also two **youth hostels** within the walls of the old city – the one on rue Ste-Ursule is surrounded by **budget hotels**. At the other end of the scale, Basse-Ville has been the site of a crop of new boutique hotels over the past few years. Always try to reserve rooms in advance, particularly during the summer months and the Carnaval in February.

Hotels

 Auberge St-Antoine 8 rue St-Antoine
☎418/692-2211 or 1-888/692-2211,
ⓦwww.saint-antoine.com. The stone walls

and chunky wood posts and beams in the common areas of this swish hotel are as authentic as the artefacts on display at the Musée de la Civilisation next door. The pricier of the sleekly modern rooms in the newer wing have private terraces, while the older part has an elegant contemporary decor with French doors overlooking the courtyard or, in the more expensive rooms, river views. The restaurant, *Panache*, serves delectable regional cuisine in a stone-walled, wood-beamed former warehouse. $259.

Auberge St-Louis 48 rue St-Louis ☎418/692-2424 or 1-888/692-4105, 🅦 www.aubergestlouis .ca. This simple inn along rue St-Louis is centrally located and comprises two three-storey houses dating from the 1830s whose muted olive-coloured rooms feature IKEA-style furnishings but are comfy nonetheless. Cheaper rooms have shared bath and don't have a/c. $89 (shared bath); $119.

Fairmont Le Château Frontenac 1 rue des Carrières ☎418/692-3861 or 1-800/441-1414, 🅦 www.fairmont.com. This opulent Victorian "castle" opened in 1893 and has accommodated such dignitaries as Churchill, Roosevelt, Madame Chiang Kai-shek and Queen Elizabeth II. It's the most expensive place in town and has magnificent views over the city and the St Lawrence, elegant dining halls, a tiled swimming pool and impeccably well-furnished rooms. If you can't afford to stay, you can still take a guided tour (see p.260). Specials can be less than half the standard price, even in high season. $599 (river view); $399.

Hôtel 71 71 rue St-Pierre ☎418/692-1171 or 1-888/692-1171, 🅦 www.hotel71.ca. A recent addition to Basse-Ville's clutch of boutique hotels, this chic property has loft-like rooms with waxed wood floors, earth tones, and exposed pipes and beams on the distant ceilings. There are lots of nice touches, such as beds piled with pillows and thick duvets, watering-can showerheads and bathrobes. Great views of the river or upper town. Buffet breakfast included. $200–225.

L'Hôtel Belley 249 rue St-Paul ☎418/692-1694, 🅦 www.oricom.ca/belley. It's easy to see why this place dubs itself "particulier" – rooms have eclectic touches like an Art Deco–style, double-length sofa (sleeps two, head-to-toe) and stained-glass panels. It's a bit like staying in a cool but slightly scruffy, well-off student's pad, perched atop a bar with pool table and terrace. $100.

Hôtel Cap-Diamant 39 av Ste-Geneviève ☎418/694-0313, 🅦 www.hcapdiamant.qc.ca. Nine-bedroom guesthouse dating from

1826 with sumptuous Victorian furnishings located on a quiet street near the Jardin des Gouverneurs. All rooms are en suite and have a/c, minifridges and TVs. In summer, you can take your continental breakfast into the peaceful courtyard garden. There are another three B&B rooms ($100–185) next door. $125.

🏃 **Hôtel Le Clos St-Louis** 69 rue St-Louis ☎418/694-1311 or 1-800/461-1311, 🅦 www.clossaintlouis.com. Elegant hotel in two interconnected 1840s houses with decor to match – Victorian stuffed chairs and settees, four-poster beds in some of the rooms, gilt mirrors and lots of antiques (including the armoires where the TVs are cached), plus therapeutic baths. Continental-plus breakfast included. $195.

🏃 **Hôtel Dominion 1912** 126 rue St-Pierre ☎418/692-2224 or 1-888/833-5253, 🅦 www.hoteldominion.com. Fabulous boutique hotel with all the touches – feather pillows and duvets, subdued lighting, stylish modern decor and cool frosted-glass sinks lit from below. Windows run the lengths of the rooms, offering terrific views of the St Lawrence or Vieux-Québec from the upper floors. $205.

Hôtel La Maison Demers 68 rue Ste-Ursule ☎418/692-2487 or 1-800/692-2487. Family-run since 1962, this small hotel has just seven rooms, four with private bath. Rates include continental breakfast and free parking. $75.

Hôtel Manoir d'Auteuil 49 rue d'Auteuil ☎418/694-1173 or 1-866/662-6647, 🅦 www .manoirdauteuil.com. Lavish 1835 townhouse by the city walls, refurbished a century later with Art-Deco touches in the sixteen comfy, recently renovated rooms, which come with Wi-Fi, a/c and private bath. Friendly service and continental-plus breakfast is included. $129.

Hôtel Le Priori 15 rue de Sault-au-Matelot ☎418/692-3992 or 1-800/351-3992, 🅦 www .hotellepriori.com. The rooms in this renovated house have a bright, modern feel with deep purple carpets, cone-shaped stainless-steel wash basins and, in some of the rooms, clawfoot tubs. You can have your buffet breakfast in the hotel's tranquil courtyard. $169.

Hôtel Sainte-Anne 32 rue Ste-Anne ☎418/694-1455 or 1-877/222-9422, 🅦 www.hotelste-anne .com. Given the dead-central location – you can have breakfast (costs extra) on the terrace facing Place d'Armes – the 28

②②

rooms are a decent size in this eighteenth-century edifice. But apart from stone or brick walls, it's thoroughly modern, with contrasting dark and light earth tones in the bedrooms, and slate tiles and sleek fixtures in the bathrooms. $144.

Hôtel Terrasse-Dufferin 6 place Terrasse-Dufferin ☎418/694-9472, ⓦwww.terrasse-dufferin.com. An 1830s mansion with some original details in the twenty or so rooms, all of which have private bath. The rooms at front have striking views over the St Lawrence, and thus need to be booked months in advance. $112 (river view); $87.

Au Manoir Ste-Geneviève 13 av Ste-Geneviève ☎418/694-1666 or 1-877/694-1666, ⓦwww.quebecweb.com/msg. A small, quiet hotel facing the Jardin des Gouverneurs, with friendly staff, and original mouldings, a/c and TVs in the quaint rooms, though the bathrooms are tiny. You can eat your continental breakfast out on the balcony. $95.

Bed and breakfasts

B&B des Grisons 1 rue des Grisons ☎418/692-1704 or 1-877/692-1704, ⓦwww.bbcanada.com/2608.html. A late nineteenth-century home with high ceilings, wood-strip floors and antiques from various epochs. The larger of the five rooms have sofa beds and all have shared bath. You're unlikely to see the owners, though; they have someone in to serve the copious hot breakfasts. $85.

Maison Historique James Thompson 47 rue Ste-Ursule ☎418/694-9042, ⓦwww.bedandbreakfastquebec.com. One of Vieux-Québec's original B&Bs, this historic 1793 house is surprisingly bright and strewn with antiques; there are a pair of sleigh beds in each of two of the three large bedrooms, which all have private bath. The air-filtration system's a boon for allergy sufferers, and the friendly owner will serve breakfast until whenever. $100.

La Marquise de Bassano 15 rue des Grisons ☎418/692-0316 or 1-877/692-0316, ⓦwww.marquisedebassano.com. An 1888 house with five tastefully decorated rooms – the more expensive have private bath and perks like four-poster beds or a roof terrace. The friendly young owner prepares fresh pastries to go with the continental-plus breakfast and occasionally plays the baby grand in the comfy living room. There's a friendly dog, too. $85 (shared bath); $150.

Hostels

Auberge de la Paix 31 rue Couillard ☎418/694-0735, ⓦwww.aubergedelapaix.com. Situated just off rue St-Jean, this is by far the better of Québec City's two youth hostels, with a friendly staff and a large courtyard to hang out in. Rates – $20 per person whether in dorms or one of the two private rooms – include a serve-yourself breakfast; bedding is an extra $3 per stay ($5 deposit). It fills up fast, so book ahead.

Auberge Internationale de Québec 19 rue Ste-Ursule ☎418/694-0755, ⓦwww.aubergeinternationaledequebec.com. The city's official youth hostel (formerly known as the Centre International de Séjour de Québec), in a former hospice run by nuns, can be impersonal and fills up quickly despite offering over 300 beds in large shared rooms and dormitories ($22–26 for members, $26–30 for nonmembers) and doubles ($67/$71 for the room, $77/$81 with private bath), triples, quads, etc. It's well kitted-out for budget travellers, though, with a café/bar, kitchen and laundry facilities, Internet access ($3/hr) and luggage lockers. No curfew, but you'll need to be buzzed in after 11pm. Discounts for children under 12.

The City

Québec City's historic highlights are mostly situated beside the St Lawrence, with the main attractions evenly distributed between the upper and lower

There is no escaping history in Québec City. In addition to panels illustrated with archival photos and text (mainly in French) scattered throughout the city, more than a dozen museums, interpretation centres and historic buildings each provide their own take on the past, based on a particular person, religious movement or district – we cover the best ones for a short visit. Most have loads of activities aimed at kids, including replica costumes to try on and use to re-enact the life of former days – an adult version is even on offer in the form of a mystery dinner in the **Martello Tower No. 2** ($35; ☎418/649-6157).

On top of all of this, there are at least half a dozen multimedia shows at various attractions, though many of these are rather patchy or painfully hokey. The most whiz-bang is the 3-D **Québec Experience**, 8 rue du Trésor, second floor (daily: mid-May to mid-Oct 10am–10pm; mid-Oct to mid-May 10am–5pm; $7.50; call for show schedules ☎418/694-4000, ⊛www.quebecexperience.com), whose half-hour shows are aimed at people with short attention spans.

Although hardly cutting-edge (think LED lights), the 37-square-metre model of Québec City, circa 1750, that forms the sole exhibit of the **Musée du Fort** at 10 rue Ste-Anne (April–Oct daily 10am–5pm; Feb–March Thurs–Sun 11am–4pm; $7.50; call for schedules ☎418/692-2175, ⊛www.museedufort.com) gives the most detailed account of the six battles fought here (the gift shop also has a decent selection of history books in English).

Finally, there are a host of **tours**, ranging from the colourful banter of the *calèche* drivers ($75 for a 35-minute tour; departures from in front of the *Château Frontenac*, Porte St-Louis or Parc de l'Esplanade near rue Ste-Anne) to pedicab tours of Basse-Ville, departing from Place de Paris (9.30am–11pm; $35 for 40min tour; ☎418/655-5836, ⊛www.toursludovica.com), as well as the standard bus circuits of the sights (you can compare the offerings at either tourist office – see p.256). On foot, in addition to an array of thematic tours (ghost, literary, historical), there are also walking tours of specific areas, like the free self-guided visit of Place Royale available from the interpretation centre (see p.270). Parks Canada run two ninety-minute trips along the **fortifications** led by a costumed guide – the "Fortified City" tour leaves from the *Frontenac* kiosk on Terrasse Dufferin, while "Defensive City" focuses more on military history and leaves from the fortifications interpretation centre next to the Porte St-Louis (June to early Oct 1–3 tours daily; $10, under-16s $5; ☎418/648-7016, ⊛www.parkscanada.gc.ca/fortifications).

QUÉBEC CITY | The City

㉒

portions of **Vieux-Québec** (Old Québec). Perched atop Cap Diamant and encircled by the city walls, **Haute-Ville** (Upper Town) forms the Québec City of tourist brochures, dominated appropriately enough by a hotel – the towering *Château Frontenac*. Its stupendous clifftop location accounts for part of its allure, and the wide boardwalk of the Terrasse Dufferin running along the front provides fantastic views over the St Lawrence River and **Basse-Ville** (Lower Town). Steep stairs and a funicular provide access to Basse-Ville, the site of some of the city's oldest and best-preserved buildings, as well as the worthwhile Musée de la Civilisation. Back away from the cliff edge, amid the jumble of streets in the middle of Haute-Ville are a number of museums and the city's most dramatic churches, while the fortifications are best seen at the western end of Vieux-Québec. You can follow them along to the star-shaped Citadelle, protecting the city from attack across the Plaines d'Abraham, although the only clashes there now are the bold colours of modernist paintings in the Musée National des Beaux-Arts du Québec at the far end of the former battlefield.

Haute-Ville

Most visitors begin their tour of **Vieux-Québec** in the walled upper town – **Haute-Ville** – drawn by the castle-like **Château Frontenac** and magnificent vistas over the St Lawrence from the **Terrasse Dufferin** running along in front. If you're only here for a short time, drop down into Basse-Ville (see p.269) before exploring the wealth of museums and sites on the narrow streets spreading out from **Place d'Armes** that convey the city's religious and military history. An imposing cathedral and seminary, along with a number of churches and convents, are reminders of the former, while the latter is most literally set in the stones that make up the encircling **fortifications** and massive **Citadelle** guarding the old town's southern flank.

Château Frontenac

Champlain established his first fort in 1620 on the site now occupied by the gigantic **Château Frontenac**, dominating the south side of Place d'Armes and probably Canada's most photographed building. New York architect Bruce Price drew upon the local French-Canadian architectural style to produce a pseudo-medieval, red-brick pile crowned with a steep copper roof. Although the hotel he designed was inaugurated by the Canadian Pacific Railway in 1893, its distinctive main tower was only added in the early 1920s, resulting in an over-the-top design that makes the most of the extreme location atop Cap Diamant. Numerous celebrities and royalty, including Queen Elizabeth II, have stayed here, and the hotel has hosted at least one pair of newlyweds every night since it opened. If the steep prices are beyond your budget (see p.257), there are fifty-minute guided tours departing on the hour from the lower level (May to mid-Oct daily 10am–6pm; mid-Oct to April Sat & Sun noon–5pm, call for weekday times; $8; reservations recommended ✆418/691-2166, Ⓦwww.tourschateau.ca).

Terrasse Dufferin

Fronting the *Château Frontenac*, the wide clifftop boardwalk of the **Terrasse Dufferin** overlooks the *kebec* ("where the river narrows" in the Algonquin language), which is the source of the city's (and the province's) name. Underlying part of the boardwalk are the foundations of Frontenac's Château St-Louis, which

△ Château Frontenac

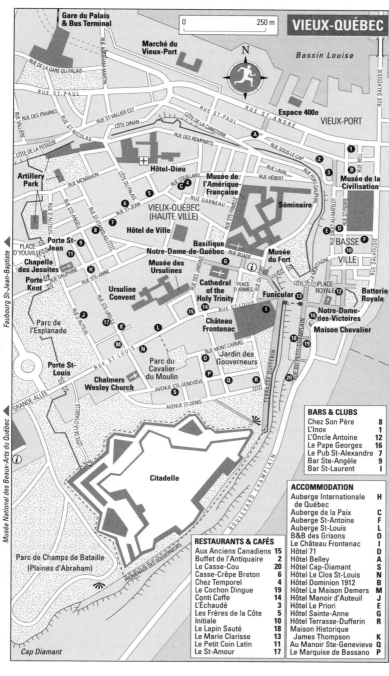

VIEUX-QUÉBEC

0 — 250 m

Bassin Louise

VIEUX-PORT

Gare du Palais & Bus Terminal

Marché du Vieux-Port

Espace 400e

Hôtel-Dieu

Artillery Park

Musée de l'Amérique-Française

Musée de la Civilisation

Séminaire

VIEUX-QUÉBEC (HAUTE VILLE)

Hôtel de Ville

Basilique Notre-Dame-de-Québec

BASSE VILLE

Porte St-Jean

Chapelle des Jesuites

Musée des Ursulines

Musée du Fort

Porte Kent

Ursuline Convent

Cathedral of the Holy Trinity

Funicular

PLACE ROYALE

Batterie Royale

Parc de l'Esplanade

Château Frontenac

Notre-Dame-des-Victoires

Maison Chevalier

Porte St-Louis

Parc du Cavalier du Moulin

Jardin des Gouverneurs

Chalmers Wesley Church

Citadelle

Parc de Champs de Bataille (Plaines d'Abraham)

Cap Diamant

Faubourg St-Jean-Baptiste

Musée National des Beaux-Arts du Québec

QUÉBEC CITY | Haute-Ville

22

261

BARS & CLUBS

Chez Son Père	8
L'Inox	1
L'Oncle Antoine	12
Le Pape Georges	16
Le Pub St-Alexandre	7
Bar Ste-Angèle	9
Bar St-Laurent	I

ACCOMMODATION

Auberge Internationale de Québec	H
Auberge de la Paix	C
Auberge St-Antoine	F
Auberge St-Louis	L
B&B des Grisons	O
Le Château Frontenac	I
Hôtel 71	D
Hôtel Belley	A
Hôtel Cap-Diamant	S
Hôtel Le Clos St-Louis	N
Hôtel Dominion 1912	B
Hôtel La Maison Demers	M
Hôtel Manoir d'Auteuil	J
Hôtel Le Priori	E
Hôtel Sainte-Anne	G
Hôtel Terrasse-Dufferin	R
Maison Historique James Thompson	K
Au Manoir Ste-Geneviève	Q
Le Marquise de Bassano	P

RESTAURANTS & CAFÉS

Aux Anciens Canadiens	15
Buffet de l'Antiquaire	2
Le Casse-Cou	20
Casse-Crêpe Breton	6
Chez Temporel	4
Le Cochon Dingue	19
Conti Caffe	14
L'Échaudé	3
Les Frères de la Côte	5
Initiale	10
Le Lapin Sauté	18
Le Marie Clarisse	13
Le Petit Coin Latin	11
Le St-Amour	17

served as the governor's residence for two centuries until a fire destroyed it in 1834. The leafy park running alongside the boardwalk was the château's garden – hence its name, the **Jardin des Gouverneurs** (see also p.265).

The boardwalk heads south from here, past the Charles Baillairgé–designed open-air pavilions and streetlamps, first electrified in 1885, and ends where the cliff rises to the Citadelle (see p.266). You can continue past it by taking a long flight of stairs up to the **Promenade des Gouverneurs**, a narrow boardwalk perched precariously on the cliff face below the Citadelle that leads to the Plaines d'Abraham. At the northern end of the walkway, near the *Château Frontenac*, you can access the funicular and staircase that lead down to Basse-Ville (see p.269). Nearby, the terrace broadens into a plaza lorded over by a romantic statue of **Champlain** and, beside it, a modern sculpture symbolizing Vieux-Québec's status as a UNESCO World Heritage Site.

Place d'Armes

Terrasse Dufferin's northern end flows into Vieux-Québec's main square, **Place d'Armes**, which features a central fountain of Gothic arches and flying buttresses topped by a monument to the Récollet missionaries who arrived here in 1615, and is surrounded by a number of notable historic buildings. One of the finest, to the right of the *Château Frontenac* at 17 rue St-Louis, is the **Maison Maillou**, which houses the Québec Chamber of Commerce. This 1736 grey-limestone house, with metal shutters for insulation and a steeply slanting roof, displays the chief elements of the climate-adapted architecture brought over to Canada by the Norman settlers.

Among the hotels and restaurants on the square's north side is the entrance to the narrow alley of **rue du Trésor**, where French settlers once paid their taxes to the Royal Treasury; nowadays it's a touristy artists' market with vendors hawking saccharine cityscapes. You'll do better to visit the courtyard just west of Place d'Armes between rue Ste-Anne and the Cathedral of the Holy Trinity, where Québec-based artisans operate small crafts and clothes stalls daily in summer. To the east of the alley, the former Union Hotel, built in 1803, houses the **Infotouriste** office (see p.256).

Basilique-Cathédrale Notre-Dame de Québec

From Place d'Armes, you can follow rue du Trésor directly towards the impressive bulk of the **Basilique-Cathédrale Notre-Dame de Québec** (daily 10am–6pm, Fri until 5pm; free). Focal point for the oldest parish north of Mexico, the church was burnt to the ground in 1922 – one of many fires it has suffered – and was rebuilt to the original plans of the post-Conquest version (the original 1647 church on this site was much smaller and insulated with furs). Absolute silence within the basilica heightens the impressiveness of the creamy Rococo-inspired interior, which culminates in a painted ceiling of blue sky and billowy clouds. The altar, a gilded replica of St Peter's, is surmounted by an elaborate baldachin by François Baillairgé that's uncharacteristically supported by angelic caryatids rather than columns due to the narrow space, and is topped by a statue of Jesus standing on a gilded sphere. The pewter sanctuary lamp, to the right of the main altar, was a gift from Louis XIV and is one of the few treasures to survive the fire. Nearby, in a chapel along the right aisle, a bronze effigy of Laval (see opposite) rests above where the bishop's remains were re-interred in 1993.

Underneath much of the area surrounding the cathedral and the Hôtel de Ville (City Hall) across the square are the largely forgotten cemeteries of the colony's early days. The basilica's crypt itself holds more than nine hundred bodies, including Frontenac, three other governors and most of Québec's bishops. (Champlain was rumoured to be buried there, his remains hidden to prevent desecration by the British invaders, but DNA tests proved that it wasn't him; no one knows where he was laid to rest.) Unfortunately, the only part of the crypt you can see on the informative **guided tours** (Mon–Thurs 10am–5pm, Fri 10am–4pm, Sun noon–5pm; every half-hour; by donation) is a ho–hum modern corridor – skip it and save a dollar.

Opposite the basilica, Côte de la Fabrique leads down to Vieux-Québec's lively main commercial strip, rue St-Jean, which is filled with a plentiful selection of restaurants and bars (see "Eating, drinking and nightlife", p.273) interspersed with some decent boutiques.

Séminaire de Québec

The wrought-iron gates beside the basilica lead into a large courtyard flanked by austere white buildings with handsome mansard roofs, where the vast **Séminaire de Québec** – founded by the aggressive and autocratic Monseigneur François de Laval-Montmorency in 1663 – spreads out to the north. In the three decades he was in office, Laval secured more power than the governor and intendant put together, and any officer dispatched from France found himself on the next boat home if Laval did not care for him. With the founding of the Diocese of Québec in 1674, Laval became the first bishop of New France and undertook a pilgrimage to see his See – a long jaunt given that it spread as far as Louisiana in those days. Laval retired early due to ill health, brought on by a religious fervour that denied him blankets and proper food. He finally died in 1708 after his feet froze on the stone floor of the chapel during his morning prayer session.

The seminary was the finest collection of buildings the city had seen, causing Governor Frontenac to grouse that the bishop was now housed better than he. Primarily a college for priests, the seminary also educated young men pursuing other professions, and in 1852 it became Laval University, the country's first Francophone Catholic university. Today, it still houses the faculty of architecture, while other buildings in the complex include the Petit Séminaire, now a school, and the Archbishop's Residence, neither of which is accessible to the public.

The Séminaire's main areas of interest – and the departure point for one-hour guided tours of the seminary (or of the collections, outside of summer) – can be found in the **Musée de l'Amérique Française** (late June to early Sept daily 9.30am–5pm; early Sept to late June Tues–Sun 10am–5pm; $5, free on Tues Nov–May. Guided tours: weekends from mid-May to mid-Oct, daily in summer; included in entry fee; ☎418/692-2843, ⓦwww.mcq.org), whose main entrance is in the **Maison du Coin**, on your left as you face the main gate. The Maison du Coin contains a small upstairs exhibition on the early colonists associated with the site. It also adjoins the high and narrow Roman-style **chapel**, whose Second-Empire interior holds Canada's largest collection of religious relics, a few of which are on display. A side-chapel contains Laval's ornate marble tomb, but not his remains, which were moved to the basilica when the main chapel was deconsecrated in 1993. The whole interior is a bit of a sham, overall – fed up with rebuilding after the chapel burnt down yet again in 1888, the church authorities decided to construct the pillars and coffered ceilings out of tin and paint over them; the stained-glass windows have been painted on single panes of glass and even the "tapestries" are just the result of some deft brushwork.

From the chapel, an underground corridor runs to the **Pavillon Jérôme-Demers**, which displays a number of well-presented, historical exhibitions. On the ground floor, the evocatively lit **L'Oeuvre du Séminaire de Québec** exhibition captures the history of seminary life with objects ranging from the simple items a student would have owned, to more elaborate flaming devotional hearts, an Episcopal throne and Laval's silver and gold chalice. Tucked away on the Pavillon's first and second floors is a tiny sample of the eclectic items gathered by Québec's bishops and the academics at Laval: elaborate nineteenth-century scientific instruments, an Egyptian mummy, a small collection of European and Canadian paintings, as well as more ecclesiastical silverware and some of Laval's personal belongings.

The museum's name derives from the main exhibition on the second floor, **The Settling of French America**, which details the history of the settlement and emigration of the more than nineteen million North Americans of French stock. It may come as a bit of a surprise – given how thoroughly Franco-Americans have melted into the pot – that throughout the nineteenth century nearly two hundred French newspapers were established in New England to serve the region's Francophone population. If yours is a French surname, you can search through the exhibition's genealogical panels to find your ancestors – the prolific Tremblays alone are responsible for some 85,000 households today.

Couvent des Ursulines

Heading south from the basilica along rue des Jardins brings you to narrow rue Donnacona, where a sculpted hand holding a quill – a monument to the women who, since 1639, have dedicated their lives to teaching Québec's young – rests on a pedestal. It points toward the **Couvent des Ursulines** on rue Donaconna, built by a tiny group of Ursuline nuns who arrived in Québec in 1639 calling themselves "the Amazons of God in Canada". Their task was to bring religion to the natives and later to the daughters of the settlers, a mission carried out in the classrooms of North America's first girls' school – the buildings still house a private school, run by the nuns.

The remains of the Ursulines' first mother superior, **Marie Guyart de l'Incarnation**, are entombed in the oratory adjoining the **chapel** (May–Oct Tues–Sat 10–11.30am & 1.30–4.30pm, Sun 1.30–4.30pm). Rebuilt in 1902, the chapel retains the sumptuous early-eighteenth-century altar and sculptures by Pierre-Noël Levasseur and a collection of seventeenth- and eighteenth-century paintings acquired from post-Revolution France in the 1820s. If you stand at the altar rail and look to the right, you can see the ornate, domed sisters' choir, positioned so that the nuns can remain cloistered while worshiping. A plaque nearby indicates General Montcalm's former resting place – he was buried in a hole created by a cannonball that punched through the roof of the chapel. However, during renovations some years later only his skull was to be found (it was recently moved to a military cemetery in the suburbs).

The lives of the early Ursulines, and Marie Guyart de l'Incarnation in particular, are the focus of the art and history **museum** (May–Sept Tues–Sat 10am–noon & 1–5pm, Sun 1–5pm; Oct–April Tues–Sun 1–4.30pm; $6; ⊤418/694-0694), opposite the chapel. Amongst the religious paraphernalia are gilded reliquaries containing partial skulls and bone fragments of a number of saints, while documents and household items stand as testament to the early colony's harsh living conditions. The collection of paintings includes a posthumous portrait of Marie, and Frère Luc's re-imagining of the Holy Family: Joseph presents a Huron girl to Mary as the St Lawrence flows past Cap Diamant in the background. What makes the entrance fee worthwhile, however, is the third-floor display of seventeenth- and eighteenth-century **liturgical ornaments** made by the nuns – wool and silk altar frontals shot through with gold and silver threads and equally richly embroidered vestments. (Note that the third-floor exhibition changes every eighteen months, and might contain sacred paintings, embroidery or other works by the nuns.)

Rue St-Louis and around

A short walk from the convent along rue des Jardins brings you to the intersection of **rue St-Louis** – Vieux-Québec's main tourist strip, teeming with overpriced and mostly uninteresting restaurants occupying dour grey-stone eighteenth- and nineteenth-century townhouses. On the corner at no. 34 stands **Maison Jacquet**, occupied by the restaurant *Aux Anciens Canadiens* (see p.274). The building's name comes from Québec's first novel, whose author, Philippe Aubert de Gaspé, lived here for a while in the middle of the nineteenth century. Dating from 1677, the house's thick stone walls, steeply sloping roof and dormer windows are typical features of seventeenth-century New France architecture, characteristics shared by the blue-and-white **Maison Kent**, at no. 25 on the other side of rue St-Louis, which was built in 1649. Once home to Queen Victoria's father, the Duke of Kent, it's best known as the place where the capitulation of Québec was signed in 1759 and now ironically houses the French consulate.

If you fancy a bit of greenery after all the grey stone of Vieux-Québec, take a detour up rue Haldimand (off rue St-Louis, just to the east of the museum) to the **Jardin des Gouverneurs**, overlooking the Terrasse Dufferin and formerly the preserve of the governors who inhabited the Château St-Louis. The monument to Wolfe and Montcalm, an obelisk erected in 1828, is rare in paying tribute to both the victor and the vanquished. A more intimate spot is the **Parc du Cavalier du Moulin**, a quiet little park two minutes west of the Jardin on rue Mont-Carmel and built on the remnant of the earlier French fortifications. The surrounding streets are home to some of the old town's most handsome residences – including those on rue de La Porte, on the Jardin's west side, and on parallel rue des Grisons. Both streets intersect with avenue Ste-Geneviève, from where you can ultimately work your way back to rue St-Louis near the city walls.

The fortifications and Artillery Park

Rue St-Louis leads directly from Place d'Armes to the **Porte St-Louis** (keep an eye out for the cannonball lodged in the tree roots at the corner of rue Corps-de-Garde along the way). The oldest (1878) of the four gates in the city wall, Porte St-Louis is surrounded by **Parc de l'Esplanade**, the main site for the Carnaval de Québec (see box, p.271) and departure point for the city's smart horse-drawn *calèches*, not to mention a good spot to begin the 4.5-kilometre stroll around the **fortifications** ringing the city (see box, p.259, for guided tours).

To the north lies the bulwark of the Citadelle (see p.266), while to the south, you can wander along the walls over the Porte Kent to Porte St-Jean, which separates the boutiques and restaurants of rue St-Jean from **Place d'Youville**, scene of outdoor concerts and a winter skating rink. Further to the west, beyond Place d'Youville, rue St-Jean is the main street of the **Faubourg St-Jean-Baptiste** neighbourhood, whose studenty vibe, tiny gay district and down-to-earth restaurants and bars can be a welcome change from the history-steeped old town. It overlooks the **St-Roch** district, Québec City's old downtown, which is becoming trendy again with chic new lounges, restaurants and boutiques after decades of neglect.

Immediately south of the Porte St-Jean lie the defensive structures of **Artillery Park**, raised in the early 1700s by the French in expectation of a British attack from the St Charles River, and subsequently a barracks for the Royal Artillery Regiment for more than a century. In 1882 it became a munitions

22

factory, providing the Canadian army with ammunition in both world wars. The foundry, added in 1902, now houses an interpretation centre (April to early Oct daily 10am–5pm; $4; ☎ 418/648-4205, ⓦ www.pc.gc.ca/artillery), which has displays on the military pedigree of the city, including a vivid model of Québec City in 1808. It's also the starting point for one-hour guided tours ($4 extra) and visits of the site's four buildings, including the Officers' Quarters, furnished as it was in 1830, and the massive Dauphine Redoubt. The latter typifies the changes of fortune here: used by the French as the barracks for their garrison, it became the officers' mess under the British and then the residence of the superintendent of the Canadian Arsenal.

The Citadelle

Towering over the southern section of Vieux-Québec, the massive, star-shaped **Citadelle** (still a working military base) can only be visited on one of the worthwhile guided tours (departing hourly: April 10am–4pm, May & June 9am–5pm, Sept 9am–4pm, Oct 10am–3pm; every half-hour: July & Aug 9am–6pm; once per day: Nov–March Mon–Fri 1.30pm; $8; ☎ 418/694-2815, ⓦ www.lacitadelle.qc.ca). The tour de force of Québec City's fortifications, the Citadelle occupies the highest point of Cap Diamant, 100m above the St Lawrence. This strategic site was first built on by the French, but most of the buildings still extant were constructed by the British under orders from the Duke of Wellington, who was anxious about American attack after the War of 1812.

The complex of 25 buildings covers 40 acres and is the largest North American fort still occupied by troops – it's home to the Royal 22nd Regiment, Canada's only French-speaking regiment. Around the parade ground are ranged various monuments to the campaigns of the "Van-Doos" (*vingt-deux*), as well as the summer residence of Canada's governor general and two buildings dating back to the French period: the Cap Diamant Redoubt, built in 1693, and thus the oldest part of the Citadelle, and the 1750 powder magazine. The latter is now a mundane museum of weaponry from the eighteenth century to the present, military costumes and other artefacts – including a stuffed white goat, Batisse IV (an ancestor of the current regimental mascot). Other highlights of the tour are the views alongside the cannon atop the King's Bastion and the long, dank tunnel to the vaulted shooting gallery used to defend the external walls.

In addition to mandatory but entertaining hour-long guided tours (see above) around the Citadelle, other activities included in the admission price are the colourful **Changing of the Guard** (late June to early Sept daily 10am), which you can catch at the end of a 9am tour (otherwise arrive by 9.45am) and the **Beating of the Retreat** tattoo (July & Aug Fri–Sun 7pm), likewise at the end of the 5.45pm tour. A guided tour (free) is also the only way you can visit the **Residence of the Governor General of Canada** (May to late June Sun 10am–4pm; late June to early Sept daily 11am–4pm; early Sept to Oct Sat & Sun 10am–4pm; ☎ 418/648-4322 or 1-866/936-4422, ⓦ www.gg.ca), whose Canadian art collection and fine setting have only recently been made accessible to the public.

Outside the walls

Beyond the confines of Vieux-Québec's enveloping walls, most of the sights in the modern city lie directly to the west in what is technically also Haute-Ville as it's on the same escarpment. The area surrounding Grande-Allée, the westward continuation of rue St-Louis, is also known as Parliament Hill, much to the ire of English-speaking Canadians who feel the name should be reserved for the Canadian Parliament's setting in Ottawa. However, the provincial parliament is here, its **Hôtel du Parlement** meeting-place lying north of Grande-Allée's sweep of bars and cafés, while to the south unfurls the broad expanse of the **Plaines d'Abraham**, culminating with the city's premier art museum. The rest of the area makes for a good respite from the tourist hype, with the Faubourg St-Jean-Baptiste filling the gap between the parliament and the northern edge of the plateau, which overlooks the trendy-again St-Roch district, which was the commercial heart of the city for much of the twentieth century. To the west near the **Musée National des Beaux-Arts du Québec**, avenue Cartier brims with boutiques and mid-range restaurants popular with locals.

Hôtel du Parlement

Sweeping out from Porte St-Louis and flanked by grand Victorian mansions, the tree-lined boulevard of **Grande-Allée** bustles with restaurants, hotels and bars. At its eastern end stand the stately buildings of the **Hôtel du Parlement** (late June to early Sept Mon–Fri 9am–4.30pm, Sat & Sun 10am–4.30pm; early Sept to late June Mon–Fri 9am–4.30pm; ☎418/643-7239 or 1-866/337-8837, ⓦwww.assnat.qc.ca), designed by Eugène-Étienne Taché in 1877, using the Louvre for inspiration. Inside, finely carved and gilded walnut panels in the entrance hall depict important moments in Québec's history. From here the corridor of the Presidents' Gallery, lined with portraits of all the Legislative Assembly's speakers and presidents, leads to the Chamber of the National Assembly, where the 125 provincial representatives meet for debate. You can't see much, though, unless you take one of the free half-hour guided tours – call ahead as the schedule changes daily.

Among the government buildings clustered to the west of here, the Édifice Marie-Guyart, 1037 rue de la Chevrotière, is the tallest structure in the city. On its 31st floor, the **Observatoire de la Capitole** (late June to mid-Oct daily 10am–5pm; mid-Oct to late June Tues–Sun 10am–5pm; $5; ☎418/644-9841 or 1-888/497-4322, ⓦwww.observatoirecapitale.org) offers a 360-degree panoramic view over Vieux-Québec, the Citadelle and beyond, with panels providing useful background info on what you can see.

The Plaines d'Abraham

West of the Citadelle are the rolling grasslands of the **Parc des Champs-de-Bataille** (Battlefields Park), a sizeable chunk of land stretching along the cliffs above the St Lawrence. The park encompasses the historic **Plaines d'Abraham**, which were named after Abraham Martin, the first pilot of the St Lawrence River in 1620, and were the site on which Canada's history was rewritten (see p.253). The best place to start out is the park's **Discovery Pavilion**, below the tourist office at 835 av Wilfrid-Laurier E (late June to early Sept daily 8.30am–5.30pm; early Sept to late June Mon–Fri 8.30am–5pm, Sat 9am–5pm, Sun 10am–5pm; ☎418/648-4071, ⓦwww.ccbn-nbc.gc.ca), with maps, information panels and a short film on the site's history. It offers a multimedia history show (10am–close; $8, $10 combined ticket including bus and Martello Tower entry – see below), which, although featuring irksome 3-D-enhanced "interviews" with Wolfe, Montcalm and other historical personages, nevertheless does a reasonable job of covering the after-effects of the Conquest, leading to the formation of Canada today. Standing out amid the landscaped gardens, scenic drives, nature trails and jogging paths (cross-country ski trails in winter) of the wooded parklands designed by Frederick G. Todd in the 1930s is the **Martello Tower 1**, built in 1808 for protection against the

Americans and today containing an unmemorable exhibition. You can listen to free music performances at the Edwin-Bélanger bandstand, towards the park's western edge, on summer evenings (mid-June to mid-Aug Thurs–Sun 8pm; T 418/648-4050).

Musée National des Beaux-Arts du Québec

Canadian art had its quiet beginnings in Québec City and the full panoply of this output can be found on the western edge of the Parc des Champs-de-Bataille in the **Musée National des Beaux-Arts du Québec** (June to early Sept daily 10am–6pm, Wed until 9pm; early Sept to June Tues–Sun 10am–5pm, Wed until 9pm; permanent collection free, special exhibitions $12; required baggage check $1; audio guide $3; T 418/643-2150 or 1-866/220-2150, W www.mnba.qc.ca; bus #11). The Grand Hall, with its cruciform skylight, connects the museum's two buildings (its original home, the Pavillon Gérard-Morisset, and a renovated Victorian prison renamed the Pavillon Charles-Baillairgé) and also serves as the main entrance.

For a chronological tour, start with Gallery 8 on the second floor of the **Pavillon Gérard-Morisset**, which provides a good survey of Québécois art from the early seventeenth through the late nineteenth centuries. As Québec churches were the primary art commissioners at the time, most of the earliest works are **religious art**, including the output of **Frère Luc**, represented here by *The Guardian Angel*, a painting depicting the story of Tobias and the archangel Raphael. The most notable contributions to the collection are by two dynasties: the works of brothers **Pierre-Noël** and **François-Noël Levasseur** from the mid-1700s and the three generations of **Baillairgés** who succeeded them, their copious output including the architecture of churches as well as their interior decoration. Under the British, the subject matter broadened to include portraiture, seen here in **Antoine Plamondon**'s mannered *Andrew Laughlin Fraser*, and Canadian landscapes by Québec-born **Joseph Légaré** and, more famously, Amsterdam-born **Cornelius Krieghoff**, noted for his romanticized landscapes of landmarks in the region.

Gallery 7, opposite, covers the period spanning 1860 to 1945, from the late-nineteenth-century **salons** to the development of **modernist art**. In the first room, paintings fight for space on the walls; one that grabs your attention as you enter is **Marc-Aurèle de Foy Suzor-Coté**'s *Jacques Cartier Meeting the Indians at Stadcona, 1535*, its classicism – a historical subject and depiction of natives cringing before the light-bathed French – contrasting with a more Impressionistic style of brush strokes. More sympathetic to its subject is **Horatio Walker**'s *Milking, Early Morning*, a romantic vision of the lives of the French-Canadian *habitants* who so engrossed him that he repudiated his Ontario roots. The tug-of-war of styles in Europe is played out in many of the subsequent works, including **Maurice Cullen**'s Impressionist-influenced view onto Basse-Ville, *Wolfe's Cove*, and the evocative scene of a horse-drawn carriage in a snowstorm, *Craig Street, Montréal*. Urban life is also admirably recorded in the next room by **Adrien Hébert**'s *Rue St-Denis*, which wonderfully captures the spirit of Montréal in the 1920s.

Downstairs, in Gallery 2, the impact of **Alfred Pellan**, who returned from Paris in 1940 to teach at Montréal's École des Beaux-Arts, plays out in the development of postwar **figurative** and **abstract art**. He introduced the modernism of Matisse and Picasso to Canada, and his comparative radicalism, evident in his Cubist-influenced still life, *Flowers and Dominoes*, was the catalyst for a generation of Québécois artists who flocked to Europe to pick up on the avant-garde movements of the time. The move to nonfigurative representation can be seen in **Jean**

22

Dallaire's softly muted abstract figures in his 1957 *Julie*, which contrasts with his surreally colourful and strident *Coq Licorne* (Unicorn Rooster) painted five years earlier. The process reaches its apogee with the Neo-Plasticism represented by **Fernand Leduc**'s boldly coloured geometric abstract *The Mountain Climber*.

At the same time, two of Québec's best-known artists were developing their signature styles. **Paul-Émile Borduas** applied the automatic-writing technique of the surrealists to painting – his *Cabalistic Signs* is almost a doodle in oils. His progression to the increasingly spare canvases that have rooms devoted to them in Montréal's museums (see p.55 & p.64) can also be noted here. Gallery 3, across the hall, is devoted solely to the work of **Jean-Paul Riopelle**. The gallery's highlight is his *L'Hommage à Rosa Luxemburg* (1992) – a forty-metre-long triptych in thirty segments, with ghostly spray-painted outlines of birds and man-made objects – though the chunky blocks of colour slathered with a palette knife across *Sun Spray* (1954) is more typical of his work.

In the **Pavillon Charles-Baillairgé**, the red-brick interior walls of the former jail have been spruced up, creating a warm atmosphere surprisingly conducive to displaying art. **Armand Vaillancourt**'s *Tree on rue Durocher* sweeps up into the atrium, which then leads visitors into the galleries and a few of the old prison cells. These lie en route to Gallery 10, where "Je me souviens" portrays the personages and events in Québec's history through paintings and sculptures by some of the province's leading artists, and includes the Rodin-esque studies for public works by sculptors **Louis-Philippe Hébert** and **Alfred Laliberté**. In the prison's tower, Montréal sculptor **David Moore** has created a unique two-storey sculpture of bodies scaling walls – just what you might expect in an old prison.

Gallery 12 on the third floor is devoted to Québec-born painter **Jean-Paul Lemieux**. His style varied wildly, from landscapes inspired by the Group of Seven, through a phase of folk-art-style painting, to end with a series of uncluttered Expressionist portraits. The focus here is on the latter, with other works from his "classical period" (1950–75) including *Les Ursulines*, an eerily abstract gaggle of nuns next to whitewashed, windowless buildings, and *La Rapide*, a sparse winter landscape with a dark mass in the corner suggestive of an oncoming train.

Nearby, Gallery 11 became the permanent home in September 2006 of the **Collection d'Art Inuit Brousseau**, donated by local gallerist and collector Raymond Brousseau. On display are a couple of hundred works: traditional hunters, Arctic birds and fauna, and abstracts carved from basalt, serpentine, whalebone and animal horn by contemporary Inuit sculptors.

Basse-Ville

The birthplace of Québec City, **Basse-Ville** (Lower Town), can be reached from Terrasse Dufferin by the **funicular** opposite the *Château Frontenac* and Place d'Armes, but it's best to save that for the weary journey back up. Instead, take the stairs at the north end of the terrace down to Porte Prescott (reconstructed in the 1980s – over a century after the original gate was demolished), where a path continues across the top of the gate to **Parc Montmorency**, the meeting place of Québec's first legislature in 1694. Descend the steps before crossing the gate, though, to reach the winding Côte de la Montagne from where the steep **Escalier Casse-cou** (Breakneck Stairs) leads to lively rue du Petit-Champlain (see p.272). Resist the temptation to descend it and carry another few metres along to where an unassuming staircase leads down to Place Royale, opening onto a lovely square of seventeenth-century stone buildings that offers perhaps the best introduction to Basse-Ville.

Place Royale and around

Champlain built New France's first permanent settlement at **Place Royale** in 1608, to begin trading fur with the native peoples. The square remained the focal point of Canadian commerce until 1759, and after the fall of Québec the British continued using the area as a lumber market, vital for shipbuilding during the Napoleonic Wars. After 1860, Place Royale was left to fall into scruffy disrepair until renovation began in the 1970s. Today, its pristine stone houses, most of which date from around 1685, are undeniably photogenic, with their steep metal roofs, numerous chimneys and pastel-coloured shutters, but it's a Legoland townscape, devoid of the scars of history. Fortunately the atmosphere is enlivened in summer by entertainment ranging from classical orchestras to juggling clowns, and by the Fêtes de la Nouvelle-France (see box opposite), when everyone dresses in period costume and Place Royale briefly relives its past as a chaotic marketplace.

In Maison Hazeur, at 27 rue Notre-Dame, a merchant's house dating in part to 1684, the **interpretation centre** (late June to early Sept daily 9.30am–5pm; early Sept to late June Tues–Sun 10am–5pm; $4, free on Tues Nov–May; ☏418/646-3167) outlines the history of Place Royale. Domestic objects and arrowheads are exhibited on the upper floors, while the original vaulted cellars have modern-looking stage sets of 1800s domestic scenes; kids will enjoy trying on the period costumes and acting out a role. The hokey multimedia show may also appeal to them, but the same ground is better covered in a tucked-away exhibit on level one illustrating the growth of the colony. The centre also runs free guided tours of the Place Royale area.

The **Église Notre-Dame-des-Victoires** (daily 9am–5pm), on the west side of the square where Champlain's residence once stood (the site of a former turret is outlined in paving stones in front of the church), was first built by Laval (see p.263) in 1688 but has been completely restored twice – after being destroyed by shellfire in 1759 and following a fire in 1969. Inside, the fortress-shaped altar alludes to the two French victories over the British navy that gave the church its name: the destruction of Admiral Phipp's fleet by Frontenac in 1690 and the sinking of Sir Hovenden Walker's fleet in 1711. Paintings depicting these events

△ Place Royale

Québec City festivals

Québec City is renowned for its massive annual **festivals**. The **Carnaval de Québec** (☎418/626-3716 or 1-866/422-7628, ⊛www.carnaval.qc.ca) takes place over eleven freezing days in early February, when large quantities of the warming Caribou – a lethal mix of red wine, spirits and spices – are consumed amid parades and ice-sculpture competitions.

In early to mid-July, the ten-day **Festival d'Été** (☎418/529-5200 or 1-888/992-5200, ⊛www.infofestival.com) is an equally cheery affair. The largest festival of Francophone culture in North America attracts hundreds of performers – many of them from the US and overseas – for this musical celebration.

The **Fêtes de la Nouvelle-France** (☎418/694-3311 or 1-866/391-3383, ⊛www.nouvellefrance.qc.ca) returns Vieux-Québec's Basse-Ville to the seventeenth and eighteenth centuries in early August. It's great fun as thousands of Québécois from around the province dress up in period costume to crowd around the Place Royale's market stalls and engage in street theatre.

Québec City celebrates its **400th anniversary** (⊛www.quebec400.qc.ca) in 2008 with a roster of events throughout the city from May to October, including special celebrations around July 3, the date the colony was founded. Party central is the **Espace 400e**, which takes over the Centre d'interprétation du Vieux-Port-de-Québec building (100 quai St-André) and the adjoining quays jutting into the Bassin Louise, from where you'll be able to see a Robert Lepage multimedia show projected onto the grain elevators opposite.

hang above the altar, while the aisles are lined with copies of religious paintings by Van Dyck, Van Loo and Rubens, gifts from early settlers to give thanks for a safe passage. The large model ship hanging over the nave is similarly an *ex voto*, donated by the Marquis de Tracy, the viceroy who commanded the Régiment de Carignan against the Iroquois in 1665–66.

Place Royale leads east past rue St-Pierre to **Place de Paris**, where a white cubic sculpture called *Dialogue with History* marks the disembarkation place of the first settlers from France. Further east beyond rue Dalhousie, you can see the promenade along the St Lawrence that passes the restaurants and attractions of the **Vieux-Port de Québec**, while to the south (past the Batterie Royale – see p.272) is the terminal for the **ferry** to Lévis (daily 6.30am–2am; $2.60 each way; ☎1-877/787-7483, ⊛www.traversiers.gouv.qc.ca). A quick round-trip affords great views of Québec City's impressive skyline.

Musée de la Civilisation

A walk north along rue Dalhousie from Place de Paris brings you to one of Québec City's most impressive museums, the **Musée de la Civilisation**, 85 rue Dalhousie (late June to early Sept daily 9.30am–6.30pm; otherwise Tues–Sun 10am–5pm; $8, free on Tues Nov–May; combo ticket with Musée de l'Amérique Française or Centre d'Interprétation de Place-Royale $10, all three sites $13; ☎418/643-2158, ⊛www.mcq.org). Designed by prominent Canadian architect Moshe Safdie (who built Habitat '67 and the addition to the Musée des Beaux-Arts in Montréal), the museum references the steep-pitched roofs of the early settlers in a structure that incorporates a rooftop terrace with great views and three historic buildings. In the main foyer, a 1730s barque discovered on the site is displayed between a stone wall (the edge of the quay built a couple of decades later) and Astri Reusch's *La Débâcle*, a sculpture that symbolizes the break-up of the ice in the spring thaw.

Concentrating primarily on Canadian subjects but also diversifying into worldwide perspectives the museum presents worthwhile temporary exhibitions that have ranged from whimsical pop-culture interests to serious looks at earlier historical periods. The first of the two permanent exhibitions, **People of Québec... Then and Now**, expertly displays life in Québec from the early days of the settlers to the present with a central timeline illustrated by artefacts (from Laval's skull cap to Jacques Plante's Stanley Cup bowl), accompanied by films cheerily extolling the virtues of life in the province. Upstairs, the **Encounter with the First Nations** exhibition was set up in consultation with all eleven of the First Nations of Québec. It presents the history and culture of these earlier residents using artefacts and videotaped oral histories; the larger items – including a *rabaska*, an enormous birch-bark canoe – were crafted in recent years. On the same floor, the museum's café (9am–6.30pm) serves decently priced sandwiches and snacks. Elsewhere, there are weekend workshops for kids (daily in summer).

Be sure to check out the gift shop in the 1751 **Maison Estèbe**, which survived the British bombardment, adjacent to the museum's secondary entrance on rue St-Pierre. Even if you're not interested in reproductions of original tableware, the vaulted cellars are worth a peek (ask for the leaflet detailing the house's history).

Batterie Royale and Maison Chevalier

Depart the Musée de Civilisation by its secondary exit next to the Maison Estèbe onto rue St-Pierre. The heart of Québec City's turn-of-the-century financial district, rue St-Pierre leads south between Place Royale and Place de Paris to end at rue Sous-Le-Fort. Here, a gate provides the sole access to the **Batterie Royale**, a crenellated rampart that took a battering from the British during the siege of 1759 and was only restored (and a new array of cannons installed) in the 1970s.

Back on rue Sous-le-Fort, you can duck through the narrow stone vaulted passageway a few feet along, or turn left onto rue Notre-Dame, to reach narrow rue du Cul-de-Sac, which wraps around the 1752 **Maison Chevalier** (May to late June & early Sept to Oct Tues–Sun 10am–5pm; late June to early Sept daily 9.30am–5pm; Nov–April Sat & Sun 10am–5pm; free). An *hôtel particulier* (a somewhat grand townhouse) that served a stint as the London Coffee House, where merchants would meet up throughout the nineteenth century, it's now an annex to the Musée de la Civilisation (see above). The entrance is through what was originally the rear of the house and leads to rooms displaying interior scenes that comprise period furniture, costumes and domestic objects. The plush drawing room and bedroom of a typical nineteenth-century bourgeois family contrast with the all-in-one common room that a tradesman and his family might have occupied a century earlier. In summer, join a half-hour guided tour (three daily) to get the most out of it.

Quartier du Petit-Champlain

Maison Chevalier lies on the edge of the **Quartier du Petit-Champlain** (ⓦ www.quartier-petit-champlain.qc.ca), the oldest shopping area in North America. Although there are a few dining and browsing distractions along boulevard Champlain leading south, you're better to take any of the stairways tucked between its buildings to the parallel and more atmospheric **rue du Petit-Champlain**. Dating back to 1685, this narrow, cobbled street is the city's oldest. The boutiques and art shops in the quaint seventeenth- and eighteenth-century

Hitting the slopes

Québec City makes a charming base for a ski holiday at one of the three surrounding resorts that are within an hour's drive. The largest, **Mont-Ste-Anne** (ⓦwww .mont-sainte-anne.com), lies 40km to the east and offers a variety of good terrain at all skill levels, particularly intermediate runs and challenging expert terrain, and night skiing until 10pm. A further 33km east, **Le Massif** (ⓦwww.lemassif.com) draws skiers as much for the spectacular vistas over the St Lawrence as for its intermediate-level carving slopes and some challenging expert runs. Beginners are best off at the locals' mountain, **Stoneham** (ⓦwww.ski-stoneham.com), whose three interconnected peaks are just 6km north of Québec City's limits and also offer a good range of intermediate runs.

Mont-Ste-Anne has the most in the way of slope-side accommodation, but with Québec City and its array of dining and nightlife so close, you can easily make day-trips to any of the hills by car or with the Hiver-Express ski shuttle service ($23 return; ☏418/525-5191, ⓦwww.taxicoop-quebec.com) to Stoneham or Mont-Ste-Anne. These two resorts along with the city tourist board offer ski packages and interchangeable lift tickets (☏418/827-5281 or 1-866/386-2754, ⓦwww.fun2ski .com). For up-to-date ski conditions, visit ⓦwww.quebecskisurf.com or listen out for regular updates on the radio.

For more comprehensive descriptions of runs, terrain, lift passes, facilities and the like, pick up a copy of *The Rough Guide to Skiing & Snowboarding in North America*.

houses are not as overpriced as you'd think, and they offer an array of excellent crafts, from weird and wonderful ceramics to Inuit carvings. The glass-blowing workshop and gallery, **Verrerie La Mailloche** (ⓦwww.lamailloche.com), where the street meets the base of the *escalier casse-cou* is particularly interesting – you can watch the craftsmen blow glass straight out of the 1100°C furnace and purchase the gorgeous and unique result. Nearby is the Maison Louis-Jolliet, which was built in 1683 for its namesake, the retired discoverer of the Mississippi. It now houses the base station for the **funicular** (daily 7.30am–11pm, until midnight in summer; $1.50) – the least taxing way to scale the cliff back up to Terrasse Dufferin and Place d'Armes in Haute-Ville (see p.262).

Eating, drinking and nightlife

The French ancestry of the Québécois truly hits all the senses when it comes to **eating** in Québec City: the city's restaurants present a fine array of culinary delights adopted from the mother country, from lovingly presented gourmet dishes to humble baguettes. Quite a few places mix French and Italian on their menus, and there are increasing numbers of ethnic spots, from Indian to Moroccan, for a change of taste. **Nightlife** in Québec City is more relaxed than in Montréal: an evening spent in an intimate bar or a jazz or blues soiree is more popular than a big gig or disco – although many a young student would beg to differ.

Cafés·and restaurants

Vieux-Québec is home to many old-school gourmet **restaurants** and **cafés** aimed largely at the tourist market, as is Basse-Ville, though the latter is increasingly popular with locals for its contemporary French restaurants helmed by inventive chefs preparing *cuisine du terroir* (typically fusion or *nouvelle cuisine* with an emphasis on regional produce). Other areas, just outside the city walls – notably along rue St-Jean (quirky and cheaper), Grande-Allée (generally touristy and expensive) and downhill in St-Roch (trendy bistros and varied cuisine) – also have their fair share of places to eat. Your best bet for moderately priced restaurants, though, is to do as the locals do: head for avenue Cartier a kilometre west of the walls (buses #11, 800 or 801) near the Musée National des Beaux-Arts du Québec, and check out the menus of the numerous terrace-fronted restaurants. Note that, especially in Vieux-Québec, you sometimes don't save much with the *table d'hôte* – it's worth comparing what you'd get instead by ordering à la carte.

Haute-Ville

Aux Anciens Canadiens 34 rue St-Louis ☎ 418/692-1627, ⊛ www.auxancienscanadiens .qc.ca. Touristy and overly expensive (*table d'hôte* starts at \$40), it's nonetheless popular due to its charming location in the city's oldest house and the menu of Québécois specialities like *tourtière* (meat pie) and *pattes de cochon* (pigs' trotters) prepared more finely than how the original *habitants* could have afforded. Lunch is a much better deal at around \$15 for a drink and three courses.

🏃 **Casse-Crêpe Breton** 1136 rue St-Jean ☎ 418/692-0438. Diner-style restaurant where \$5 crepes are filled with items like cheese, ham and vegetables for a savoury snack, or fruit and chocolate for something sweeter. There's often a queue, but it moves quickly. Open from 7am to around 11pm.

Chez Temporel 25 rue Couillard ☎ 418/694-1813. Bowls of steaming café au lait, croissants and chocolatines make this café, a few doors from the *Auberge de la Paix* hostel, a perfect place for breakfast (from 7am) or a late afternoon pit-stop. Soups and sandwiches are also available until midnight.

Conti Caffe 32 rue St-Louis ☎ 418/692-4191. An offshoot (and sharing the kitchen) of the good but more expensive and formal *Le Continental* next door, this stylish but casual Italian eatery is the best choice on a street swamped with mediocre, touristy restaurants. Veal is a speciality – the medallions in

porcini mushroom sauce (\$20.50) are rich and succulent. Lunch specials for \$10–13.

🏃 **Les Frères de la Côte** 1190 rue St-Jean ☎ 418/692-5445. A friendly and crowded bistro that draws locals as well as tourists for steaks, smoked salmon and great mussels and pizzas, as well as an excellent steak tartare. Make sure to check the daily specials (mains \$14–17) on the blackboard.

Le Petit Coin Latin 8.5 rue Ste-Ursule ☎ 418/692-2022. Yellow-orange walls brighten up the exposed stone in this cozy café-bistro but, in nice weather, the secluded courtyard is the place to be. Raclette is a speciality, but they also serve steaks and a caribou *tourtière* (meat pie) for heartier appetites (*table d'hôte* around \$22). Breakfast (7.30–11.30am, until 4pm weekends) ranges from straightforward fry-ups to eggs Benedict, while the two-course weekday lunches are good value starting at \$10.

Le St-Amour 48 rue Ste-Ursule ☎ 418/694-0667, ⊛ www.saint-amour.com. As the name suggests, this is one of Québec City's most romantic restaurants, with a suitably elegant decor to match the finely wrought French recipes applied to local produce – the foie gras (\$29) is exceptional. Ask for a table in the winter garden. Allow at least three hours if you want to splash out on the ten-course Ménu Découverte (\$95); lunch specials (mostly \$16–19) are more affordable.

Outside the walls

Café Krieghoff 1089 av Cartier ☎ 418/522-3711, ⊛ www.cafekrieghoff.qc.ca. This French café-bistro, less than a ten-minute walk north of the Musée National des Beaux-Arts du Québec, serves up some of the

city's best coffee, big breakfasts and light meals like chicken caesar salad, quiche lorraine and traditional *croutons* (a baguette topped with garlic butter and melted cheese) for around \$11–12 for two courses at lunch. There's more substantial bistro fare for dinner.

Chez Victor 145 rue St-Jean ☎418/529-7702. Although it's isolated half-way between the rue St-Jean strip and avenue Cartier, locals still gravitate here for what are arguably the best burgers in the city. There are salads and sandwiches, too.

Le Commensal 860 rue St-Jean ☎418/647-3733. It's a similar deal here as in the Montréal branches (see p.157) of this great vegetarian chain: spoon out portions from an array of savoury and sweet dishes, then pay by weight ($1.80/100g, $2.05/100g for desserts). You can also bring your own wine or beer (there's an SAQ across the street).

🏃 **Cosmos Café** 575 Grande-Allée E ☎418/640-0606, ⓦ www.lecosmos .com. This café's cool decor and imaginative menu, with specials like trout with blueberries as well as a range of burgers, salads and pizzas, make it by far the best spot on the Grande-Allée. Crowded and lively at lunch and for the 5 à 7 cocktail hour.

Le Hobbit 700 rue St-Jean ☎418/647-2677. A popular local spot where a mixed crowd of residents and tourists come for a decent range of vegetarian options, in addition to burgers, pasta and bistro dishes – the "Osez…" (dare you…) menu includes *bavette de wapiti* (elk flank steak). Most mains are under $15.

Largo 643 rue St-Joseph E ☎418/529-3111, ⓦ www.largorestoclub.com. Oversized, plush red banquettes overhung by chandeliers

set the mood for nightly jazz sessions in this otherwise sleekly modern bistro in the trendy St-Roch district, where the Mediterranean cuisine might include ravioli stuffed with trout, bouillabaisse or sautéed veal. Mains $16–35.

Momento 1144 av Cartier ☎418/647-1313, ⓦ www.bistromomento.com. Oversized gold fluted columns and swooping curves add a playful touch to this chic Italian restaurant, serving pastas, pizzas and substantial fish, veal and other meat dishes for around $20–30 for a four-course dinner, $11–16 for lighter lunches.

La Noce 102 boul René-Lévesque O ☎418/529-6646. In a cute house on the corner of avenue Cartier, this new addition to the scene has a bit of a twist to the menu. All of the dishes are available as a starter or as a main course – choose from the likes of fried calamari ($8/$15) or pork medallions with roasted garlic ($10/$19) – and the same applies to whether you want a portion or *une bouchée* (mouthful) of dessert. Closed Sun & Mon; no lunch Sat.

Pizzédélic 1145 av Cartier ☎418/525-5981. A five-or-so-minute walk north of the fine-arts museum, this trendy spot dishes up creative pizzas (try the mascarpone and Black Forest ham or the salmon carpaccio) and pastas like linguini with red Thai curry and black tiger shrimp for $10–13. The large, packed terrace is definitely the most fun of those lining the av Cartier strip.

Basse-Ville

Buffet de l'Antiquaire 95 rue St-Paul ☎418/692-2661. An old-school diner popular with locals for breakfast (served from 6am) and inexpensive, home-cooked comfort food like *poutine*, *ragoût* (pork stew) and *cipaille* (meat pie) as well as burgers and club sandwiches.

Le Café du Monde 84 rue Dalhousie ☎418/692-4455, ⓦ www.lecafedumonde.com. This large and sleek Parisian-style bistro may be in the cruise-ship terminal, but it's a hit with locals for its brash atmosphere and fantastic terrace overlooking the St Lawrence. And the food – mussels, veal sweetbreads, *confit de canard*, steak tartare and the like – is quite good, too.

Le Casse-Cou 90 rue du Petit-Champlain ☎418/694-1121. A brightly painted, casual

café at the far end of the pedestrian street serving fry-up breakfasts from 8.30am and inexpensive light meals (including burgers, *croquette*, *poutine* and pizza) throughout the day and evening.

Le Cochon Dingue 46 boul Champlain ☎418/692-2013, ⓦ www.cochondingue.com. Casual restaurant with tiled floors and checkerboard tablecloths, where young and friendly staff serve mains such as pasta, mussels, *bavette* and steak frites for $13–16, as well as back ribs ($18–24). There's a second branch at 46 boul René-Lévesque O (☎418/523-2013), near avenue Cartier.

🏃 **L'Échaudé** 72 rue du Sault-au-Matelot ☎418/692-1299, ⓦ www.echaude.com. Upscale but unpretentious bistro with a terrace on the pedestrian portion of rue

22

du Sault-au-Matelot. A good selection of vintages – the owner hosts a radio show on wine – accompanies classic mains like *confit de canard*, steak tartare and stuffed quail (in season), as well as daily fish specials, mostly in the $20–32 range.

Initiale 54 rue St-Pierre ☎418/694-1818, ⓦ**www.restaurantinitiale.com**. Subdued earth-tones help create a hushed atmosphere where the focus is on fine French cook-:ng based around regional produce. The seasonally changing menu might include roasted suckling pig, venison medallions or Arctic char. Mains are around $38 but gourmets will want to investigate the chef's menus (starting at $59).

Le Lapin Sauté 52 rue du Petit-Champlain ☎418/692-5325, ⓦ**www.lapinsaute.com**. As the name suggests, they serve rabbit in a variety of ways at this country-style bistro, including the classic *lapin à la moutarde* ($18), but there is also steak, duck and salads, and a largely rabbit-free breakfast menu. The flagstone terrace is an ideal spot from which to watch the passing parade.

Le Marie Clarisse 12 rue du Petit-Champlain ☎418/692-0857. Named after an old schooner, the specialty in this late seventeenth-century stone house with a terrace at the foot of the *escalier casse-cou* is market-fresh seafood. Try the large pan-seared bay scallops, served in a lobster and beet sauce with a touch of saffron or the house *marmite* – a fish stew similar to a bouillabaisse. The lunchtime *table d'hôte* is a good deal at under $20; a five-course dinner costs $50. With only twelve tables, you'll need to make a reservation.

Bars and clubs

Compared to Montréal, Québec City's **nightlife** feels quite laid-back, with plenty of quiet bars and the few louder ones – venues for folk, rock or jazz – being on the small side. That said, the clubs at either end of the Grand-Allée strip are a frenzy on summer weekends, drawing a young, dressed-up crowd who wouldn't be caught dead with one of the gimmicky drinks (like half-yards of ale) offered on the restaurant terraces along the way. The bars along rue St-Jean, especially beyond the walls, tend to be more down-to-earth.

Haute-Ville

Bar Ste-Angèle 26 rue Ste-Angèle ☎418/692-2171. A dark, neighbourhood bar with a beamed ceiling and cozy nook that doesn't seem to realize it's in the middle of tourist central. Cheap bottles of beer ($3.75) and single malts make it a popular student hangout as well. Open from 8pm.

Bar St-Laurent 1 rue des Carrières ☎418/266-3906. The *Château Frontenac* address may be a bit stuffy, with glasses of wine and pints of beer costing $9–12 and a whopping $9, respectively, at the polished octagonal bar, but you don't need to dress to the nines and the view from the terrace is stupendous.

Chez Son Père 24 rue St-Stanislas ☎418/692-5308, ⓦ**www.barchezsonpere.qc.ca**. Québécois folk singers keep things humming in this lively bar just off rue St-Jean in Vieux-Québec. Nightly specials like $10 pitchers (Fri & Sat before 10pm) add to the buzz. Free admission; open from 8pm.

Le Pub St-Alexandre 1087 rue St-Jean ☎418/694-0015, ⓦ**www.pubstalexandre .com**. Yuppie English-style pub with a long mahogany bar set against the exposed-brick walls. With 40 single malts, 25 beers on tap – including Bass, Tartan and Newcastle Brown from $7.50 a pint – and nearly ten times that many in bottles, it's a good spot to down a few. Decent pub grub, too.

Outside the walls

L'Amour Sorcier 789 Côte Ste-Geneviève ☎418/523-3395. Popular and intimate, this mainly lesbian bar offers cheap beers and soft music (which gets louder and more danceable on weekend evenings) in a two-storey, exposed-brick interior with a great roof-terrace in summer. A ten-minute walk west of the Porte St-Jean.

Boudoir 441 rue du Parvis ☎418/524-2777, ⓦwww.boudoirlounge.com. A hip place to hang out, whether on the terrace of this short pedestrianised street lined with restaurants or inside, where you can lounge in svelte armchairs and admire the giant rose window. The floor in front rises to become a stage for cabaret-style crooning and rock bands ($5–15); there's a disco downstairs (Thurs–Sat) and the kitchen dishes up East-meets-West cuisine.

Dagobert 600 Grande-Allée E ☎418/522-0393, ⓦwww.dagobert.ca. This sprawling old house has been one of the city's most raucous nightspots for decades. Young dressed-up-for-it clubbers head upstairs for the large dance floor, which feels trapped in the past decade with its smoke machine and flashing lights. Downstairs an only slightly older crowd sit at tiered tables to catch cover bands playing popular tunes from 10.30pm. There's a cover charge.

Le Drague 815 rue St-Augustin ☎418/649-7212, ⓦwww.ledrague.com. Situated in Québec City's tiny gay district ten minutes west from the Porte St-Jean; beyond the front terrace there's a café, a basement nightclub with wraparound mezzanine, a men-only leather bar and a showbar – the Thursday-and Sunday-night drag shows are great fun.

Maurice 575 Grande-Allée E ☎418/647-2000, ⓦwww.mauricenightclub.com. Happening club with a rotating crew of DJs that attracts a stylish twenty- to mid-thirty-something crowd for R&B and house nights (Wed–Sun only in winter). Dress up to get by the selective door policy. The cover charge (around $4) also gets you into the more laid-back *Charlotte* upstairs, with couches for chilling out or smoking a cigar, though on the funk and latino nights it can be just as hopping.

Pub Java 1112 av Cartier ☎418/522-5282. There's a good selection of imported and draught beers at this pub, that also draws locals for lunch (from $10) and breakfasts (8am–noon, until 4pm weekends). For cosier surroundings, head upstairs to the *Salon Galway* (Wed–Sat), done up like an Irish pub with dark woods, large armchairs by the fireplace and a pool table.

Sacrilège 447 rue St-Jean ☎418/649-1985, ⓦwww.lesacrilege.net. Friendly and often packed watering-hole drawing students and locals, especially for the cheap beer specials ($4.25 a pint) and popular courtyard terrace in back. It's in the Faubourg St-Jean-Baptiste district, less than fifteen minutes west of Place D'Youville.

Basse-Ville

L'Inox 37 quai St-André ☎418/692-2877, ⓦwww.inox.qc.ca. If Québec City's original brewpub seems a bit empty aside from the pool tables, you've probably missed the popular terrace alongside. There, on warm nights, tourists and locals snack on artisanal cheeses and European sausages to accompany fine ales such as the brown Scottiche (a winter warmer only) and Trouble-Fête, a refreshing Belgian blonde with coriander and lime.

L'Oncle Antoine 29 rue St-Pierre ☎418/694-9176. A pair of stone-vaulted rooms in a mid-eighteenth-century warehouse provides an atmospheric venue for consuming local microbrewery Barberie's output as well as giant bottles of Molson and Labatt beers. There's a street-side terrace in summer and roaring fireplace in winter.

Le Pape Georges 8 1/4 rue Cul-de-Sac ☎418/692-1320, ⓦwww.papegeorges .com. There's barely room for the guitarist squashed against the fireplace in this tiny cellar of a bar. If you're claustrophobic, you can have your wine or beer (along with a cheese plate) on the equally atmospheric terrace in front. Free live acts start up around 9 or 10pm Wed–Sun (Thurs–Sun in winter).

22

Contexts

Contexts

A brief history of Montréal

The struggle between French and English has been a constant theme throughout most of Montréal's **history**, shaping it culturally, politically, socially and even physically. After seizing Québec City from the French in 1759, the British gained the upper hand, yet passage of the Québec Act in 1774 ensured the survival of the province's French culture. In the nineteenth century, British influence was most strongly felt in the increasing commercialization of Montréal, which made it Canada's largest and wealthiest city before it evolved into Canada's "sin capital" during Prohibition. The subsequent influx of immigrants has resulted in a great ethnic mix, a rich culture and an array of festivities that make this cosmopolitan city one of the continent's most fun and unique places to visit.

Beginnings

Little is known about the earliest peoples who roamed this part of Québec beyond that they were nomadic groups of **hunter–gatherers**, living off a plentiful supply of fish, fowl, moose, deer and caribou. What is known is that by around 1000 BC Iroquois-speaking peoples lived in the area, though it took another two millennia for these Iroquois nations to develop a sedentary life-style, cultivating crops – primarily corn, beans and squash – and making pottery in which to store food. These tribes surrounded their villages with wooden palisades, inside of which up to 1500 people would live in communal, bark-covered longhouses some twenty to thirty metres long.

It was such a settlement, named **Hochelaga** ("Place of the Beaver"), situated at the base of the mountain and occupied by the St Lawrence Iroquois, that **Jacques Cartier** stumbled across on his second trip to North America in 1535. The year before, he had claimed all of Canada for Francis I of France and had returned to look both for gold and a shorter trade route to Asia. While he found neither, he did manage to provide the source for Montréal's name, labelling the hill that towered over Hochelaga **Mont Royal** (although some argue he actually named it Monreale, for the bishop of that town who was one of his trip's sponsors).

The founding of Ville-Marie

It's uncertain whether warfare with other tribes or disease brought by the Europeans was at fault, but in the latter half of the sixteenth century the population of St Lawrence Iroquois plummeted. By the time French explorer **Samuel de Champlain** arrived in 1603, all traces of Hochelaga had vanished. Champlain briefly left the scene as well, travelling east to found Québec City in 1608, but he returned three years later to the Montréal area to begin the first European construction on the island at Pointe-à-Callière, naming the immediate area Place Royale. Champlain then turned his energies to the smaller island just offshore, naming it in honour of his twelve-year-old bride, Hélène – a decent thing to do given that he purchased it with her dowry.

The next few decades saw only intermittent European activity, the French settlement at Place Royale being little more than a small garrison. The Récollets (reformed Franciscans) and Jesuit missionaries – called the "Black Robes" by the natives who suspected them of sorcery – also maintained a small presence on the island, attempting to convert the Iroquois, more often than not being put to death for their pains. The priests' tasks were not made any easier by the fact that the French had aligned with the Algonquin and Huron nations to gain access to their **fur-trading networks**, while those groups' traditional enemies, the Iroquois Confederacy, had formed alliances with the Dutch and subsequently the British. Periodic bouts between the factions over control of the industry would continue over the next half-century.

Meanwhile, a group of French aristocrats and merchants soon obtained a title from Louis XIII to colonize Canada for commercial gain, and Paul de Chomedey, **Sieur de Maisonneuve**, was chosen to lead the mission. After wintering in Québec City, he established the colony of Ville-Marie on the site of Champlain's Place Royale along with some fifty settlers on either May 16 or 17 in 1642. That winter the settlement – which would before too long be known as Montréal – seemed destined to disappear as quickly as it came due to the impending threat of rising floodwaters. De Maisonneuve's fervent prayers were answered on Christmas Day when the waters receded, and in gratitude, he planted a **cross** near the mountain's summit, a gesture commemorated by the present-day landmark. Floods, though, were only the beginning of de Maisonneuve's problems, as native attacks plagued the colony; even after the Frenchman bested an Iroquois chief in single combat in 1644, settlers risked ambushes for the next two decades.

New France

Ville-Marie's survival remained tenuous until Louis XIV made Québec a royal province in 1663 (and granted the seigneury of the island of Montréal to the **Sulpicians**, an order of missionaries who would be the city's de facto landlords for roughly the next two hundred years; see box, p.72). The area's new status allowed for the dispatch of a thousand French troops, whose arrival further widened the existing gender gap. In order to rectify this imbalance, unmarried Frenchwomen, the so-called **filles du roi**, were shipped over by the boatload throughout the next decade (see box, p.129). Still, even with the much stronger military presence, periodic skirmishes between the French and British and their native allies continued to be a destabilizing factor, stunting the growth of the colony. Matters were resolved somewhat when 1200 colonists met with an even greater number of natives from across eastern North America at Pointe-à-Callière to sign **La Grande Paix**, the Great Peace treaty of 1701 between the French and 39 Indian nations. The signing of the Treaty of Utrecht with the British a decade later further allowed the fur trade to flourish, greatly increasing the town's fortunes.

It wasn't until mid-century that further serious conflict broke out, with the British and French again at odds in the **Seven Years' War** (also known as the French and Indian War). Although the early years of fighting were concentrated in the Atlantic colonies, the turning point took place in 1759 when, after a summer of punishing bombardment at Québec City, General James Wolfe defeated the French under the Marquis de Montcalm in the twenty-minute **Battle of the Plains of Abraham**. When Québec City fell, Montréal briefly served as the capital of New France, until the Marquis de Vaudreuil surrendered to the Brits a year later, without a shot being fired.

British rule and the birth of a city

The transfer to **British rule** saw little change in the life of most Québécois, except for the fleeing of a few upper-class merchants. But when an attempt was made in 1763 to impose British administrative structures that threatened the status of the powerful Catholic clergy, grumbles rose from the largely Francophone and rural population. Worried that unrest similar to that occurring in the American colonies might be played out here, the British enacted the 1774 **Quebec Act**, a stopgap measure that allowed the French to maintain their language, civil code, seigneurial system and religion. This short-term solution was largely responsible for Québec's unique character, as well as the tensions that would continue to flare up throughout its future.

The British occupation suffered a brief hiccup in the mid-1770s when **American** soldiers, led by General Richard Montgomery, took over the city, and the likes of **Benjamin Franklin** tried to convince a skeptical populace to join the American struggle against the British. The Americans were soon defeated in Québec City, but after they won independence from Britain in their own land, a flood of British Loyalists fled across the Canadian border, settling primarily in the Eastern Townships and present-day Ontario.

These new Anglophone residents, as well as the Francophone bourgeoisie, chafed under the terms of the Quebec Act, and both wanted an elected assembly. The British response to these demands was the 1791 **Constitutional Act**, which divided the territory into Lower and Upper Canada (present-day Québec and Ontario), giving both a legislative assembly. The act emphasized the inequalities between Anglophones and Francophones, however, as real power lay with the so-called **Château Clique** – an assembly composed mainly of members of the wealthy establishment and answerable to a British governor and a council appointed in London.

Around this time, the city walls were becoming a serious impediment to growth, and their demolition was carried out between 1804 and 1809, with all traces of their existence wiped out by 1817. During this period, the first steamships began sailing between Montréal and Québec City, leading to further growth and, despite fears of an American invasion during the War of 1812, the city continued to prosper.

The town by now was well on its way to becoming Canada's commercial centre, a fact confirmed with the establishment of the **Banque de Montréal** in 1817. From around 1815, waves of British and Irish immigrants swelled the population enough that by the 1820s Montréal's total passed that of Québec City and in 1831 Anglophones formed the majority of Montréal's residents.

Resentment, however, was brewing just under the surface as the Château Clique vetoed bills passed in the Francophone-dominated assembly, occasionally resulting in riots. Francophone anger – exacerbated by a severe depression and punitive import taxes on British goods, as well as the favouritism shown Anglophones – boiled over in 1837, when the French **Patriotes** led by **Louis-Joseph Papineau** rose up against the British. Their insurgency failed, resulting in hangings, exiles and a particularly murderous punitive episode in St-Eustache (see p.233), and led to an investigation by the British-appointed governor general, **Lord Durham**, who concluded that English and French relations

C

were akin to two nations warring within the bosom of a single state. His prescription for peace was immersing French Canadians in the English culture of North America; the subsequent establishment of the **Province of Canada** with the 1840 Act of Union can be seen as a deliberate attempt to marginalize Francophone opinion within an English-speaking state. In 1844, Montréal became the capital of Canada, a role it held only until 1849 when a protesting mob of Anglophone Tories torched the parliament building (a former market on Place d'Youville) in anger at legislation compensating Francophones for damages caused by the British army in quelling the Patriotes' rebellion.

Industrialization and expansion

The mid-nineteenth century was a time for **industrialization** in Montréal – much as it was in urban areas across Canada and the US – spurred by the deepening of the channel between Montréal and Québec City and the construction of the Grand Trunk Railway, which reached from the ice-free port of Portland, Maine, to the island of Montréal itself when the Victoria Bridge was completed in 1859. Vast tracts of factories sprouted up along the **Lachine Canal** and in east-end towns like Hochelaga, refining grain and sugar, producing shoes and other leather goods, textiles, and heavy machinery for the rail and ship industries. Simultaneously, massive blocks of substandard rowhouses were built to accommodate, in part, the masses of rural Francophones who flooded into Montréal looking for work in the factories – by 1866 Montréal's language scale had tipped, leaving **Francophones in the majority** for good.

The city's hold on the national economy was further strengthened by the completion of the coast-to-coast **Canadian Pacific Railway** in the 1880s, and the city continued to jump its boundaries, absorbing 22 adjacent municipalities between 1883 and 1918. Meanwhile, the commercial centre of the city shifted to the present-day Downtown and an electric streetcar network began running in 1892, connecting the growing metropolis. Pogroms in Eastern Europe sent thousands of **Jews** fleeing to Montréal and with a continued exodus from the rural areas the city's population reached half a million in 1911, doubling in the next two decades with an influx of émigrés from war-torn Europe.

Morality and the early 1900s

For the first half of the twentieth century, Montréal's liberated mores stood out against the staid Puritanism of other Canadian cities, earning it a reputation as Canada's **"sin city"**. US Prohibition in the 1920s allowed Québec to become the continent's main **alcohol supplier** – the Molsons (brewers), Bronfmans (owners of Seagram distillers) and their ilk made their fortunes here – while prostitution and gambling thrived under the protection of city and police officials.

Even the Great Depression couldn't dampen the carousing, in part because **Camillien Houde**, the off-and-on mayor of Montréal between 1928 and 1954, mitigated much of its effects with massive **public works projects** (like the construction of the Jardin Botanique). His magnanimity bankrupted the city, though, and it was forced into trusteeship by the province in 1940. Yet despite this, and the jail term he served for urging citizens to resist conscription for World War II, Houde's popularity did not cease, and he returned to power for another decade. With the war, the economy picked up again and by this time Montréal had forty nightclubs and lounge bars, whose lavish floor-shows, big bands and visiting entertainers – including Harlem jazz acts at the famous Rockhead's Paradise – pulled in crowds until dawn.

The pace only let up when Pacifique "Pax" Plante became head of the **Morality Squad** in 1946. Whereas his predecessors had pretty much gone along with the times, organizing sham raids and scaring no one, Plante surprised everyone by shutting down the gambling joints and whorehouses virtually overnight. But rather than receive praise, he was ousted eighteen months later, and the city roared back to life. It wasn't until 1950 that citizens' outrage finally sparked a four-year-long judicial inquiry into corruption and other matters, and on the strength of its damning report, prosecuting lawyer **Jean Drapeau** won a landslide victory in the October 1954 mayoral race with his promise to clean up Canada's wide-open city.

The Drapeau years and the Quiet Revolution

Drapeau's reforming zeal did not sit well with the premier of Québec, **Maurice Duplessis**, who used his organizational might to fix the 1957 election against him. It was hardly a stretch for Duplessis, who had the support of both the Anglophone business elite and the clergy. Rural Québec at this time was almost a feudal state, held under the thrall of both the Church and the State, and despite their demographic strength, Francophones continued to be ill-paid and badly housed in comparison to their Anglo counterparts. Frustrated by this disparity, a French-speaking middle class began articulating the workforce's grievances, leading to the so-called **Quiet Revolution** that began in 1960. The provincial government, led by **Jean Lesage** and his Liberal Party of Québec, took control of welfare, health and education away from the Church and, under the slogan "*Maîtres chez-nous*" (Masters of our own house), established state-owned industries that kick-started the development of a **Francophone business class**.

In 1960, Drapeau returned to power and set about attending to his legacy: in large part, this meant changing Montréal's physical appearance during his next 26 years as mayor. He, like Camillien Houde before him, is remembered for the megaprojects bestowed on the city, such as Place Ville-Marie, the Underground City (RÉSO), Place des Arts and the **Métro system**. The first underground trains began running in 1966, just in time for the hugely successful 1967 Universal Exposition – better known as **Expo '67** – a world's fair that attracted fifty million guests and catapulted the city to international status.

One of those visitors was Charles de Gaulle, who made his famous "**Vive le Québec libre!**" speech from the balcony of the Hôtel de Ville, echoing the sentiments of nationalists who, woken by the social and cultural possibilities of the Quiet Revolution, were intent on achieving political results as well. Despite inroads into the corridors of real power, many still felt that it was Montréal's Anglophones who were benefiting from the prosperity of the boom that accompanied the Expo and the city's rapid expansion, and beneath the smooth surface Francophone frustrations were reaching dangerous levels.

The crisis peaked in October 1970, when the radical **Front de Libération du Québec** (FLQ) kidnapped the British trade commissioner, James Cross, and

△ Stade Olympique

then a Québec cabinet minister, Pierre Laporte. As ransom, the FLQ demanded the publication of the FLQ manifesto, the transportation to Cuba of 25 FLQ prisoners awaiting trial for acts of violence and $500,000 in gold bullion. Prime Minister **Pierre Trudeau** responded with the War Measures Act, suspending civil liberties and putting troops on the streets of Montréal. The following day, Laporte's body was found in the trunk of a car. By December, the so-called October Crisis was over: Cross had been released, and his captors and Laporte's murderers arrested. But the reverberations shook the nation, having an impact on politics not just in Québec, but Canada as a whole.

At last recognizing the need to redress the country's social imbalances, the federal government poured money into countrywide schemes to promote French-Canadian culture, while in Montréal, Drapeau funnelled money into the last of his grand projects – hosting the **1976 Summer Olympics**.

The ongoing threat of Separatism

Francophone discontent found a political voice in the Parti Québécois, founded by **René Lévesque** in 1968 with the chief goal of Québec sovereignty – still one of the party's main platforms today. Their message finally won the support of voters in the provincial election of 1976, and the consequent language law – the Charte de la langue française, better known as **Bill 101** – was enacted the following year. It established French as the province's official language, making it a compulsory part of the school curriculum and banning English-only signs on business premises (subsequently eased so that all signs had to at least be bilingual, with the French printed twice as large as the English). Tens of thousands of Anglophones promptly began an **exodus** from Montréal. Over a hundred companies, several head offices and a massive amount of capital moved west to Toronto, provoking a steep decline in housing prices, a halt on construction work and the withdrawal of investment.

For Québec to shape its own future, many nationalists felt the province needed control over laws and taxes, although they wanted to maintain an economic association with Canada. In 1980, a **referendum on sovereignty association** was held, but still reeling from the terrorist activities of the FLQ and scared that separatism would leave Québec economically adrift, the 6.5-million population voted 60/40 against. Prime Minister Trudeau then set about repatriating the country's **Constitution** in the autumn of 1981. Trudeau called a late-night meeting on the issue and did not invite Lévesque, literally denying Québec a seat at the table. "The night of the long knives", as the event became known, wound up imposing a Constitution on the province that placed its language rights in jeopardy and removed its veto power over constitutional amendments. Accordingly, the provincial government refused to sign it – and still hasn't to this day.

In October 1993, Québec's displeasure with federalism was evident in the election of Lucien Bouchard's Bloc Québécois to the vastly ironic status of Her Majesty's Loyal Opposition in Ottawa. The cause received added support in 1994 when the Parti Québécois was returned to provincial power after vowing to hold a **province-wide referendum** on separation from Canada. The referendum was held a year later, and the vote was so close – the province opted to remain a part of Canada by a margin of less than one percent – that calls immediately arose for a third referendum (prompting pundits to refer to the process as the "neverendum").

Contemporary Montréal

Political uncertainty and continuing tensions, combined with a Canada-wide economic recession, had Montréal on shaky ground in the mid-1990s. After the 1995 referendum, however, a tacit truce was made on the issue of separation. The more stable political climate – the result of Francophones increasingly confident with their lot and Anglophones who have remained and adjusted to the turbulence and change – coincided with restored **economic confidence** that led to a good deal of rejuvenation on the city's commercial streets. Boarded-up shops that lined rue Ste-Catherine in the mid-1990s, for example, reopened and continue to do bustling business. Derelict pockets on the edges of Downtown and Vieux-Montréal have been renovated to house the growing multimedia industry, just one element of the city's transition to a **new economy**. The industry was seemingly less affected by the burst of the dot-com bubble than many other cities thanks to specialization in animation and special-effects software, though the amount of new building in the Cité Multimédia and the towers of the Cité du Commerce Électronique (E-Commerce Place) has proven over-optimistic.

Even though most Quebecers – and certainly most Montrealers – have for now put the separatist dream on hold, Montréal still seems doomed to ongoing political squabbles. Not long after Lucien Bouchard stepped down as the leader of the Parti Québécois in January 2001, claiming that Quebecers weren't ready for sovereignty, and separatist firebrand Bernard Landry took his place, **Pierre Bourque**, the mayor since 1994, led the drive to create "One Island, One City". Proponents of a **Mega-City** that would merge Montréal and the island's patchwork of 27 other towns and cities claimed everyone would benefit from economies of scale. The idea did not sit well with the English-speaking municipalities in the West Island, who worried that they would not only pay more taxes for fewer services, but that the move was also an attempt to deprive many areas of bilingual status through re-districting. Mayor Bourque lost the November 2001 election, due largely to his support of the scheme, but the provincial government pushed the bill through anyway, creating the new island-wide city of Montréal on January 1, 2002.

Courting suburban voters with the carrot of possible referendums to overturn the merger may have played a part in the election of **Jean Charest** and his Liberal party in April 2003. For most Quebecers, though, the reasons for casting out the Parti Québécois probably had more to do with meat-and-potato issues – fixing an ailing healthcare system, funnelling money into education and promising to reduce taxes in the highest-taxed province in the country – not to mention a well-earned rest from separatism, at least at the provincial level. True to his word, Charest allowed referenda to be held on the issue, and fifteen municipalities subsequently opted for a "**demerger**", leaving Montréal smaller but still twice the area it encompassed prior to 2002. Voters have been less impressed with Charest's progress on other fronts, however, and there's a good chance that the Parti Québécois, under their youthful and openly gay leader **André Boisclair**, could resume power in the next election (by 2008), bringing up the issue of separatism yet again.

While the merger and demerger have had little impact on visitors to Montréal – the new *arrondissements* (boroughs) conform largely to the same boundaries that existed beforehand – a decision made by current mayor, **Gérald Tremblay**, may require you to alter some of the maps in this book. With minimal consultation, Tremblay announced in October 2006 that historic avenue du Parc would be renamed in honour of the late premier Robert Bourassa. Within a week, online petitions had already garnered 20,000 names against the move, still awaiting a vote by city council (in which Tremblay's Montreal Island Citizens Union has a solid majority) as this guide went to press.

Books

The listings below represent a highly selective reading list on Montréal, with a couple of broader Québec-specific books thrown in. Wherever possible, they've been listed by their most recent edition and most accessible publisher; many should be readily available in Canada, the US and the UK. If they can't be found in bookstores, try to order through the publisher, or online from Montréal bookstores (see p.201). Of particular note is local publisher Véhicule Press; in addition to putting out a number of Montréal-related titles, they provide further background on the city's writers on their website (Ⓦ www.vehiculepress.com/montreal). Highly recommended titles are signified by 🎄. Out-of-print titles are indicated by o/p.

History, society and politics

Pierre Anctil *Saint-Laurent: Montréal's Main* (Les Éditions du Septentrion, Canada). Based on research for an exhibition at the Musée d'Archéologie, this history of Montréal's most vibrant street is in many ways a microcosm of the city's history itself – the Main always reflecting current trends if not actually instigating them.

Lucien Bouchard *On the Record* (Stoddart, Canada). A recording of the sovereignty movement's *raison d'être*, written by one of its most charismatic leaders; so persuasive you may wish to join up – that is, until you read Lawrence Martin's *The Antagonist* (see opposite).

Bill Brownstein *Schwartz's Hebrew Delicatessen: The Story* (Véhicule Press, Canada). The *Gazette* columnist's look at the venerated smoked-meat emporium is as much a social history of the Main as it is about brisket of beef and those who've served it.

Edgar Andrew Collard *Montreal Yesterdays* (o/p). Collard's light-hearted tomes often blend momentous stories with quirky anecdotes, and this volume, which combines a chapter on Mark Twain's visit to the *Windsor Hotel* with tales of haunted houses and reclusive hermits, is no exception.

John A. Dickinson and Brian Young *A Short History of Quebec* (McGill-Queen's University Press, Canada). Though not especially short, this book is nonetheless a readable trawl through the province's social, economic, governmental, cultural and religious histories with loads of suggestions for further reading.

John Gilmore *Who's Who of Jazz in Montreal* (Véhicule Press, Canada). A jazz-aficionado handbook with hundreds of biographies of musicians that worked in the city from the dawn of the jazz era to 1970, including home-grown talents like Oscar Peterson and Americans like Louis Metcalfe and Slap Rags White.

Lawrence Martin *The Antagonist* (Viking, Canada). Martin's excellent biographies of influential Canadian politicians generally hinge on a controversial hypothesis; here he psychoanalyses former Separatist leader Lucien Bouchard as having "esthetic character disorder" – pyschobabble for highly unstable.

Jennifer Robinson (ed) *Montreal's Century* (Éditions du Trécarré, Canada). A good potted history of twentieth-century Montréal with essays on city life, politics and sports supplemented by scads of colour photographs from both the *Montreal Gazette* and *Journal de Montréal's* archives.

William Weintraub *City Unique* (McClelland and Stewart, Canada). This riveting narrative of the city in the 1940s and 1950s is full of salacious stories of corruption, sex and boozing, with an especially juicy section on the stripteaser Lili St-Cyr.

Architecture and photography

Pierre Phillipe Brunet and Jean O'Neil *Les Escaliers de Montréal* and *Les Couronnements de Montréal* (Hurtubise HMH, Canada). A pair of photo books focusing on some of the city's unique architectural details – the former captures the staircases that are such a prominent feature of Montréal's residential streets, while the latter looks up at the city's rooflines and their fanciful parapets, dormers and *tourelles*. Text is in French only.

Sandra Cohen-Rose *Northern Deco – Art Deco Architecture in Montreal* (Corona, Canada). This glossy pictorial study beautifully captures the city's finest Art-Deco buildings, including the interior of the private Maison Cormier (see box, p.61).

Bryan Demchinsky *Montréal Then and Now* (Éditions du Trécarré, Canada). A photo essay that captures the city's history in architectural terms – how spaces are used differently, what has passed away and what's surprisingly unchanged. Curiously, many of the century-old photos from *The Gazette*'s photographers look crisper than the modern-day ones. Bilingual text.

Isabelle Gournay and France Vanlaethem *Montréal Metropolis* (Stoddart, Canada). The definitive analysis of Montréal's architectural evolution from 1880 to 1930, complete with a studied collection of black-and-white photographs and layout plans (including projects never built).

Phyllis Lambert and Alan Stewart *Opening the Gates of Eighteenth-Century Montreal* (Canadian Centre for Architecture, Canada). A thorough, if academic, volume documenting the impact of Vieux-Montréal's fortifications on urban planning.

Andrzej Maciejewski *After Notman: Montreal Views – A Century Apart* (Firefly Books, Canada). Prolific late-nineteenth-century photographer William Notman documented a great deal of Montréal life and architecture. Here, his images from the Musée McCord's archives are placed side-by-side with Maciejewski's contemporary shots of the same scenes, giving a fascinating insight into how the city has changed.

Nancy Marrelli *Stepping Out: The Golden Age of Montreal Night Clubs* (Véhicule Press, Canada). A trove of archival photos from the city's jazz age displays the wild history of Montréal's nightlife in vivid detail.

Jean-Claude Marsan *Montreal in Evolution* (McGill-Queen's University Press, Canada). An analysis of Montréal's architectural trends and urban planning motifs that spans three centuries and culminates with an exhaustive look at the orchestration of Expo '67.

Jean–Eudes Schurr and Louise Larivière (eds) *Montréal Métropole* (Aux Yeux du Monde, Canada). A coffee-table book showcasing evocative photographs of the city taken by thirty photojournalists during a three-day blitz in the autumn of 1999.

Impressions, travel and specific guides

Nick Auf der Maur *Nick: A Life* (Véhicule Press, Canada). This regaling collection of works by the *Montreal Gazette*'s most illustrious columnist is as much about the late Auf der Maur's boisterous life as it is about Montréal.

Joe Fiorito *Tango on the Main* (Nuage Editions, Canada). Winner of the 1996 National Newspaper Award, Fiorito's compiled columns about the city's people, places and things make great, if sentimental, reading.

🏃 **Kristian Gravenor and John David Gravenor** *Montreal: The Unknown City* (Aresnal Pulp Press, Canada). A book full of fascinating trivia on all aspects of the city, including its scandals, quirkier personalities, hidden treasures and hare-brained ideas for projects that, if built, would have made the Big O look like a stroke of genius.

🏃 **Johnson and David Widgington** *Montréal Up Close* (Cumulus Press, Canada). Two great walking tours through the city that give the low-down on every gargoyle, frieze and bas-relief carving throughout Vieux-Montréal and

Downtown; comes with a handy fold-out map.

Leif R. Montin *Get Outta Town* (No Fixed Address Publications, Canada). A terrific day-trip guide to 52 attractions within driving distance of Montréal.

Stuart Nulman *Beyond the Mountain: True Tales About Montreal* (Callawind Publications, Canada). Detailed explorations of quirky historical tidbits about the city's buildings, institutions and personages, though the question-and-answer format is annoying.

Sandra Phillips *Smart Shopping Montréal.* If you're serious about shopping in Montréal this guide (currently in its ninth edition) covers a myriad of ways to spend your money, with a focus on discount and specialist shops. Also available online (Ⓦ www.smartshopping.net).

John Symon *The Lobster Kids' Guide to Exploring Montréal* (Lobster Press, Canada). A comprehensive guide to kids' activities around and outside the city with listings of child-friendly restaurants, playlands, and the like.

Fiction and drama

Yves Beauchemin *The Alley Cat* (McClelland and Stewart, Canada). An engaging story centred on the *Binerie* restaurant (see p.161) and owner Florent Boissonneault's struggles to keep the place and his personal life afloat while one sinister Egon Ratablavasky strives to bring him down.

Andy Brown and Rob McLennan *You and Your Bright Ideas: New Montreal Writing* (Véhicule Press, Canada). Contemporary stories by mainly young local authors, many of

whom are part of the city's energetic spoken-word scene.

🏃 **Roch Carrier** *The Hockey Sweater* (Tundra Books, Canada). Every kid in Québec has read this story about a boy who longs for a Montréal Canadiens hockey jersey but gets a Toronto Maple Leafs one instead, much to the scorn of his fellow shinny-players. A must if you have children in tow.

🏃 **Leonard Cohen** *The Favourite Game* (McClelland and Stewart,

Canada). Songwriter Cohen's debut novel chronicles the escapades of the irresistible Lawrence Beavman through the streets, sheets and bars of Montréal and New York City, in punchy and lyrical prose. His follow-up, *Beautiful Losers* (McClelland and Stewart, Canada), a more uninhibited and experimental work, is a cult classic.

John Farrow *City of Ice* (Harper-Collins, Canada). A tense thriller about the city's biker gangs with all the criminal activity you'd expect – CIA plants, crooked cops, dodgy lawyers and the like – set during a bone-chilling Montréal winter.

David Fennario *Balconville* (Talonbooks, Canada). This play adroitly captures the social interaction fostered by the facing balconies of Montréal's paired triplex apartment-buildings. Set in Pointe-St-Charles, the Anglophone and Francophone neighbours talk of day-to-day things, separatism and the Expos.

Charles Foran *Butterfly Lovers* (HarperCollins, Canada). Ailing and embittered David LeClair's meandering narrative of self-discovery starts and ends in a Mile End bar called Remys, but spends a good chunk in China, where his relationship with a married woman prompts a profound metamorphosis.

Hugh MacLennan *Two Solitudes* (McClelland and Stewart, Canada). The story of Canada's French–English relations is mapped onto the equally epic but more poignant narrative of Paul Tallard's struggles as the son of a French-Canadian father and Irish mother; an even-handed and enlightening

read. His wonderfully sentimental *The Watch that Ends the Night* is also worth picking up.

Kathy Reichs *Déjà Dead* (Pocket Books, US/Arrow Books, UK). A chilling forensic crime novel about one woman's attempts to track down a serial killer fond of dismembering women's bodies and stashing them about town; a serious page-turner that spawned a series of sequels.

Mordecai Richler *Barney's Version* (Alfred A. Knopf, Canada/Washington Square Press, US/Random House, UK). The late Richler's last novel, *Barney's Version*, is as much about himself as it is Barney Panofsky, his affable protagonist whose passions – hockey and Anglophone rights in Montréal – often get side-tracked by his fondness for women. Richler's debut, *The Apprenticeship of Duddy Kravitz* (McClelland and Stewart, Canada/Washington Square Press, US), introduced Canadian literature's greatest scoundrel, whose capers are told here in witty style.

Gabrielle Roy *The Tin Flute* (McClelland and Stewart, Canada). The houses crammed together on rue St-Augustin, with their backs to the railway tracks, inspired this touching novel about an impoverished family's struggles during World War II.

Michel Tremblay *The Fat Woman Next Door is Pregnant* (Talonbooks, Canada). A great title for a wonderful book chronicling the events of one day, May 2, 1942, in the life of a Plateau family; no one captures the ethos of working-class Francophone Montréal better.

Montréal on film

ow production costs, varied architecture and skilled locals had all made Montréal an in-demand locale for film shoots – including major productions like *Snake Eyes*, *The Aviator* and *The Art of War* – though ongoing labour disputes have cooled things of late. But other than fleeting glimpses – the Jacques-Cartier bridge in *Johnny Mnemonic*, the Big O in the Super Bowl scene of *The Sum of All Fears* and a post-apocalyptic McGill Arts Building in the atrocious *Battlefield Earth*, the city rarely appears as itself. There are some good films with Montréal in the starring role, though – a selective list appears below. Note that many of these were shot in French, but are available with either English subtitles or dubbed into English (alternate release titles indicated in parentheses followed by director and year of release).

The Apprenticeship of Duddy Kravitz (Ted Kotcheff 1974). Richard Dreyfuss plays Mordecai Richler's larger-than-life scamp as he schemes his way through Jewish Montréal and the Laurentians in the 1940s.

Bon Cop, Bad Cop (Eric Canuel 2006). The premise of mismatched cops forced to work together may not be new – though in this case, overlapping jurisdictions arise from a body being found on the "Bonjour!" sign as you cross into Québec from Ontario. One of the few bilingual movies made in Québec, it's a good-humoured affair that did well at Canadian (and especially Québec) box offices.

Le Confessional (*The Confessional*; Robert Lepage 1995). Top Québec playwright Lepage turns his hand to film with excellent results. The action flips back and forth between the present, as the main characters try to make sense of their roots, and the secrets and events four decades earlier during the filming of Alfred Hitchcock's *I Confess* in Québec City in 1952.

C.R.A.Z.Y. (Jean-Marc Vallée 2004). The story of Zac, the fourth of five sons, whose coming to terms with his homosexuality mirrors the cultural changes occurring in the 1960s and 70s, and is accompanied by a kicking soundtrack.

Le Déclin de l'Empire Américain (*Decline of the American Empire*; Denys Arcand 1986). Grand themes of sex and society pervade this tale of a group of middle-class baby-boomers – the generation that transformed Québec with the Quiet Revolution.

Les Invasions Barbares (*The Barbarian Invasions*; Denys Arcand 2003). The characters (and cast) of *Déclin* reunite in Montréal nearly two decades later at the deathbed of the family patriarch. Older and wiser, they reflect on life and morality in twenty-first-century Montréal and wonder where their dreams went and how the next generation turned out so different.

Jésus de Montréal (*Jesus of Montreal*; Denys Arcand 1989). Lothaire Bluteau plays an actor hired to stage the passion play – but his updated retelling, which re-examines Christ's story and principles in a contemporary context, infuriates church officials.

Léolo (Jean-Claude Lauzon 1992). Delightful and occasionally surreal film whose slightly mad child protagonist is convinced he's Italian – despite being born into a large, poor Francophone family in 1950s Montréal.

Maurice Richard (*The Rocket*; Charles Binamé 2005). Biopic about the Montréal Canadiens captain, one of the greatest ice-hockey players of all time and a Québécois hero.

Scanners (David Cronenberg 1981). Canadian horror-meister Cronenberg's thriller has telepaths using their psychic powers to battle it out with head-popping results, all beneath the ominous sweep of Place Ville-Marie's searchlights.

The Score (Frank Oz 2001). Vieux-Montréal features prominently as the setting for a jazz club owned by Robert De Niro, a safe-cracker who even speaks a bit of French in this one-last-heist flick co-starring Edward Norton.

Language

Language

French language and glossary

N o amount of French training will prepare you for the vagaries of the Québécois dialect – even the European French have difficulty understanding the slurring drawl that's spoken here at lightning speed. Don't be embarrassed to ask people to repeat themselves more slowly (*s'il vous plaît, répétez plus lentement*), or just ask if they speak English (*parlez-vous anglais?*); most in Montréal do and they won't be offended at your asking. With **pronunciation** there's little point trying to mimic the local dialect – just stick to the classic French rules. Consonants at the ends of words are usually silent and at other times are much like English, except that **ch** is always sh, **ç** is s, **h** is silent, **th** is the same as t, **ll** is like the y in yes and **r** is growled. Vowel-wise, **é** resembles a long a, **è** is eh and **a** is ah. If you plan on spending much time in the province, consider the pocket-sized *Rough Guide to French* (Penguin, UK/US), in a handy A–Z format.

Words and phrases

Basics

Good morning/Hello	Bonjour	Today	Aujourd'hui
Good evening	Bonsoir	Tomorrow	Demain
Good night	Bonne nuit	Yesterday	Hier
Goodbye	Au revoir	Morning	Matin
Yes	Oui	Afternoon	Après-midi
No	Non	Evening	Soir
Please	S'il vous/te plaît	Night	Nuit
Thank you	Merci	Monday	Lundi
You're welcome	Bienvenue/De rien	Tuesday	Mardi
OK	D'accord	Wednesday	Mercredi
How are you?	Comment allez-vous?/Ça va?	Thursday	Jeudi
		Friday	Vendredi
Fine, thanks	Très bien, merci	Saturday	Samedi
Do you speak English?	Parlez-vous anglais?	Sunday	Dimanche
I don't speak French	Je ne parle pas français	Except	Sauf
		Here/there	Ici/là
I don't understand	Je ne comprends pas	With/without	Avec/sans
Excuse me	Je m'excuse	Near/far	Près (pas loin)/loin
Sorry	Pardon/Désolé(e)	More/less	Plus/moins

Questions

Where?	Où?	What?	Quoi?
When?	Quand?	What is it?	Qu'est-ce que c'est?
Why?	Pourquoi?	What time is it?	Il est quelle heure?
How much/many?	Combien?	What time does it open?	À quelle heure ça ouvre?
How much does it cost?	Ça coûte combien?		

Numbers

1	un/une	14	quatorze
2	deux	15	quinze
3	trois	16	seize
4	quatre	17	dix-sept
5	cinq	18	dix-huit
6	six	19	dix-neuf
7	sept	20	vingt
8	huit	21	vingt-et-un
9	neuf	100	cent
10	dix	110	cent-dix
11	onze	500	cinq cents
12	douze	1000	mille
13	treize	2000	deux milles

Accommodation

Hotel	Hôtel	...for one/two weeks	...pour une/deux semaine(s)
Inn	Auberge	How much is it?	C'est combien?
Youth hostel	Auberge de jeunesse	Can I see it?	Est-ce que je peux la voir?
B&B	Gîte (du Passant)	Do you have anything cheaper?	Avez-vous quelque chose de moins cher?
room with a double bed	chambre avec un lit double	Is breakfast included?	Est-ce que le déjeuner est compris?
...with a shower /bath	...avec douche/salle de bain		
...for one/two/three nights	...pour une/deux/trois nuit(s)		

Transport

Aeroplane	Avion	Railway station	Gare centrale
Bus	Autobus	Ferry terminal	Quai du traversier
Train	Train	I'd like a ticket to...	J'aimerais un billet pour...
Car	Voiture		
Taxi	Taxi	One-way/return	Aller simple/aller-retour
Bicycle	Vélo		
Ferry	Traversier	Transfer	Correspondance
Bus station	Terminus d'autobus/ gare des autobuses	Freeway (motorway)	Autoroute

Eating and drinking

Do you have an English menu?	Avez-vous un menu en anglais?	Mussels	Moules
Set menu	Table d'hôte	Lobster	Homard
Lunch special	Spécial du midi	Fish	Poisson
Breakfast	Déjeuner	Chicken	Poulet
Lunch	Dîner	Duck	Canard
Dinner	Souper	Pork	Porc
Appetiser	Entrée	Ham	Jambon
Main course	Plat principal	Beef	Bœuf
Dessert	Dessert	Veal	Veau
Sugar	Sucre	Pasta	Pâtes
Milk	Lait	Potato	Patate
Butter	Beurre	Fries	Frites
Salt	Sel	Apple	Pomme
Pepper	Poivre	Lemon	Citron
Bread	Pain	Salad	Salade
Coffee	Café	Lettuce	Laitue
Tea	Thé	Beer	Bière
Eggs	Oeufs	On tap	En fût
Sausages	Saucissons	Glass	Verre
Bacon	Bacon	Pitcher	Pichet
Meat pie	Tourtière	White wine	Vin blanc
Baked beans	Fèves au lard	Red wine	Vin rouge
Shrimp	Crevettes	Check, please	L'addition, s'il vous plaît

Glossary of Montrealisms

Because of the interweaving of Francophone and Anglophone cultures, it's not surprising that English-speaking Montrealers often throw the occasional French word or expression into a conversation. This glossary lists the most common of these occurrences, as well as local English slang and idioms you're likely to encounter.

2 & 20 Hwy-20; called that by older Montrealers as it used to link to Hwy-2 in Ontario.

450 (four-five-oh) Area code for off-island suburbs; derogatory term used for the people who live there (also "bridge and tunnel people").

5 à 7 (cinq à sept) Happy hour.

Allongé Long (or "stretched") espresso but still stronger than an Americano.

Allophone Montrealer whose ethnicity and/or native tongue is neither English nor French.

Als Montréal Alouettes football team.

Anglophone English-speaker.

Angryphone Vocal Anglophone complaining about erosion of rights for English-speakers, especially on talk-radio phone-ins.

Apportez votre vin Bring your own wine; many smaller restaurants do not have a liquor license, but will uncork any bottle you bring.

Arrêt Stop (in theory – to Montréal drivers, it seems to mean slow down); unique to Québec – in France, signs say "Stop".

Arrondissement Borough.

Balconville Social space created by the proximity of balconies in many of the city's typical triplex houses.

Bavette Flank steak – the classic version is served with shallots.

Big O Stade Olympique.

Bill 101 Law promoting the use of French (and restricting the use of English).

Bio/biologique Organic.

Boîte à chanson Small folk-music bar.

Buanderie Laundromat.

Cabane à sucre Sugar shack; where maple syrup and its derivatives are produced in spring; usually open to the public to try out some samples.

Café au lait Espresso with steamed milk (similar, if not identical, to a caffè latte); often served in a bowl (*bol*).

Caisse pop Abbreviation of *caisse populaire*; credit union.

Calèche Horse-drawn carriage.

Casse-Croûte Snack bar.

CÉGEP Acronym for Collège d'enseignement général et professionel, a junior college (in Québec, this replaces the final year of high school and first year of university, as compared to other provinces and states).

Centre-ville Downtown.

CLSC Acronym of Centres locaux de services communautaires; health clinic.

The Conquest English capture of Québec City in 1759 (and their take-over of the rest of New France the following year).

Courriel Email.

Demerger The act of partially undoing the merger that created the Mega-City.

Dep Abbreviation of *dépanneur*; convenience store or cornershop.

Équitable Fair-trade.

First Nations Generally preferred term for Native Canadian or Indian.

FLQ Front de Libération du Québec; 1960s separatist terrorist group – see p.285.

Francophone French-speaker.

Fripperie Secondhand-clothes store.

GST/TPS Goods and Services Tax.

Guichet (automatique) ATM.

Habs Montréal Canadiens hockey team.

Hôtel de ville City hall.

Hydro Electricity (supplied by Hydro-Québec); some Anglo Montrealers also refer to natural gas as *gaz*, as the bills are from Gaz Métropolitain.

Je me souviens "I will remember"; motto on the Québec license plates and coat of arms. Although it is read as being a nationalist slogan, the three-line poem from which it comes is open to interpretation: *Je me souviens / que né sous le lys, / je croîs sous la rose* (I remember / that born under the [French] lily / I grow under the [English] rose).

Joual Thick Québécois regional accent.

Language police Office de la Langue Français; they enforce the rules governing the size of English signs (they must be no larger than half the size of the French) and other vital matters.

Lavoir Laundromat.

Loonie Dollar coin; the two-dollar coin, released later, thus became known as a toonie.

Magasiner To go shopping.

The Main Boulevard St-Laurent.

Mega-City The amalgamation of all the island of Montréal municipalities into one.

The Met Short for the Metropolitan (Autoroute Métropolitaine); the portion of Hwy-40 on the eastern half of the island.

Monnaie French for coins or spare change.

The mountain In Montréal, apparently any land mass that's at least 233m high; Mont Royal; Parc du Mont-Royal; the combined summits of Mont Royal, Westmount and Outremont.

National What qualifies in other provinces as provincial (eg the Québec provincial parliament calls itself the Assemblée Nationale).

Patriotes Insurgents, mainly Francophone, in the early nineteenth century.

Pepsi Derogatory term for Francophones (due to their preference for Pepsi over Coke).

Péquiste A member or supporter of the PQ (Parti Québécois); sometimes used to refer to separatists in general.

Piastre French slang for dollar.

Poutine French fries topped with cheese curds and gravy; artery-busting and alcohol-absorbing.

Pur laine Pure wool; old-stock, hundred percent Francophone.

QST/TVQ Québec Sales Tax.

Quiet Revolution 1960s arising of an articulate, mainly Francophone, intellectual and political class against the domination of Church and State.

Refus global Artists' manifesto published in 1948 that had profound effects on Québec culture - see box, p.56.

Resto Restaurant.

Rez-de-chaussée Ground floor.

SAQ Société des Alcools du Québec; runs the provincial liquor outlets.

Seigneury Land granted by the crown to an individual or group; the *seigneur* then let parcels of the land to tenants (rural farmers of this sort were known as *habitants*).

Smoked meat Brine-cured and smoked beef brisket similar to pastrami; served on rye with a pickle on the side.

Sous French for cent(s).

South Shore Suburbs geographically east of the St Lawrence from Downtown.

Stationnement Parking; a "P" is used on traffic signs, however.

Steamée Hot dog – the classic Montréal version is steamed (rather than grilled or boiled) and served with mustard and shredded cabbage.

STM Société des Transports de Montréal (Montréal Transit Commission).

Tam-tams Tribal drum sessions (specifically the percussion jams on the mountain – see p.103).

Terrasse Terrace (patio/pavement seating); *terrasse en arrière* indicates there's a terrace in the back garden or courtyard.

Tisane Herbal tea; also *infusion*.

Tourelle Turret-like dormer window.

T-Can / Trans-Canada Autoroute Trans-Canadienne; the portion of Hwy-40 on the western half of the island.

Triplex Townhouse with three apartments, one above the other.

Vielle souche Old-stock Québécois, descended from the original French settlers.

West Island Mainly Anglophone suburbs on the western half of the island of Montréal.

Travel
store

UK & Ireland
Britain
Devon & Cornwall
Dublin **D**
Edinburgh **D**
England
Ireland
The Lake District
London
London **D**
London Mini Guide
Scotland
Scottish Highlands
  & Islands
Wales

Europe
Algarve **D**
Amsterdam
Amsterdam **D**
Andalucía
Athens **D**
Austria
Baltic States
Barcelona
Barcelona **D**
Belgium &
  Luxembourg
Berlin
Brittany & Normandy
Bruges **D**
Brussels
Budapest
Bulgaria
Copenhagen
Corfu
Corsica
Costa Brava **D**
Crete
Croatia
Cyprus
Czech & Slovak
  Republics
Denmark
Dodecanese & East
  Aegean Islands
Dordogne & The Lot
Europe
Florence & Siena
Florence **D**
France
Germany
Gran Canaria **D**
Greece
Greek Islands

Hungary
Ibiza & Formentera **D**
Iceland
Ionian Islands
Italy
The Italian Lakes
Languedoc &
  Roussillon
Lanzarote &
  Fuerteventura **D**
Lisbon **D**
The Loire Valley
Madeira **D**
Madrid **D**
Mallorca **D**
Mallorca & Menorca
Malta & Gozo **D**
Menorca
Moscow
The Netherlands
Norway
Paris
Paris **D**
Paris Mini Guide
Poland
Portugal
Prague
Prague **D**
Provence
  & the Côte D'Azur
Pyrenees
Romania
Rome
Rome **D**
Sardinia
Scandinavia
Sicily
Slovenia
Spain
St Petersburg
Sweden
Switzerland
Tenerife &
  La Gomera **D**
Turkey
Tuscany & Umbria
Venice & The Veneto
Venice **D**
Vienna

Asia
Bali & Lombok
Bangkok
Beijing

Cambodia
China
Goa
Hong Kong & Macau
Hong Kong
  & Macau **D**
India
Indonesia
Japan
Laos
Malaysia, Singapore
  & Brunei
Nepal
The Philippines
Singapore
Singapore **D**
South India
Southeast Asia
Sri Lanka
Taiwan
Thailand
Thailand's Beaches
  & Islands
Tokyo
Vietnam

Australasia
Australia
Melbourne
New Zealand
Sydney

North America
Alaska
Baja California
Boston
California
Canada
Chicago
Colorado
Florida
The Grand Canyon
Hawaii
Las Vegas **D**
Los Angeles
Maui **D**
Miami & South Florida
Montréal
New England
New Orleans **D**
New York City
New York City **D**
New York City Mini
  Guide

Orlando & Walt
  Disney World® **D**
Pacific Northwest
San Francisco
San Francisco **D**
Seattle
Southwest USA
Toronto
USA
Vancouver
Washington DC
Washington DC **D**
Yellowstone & The
  Grand Tetons
Yosemite

Caribbean
& Latin America
Antigua & Barbuda **D**
Argentina
Bahamas
Barbados **D**
Belize
Bolivia
Brazil
Cancún & Cozumel **D**
Caribbean
Central America
Chile
Costa Rica
Cuba
Dominican Republic
Dominican Republic **D**
Ecuador
Guatemala
Jamaica
Mexico
Peru
St Lucia **D**
South America
Trinidad & Tobago
Yúcatan

Africa & Middle East
Cape Town & the
  Garden Route
Dubai **D**
Egypt
Gambia
Jordan

D: Rough Guide
DIRECTIONS for
short breaks

For more information go to www.roughguides.com

ROUGH GUIDES

Small print and

Index

A Rough Guide to Rough Guides

Published in 1982, the first Rough Guide – to Greece – was a student scheme that became a publishing phenomenon. Mark Ellingham, a recent graduate in English from Bristol University, had been travelling in Greece the previous summer and couldn't find the right guidebook. With a small group of friends he wrote his own guide, combining a highly contemporary, journalistic style with a thoroughly practical approach to travellers' needs.

The immediate success of the book spawned a series that rapidly covered dozens of destinations. And, in addition to impecunious backpackers, Rough Guides soon acquired a much broader and older readership that relished the guides' wit and inquisitiveness as much as their enthusiastic, critical approach and value-for-money ethos.

These days, Rough Guides include recommendations from shoestring to luxury and cover more than 200 destinations around the globe, including almost every country in the Americas and Europe, more than half of Africa and most of Asia and Australasia. Our ever-growing team of authors and photographers is spread all over the world, particularly in Europe, the USA and Australia.

In the early 1990s, Rough Guides branched out of travel, with the publication of Rough Guides to World Music, Classical Music and the Internet. All three have become benchmark titles in their fields, spearheading the publication of a wide range of books under the Rough Guide name.

Including the travel series, Rough Guides now number more than 350 titles, covering: phrasebooks, waterproof maps, music guides from Opera to Heavy Metal, reference works as diverse as Conspiracy Theories and Shakespeare, and popular culture books from iPods to Poker. Rough Guides also produce a series of more than 120 World Music CDs in partnership with World Music Network.

Visit www.roughguides.com to see our latest publications.

Rough Guide travel images are available for commercial licensing at www.roughguidespictures.com

Rough Guide credits

Text editor: Patricia Cunningham, AnneLise Sorensen
Layout: Jessica Subramanian
Cartography: Amod Singh, Maxine Repath, Katie Lloyd-Jones
Picture editor: Jj Luck
Production: Aimee Hampson, Katherine Owers
Proofreader: Diane Margolis
Cover design: Chloë Roberts
Photographer: Tim Draper
Editorial: London Kate Berens, Claire Saunders, Joanna Kirby, Ruth Blackmore, Polly Thomas, Richard Lim, Alison Murchie, Karoline Densley, Andy Turner, Keith Drew, Edward Aves, Nikki Birrell, Alice Park, Sarah Eno, Lucy White, David Paul, James Smart, Sam Cook, Joe Staines, Duncan Clark, Peter Buckley, Matthew Milton, Tracy Hopkins, Ruth Tidball; **New York** Andrew Rosenberg, Steven Horak, April Isaacs, Amy Hegarty, Ella Steim, Anna Owens, Joseph Petta, Sean Mahoney
Design & Pictures: London Scott Stickland, Dan May, Diana Jarvis, Mark Thomas, Harriet Mills,

Nicole Newman; **Delhi** Madhavi Singh, Umesh Aggarwal, Ajay Verma, Ankur Guha, Pradeep Thapliyal, Sachin Tanwar, Anita Singh
Production: Lauren Britton
Cartography: London Ed Wright; **Delhi** Jai Prakash Mishra, Rajesh Chhibber, Ashutosh Bharti, Animesh Pathak, Rajesh Mishra, Jasbir Sandhu, Karobi Gogoi, Alakananda Bhattacharya, Athokpam Jotinkumar
Online: New York Jennifer Gold, Kristin Mingrone; **Delhi** Manik Chauhan, Narender Kumar, Rakesh Kumar, Amit Verma, Amit Kumar, Rahul Kumar, Ganesh Sharma, Debojit Borah
Marketing & Publicity: London Niki Hanmer, Louise Maher, Anna Paynton, Jess Carter, Libby Jellie; **New York** Geoff Colquitt, Megan Kennedy, Katy Ball; **Delhi** Reem Khokhar
Special projects editor: Philippa Hopkins
Manager India: Punita Singh
Series editor: Mark Ellingham
Reference Director: Andrew Lockett
Publishing Coordinator: Megan McIntyre
Publishing Director: Martin Dunford

Publishing information

This third edition published April 2007 by
Rough Guides Ltd,
80 Strand, London WC2R 0RL
345 Hudson St, 4th Floor,
New York, NY 10014, USA
14 Local Shopping Centre, Panchsheel Park,
New Delhi 110017, India
Distributed by the Penguin Group
Penguin Books Ltd,
80 Strand, London WC2R 0RL
Penguin Putnam, Inc.
375 Hudson Street, NY 10014, USA
Penguin Group (Australia)
250 Camberwell Road, Camberwell,
Victoria 3124, Australia
Penguin Books Canada Ltd,
10 Alcorn Avenue, Toronto, Ontario,
Canada M4V 1E4
Penguin Group (NZ)
67 Apollo Drive, Mairangi Bay, Auckland 1310,
New Zealand
Cover concept by Peter Dyer.

Typeset in Bembo and Helvetica to an original design by Henry Iles.

Printed and bound in China

© John Shandy Watson and Arabella Bowen 2007

320pp includes index
A catalogue record for this book is available from the British Library
ISBN 9-78184-353-775-5

3   5   7   9   8   6   4   2

SMALL PRINT

Help us update

We've gone to a lot of effort to ensure that the third edition of **The Rough Guide to Montréal** is accurate and up-to-date. However, things change – places get "discovered", opening hours are notoriously fickle, restaurants and rooms raise prices or lower standards. If you feel we've got it wrong or left something out, we'd like to know, and if you can remember the address, the price, the time, the phone number, so much the better. We'll credit all contributions, and send a copy of the next edition (or any other Rough Guide if you

prefer) for the best letters. Everyone who writes to us and isn't already a subscriber will receive a copy of our full-colour thrice-yearly newsletter. Please mark letters: **"Rough Guide Montréal Update"** and send to: Rough Guides, 80 Strand, London WC2R 0RL, or Rough Guides, 4th Floor, 345 Hudson St, New York, NY 10014. Or send an email to **mail@roughguides.com**
Have your questions answered and tell others about your trip at
www.roughguides.atinfopop.com

Acknowledgements

John Shandy Watson: A big thank you to Gilles Bengle and the staff at Tourisme Montréal, Richard Séguin and the staff at the Greater Québec Area Tourism and Convention Bureau, Roselyne Hébert at Tourisme Québec, Caroline Jalbert at Tourisme Laurentides and Ronald Poiré for the city tour and gastronomic update. Thanks also to Neil Hartlen, Pierre-Yves Legault and especially Stephanie Halley for hitting the town with me, and Darren Henriet and Angela Songui for providing homes for me to come back to afterwards. Cheers to friends in London for their support and patience – notably Neville Walker and Geoff Hinchley for taking me in when I got back. Thanks also to VIA Rail for assistance in getting around, Christian Williams for ski info, ilesansfils.org and the staff at ArtJava for keeping me wired and to the lovely folks at I-Technique for saving my hard drive. I couldn't have done it without the able assistance of the RG staff – thanks to Hunter Slaton for getting things rolling and Patricia Cunningham and AnneLise Sorensen for fine-tuning the text and to Tim Draper for snapping just the right pics. And, finally, a big thanks to Arabella Bowen for sharing the research and writing.

Arabella Bowen: Great thanks to the inimitable Natasha Hall for sharing her flat and to the delightful Warren Wilansky for office space. Additional gratitude goes to co-author John Shandy Watson for taking on the majority of the book (again) and to the editor, Patricia Cunningham, for shepherding it to completion.

The editor: Thanks to John Shandy Watson and Arabella Bowen for all their hard work and general pleasantness. Special thanks go to the fine folks at Rough Guides: Jj Luck, Jessica Subramanian, Chloë Roberts, Andrew Rosenberg and the incomparable AnneLise Sorensen.

Readers' letters

Thanks to the readers of the second edition who took the time to write in with their amendments and additions. Apologies for any misspellings or omissions.

Richard Cowan, Jaye Imrie, Keith Rohman, David Saville, Rose-Marie Tonk.

SMALL PRINT

Photo credits

All photos © Rough Guides except the following:

Full page
The Plateau's avenue Coloniale © M.H. Jackson

Things not to miss
06 The Plateau © M.H. Jackson
09 Formula One Grand Prix of Canada in Montréal © David Boily/AFP/Getty Images
14 Montréal International Jazz Festival © Sean O'Neill/Alamy
15 Skiing Mont Tremblant, Laurentides, Quebec © Publiphoto Diffusion Inc/Alamy
21 Montréal Canadiens against the Buffalo Sabres © Rick Stewart/Getty Images

Taste of Montréal colour section
Beer mug © Marshall Ikonography/Alamy

Summer festivals colour section
Montréal International Jazz Festival crowd © Pierre Roussel/Getty Images

Montréal International Jazz Festival concert © Blaine Harrington III/Alamy
Fireworks display © Earl & Nazima Kowall/Corbis
Just for Laughs festival © SPG/www.esselab.com
Gay Pride Parade drummers © Sebastien Baussais/Alamy
Cherokee dancers, Montréal First Peoples' Festival © Terres en vues

Black and whites
p.193 Cirque du Soleil, Montréal © M.H. Jackson
p.212 Montréal Alouettes © Reuters/Corbis
p.223 La Fête des Neiges © Rubens Abboud/Alamy
p.226 Rogers Cup © Matthew Stockman/Getty Images
p.240 Mont Tremblant, Quebec © Rubens Abboud/Alamy

SMALL PRINT

Index

Map entries are in colour.

INDEX

313

INDEX

317

Map symbols

maps are listed in the full index using coloured text

▪▪▪▪▪	International boundary	*(i)*	Information office
▬ ▬ ▬	Chapter boundary	⊞	Hospital
⟨10⟩	Autoroute	◉	Accommodation
⟨5⟩	US interstate highway	▣	Restaurant
⟨5⟩	Provincial highway	🏛	Monument
	Major road	⊙	Statue
	Minor road	⅏	Viewpoint
	Pedestrianized street	♜	Fort
▬▬▬	Steps	♠	Monastery
	Bridge	⚡	Ski resort
===	Underground tunnel	Ⓜ	Métro station
- - - - -	Path	P	Parking
··········	Bike path	★	Bus stop
▬▪▬	Railway	⊠	Gate
- - - - -	Gondola	▬	Building
	Coastline/river	⊞	Church
— —	Ferry	⬭	Stadium
	Wall	⊔	Cemetery
◆	Point of interest	▨	Park
✈	International airport	⣿	Beach
⌐⌐⌐	Cliff		

MAP SYMBOLS

I

319

We're covered. Are you?

ROUGH GUIDES Travel Insurance

Visit our website at www.roughguides.com/insurance or call:

COLUMBUS DIRECT
Travel Insurance

ROUGH GUIDES

- Ⓣ UK: 0800 083 9507
- Ⓣ Spain: 900 997 149
- Ⓣ Australia: 1300 669 999
- Ⓣ New Zealand: 0800 55 99 11
- Ⓣ Worldwide: +44 870 890 2843
- Ⓣ USA, call toll free on: 1 800 749 4922

Please quote our ref: *Rough Guides books*

Cover for over 46 different nationalities and available in 4 different languages.

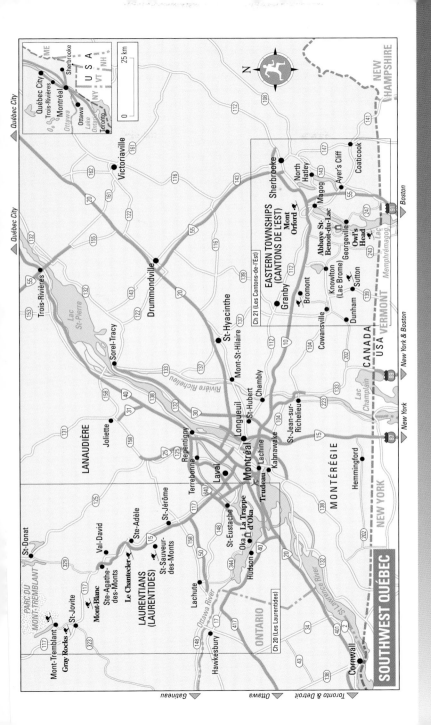

SOUTHWEST QUÉBEC

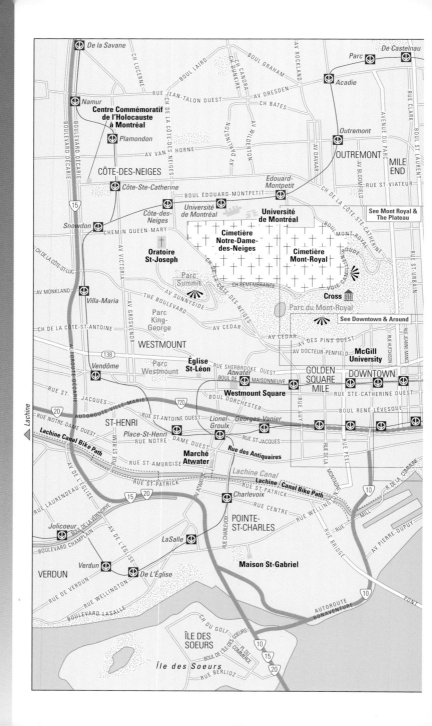

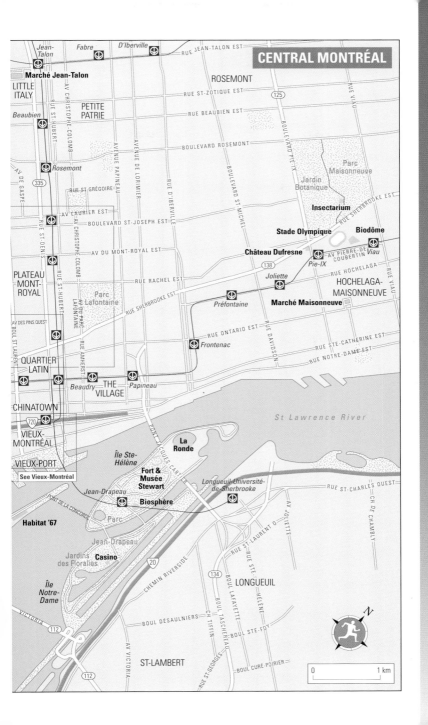

CENTRAL MONTRÉAL

Jean-Talon
Fabre
D'Iberville
RUE JEAN-TALON EST
Marché Jean-Talon
ROSEMONT
LITTLE ITALY
RUE ST-ZOTIQUE EST
125
PETITE PATRIE
RUE BEAUBIEN EST
Beaubien
AV CHRISTOPHE-COLOMB
RUE ST-HUBERT
BOULEVARD ROSEMONT
BOULEVARD PIE-IX
RUE VIAU
Parc Maisonneuve
AVENUE PAPINEAU
AVENUE DE LORIMIER
Jardin Botanique
Rosemont
335
RUE ST GRÉGOIRE
AV DE GASPE
Insectarium
RUE SHERBROOKE EST
AV LAURIER EST
RUE D'IBERVILLE
RUE ST-DENIS
BOULEVARD ST-JOSEPH EST
BOULEVARD ST-MICHEL
Stade Olympique
Biodôme
AV DU MONT-ROYAL EST
Château Dufresne
AV PIERRE-DE COUBERTIN
Viau
PLATEAU MONT-ROYAL
AV CHRISTOPHE-COLOMB
RUE ST-HUBERT
RUE RACHEL EST
138
Pie-IX
RUE HOCHELAGA
RUE VIAU
Joliette
HOCHELAGA-MAISONNEUVE
Parc Lafontaine
RUE SHERBROOKE EST
Préfontaine
Marché Maisonneuve
AV DES PINS OUEST
AV DU PARC LAFONTAINE
RUE AMHERST
RUE ONTARIO EST
RUE DAVIDSON
QUARTIER LATIN
BOUL ST LAURENT
Frontenac
RUE STE-CATHERINE EST
RUE NOTRE-DAME EST
Beaudry
THE VILLAGE
Papineau
CHINATOWN
720
VIEUX-MONTRÉAL
PONT JACQUES-CARTIER
St Lawrence River
VIEUX-PORT
See Vieux-Montréal
La Ronde
Île Ste-Hélène
Fort & Musée Stewart
Longueuil-Université-de-Sherbrooke
RUE ST-CHARLES OUEST
CH DE CHAMBLY
Jean-Drapeau
Biosphère
AV JOLIETTE
PONT DE LA CONCORDE
Habitat '67
Parc
Jean-Drapeau
RUE ST-LAURENT O
RUE ST-LAURENT
BOUL STE-HÉLÈNE
Jardins des Floralies
Casino
20
CHEMIN RIVERSIDE
134
BOUL LAFAYETTE
LONGUEUIL
Île Notre-Dame
CH TIFFIN
BOUL TASCHEREAU
BOUL STE-FOY
VICTORIA
112
BOUL DÉSAULNIERS
AV VICTORIA
RUE ST-GEORGES
BOUL CURÉ-POIRIER
ST-LAMBERT
112
N

0   1 km

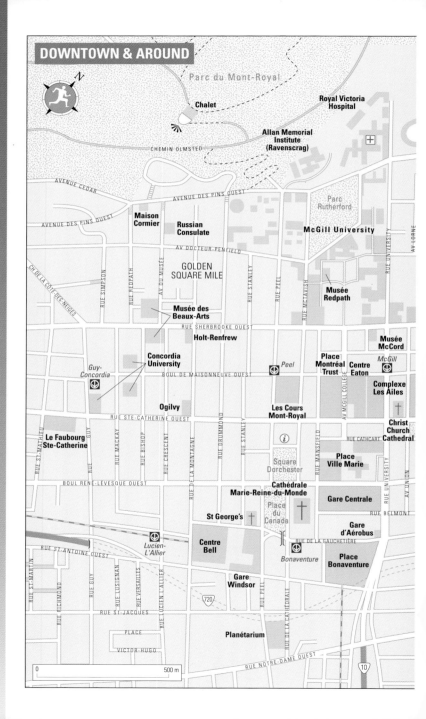

DOWNTOWN & AROUND

N

Parc du Mont-Royal

Chalet

Royal Victoria Hospital

Allan Memorial Institute (Ravenscrag)

CHEMIN OLMSTED

AVENUE CEDAR

AVENUE DES PINS OUEST

AVENUE DES PINS OUEST

Maison Cormier

Russian Consulate

AV DOCTEUR-PENFIELD

Parc Rutherford

McGill University

CH DE LA CÔTE-DES-NEIGES

RUE SIMPSON

RUE REDPATH

AV DU MUSÉE

GOLDEN SQUARE MILE

RUE STANLEY

RUE PEEL

RUE MCTAVISH

AV LORNE

RUE UNIVERSITY

Musée Redpath

Musée des Beaux-Arts

RUE SHERBROOKE OUEST

Holt-Renfrew

Musée McCord

Concordia University

Guy-Concordia

BOUL DE MAISONNEUVE OUEST

Peel

Place Montréal Trust

Centre Eaton

McGill

AV MCGILL COLLÈGE

Complexe Les Ailes

Ogilvy

RUE STE-CATHERINE OUEST

Les Cours Mont-Royal

Christ Church Cathedral

RUE CATHCART

RUE ST-MATHIEU

RUE MACKAY

RUE BISHOP

RUE CRESCENT

RUE DE LA MONTAGNE

RUE DRUMMOND

RUE STANLEY

RUE MANSFIELD

RUE UNIVERSITY

AV UNION

Le Faubourg Ste-Catherine

Square Dorchester

Place Ville Marie

BOUL RENÉ-LÉVESQUE OUEST

Cathédrale Marie-Reine-du-Monde

Place du Canada

Gare Centrale

RUE BELMONT

St George's

RUE ST-MARTIN

RUE RICHMOND

RUE GUY

RUE LUSIGNAN

RUE VERSAILLES

RUE LUCIEN L'ALLIER

Lucien-L'Allier

RUE ST-ANTOINE OUEST

Centre Bell

RUE DE LA GAUCHETIÈRE

Bonaventure

Gare d'Aérobus

Place Bonaventure

Gare Windsor

RUE ST-JACQUES

720

RUE PEEL

RUE DE LA CATHÉDRALE

PLACE VICTOR-HUGO

Planétarium

RUE NOTRE-DAME OUEST

0   500 m

10

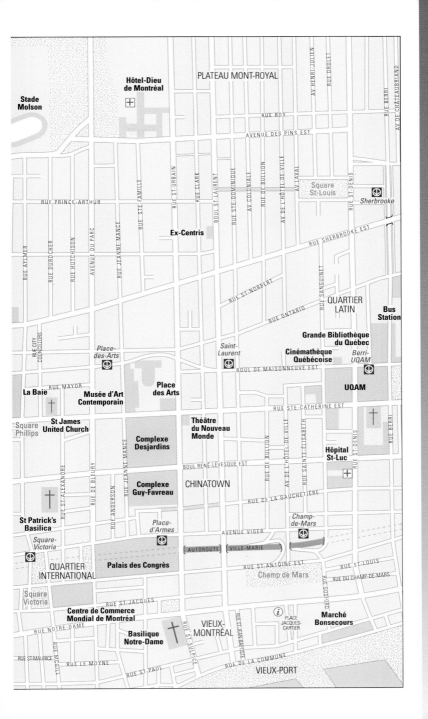

VIEUX-MONTRÉAL

0   250 m

N

St Lawrence River

Bassin Bonsecours

Quai de l'Horloge

Quai Jacques-Cartier

Quai King-Edward

Quai Alexandra

Centre des Sciences de Montréal

VIEUX-PORT
Promenade du Vieux-Port

Lieu Historique Sir-George-Étienne-Cartier

Chapelle Notre-Dame-de-Bon-Secours

Marché Bonsecours

Maison du Calvet

Château Ramezay

Hôtel de Ville

Place Vauquelin

Old Courthouse

Palais de Justice

Aldred Building

Basilique Notre-Dame

Centaur Theatre

Old Customs House

Musée d'Archéologie et d'Histoire de Montréal

Youville Stables

Musée Marc-Aurèle Fortin

Centre d'Histoire de Montréal

Séminaire de Saint-Sulpice

Banque de Montréal

Palais des Congrès

Centre de Commerce Mondial de Montréal

La Joute

Bourse de Montréal

Hôpital Général des Soeurs-Grises

CITÉ DU MULTIMÉDIA

QUARTIER INTERNATIONAL

Square-Victoria

Place-d'Armes

Champ-de-Mars

PLACE JEAN PAUL RIOPELLE

PLACE D'ARMES

PLACE JACQUES-CARTIER

PLACE ROYALE

PLACE D'YOUVILLE

RUE ST-HUBERT

RUE BERRI

RUE ST-DENIS

RUE ST-LOUIS

RUE DU CHAMP-DE-MARS

RUE GOSFORD

RUE ST-ANTOINE EST

AUTOROUTE VILLE-MARIE

Old Champ de Mars

RUE BONSECOURS

RUE NOTRE-DAME EST

RUE ST-VINCENT

RUE ST-GABRIEL

ST-JEAN-BAPTISTE

ST-LAURENT

BOULEVARD

ST-DIZIER

RUE DE BRÉSOLES

RUE ST-SULPICE

COURS LE ROYER

RUE DE LA COMMUNE

RUE ST-AMABLE

RUE ST-PAUL EST

RUE ST-PAUL OUEST

RUE ST-FRANÇOIS-XAVIER

RUE ST-JACQUES

RUE DE L'HÔPITAL

RUE DU ST-SACREMENT

RUELLE DES FORTIFICATIONS

RUE ST-ANTOINE OUEST

A.V. VIGER

A.V. VIGER

RUE NOTRE-DAME OUEST

RUE DOLLARD

RUE DES RÉCOLLETS

RUE STE-HÉLÈNE

RUE LE MOYNE

RUE ST-PIERRE

DU PORT

RUE MCGILL

RUE NORMAND

RUE DES SOEURS-GRISES

RUE DE LONGUEUIL

RUE ST-MAURICE

RUE ST-HENRI

RUE WILLIAM

RUE KING

RUE QUEEN

RUE PRINCE

RUE DE WELLINGTON

RUELLE ROYER

Downtown ▲

Chinatown ▲

Quartier Latin ▲

Lachine Canal ▶

Parc des Écluses ▶

MONT ROYAL & THE PLATEAU

Stade Olympique & Jardin Botanique (3.2km)

Little Italy

MILE END

OUTREMONT

Oratoire St-Joseph

The Village

Quartier Latin

Place des Arts

Downtown

0   500 m

Streets and locations:

RUE MARQUETTE
AVENUE ÉMILE-DUPLOYÉ
RUE CHAMPLAIN
RUE ALEXANDRE-DESÈVE
RUE FABRE
RUE GARNIER
RUE PLESSIS
RUE DE LANAUDIÈRE
RUE PANET
RUE CHAMBORD
RUE DE LA VISITATION
RUE DE BRÉBEUF
RUE DE LA ROCHE
AV CHRISTOPHE-COLOMB
RUE BOYER
RUE DE MENTANA
RUE ST-ANDRÉ
RUE ST-CHRISTOPHE
RUE ST-HUBERT
AV DE CHÂTEAUBRIAND
RUE BERRI
RUE RIVARD
RUE ST-DENIS
RUE DROLET
AVENUE HENRI-JULIEN
AVENUE LAVAL
AVENUE DE L'HÔTEL-DE-VILLE
RUE DE BULLION
AVENUE COLONIALE
RUE ST-DOMINIQUE
BOULEVARD ST-LAURENT
RUE CLARK
RUE ST-URBAIN
RUE JEANNE-MANCE
RUE HUTCHISON
AVENUE DU PARC
AVENUE DES PINS OUEST
AVENUE DES PINS EST
RUE PRINCE-ARTHUR OUEST
RUE SHERBROOKE
RUE ONTARIO EST

RUE GILFORD
PARC SIR-WILFRID-LAURIER
Laurier
Mont-Royal
Sanctuaire Très St-Sacrement
Maison de Culture
Maison des Cyclistes
Théâtre de Verdure
Parc Lafontaine
Hôpital Notre-Dame
Écomusée du Fier Monde
AVENUE DU PARC-LAFONTAINE
Agora de la Danse
Sherbrooke
Square St-Louis
Ex-Centris
Église St-Jean-Baptiste
Parc du Portugal
Parc des Amériques
Schwartz's
Hôtel-Dieu de Montréal
Parc Jeanne-Mance
Sir George-Étienne Cartier Monument
Stade Molson
Royal Victoria Hospital
Allan Memorial Institute (Ravenscrag)
McGill University
Musée Redpath
Russian Consulate
Parc du Mont-Royal
Cimetière Mont-Royal
Cross
Chalet
Maison Cormier
Hôpital Général de Montréal
Cimetière Notre-Dame-des-Neiges
Maison Smith
Lac-aux-Castors
CHEMIN OLMSTED
VOIE CAMILLIEN-HOUDE
CH DE LA CÔTE-STE-CATHERINE
CHEMIN REMEMBRANCE
CHEMIN DE LA CÔTE-DES-NEIGES
AVENUE CEDAR
RUE SIMPSON
RUE REDPATH
AV DU MUSÉE
RUE DRUMMOND
RUE PEEL
RUE UNIVERSITY
AVENUE DOCTEUR-PENFIELD
RUE STANLEY
AVENUE LORNE
RUE AYLMER
RUE DUROCHER
AVENUE DU PARC
RUE JEANNE-MANCE
RUE STE-FAMILLE
RUE MILTON
AVENUE DULUTH OUEST
AVENUE DULUTH EST
RUE RACHEL OUEST
RUE RACHEL EST
RUE MARIE-ANNE OUEST
RUE MARIE-ANNE EST
RUE NAPOLÉON
RUE ROY EST
PLATEAU MONT-ROYAL
AVENUE DE L'HÔTEL-DE-VILLE
RUE PRINCE-ARTHUR
RUE DE BIENVILLE
BOULEVARD ST-JOSEPH EST
RUE DROLET
RUE ST-JULIEN
AVENUE HENRI-JULIEN
AV DE L'HÔTEL-DE-VILLE
RUE DE BULLION
AVENUE COLONIALE
RUE ST-DOMINIQUE
RUE MARIE-ANNE OUEST
RUE CLARK
RUE ST-URBAIN
AV DE L'ESPLANADE
RUE JEANNE-MANCE
AVENUE DU MONT-ROYAL OUEST
AVENUE DU MONT-ROYAL EST
RUE CHERRIER
AVENUE LAUBIER OUEST
AV NELSON
BOUL MONT-ROYAL
AV MAPLEWOOD
RUE HUTCHISON
RUE DE LA ROCHE
RUE CALIXA-LAVALLÉE

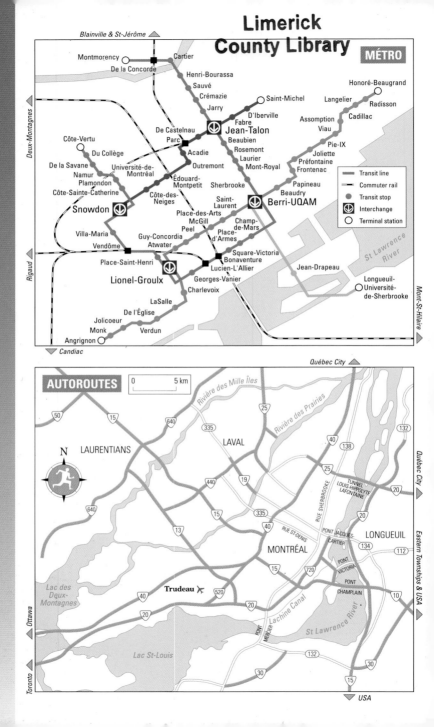